D0162110

The Censorship of British Drama 1900–1968

Volume Four: The Sixties

Winner of the Society for Theatre Research Book Prize, 2016

Published in paperback for the first time, with the addition of brief biographies of the staff in the Lord Chamberlain's Office, this is the final part of Steve Nicholson's definitive four-volume analysis of British theatre censorship from 1900 to 1968, based on previously undocumented material in the Lord Chamberlain's Correspondence Archives in the British Library and the Royal Archives at Windsor. It covers the 1960s, a significant decade in social and political spheres in Britain, especially in the theatre. As certainties shifted and social divisions widened, a new generation of theatre makers arrived, ready to sweep away yesterday's conventions and challenge the establishment.

'forensic and fascinating, rich with detail and countless examples of the hilarious and bewildering attitudes of the later censorship ...'
Dan Rebellato, Royal Holloway University of London

'Nicholson's skillful deployment of meticulous archival research is combined with an effective sense of the overall picture of theatre and performance in the 1960s and concludes with a persuasive caution against complacency about the situation after the end of pre-censorship.'
Russell Jackson, *Theatre Notebook*

'We will lament the abolition of censorship insofar as it has robbed us of another volume.'
Anne Etienne, *Studies in Theatre and Performance*

Steve Nicholson is Emeritus Professor, University of Sheffield. He is a series editor for Exeter Performance Studies and the author of *British Theatre and the Red Peril: The Portrayal of Communism, 1917–1945*, also published by UEP.

Exeter Performance Studies

Series Editors:

Helen Brooks, Reader in Theatre and
Cultural History, University of Kent

Jane Milling, Professor in Drama, University of Exeter

Steve Nicholson, Emeritus Professor, University of Sheffield

Duška Radosavljević, Reader in Contemporary
Theatre and Performance, Royal Central School of
Speech and Drama, University of London

Founding series editors and advisors: Graham Ley and Peter Thomson

A complete list of books published in the series is available from
the publishers, University of Exeter Press: www.exeterpress.co.uk

Other books by Steve Nicholson
published by University of Exeter Press

British Theatre and the Red Peril: The Portrayal of Communism
The Censorship of British Drama 1900–1968: Volume One: 1900–1932
The Censorship of British Drama 1900–1968: Volume Two: 1933–1952
The Censorship of British Drama 1900–1968: Volume Three: The Fifties

The Censorship of British Drama
1900–1968

Volume Four: The Sixties

Steve Nicholson

and

First published in 2020 by
University of Exeter Press
Reed Hall, Streatham Drive
Exeter EX4 4QR
UK
www.exeterpress.co.uk
in association with the Society for Theatre Research

Exeter Performance Studies

British Library Cataloguing in Publication Data
A catalogue record for this book is available
from the British Library.

Vol. 1 ISBN 978-1-905816-40-8
Vol. 2 ISBN 978-1-905816-41-5
Vol. 3 ISBN 978-1-905816-42-2
Vol. 4 ISBN 978-1-905816-43-9

Cover image: Peter Eyre as Prince Arthur, with the attached
skeleton of his dead conjoined twin, Prince George, in
Edward Bond's *Early Morning*: Royal Court Theatre, London, UK, 1968.
(© Douglas H. Jeffery/Victoria and Albert Museum, London)

Contents

Preface to the
2020 Paperback Edition

When George Redford resigned from his post as Reader and Examiner of plays in 1911—a position he had held since 1895—he told the Lord Chamberlain that 'seventeen years of reading bad plays is enough for any man'.[1] It is tempting to say I know what he meant. Of course, Redford's comment presented an overly cynical and jaundiced perspective of someone who had been forced unwillingly from office, and was departing in something of a huff. In a more generous mood, he would doubtless have acknowledged that he had read some good plays alongside the bad ones. A century or so later, the attempt to draw distinctions on grounds of quality seems both futile and largely irrelevant. As I have mentioned elsewhere, Arnold Wesker did once suggest to me that theatre censorship only matters if there is definite and direct evidence of the suppression of great art. I continue to maintain that censorship, and the way in which theatre is controlled, must always be significant, not least because its most effective form of silencing is to prevent those works which might be most challenging and provocative from even being created. By the same token, I realised very quickly after starting my research (which was actually quite a lot longer ago than Redford's seventeen years) that it would not be sufficient to focus my attention only on those plays which had never been licensed for performance, or on those where some sort of confrontation between the Lord Chamberlain's Office and a playwright or theatre manager or director had erupted into public consciousness. It was clear that only by looking through as many as possible of the very many texts where specific deletions or amendments had been imposed would it be possible to gain a sense of the practice and impact of the laws of 1737 and 1843 on the development of twentieth century British theatre. Moreover, to gain an understanding of the contexts and the reasons for decisions made, it was necessary to examine the Lord Chamberlain's Correspondence files for

---

[1] *New York Times*, 22 December 1911, p. 14.

evidence of the arguments and negotiations and compromises, the internal memoranda, the reports and the statements of policy, and the letters of complaint from politicians, foreign ambassadors, church leaders, public morality campaigners and members of the public received by the Lord Chamberlain's Office, criticising both what he had and had not allowed. And while one could not assume that absolutely everything had been saved in the sometimes bulging (and exploding) files which had been lovingly (or perhaps methodically) created for each and every individual play submitted for licence, since there must have been many discussions (including on the telephone) which had not been fully documented, an enormous—not to say overwhelming—amount of material had survived. While some of it was typewritten and official, much was in the form of handwritten—scribbled even—unofficial thoughts and notes, faded and at times indecipherable, but crucial to any attempt to construct a picture and tell a story.

Between 1900 and 1968, over 56,000 scripts were submitted to the Lord Chamberlain's Office for licensing. After 1909, his Examiner and Reader of Plays was required to write a report which included a reasonably detailed summary of the play, a recommendation as to whether it should be imme- diately licensed or was in need of further consideration, and a list of specific elements (subject matter, tone, individual lines, or scenes, or characters, or costumes, or actions) which the Reader thought required modification or clarification, or where a second (and sometimes third, fourth and fifth) opinion would be required before a decision could be made. The respon- sibility for licensing was always the Lord Chamberlain's, but in most cases he relied heavily on the judgments of his senior staff—the Comptroller and Assistant Comptroller of his Office—and, where he judged it appropriate, the opinions of external organisations and individuals whose views he deemed should carry weight. While probably a majority of the scripts submitted were read only by an Examiner of Plays—who judged them unproblematic, and was therefore able to recommend them for licence without the need for further opinions—in any given year there were also many which required further reading and discussion. As a researcher, it became important to consider not only those scripts which had required further consideration and changes before they were licensed, but also those which had *not* done so. Any study of censorship must take note not only of what is prevented, but also of what is allowed—especially the expression of ideas and assumptions which might have been considered entirely unproblematic when they were written, but which might at other times—including our own—be considered much more questionable.

Given that it is possible to read histories of eighteenth-century and nineteenth-century theatre censorship by the Lord Chamberlain in single volumes, it may seem questionable as to why it should take four volumes to cover just over two thirds of the twentieth century. The answer lies primarily

in the fact that we have so much more documentation from the early years
of the twentieth century onwards, which enables us to look in far closer detail
at what was happening and why. Crucially too, far more scripts were being
submitted for licensing than in previous centuries. This—I hope—goes some
way to explaining why what started out to be a single book expanded as it
did. As a series, these four volumes mark an attempt to map the territory
and the period more or less chronologically, while also identifying some of
the broad recurring themes and areas in which anxieties and confrontations
repeatedly surfaced, and examining in detail a range of specific examples. But
there remains much more to discover in these files; there are different ways
to approach the material, different questions to ask of it, different areas of
focus, and different examples which still lie hidden. The files remain a gold-
mine—not untouched, certainly, but with a great deal more to be revealed.

When my interest in the field began, I probably supposed—naively—that
theatre censorship in Britain was more or less a thing of the past. Hadn't the
1968 Theatres Act changed everything? I knew, of course, about seemingly
isolated cases; the trial at the start of the 1980s involving the production of
Howard Brenton's *Romans in Britain* at the National Theatre, or Norman
Tebbit's attempt to prevent a Theatre-in-Education company touring a
trilogy of plays about Hiroshima and cruise missiles to primary schools. I
knew, too, that theatres were being pressurised by an increasing demand to
prioritise 'bums on seats' and that, as one writer put it, 'The accountant is the
new censor'.[2] The withdrawal of Arts Council funding from theatre companies—especially, it often seemed, from those seen as pursuing an overtly
political agenda—and an increasing reliance of theatres on private business
sponsorship, was, in effect, another form of censorship. Yet this all felt to
me somehow rather different—if arguably more insidious—from the sort of
detailed vetting practised day in and day out by the Lord Chamberlain's
Office on every play seeking a public performance. And surely the moralities
and hypocrisies he had felt bound to observe had been swept away forever
by performances such as *Hair* and *Oh, Calcutta!* in the years after 1968.

It turned out not to be so. In 2018 I participated on a number of
panels at events marking the fiftieth anniversary of the ending of the Lord
Chamberlain's powers over theatre. While there was certainly a strong interest
in history and the past, many of the questions and discussions sought—
predictably and quite naturally—to focus on current, contemporary and
future questions around the censorship of performance. For as we must all
be aware, censorship has returned (if it ever went away) in forms which are
often far more active and far more dangerous. Whenever I have spoken about

---

[2]   Howard Barker, 'Fortynine asides for a tragic theatre', first published in the
Guardian, 10 February 1986, and subsequently in Howard Barker, *Arguments for
a Theatre* (London, John Calder, 1989, and subsequent editions)

theatre censorship in Britain before 1968, I have been keen to emphasise that no-one in Britain—by contrast with some other countries—was imprisoned or had their life (or the lives of their loved ones or associates) threatened because of what they had written. The worst that happened was that their play might not be put on or that they might be fined. Clearly, that is not now the case, and it is not only the law and the official authorities which the writer and theatre-maker have to fear. Nor is it easy even to know whether it is possible to argue for a theatre without any censorship if the cherished 'right to give offence' means that anyone can say or do anything on stage, without regulation or control. This is not the place to try and discuss these issues, but they are vital—and ever-evolving.

One other fact which occurs to me in writing a preface for these second editions is that it is even more striking in 2020—though it will hardly come as a surprise—that almost everyone involved in censoring plays in the Lord Chamberlain's Office was male (and, equally obviously, white). When government ministers or diplomatic ambassadors or senior religious figures were consulted for advice, they were all male (and usually white) too. At times, a Lord Chamberlain did make use of an Advisory Board (it was he, of course who selected its members) and very occasionally that might offer a (white) female voice. Indeed, in 1926 the Earl of Cromer—the then Lord Chamberlain—said he would 'personally prefer to seek two women on the board' (although one of them would 'be really a spare vote if the other happens to be away').[3] Lady Violet Bonham Carter was duly enlisted, serving for some years as an occasional adviser, and most often called upon in relation to plays seen as having a particular relevance for women. It is also true, of course, that as the servant of the Royal Household, the Lord Chamberlain's prime duty in all he did was to serve the wishes of senior members of the Royal Family, and that at certain times (especially after 1953) this very much included female members. There is some evidence of his consulting directly with them—and even of occasional interventions. Probably less acknowledged is the fact that from 1918 until 1960 a certain Ruth Webster was employed in the Lord Chamberlain's Office as a play reader's clerk, and that it was she who physically marked the scripts in blue pencil before returning them to managers and playwrights to indicate to them what had been disallowed. Another part of her job was often to type up the readers' reports, and John Johnston—who was Assistant Comptroller of the Lord Chamberlain's Office in its final years of censorship—has also indicated that it fell to Ruth Webster's successor—Mary Fisher—to phone theatre managers and read aloud to them the lines that they were required to delete. There is also some evidence that Miss Webster's long career in the

---

[3] Memorandum from Cromer to Sir Douglas Dawson, 5 June 1926. See LCO Theatre Files.

department meant that she was able to pass on information about previous plays and policies to those appointed to work there more recently. We know that from time to time—perhaps when a check was being made that actors were properly observing the Lord Chamberlain's requirements—Miss Webster or Miss Fisher might accompany a male member of staff (usually incognito) to watch a performance. However, neither enjoyed any power or authority or official status—though of course we cannot know whether their opinion may sometimes have been informally sought—and apart from the few tantalising references in the files, we know nothing of their experiences or perspectives. But maybe, if anyone in the future should conceive of writing an imaginative and (in part) fictional drama set in the Lord Chamberlain's office, it might be worth considering whether a possible way of looking at that world would actually be through the eyes (and voices) of Miss Webster and Miss Fisher.

Publication of the original editions of these volumes occurred over a period of twelve years. I have made almost no changes to the main texts of the originals, but there are a few additions. Only volume four of the original versions contained a Timeline, which allowed the possibility of connecting what was occurring in theatre censorship with historical, political and cultural contexts. Timelines have now been added to the other three volumes. Again, in the original editions, only volume three included a section of short biographies of key individuals involved in theatre censorship during the relevant period; biographies have now been added to volumes one, two and four, as appropriate, and there are minor modifications to the biographies as presented in volume three. In the case of volume four, this has also resulted in some amendments to the Afterword. Finally, while it has not been necessary to update the bibliographies individually, the following entries—which appear in volume four—are relevant across the whole period:

- Aldgate, Anthony and Robertson, James C., *Censorship in Theatre and Cinema* (Edinburgh: Edinburgh University Press, 2005)
- Freshwater, Helen, *Theatre Censorship in Britain: Silencing, Censure and Suppression* (Basingstoke: Palgrave Macmillan, 2009)
- Houchin, John, *Censorship of the American Theatre in the Twentieth Century* (Cambridge: Cambridge University Press, 2003)
- Shellard, Dominic, Nicholson, Steve, and Handley, Miriam, *The Lord Chamberlain Regrets* (London: British Library Publications, 2004)
- Thomas, David, Carlton, David and Etienne, Anne, *Theatre Censorship: from Walpole to Wilson* (Oxford: Oxford University Press, 2007)

In conclusion to this preface, I wish to express my sincere gratitude to the University of Exeter Press—especially Simon Baker, Nigel Massen and Anna Henderson—and its series editors at the time the volumes were in gestation—Peter Thomson, Graham Ley and Jane Milling—for their support and decisions, and equally to the Society for Theatre Research for all their support and encouragement, which has been crucial in making this edition possible. I also want to thank all the individual members of that society who responded to my request for suggestions of significant theatre dates to include in the timelines for this second edition. For their support through the original research and writing process, I am grateful to the AHRC (formerly AHRB), the Universities of Huddersfield and Sheffield, Kathryn Johnson and staff in the Manuscripts section of the British Library, the V&A Theatre and Performance Archives (formerly the Theatre Museum) and the Royal Archive at Windsor. I also wish to express my thanks to former colleagues who were kind enough to comment on material, and especially to my wife, Heather, for her support over many years.

TIMELINE
1960–1969
A Cultural and Political Calendar

1960

	PERFORMANCE	POLITICAL/WORLD
January		
February		Wave of anti-Semitic attacks take place in Britain (and elsewhere) British Prime Minister Harold Macmillan makes his 'Winds of Change' speech in South African parliament, attacking apartheid
March	Harold Pinter's *The Dumb Waiter* transfers to Royal Court (opened in January at Hampstead theatre club)	Sharpeville Massacre in South Africa. ANC banned
April	*The Two Gentleman of Verona* opens in Stratford—Peter Hall's first production and first season as director of RSC Harold Pinter's *The Caretaker* opens at the Arts Theatre Eugene Ionesco's *Rhinoceros* opens at Royal Court (Laurence Olivier in main role) Arnold Wesker's *I'm Talking about Jerusalem* opens in Coventry, completing his trilogy, which plays at Royal Court from June	Attempted assassination of Dr Henrik Verwoerd, South African prime minister Third CND Aldermaston march over Easter weekend against nuclear weapons culminates in huge 'ban the bomb' rally in Trafalgar Square France carries out nuclear test Civil Rights Bill passed in US
May	Terence Rattigan's *Ross* opens at Haymarket with Alec Guinness as Lawrence of Arabia	Leonid Brezhnev becomes President of the Soviet Union Soviet Union launches first unmanned space capsule American spy plane shot down over Soviet Union Nazi war criminal Adolf Eichmann captured in Argentina and sent for trial in Israel Military coup in Turkey
June	Brecht's *Galileo* opens at Mermaid Theatre Lionel Bart's *Oliver!* opens at New Theatre	Somaliland (Somalia) becomes independent of British government Congo becomes independent of Belgium
July	RSC signs lease for London base at Aldwych Theatre Robert Bolt's *A Man for All Seasons* opens at Globe Theatre	The world's first woman Prime Minister is elected in Sri Lanka (Ceylon)

1960

	PERFORMANCE	POLITICAL/WORLD
August	Theatre Workshop's *Sparrers Can't Sing* opens at Stratford East *Beyond the Fringe* opens at Edinburgh Festival	Cyprus gains independence from Britain East Germany imposes a partial blockade on West Berlin
September	Keith Waterhouse's *Billy Liar* opens at Theatre Royal, Brighton, with Albert Finney	
October	Franco Zeffirelli's production of *Romeo and Juliet* opens at Old Vic	Nigeria gains independence from Britain Britain agrees to allow US nuclear submarine bases; launch of first British nuclear submarine
November		J.F. Kennedy elected as US President Old Bailey trial of Penguin Books on grounds of obscenity for publishing D.H. Lawrence's *Lady Chatterley's Lover* ends with acquittal
December	Shelagh Delaney's *The Lion in Love* opens at Royal Court *Coronation Street* first broadcast on television	Last call up to National Service in Britain

Other countries to declare independence from former colonial regimes in 1960 include French Cameroon, Chad, Senegal, Togo, Madagascar, Ivory Coast, Dahomey, Upper Volta, Niger, Mali and Mauritania. The bloody Algerian War of Independence continues

Major Picasso exhibition takes place at the Tate; Soviet Union sends dogs into space; British government agrees to legalise betting shops; First use of traffic wardens in London; Final episode of *The Goon Show* broadcast on BBC Radio; The BBC Television Centre is opened

Significant new films released in 1960 include *Sons and Lovers, Psycho, Spartacus, The Brides of Dracula, Saturday Night and Sunday Morning, Peeping Tom, La Dolce Vita, Whatever Happened to Baby Jane, The Time Machine*

Rumour of the year in *Plays and Players*: Elvis Presley to play *Hamlet* at the Old Vic

1961

	PERFORMANCE	POLITICAL/WORLD
January		US breaks off diplomatic relations with Cuba
February	John Whiting's *The Devils* opens at the Aldwych—first RSC production of a new play Thomas Middleton's Jacobean Tragedy *The Changeling* revived at Royal Court Living Theatre's controversial production of *The Connection* opens in West End	
March	Theatre Workshop's *Sparrers Can't Sing* revived at Stratford East and transfers to Wyndham's Theatre Chancellor of Exchequer reneges on promise of funds to build National Theatre, and switches money to regions	Five people found guilty under the Official Secrets Act of spying for Soviet Union US nuclear submarine arrives at Scottish naval base of Holy Loch South Africa leaves British Commonwealth
April		Trial of Adolf Eichmann begins in Israel European Court of Human Rights opens in Strasbourg Sierra Leone declares independence from Britain Yuri Gargarin becomes first person in space and circles the earth Cuban refugees financed and trained by US invade Cuba (Bay of Pigs) in failed attempt to overthrow Castro
May	Jean Genet's *The Blacks* opens at Royal Court *Beyond the Fringe* opens in London	Amnesty International founded George Blake sentenced to 42 years in prison for spying for Russia South Africa becomes a Republic
June	Arnold Wesker's *The Kitchen* opens in full production at Royal Court	Kuwait declares independence from Britain
July	John Osborne's *Luther* opens at Royal Court, with Albert Finney Centre 42 launched (under Arnold Wesker) to stimulate working-class participation in the arts	Cyprus achieves independence from UK Extensive rioting and fighting in Algeria J.F. Kennedy declares that a Soviet attack on Berlin would be an attack on NATO

1961

	PERFORMANCE	POLITICAL/WORLD
August	RSC production of *Romeo and Juliet* at Stratford with Dame Edith Evans as Nurse Adaptation of *Lady Chatterley's Lover* staged privately at Arts Theatre Club Musical *The Lord Chamberlain Regrets* opens at Saville Theatre	East Germany closes border with West Berlin and starts construction of Berlin Wall Britain applies to join EEC
September	Joan Littlewood announces she is leaving British theatre	
October	Zeffirelli's production of *Othello* opens at Stratford with John Gielgud in title role Edward Albee double bill opens at Royal Court (*The Death of Bessie Smith* and *The American Dream*)	
November		British government introduces Commonwealth Immigrants Bill to limit immigration from former colonies
December	*The Times* publishes an article on 'Theatre of Cruelty'	Adolf Eichmann found guilty in Israel of crimes against humanity Kennedy sends US military helicopters and crews to South Vietnam Tanganyika declares independence from Britain, as Tanzania

America and Soviet Union both conduct extensive series of nuclear tests; Female contraceptive pill becomes available to (married) women in Britain on the National Health; Monday Club established by right-wing Conservative MPs; America sends chimpanzee into space; Beatles' first performance at the Cavern Club in Liverpool; Bob Dylan's first performance at Greenwich Village, New York; *Private Eye* magazine launched; *The Avengers* first screened; In tennis, the final of the women's singles championship at Wimbledon is between two British players (Angela Mortimer beats Christine Truman), a British man (Mike Sangster) also reached the semi-finals of the men's championship

Significant new films released in 1961 include *A Taste of Honey, Breakfast at Tiffany's, The Guns of Navarone, One Hundred and One Dalmatians*

1962

	PERFORMANCE	POLITICAL/WORLD
January		
February		US begins blockade of Cuba US Supreme Court bans racial segregation on public transportation
March	Anne Jellicoe's *The Knack* opens at Royal Court RSC stage Brecht's *The Caucasian Chalk Circle* at the Aldwych Caryl Churchill's *Easy Death* staged at Oxford Playhouse	Britain explodes underground nuclear device in Nevada Army seizes power in Syria
April	Arnold Wesker's *Chips with Everything* opens at Royal Court	Commonwealth Immigration Act receives royal assent, restricting access to UK
May	First performance of Benjamin Britten's *War Requiem* at Coventry Cathedral Lionel Bart's musical *Blitz* opens at Adelphi Theatre Crazy Gang retire *The Black and White Minstrel Show* opens at Victoria Palace	
June	Private RSC production of David Rudkin's *Afore Night Comes* at the Arts Theatre Club	
July	Chichester Festival Theatre opens with Sir Laurence Olivier as artistic director—the first modern thrust stage in Britain. Its acclaimed production of *Uncle Vanya* stars Olivier, Sybil Thorndike, Joan Plowright and Michael Redgrave Proposals approved for a National Theatre and a National Opera House Osborne's *Plays for England* at Royal Court American revue *The Premise* opens at Comedy Theatre, a show normally including improvisation	Algeria achieves independence from France Rally in London with Sir Oswald Moseley disrupted by anti-fascist protesters British PM Harold Macmillan sacks a third of his cabinet in 'the Night of the Long Knives' Telstar—the first communications satellite—launched. First transatlantic television programme broadcast

1962

	PERFORMANCE	POLITICAL/WORLD
August	Sir Laurence Olivier appointed as first director of National Theatre	Trinidad and Tobago achieves independence from Britain, as does Jamaica Nelson Mandela arrested in South Africa
September		Race riots at University of Mississippi when first black student admitted and prevented from taking up place
October	Stoke's Victoria Theatre opens under Stephen Joseph and Peter Cheeseman. Britain's first permanent and full-time Theatre-in-the-round	Uganda achieves independence from Britain Cuban missile crisis brings world to brink of nuclear war
November	Peter Brook's production of *King Lear* at Stratford (with Paul Scofield) Samuel Beckett's *Happy Days* opens at Royal Court Caryl Churchill's *The Ants* broadcast on radio	
December	Edward Bond's *The Pope's Wedding* staged at Royal Court in Sunday night performance	Agreement between Macmillan and Kennedy for joint nuclear strategy, and for America to sell Polaris missiles to Britain

America's first combat missions against the Vietcong take place in Vietnam; First person killed trying to escape from East Germany across Berlin Wall; Death of Marilyn Monroe; Twenty-five smallpox deaths in UK; First Sunday colour supplement starts (*Sunday Times*); Beatles release first record (*Love Me Do*); First James Bond movie released (*Doctor No*) with Sean Connery as Bond; Centigrade first used to record temperatures in Britain; Andy Warhol's soup cans exhibited; Publication of Rachel Carson's *Silent Spring*, launching the environmental movement

New television programmes first broadcast in 1962 include *That Was the Week That Was, University Challenge, Top of the Form, Z Cars, Steptoe and Son, Dr Finlay's Casebook, Animal Magic*

Significant new films released in 1962 include *Dr No, How the West Was Won, The Loneliness of the Long Distance Runner, Lawrence of Arabia*

1963

	PERFORMANCE	POLITICAL/WORLD
January	Lord Cobbold replaces Lord Scarbrough as the Lord Chamberlain Traverse Theatre Club opens in Edinburgh in former brothel/doss house	Death of Hugh Gaitskell, leader of Labour Party. Harold Wilson becomes leader . French President General De Gaulle rejects UK application to join the EEC
February		
March	Theatre Workshop's *Oh! What a Lovely War* opens at Stratford East Kenneth Tynan appointed as Literary Manager for National Theatre *Half a Sixpence* (starring Tommy Steele) opens at Cambridge Theatre	Report by Dr Beeching published recommending huge cuts to the British rail network, leading to closure of over 2000 stations
April	Frank Wedekind's much banned *Spring Awakening* staged for Sunday night only at Royal Court US comedian Lenny Bruce banned by Home Office from entering and performing in Britain	Violence and arrests in Whitehall following Aldermarston CND march
May		Race riots in Birmingham, Alabama Thirty-two African nations form Organisation of African Unity Jomo Kenyatta elected to be first Prime Minister of independent Kenya
June	Theatre Workshop's *Oh! What a Lovely War* transfers to West End John Arden's *Workhouse Donkey* opens at Chichester More than forty British playwrights refuse permission for plays to be staged to segregated audiences in South Africa (or any theatres 'where discrimination is made among audiences on grounds of colour')	British Minister of War John Profumo resigns following Christine Keeler scandal and lying to Parliament US President J.F. Kennedy makes famous 'Ich bin ein Berliner' speech
July	Barry Reckord's *Skyvers* opens at Royal Court	Arrest of ANC leaders in South Africa British spy Kim Philby revealed as third Briton in Soviet spy ring, with Guy Burgess and Donald Maclean US, Russia and Britain sign nuclear test ban treaty

1963

	PERFORMANCE	POLITICAL/WORLD
August	RSC's *Wars of the Roses* cycle of Shakespeare's History plays opens at Stratford (John Barton & Peter Hall)	200,000 march for African American civil rights in Washington, DC; Martin Luther King delivers his 'I have a dream' speech Hotline communication set up between the Pentagon and the Kremlin to help prevent nuclear confrontations
September	RSC production of Rolf Hochhuth's *The Representative* opens at the Aldwych Eugène Ionesco's *Exit the King* opens at Royal Court with Alec Guinness International Drama Conference in Edinburgh culminates in staged 'Happening' and 'nude girl incident', co-ordinated by Charles Marowitz and John Calder	
October	First National Theatre production opens at the Old Vic (*Hamlet* with Peter O'Toole) *At the Drop of Another Hat* (Flanders and Swann) opens at Haymarket	In South Africa, trial of Nelson Mandela and other ANC leaders begins In Britain, Harold Macmillan resigns as PM on health grounds. Alec Douglas-Home replaces him as Tory PM
November	Alan Ayckbourn's *Mr Whatnot* opens at Victoria Theatre, Stoke Rodgers and Hart musical *Boys from Syracuse* (based on Shakespeare's *Comedy of Errors*) opens at Drury Lane	Assassination in Texas of President of USA, J.F. Kennedy. Lyndon Johnson becomes President
December	Nottingham Playhouse opens with production of *Coriolanus*, starring John Neville and directed by Sir Tyrone Guthrie	Zanzibar and Kenya both achieve independence from Britain

£2.6 million stolen in Great Train Robbery from Glasgow to London train; Sindy fashion doll first appears in shops; Publication of Robbins Report recommending major expansion of British Higher Education; Great Britain ends its amateur-professional divide in cricket; Beatles release *I Want to Hold Your Hand*

Significant new films released in 1963 include *The Birds*, *This Sporting Life*, *From Russia with Love*, *The Pink Panther* and Cliff Richard in *Summer Holiday*

New television programmes first broadcast in 1963 include *Ready Steady Go* and *Doctor Who*

1964

	PERFORMANCE	POLITICAL/WORLD
January	Theatre of Cruelty season (including Artuad's *Spurt of Blood*) opens at LAMDA, under Peter Brook and Charles Marowitz	Kenneth Kaunda becomes President of Zambia (Northern Rhodesia)
February	RSC's *The Rebel* presented at Aldwych Edward Albee's *Who's Afraid of Virginia Woolf?* opens at Piccadilly Theatre	France and Britain agree to build Channel Tunnel Fighting between Greece and Turkey in Cyprus
March	Theatre Workshop's *A Kayf Up West* (by Frank Norman) opens at Stratford East	Married Women's Property Act passed, allowing married women to keep half of any savings they had made from the allowance paid to them by their husbands
April	Samuel Beckett's *Play* first staged by NT at Old Vic John Dexter/Laurence Olivier NT production of *Othello* opens at Old Vic First international 'World Theatre' season presented at the Aldwych, produced by Peter Daubeny	Ian Smith becomes Prime Minister of Rhodesia
May	*Entertaining Mr Sloane* opens—Joe Orton's first play RSC Experimental Group stage Genet's *The Screens*, Donmar Rehearsal Room	State of emergency in British Guiana PLO formed
June	RSC full production of David Rudkin's *Afore Night Come* at Aldwych Brecht's *Saint Joan of the Stockyards* staged at Queen's Theatre	Nelson Mandela and seven others sentenced to life imprisonment in Rivonia trial, Pretoria
July		President Johnson signs Civil Rights Act in America Malawi (formerly Nyasaland) declares independence from UK
August	Peter Brook's RSC production of Weiss's *Marat/Sade* opens at Aldwych 'Dirty Plays' controversy—attack on Peter Hall and RSC	

1964

	PERFORMANCE	POLITICAL/WORLD
September	Living Theatre's *The Brig* opens in London John Osborne's *Inadmissible Evidence* opens at Royal Court with Nicol Williamson	Malta becomes independent from Britain
October	Ill health forces George Devine to resign as artistic director at Royal Court. Succeeded by Bill Gaskill Windmill Theatre closes	Labour under Harold Wilson win General Election with majority of four seats Nikita Kruschev replaced as leader of the Soviet Union by Alexei Kosygin and Leonid Brezhnev Martin Luther King awarded Nobel Peace Prize
November		Lyndon Johnson wins presidential election in America
December	Peter Shaffer's *Royal Hunt of the Sun* opens—NT production, with Robert Stephens	

Total of over 300 years in prison sentences given to twelve men found guilty of involvement in Great Train Robbery; Typhoid outbreak in Aberdeen; Report in US links smoking with cancer; Violence and fighting take place between mods and rockers over bank holiday weekends at Clacton, Margate, Brighton and Bournemouth with many arrests; Five new universities open in Britain; *Daily Herald* closes down; *The Sun* begins publishing; *Jackie* first published; First pirate radio station (Radio Caroline) launched; Drilling for oil and gas in the North Sea approved; Cassius Clay becomes World Heavyweight Champion and joins the Nation of Islam, changing his name to Muhammad Ali; First Habitat shop opens; Bull Ring, Birmingham opens; Topless dresses appear in London

Ariane Mnouchkine's Théâtre du Soleil founded; Jan Kott's, *Shakespeare Our Contemporary* published; According to *Plays and Players* 'Theatre of Cruelty replaced Theatre of the Absurd as the number one talking point'; ICA exhibition: Violence in Society, Nature and Art

New television programmes first broadcast in 1964 include *Top of the Pops*, *Match of the Day*, *Playschool*, *The Wednesday Play* and *The Man from U.N.C.L.E.*; Peter Watkins's *Culloden* broadcast

Significant new films released in 1964 include *Goldfinger*, *Dr Strangelove*, *Hard Day's Night*, *Zulu*, *Mary Poppins*

Top singles in the UK include Rolling Stones, *Not Fade Away* and *It's All Over Now*; Animals, *House of the Rising Sun*; Kinks, *You Really Got me*; Beachboys, *I Get Around*

1965

	PERFORMANCE	POLITICAL/WORLD
January	Jerzy Grotowski founds Laboratory Theatre in Wroclaw	Death of Sir Winston Churchill
February	Joe Orton's *Loot* opens at Cambridge Arts Theatre	Jenny Lee appointed as first Minister for the Arts Gambia becomes independent from the United Kingdom Assassination of American black nationalist leader, Malcolm X
March		Russian cosmonaut becomes the first person to walk in space US confirms it has been using chemical weapons in Vietnam
April	First public performance in Britain (with cuts) of Wedekind's *Spring Awakening* (Royal Court) Frank Marcus's *Killing of Sister George* opens in Bath—later transfers to West End	Creation of Greater London Council (GLC)
May	*Mother Courage and Her Children* opens at Old Vic—NT's first production of a play by Brecht Baldwin's *Blues for Mr Charlie* staged at Aldwych in World Theatre season	
June	Harold Pinter's, *The Homecoming* opens at the Aldwych (RSC), following tour Arnold Schoenberg's *Moses and Aaron* staged at Royal Opera House	
July	Royal Court becomes a private club to stage John Osborne's, *A Patriot for Me* Alan Ayckbourn's *Relatively Speaking* premieres at Scarborough	Edward Heath replaces Alec Douglas-Home as leader of Conservative Party
August	Berliner Ensemble perform series of Brecht plays at the Old Vic Soyinka's *The Road* staged at Theatre Royal, Stratford East BBC cancels showing of Watkins' *War Game*	

1965

	PERFORMANCE	POLITICAL/WORLD
September	First Theatre-in-Education programme in UK presented by Coventry Belgrade Theatre Wole Soyinka's *The Road* staged at Theatre Royal, Stratford East in Commonwealth Arts Festival	
October	Pete Weiss's *The Investigation* staged at Aldwych by RSC	Unsuccessful series of talks to try and resolve Rhodesia crisis between Harold Wilson and Ian Smith Bodies of murdered children found in Lancashire, Myra Hindley and Ian Brady committed for trial
November	Edward Bond's *Saved* staged in club conditions at Royal Court Kenneth Tynan says 'fuck' on television	Capital Punishment in Britain abolished for trial five-year period In Rhodesia, Ian Smith declares UDI from Britain. British government declares his regime illegal and imposes economic sanctions
December	Theatre Workshop/Joan Littlewood production of *Twang!* opens in London *The Curse of the Daleks* opens at Wyndham's Theatre *Hello, Dolly!* opens at Theatre Royal, Drury Lane	Race Relations Act becomes law in Britain, making racial discrimination in public places illegal

Massive escalation by US in Vietnam war, involving bombers, ground troops and chemical weapons; Civil Rights marches, protests and violence in several states in America; Barbara Castle becomes the first female Secretary of State in the UK (Department of Transport); The intention to adopt the metric system is announced; North Sea gas is discovered; A 70 m.p.h. speed limit is imposed; The Post Office Tower opens; Local authorities are instructed to submit plans for comprehensive schools; Mary Whitehouse founds the National Viewers' and Listeners' Association; Miniskirts appear (Mary Quant); Beatles awarded MBEs

First performances by fringe theatre companies The People Show and Cartoon Archetypal Slogan Theatre (CAST); Death of George Devine, director of English Stage Company and the Royal Court 1956–1965; First International Poetry Incarnation held at the Royal Albert Hall

Significant new films released in 1965 include *Help* (Queen attends premiere), *Dr Zhivago*, *The Sound of Music*

Top singles in the UK include Rolling Stones, *Satisfaction*, *The Last Time* and *Off of My Cloud*; The Who, *My Generation*; The Byrds, *Mr Tambourine Man*; Tom Jones, *It's Not Unusual*; Moody Blues, *Go Now*

New television programmes broadcast in 1965 include *Not Only . . . But Also* (Peter Cooke and Dudley Moore), *Going for a Song*, *Tomorrow's World*, *Jackanory*, *The Magic Roundabout*

Dylan releases *Like a Rolling Stone* and starts to use electric guitar

1966

	PERFORMANCE	POLITICAL/WORLD
January		Indira Gandhi becomes first woman prime minister in India
February	Theatre Workshop's *Twang!* opens at Shaftesbury Theatre	In Ghana, a military coup removes the country's first post-independence leader Russian spacecraft lands on moon
March	David Halliwell's *Little Malcolm and his Struggle Against the Eunuchs* opens at the Garrick Theatre Peter Shaffer's *Black Comedy* at National Theatre	IRA blow up Nelson's column in Dublin World Cup stolen from central London
April	Peter Hall's RSC production of *Hamlet* opens at Aldwych (with David Warner in title role) John McGrath's, *Events While Guarding the Bofors Gun* first staged at Hampstead Theatre Club	Labour under Harold Wilson re-elected in general election with increased majority (97) Myra Hindley and Ian Brady found guilty of 'moors murders' and sentenced to life imprisonment
May	Arnold Wesker's *Their Very Own and Golden City* opens at Royal Court	*The Times* begins publishing news on its front page Guyana declares independence from UK
June	Peter Handke's *Offending the Audience* first staged in Frankfurt	David Steele introduces Medical Termination of Pregnancy Bill to the House of Commons, which will lead to first limited legalisation of abortion the following year
July	*The Knotty* (Peter Cheeseman and Peter Terson's devised musical documentary about the North Staffordshire Railway) opens at Victoria Theatre, Stoke-on-Trent	Leo Abse introduces Sexual Offences Bill to the House of Commons, which will lead the following year to decriminalisation of homosexuality for consenting adults over 21 Big anti-war demonstration outside US Embassy in London Race riots in Nebraska and Chicago
August	Tom Stoppard's *Rosencrantz and Guildenstern* first performed at Edinburgh Fringe Festival	Start of cultural revolution in China

1966

	PERFORMANCE	POLITICAL/WORLD
September	Joe Orton's *Loot* staged at Jeanette Cochrane Theatre In a co-ordinated campaign, protestors against the war in Vietnam interrupt a series of performances in London's West End by infiltrating the stage and making political speeches Covent Garden hosts controversial 'Destruction in Art' event	Assassination of Dr Henrik Verwoerd, the South African Prime Minister and architect of apartheid system, in Cape Town parliament Albert Speer, Hitler's architect and Nazi war criminal, released from Spandau Prison Botswana declares independence from UK
October	Peter Brook/RSC production of *US* opens at Aldwych Trevor Nunn's production of *The Revenger's Tragedy* opens at Stratford RSC present *The Matter of J. Robert Oppenheimer* in private performances at Hampstead	Lesotho declares independence from UK
November	*The Matter of J. Robert Oppenheimer* licensed and transfers to West End (Fortune Theatre) David Mercer's *Belcher's Luck* opens at Aldwych (RSC) Henry Livings's *Little Mrs Foster Show* opens at Liverpool Playhouse Ken Loach's *Cathy Come Home*—a drama about homelessness—first broadcast on television	Barbados achieves independence from UK
December	Wole Soyinka's *The Lion and the Jewel* at the Royal Court	Shelter charity founded

Centre Point, a 32-floor office building at St Giles Circus in London, designed by Richard Seifert for property speculator Harry Hyams, is completed. It remains empty for around a decade; Aberfan disaster—coal tip collapses and destroys school (116 children killed); London School of Contemporary Dance founded

New television programmes broadcast in 1966 include *Softly Softly* and *Till Death Us Do Part*

Significant new films released in 1966 include *Alfie, The Battle of Algiers, Blow-Up, Born Free, The Good, the Bad, and the Ugly, A Man for All Seasons, Who's Afraid of Virginia Woolf?*

Top singles in the UK include Frank Sinatra, *Strangers in the Night*; Beatles, *Eleanor Rigby/Yellow Submarine* and *Paperback Writer*; Rolling Stones, *Nineteenth Nervous Breakdown* and *Paint it Black*; Beach Boys, *Sloop John B, Good Vibrations* and *God Only Knows*; Kinks, *Sunny Afternoon* and *Dedicated Follower of Fashion*; Dusty Springfield, *You Don't Have to Say you Love Me*; Ike and Tina Turner, *River Deep, Mountain High*; Troggs, *Wild Thing*; The Who, *Substitute*

1967

	PERFORMANCE	POLITICAL/WORLD
January	John McGrath's *Events While Guarding the Bofors Gun* opens at Edinburgh Lyceum (directed by Richard Eyre)	Jeremy Thorpe replaces Joe Grimmond as leader of Liberal Party
February	RSC presents reading from *The Senate Hearings on Vietnam* (Aldwych) *Fiddler on the Roof* opens at Her Majesty's Theatre	Dominica gains independence from England Extreme right-wing National Front party formed in Britain
March	Alan Ayckbourn'a *Relatively Speaking* opens in London D.H. Lawrence's *The Daughter-in-Law* revived at Royal Court	St Lucia gains independence from Britain *Torrey Canyon* runs aground off Cornwall and leaks 100,000 tons of crude oil into the sea
April	Tom Stoppard's *Rosencrantz and Guildenstern are Dead* opens at National Theatre (Old Vic) Theatre Workshop's *MacBird* opens at Stratford East Edward Bond's translation of *The Three Sisters* at Royal Court National Theatre Board rules that Hochhuth's *Soldiers* is not suitable for performance	Military coup and introduction of martial law in Greece Muhammad Ali refuses US army draft and is stripped of world boxing title In Britain, Political Economic Planning survey produces report identifying a significant colour bar operating in British society
May	Peter Nichols's *A Day in the Death of Joe Egg* opens in Glasgow Centre 42: *What About the Workers*	Biafra declares independence from Nigeria President De Gaulle again vetoes British application to join EEC
June	Joe Orton's *Ruffian on the Stair* and *The Erpingham Camp* open at Royal Court	Six Day War between Israel and neighbouring Arab countries China explodes country's first hydrogen bomb Muhammad Ali/Cassius Clay sentenced to five years in prison for refusing to serve in US army
July/August	Peter Hall directs *Macbeth* for RSC, with Paul Scofield and Vivien Merchant (Stratford) Jean-Claude van Itallie's *America Hurrah* opens at Royal Court Leading New York experimental company La MaMa stage *Futz* at Edinburgh Festival Peter Terson's *Zigger Zagger* first staged by National Youth Theatre at Jeanetta Cochrane Theatre Joe Orton murdered	British Parliament approves bill legalising abortion Sexual Offences Act comes into force (legalising homosexuality for consenting adults) British Steel Industry re-nationalised Biafran war/Nigerian civil war begins

1967

	PERFORMANCE	POLITICAL/WORLD
September	La MaMa present Paul Foster's *Tom Paine* at Vaudeville Theatre *Mrs Wilson's Diary* (John Wells and Richard Ingrams) opens at Stratford East The Arts Lab opens in Drury Lane (founded by Jim Haynes) as a centre for experimental and avant-garde arts	George Blake revealed as a Soviet spy
October	Simon Gray's *Wise Child* opens at Wyndham's Theatre *Hair* opens off-Broadway Albert Hunt re-stages the Russian Revolution in Bradford to mark 50th anniversary	Che Guevara killed in Bolivia Criminal Justice Act comes into force in UK (including abolition of flogging in prisons) Huge anti-war protests in America, including in California and Washington, as well as in London
November	Charles Wood's *Dingo* opens at Royal Court Bolton Octagon Theatre opens Exeter Northcott Theatre opens	Aden achieves independence from Britain Publication of Street Report into racial discrimination in Britain De Gaulle rules out negotiations for Britain to join EEC British government devalues the pound
December	Paperbag Players from America perform at Royal Court *The Dragon* by Yevgeny Shvarts opens at Royal Court	Nicolae Ceaușescu becomes president (dictator) of Romania

First human heart transplant takes place (South Africa); National Health Family Planning Act passed—Pill available to all women; Entertainment Tax abolished; Breathalyser tests introduced. World's first ATM installed in London; Laura Ashley opens first shop; First Monterey pop festival (California); UK wins Eurovision song contest with Sandie Shaw's *Puppet on a String*; First British colour TV broadcasts; Radio 1 launched and other stations rebranded as Radios 2, 3 and 4; BBC local radio starts; Publication of Desmond Morris's *The Naked Ape* and *The Mersey Sound* anthology (Roger McGough, Brian Patten and Adrian Henri); *Forsyte Saga* on television; Queen Elizabeth Hall opens

Significant new films released in 1967 include *You Only Live Twice*, *The Graduate*, *Bonnie and Clyde*, *Guess Who's Coming to Dinner*, *The Jungle Book*

Beatles release *Sergeant Pepper* and *Magical Mystery Tour* albums

Top UK singles include Doors, *Light My Fire*; Procol Harum, *A Whiter Shade of Pale*; Hendrix, *Hey Joe*; Beatles, *All You Need is Love*; Royal Guardsmen, *Snoopy vs the Red Baron*

1968

	PERFORMANCE	POLITICAL/WORLD
January		
February	*Cabaret* opens at Palace Theatre (with Judi Dench as Sally Bowles)	Payment of damages by drug companies for thalidomide children agreed
March	Bond's *Early Morning* given private performance at Royal Court Peter Brook's production of Ted Hughes's version of Seneca's *Oedipus* for the National Theatre opens at the Old Vic Trilogy of D.H. Lawrence plays open at Royal Court, directed by Peter Gill (*A Collier's Friday Night*, *The Daughter-in-Law*, *The Widowing of Mrs Holroyd*)	Mauritius gains independence from Britain Riots in Grosvenor Square following demonstration against Vietnam War outside US Embassy Student riots in Nanterre British Foreign Secretary George Brown resigns My Lai massacre carried out by US troops in Vietnam
April	Trevor Nunn directs *King Lear* at Stratford (cast includes Eric Porter, Alan Howard, Ben Kingsley and Patrick Stewart) Adrienne Kennedy's *Funnyhouse of a Negro* and *A Lesson in a Dead Language* staged at Royal Court Brecht's adaptation of Marlowe's *Edward II* opens at Old Vic (NT) RSC tours London schools with production based on *Eleanor Rigby* Ambiance Lunch Hour Theatre opens in London (Ed Berman)	N Vietnam agrees to meet US to set up preliminary peace talks Assassination of Martin Luther King in Memphis, Tennessee Enoch Powell makes 'Rivers of Blood' speech, warning against dangers of (black) immigration. He is sacked by Conservative leader, Ted Heath, but achieves significant public support
May	RSC tours schools with *The Seven Ages of Woman*	Student and worker uprisings in Paris (and elsewhere in Europe)
June	Edward Bond's *Narrow Road to the Deep North* opens in Coventry RSC production of Marlowe's *Doctor Faustus* opens at Stratford, with Eric Porter in title role	Assassination of Robert Kennedy in US Attempted assassination of Andy Warhol by Valerie Solanas In London, women machinists at Fords of Dagenham go on strike for equal pay—leads to Equal Pay Act (1970)
July	Arthur Kopit's *Indians* opens at Aldwych (RSC) The Roundhouse opens as theatre venue with *Themes on the Tempest* (Brook/Reeves) as first production Trafalgar Square Festival includes performances by Agitprop Street Players/Red Ladder	US, Britain, USSR and 58 nations sign Nuclear Non-Proliferation Treaty

1968

	PERFORMANCE	POLITICAL/WORLD
August		Soviet Tanks enter Czechoslovakia to crush 'Prague Spring'
September	Christopher Hampton's *Total Eclipse* opens at Royal Court 1968 Theatres Act abolishes pre-censorship by Lord Chamberlain *Hair* opens in London Paddy Chayefsky's *The Latent Homosexual* opens at Aldwych	Swaziland gains independence from Britain
October	Alan Bennett's *Forty Years On* opens at the Apollo Theatre	Two American athletes sent home from Mexico Olympics for giving 'Black Power' salute from victory podium during US national anthem Violent clashes outside American Embassy in London between anti-war protesters and police Civil rights march in Londonderry broken up by police US halts bombing of Vietnam
November	Peter Barnes's *The Ruling Class* opens, Nottingham Playhouse Michael McClure's *The Beard* performed late night at Royal Court	Robert Nixon elected as Republican President of United States UK Race Relations Act makes it illegal to refuse housing, employment or public services on the basis of ethnic background
December	Welfare State International Theatre founded by John Fox and Sue Gill	

Britain introduces Abortion law, decimal coinage, prescription charges and second-class stamps.

Pip Simmons Theatre Group formed; Ed Berman starts Inter-Action; Grotowski's *Towards a Poor Theatre* and Peter Brook's *The Empty Space* published; *Time Out* launched, and starts fringe listings

Significant new films include *Yellow Submarine, If, 2001: A Space Odyssey, Once Upon a Time in the West, Planet of the Apes*

Top UK singles include Louis Armstrong, *What a Wonderful World*; Tom Jones, *Delilah*; Simon & Garfunkel, *Mrs Robinson*; Cliff Richard, *Congratulations*; Rolling Stones, *Jumping Jack Flash* and *Street Fighting Man*

1969

	PERFORMANCE	POLITICAL/WORLD
January	Howard Brenton's *Gum and Goo* performed by Brighton Combination	Richard Nixon inaugurated as President of USA Student protesters take over LSE in London, and the institution is closed for three weeks Beatles perform last live gig, a 42-minute concert on roof of Apple HQ, London
February	Edward Bond's *Saved* and *Narrow Road to the Deep North* open at Royal Court	Yasser Arafat becomes President of PLO
March	Joe Orton's *What the Butler Saw* first performed at Queen's Theatre Peter Barnes's *The Ruling Class* performed at Piccadilly Theatre Edward Bond's *Early Morning* opens at Royal Court	Kray brothers found guilty of murder and imprisoned
April	David Storey's *The Contractor* opens at Royal Court (directed by Lindsay Anderson) *The Enoch Show* at Royal Court— event infiltrated and disrupted by the National Front Dennis Potter's controversial *Son of Man* broadcast on BBC1 (Frank Finlay as Christ)	Massive anti-war demonstrations take place in cities across America President de Gaulle resigns in France UK voting age lowered from 21 to 18
May	Charles Marowitz's adaptation of *Macbeth* staged at the Open Space	Government and Police in America crack down on student sit-ins at Universities, using force and threats of arrest
June	Pinter's *Landscape* and *Silence* open at the Aldwych (RSC, directed by Peter Hall) Bread and Puppet Theatre perform at Royal Court Living Theatre perform at the Roundhouse with *Frankenstein*, *Mysteries*, *Antigone* and *Paradise Now* *Oh! Calcutta!* opens in New York	US starts to withdraw troops from Vietnam

1969

	PERFORMANCE	POLITICAL/WORLD
July	Middleton's *Women Beware Women* opens at Stratford (RSC), with Judi Dench as Bianca Charles Marowitz's adaptation of *Hamlet* staged at the Open Space Stephen Berkoff's *Metamorphosis* and *In the Penal Colony* at the Roundhouse	Apollo 11 launched and first men land on the moon Brian Jones (former guitarist with Rolling Stones) found dead in swimming pool
August		British government sends troops into Northern Ireland, following street violence and marches Actress Sharon Tate and others ritualistically murdered in Los Angeles by Charles Manson and others Woodstock music festival takes place in New York State Bob Dylan performs at Isle of Wight Festival
September	Howard Brenton's *Revenge* opens at Royal Court Upstairs	200 police involved in evicting squatters from a mansion in Piccadilly Shelter publishes report claiming three million people in Britain are living in slum conditions
October	Dennis Potter's *Son of Man* staged at the Leicester Phoenix Theatre	Huge anti-war marches across US in the 'Vietnam Moratorium' Divorce Bill approved by British Parliament, removing blame and making divorce easier
November	John Webster's *The White Devil* opens at Old Vic (NT)	Apollo 12—second moon landing
December		Britain confirms abolition of death penalty

Rolling Stones play free concert in Hyde Park a few days after death of guitarist Brian Jones; Concorde's maiden flight; Victoria Underground line opens; Britain introduces 50p coin; Open University established; Margaret Atwood's first novel, *The Edible Woman*

Oval House, Soho Poly and Royal Court Theatre Upstairs among new performance spaces to open

Television: BBC1 and ITV launch colour TV service; *Monty Python's Flying Circus* first broadcast; *Civilisation: A Personal View* by Kenneth Clark on BBC2 (13 parts)

Significant new films released in 1969 include *Easy Rider, Butch Cassidy and the Sundance Kid, Midnight Cowboy, Kes*

Top singles in the UK include Thunderclap Newman, *Something in the Air*; Fleetwood Mac, *Albataross*; The Who, *Pinball Wizard*; Rolling Stones, *Honky Tonk Woman*; Beatles, *Get Back*; Plastic Ono Band, *Give Peace a Chance*; George Harrison, *Something*; David Bowie, *Space Oddity*; Bob Dylan, *Lay Lady Lay*; Rolf Harris, *Two Little Boys*

INTRODUCTION

Galahad and Mordred

What might come before the public but for his Office we can only guess.[1]

In March 1961, the Assistant Comptroller in the Lord Chamberlain's Office, Eric Penn, replied to a Colonel who had sought advice on behalf of his daughter in connection with an essay on the history and practice of stage censorship she was submitting as part of her entrance examination to Oxbridge. Penn informed the Colonel that the system was very widely accepted as a necessary control, which had worked without significant problems since its inception in 1737. Indeed, the letter exuded a confidence that it remained an essential and effective practice, being in effect a natural life form ('The censorship is so old as to be almost an organic growth') which functioned on quasi-Darwinian principles: 'it selects a man (the Lord Chamberlain) who, by virtue of his position, must be a man of wide experience and great tolerance who substitutes his personal opinion for that of a committee which has the need to work with a quorum'. If this risked making the set up sound dangerously close to dictatorship, there was no need to worry: 'It gives this man autocratic powers but, as so often happens with our English system of balances, Press and other vociferous sources of protest are so strong as to constitute a very powerful safeguard against any tyrannical use of the powers granted.'[2]

These comfortable assertions may have satisfied a Colonel and his daughter—they may even have satisfied a University Admissions Officer. But in reality, pretty much everyone associated with the Lord Chamberlain's Office at St James's Palace knew that the system was crumbling. The current incumbent, the Earl of Scarbrough, had already made it patently clear to the Home Office that he wanted out—that responsibility for theatres should be removed from his portfolio of duties, in order that he could better concentrate on his other tasks, such as organising the Queen's garden parties and culling her swans. The sustained adverse publicity that had increasingly come to dominate newspaper coverage of his licensing decisions damaged not only his reputation but that of the 'establishment' he was seen to be part of, and, at least potentially, that of the monarch.

Some time, something had to give. Of course, the Lord Chamberlain was not without friends and allies. 'I hope you don't mind us taking up a light-weight cudgel on your behalf now and then' wrote the *Daily Telegraph* in 1963; 'We would not like you to think that all the Press are against you'.[3] And as in previous decades, and as Lords Chamberlain frequently pointed out, the Office probably received at least as much criticism for what it allowed as for what they turned down. But an internal memorandum written by his assistant secretary in the same month as the letter to the Colonel confirmed that 'the climate of opinion, or at least the vociferous part thereof, is against censorship', and that 'any positive action on the Lord Chamberlain's part is greeted in the Popular Press with indignation'. As the memorandum acknowledged: 'The writing is on the wall.'[4] This, remember, when the 'rebellious decade' had but barely begun.[5]

There are times during the next few years when the Lord Chamberlain and his Comptroller and Assistant Comptroller seem to have been fuelled more by a sense of obligation to fulfil their responsibilities than by a real commitment to the cause. But St James's had at least one member of staff who remained rigidly convinced both of the necessity for theatre censorship, and that the Lord Chamberlain was the right person to be doing it. Ronald John Hill had been an assistant secretary in the Office since the mid 1930s, and his enthusiasm for the cause was unwavering. He also knew more about the history and practice of censorship than anyone at St James's, and it was invariably he who supplied his superiors with details of precedents and historical policy, as well as with carefully-worded letters and briefing documents. When in 1965 he gave evidence in court for the prosecution of the Royal Court over its production of Edward Bond's *Saved*, Hill was gently mocked in the press as 'an upright, greying man with spectacles, who called both counsel "Sir"'.[6] He may have come from another era, and held to values which would be confounded by some of the ideas and practices which became acceptable—even fashionable—during the 1960s; but at least the Assistant Secretary was no jobsworth. Hill believed fundamentally in the importance and necessity of the Censor, and was resistant to the last to any substantial change or any diminution of the Lord Chamberlain's authority. Indeed, whenever he was allowed to be so he was an active campaigner for the existing system, ready to embrace alteration only where it seemed likely to increase the effectiveness of control. Hill would go down fighting, the last to leave the bridge.

Certainly, there are no documents more passionate in their advocacy of theatre censorship by the Lord Chamberlain than Hill's. In 1962, when the Lord Chamberlain was looking for a friendly journalist to write a sym-pathetic and 'Informed Article' to try and counterbalance the seemingly endless criticism, Hill, at the drop of a hat, produced eleven closely typed foolscap pages designed to persuade readers to realise the debt which the entire country owed to its Censor of Plays, and how lucky they were to have him. It was good stuff, too:

> For some time now the Lord Chamberlain in his capacity as Censor of Stage Plays has been under public attack. He has been damned with the faintest of faint praise by the more staid newspapers; abused in the most offensive terms by others; and his actions have been publicly dissected by professional controversialists on television. More understandably perhaps he has also been jeered at from the stage by those actors who revel in the atmosphere of public derision of any authority.

Hill's testimony did more than defend—it also attacked, mocking the credibility and naivety of the Office's opponents: 'If we are to believe what we read every day the Censor of stage plays is a purblind ass, unable to appreciate what is evident to the least qualified journalist or to his Readers', wrote Hill. In order to demonstrate the risibility of such assumptions, he documented Scarbrough's educational and professional and political experience, thus affirming the Earl's credentials: 'It is worth asking oneself why, immediately he becomes Lord Chamberlain, he should abandon all sensible thinking and deliver himself to the public correction of self-appointed tutors.' Hill's point, of course, was that it was not the Lord Chamberlain who was intellectually weak, but 'those whose interest is the manufacture and exploitation of journalistic Aunt Sallies' at whom they could then lob stones. Lords Chamberlain 'as a class', insisted Hill, had the ability to reach decisions with 'complete detachment', while the qualities honed in pursuance of his other duties 'make it probable, almost to the point of certainty, that he will be a tolerable, impartial, urbane and experienced man'. Moreover, their breeding and life history placed them in the fortunate position of enjoying easy access to the best contacts for advice, since their 'many ceremonial and social duties' required them to be 'continually out of doors and in the company of almost everyone who has attained eminence in government, commerce or the professions'. But the clincher was value for money. Because the Lord Chamberlain's salary was paid by the Queen, he came as a sort of free gift to serve his country. What else would offer the taxpayer such a good deal? And as an added bonus, no-one could accuse Lords Chamberlain of ideological bias since 'as Members of the Royal Household they are demonstrably politically neutral'. This supposed lack of bias and inbuilt sense of fairness differentiated Lords Chamberlain from their opponents and detractors, who, according to the assistant secretary, were motivated by class prejudice and an immature antagonism:

Could it be an irresistible incitement to them that the Censor of stage plays is an autocratically appointed Court Official—named as a member of the 'Establishment', with a theatrical history of four hundred years, and the holder of an Office which includes, with the traditional task of opening The Sovereign's carriage door, a title easily corrupted into a reference to chamber pots.

Hill's document traced much of the recent antagonism to the Earl of Scarbrough's refusal through most of the 1950s to allow any reference to homosexuality on the public stage; a refusal which had led to the banning of plays by, among others, Arthur Miller and Tennessee Williams. By the time Scarbrough had rescinded the policy, much damage had already been done. But rather than apologising, the assistant secretary did his best to recuperate the Earl's judgement.

> To the Lord Chamberlain's credit or shame, whichever way you look at it, the theatre was one of the last places of public entertainment at which this subject was aired. A review of the contemporary scene with its pervert-traitors and in London one soliciting prostitute in three convicted a man . . . will show I think that he was right at least to be dubious about falling in at once with his detractors' views.

Hill deployed sarcasm against the enemy, emphasising the decent and gentlemanly values which lay beneath the Lord Chamberlain's choices: 'He is so foolish as to think in this troubled world that some courtesy extended to the Heads of States would be helpful; he is so old fashioned as to object to blasphemy or to Christ being represented on the stage for money.' And Hill derided the altruistic motives lavished on his critics:

> It is also the claim, stated or implied, that everyone associated with any theatrical venture who is at odds with the Lord Chamberlain is actuated by nothing but the good of the theatre . . . might it not be that occasionally some of these, driven by poverty or greed, would, but for the Censor, be tempted to diverge from the high standards of the profession and stage some titillating piece of dirt, or propagate some piece of vice that would show good pickings. But no, apparently it is all Sir Galahad in the theatre with the Lord Chamberlain playing Mordred.

Hill castigated the press for collectively maintaining 'a conspiracy of silence about the more solid work that the Lord Chamberlain does'. If only more people knew what he had to deal with on a daily basis, they would realise that he was on the side of the angels. So Hill detailed some examples: 'Indecent language is a commonplace', he declared, somewhat embroidering reality: '"Cunt" and "fuck" if not daily are recurring deletions'. In fact there are very few 'cunts' to be found in the archive, and 'fucks' are relatively few and far between especially before 1962. Hill also cited examples of recent scripts where only the Lord Chamberlain's last minute interventions had spared audiences from having to endure a variety of unthinkable encounters:

> A play taking the class war into the Royal Air Force where officers are all homosexuals and the NCOs thugs . . . A play based on the pleasant theme of a young man being able to overcome any woman's virtue in five minutes whether he knew her or not . . . a sketch mocking the Crucifixion . . . a man exhibited on the stage with all the symptoms of a male orgasm . . . One set at a public school where an older boy seduces a junior boy . . . a girl of fifteen who has already slept with all the boys in the top class at school [who] runs off with one of the younger masters and starts a magnificent brothel in the West End . . . the flagellation of a woman for her own erotic fascination . . . description of a woman brought into a hospital by two policemen who have twice raped her in the back of the police car . . . a play which mocks the Holy communion which is celebrated with a bottle of Coco-cola, a wrapped sandwich, lighter fuel and an ashtray.

Even in the face of the above—and more—passing across his desk, Hill remained optimistic that the recent drift away from proper values and expectations might soon be reversed, and that the pendulum would swing again: 'So far, since the war, the movement has been all in one direction, and it has gone an astonishing way', he wrote; 'but there are slight signs of public reaction'. If that swing came, he promised, 'the Censor will move with it'. But as the sixties played out, and as more playwrights and theatres and directors and audiences refused to play by the Office's rules, the assistant secretary's hope came to look increasingly forlorn.[7]

Despite Hill's belligerence, it is probably fair to say that the battle to bring theatre censorship to an end—if we accept for a moment that this is what happened in 1968—had been largely won by the time the decade started. On that count, what we are watching in this volume is its prolonged and sometimes agonised death throes. In reality, it wasn't John Osborne or Edward Bond or the Royal Court or the Royal Shakespeare Company that did for the Lord Chamberlain—though all of these (and more) stuck in their knives and helped to finish him off. In the end, the victory had more to do with the broader cultural climate and the changes sweeping through British society and public attitudes. The election of a Labour government in 1964—with an agenda which, if not radical, was at least a modernising and reforming one—was another manifestation of a shift in outlook after thirteen years of Conservatism; it surely marked the Lord Chamberlain's card. On the other hand, it is also important to remember that his reign could have lasted longer. Certainly, it was not obvious to most people—even, perhaps, to those who were trying the hardest to bring it down—that the walls of the citadel were going to cave in when they did, or that they would collapse so completely.

The two men who held the reins at St James's Palace during the 1960s—the Earl of Scarbrough and Lord Kim Cobbold—wanted reform of the system, and responsibility for theatre censorship moved elsewhere, not abandoned. Neither really anticipated the transformation which would occur in the autumn of 1968. Significantly—and with some logic—Cobbold had wanted the remit of the government's 1966 Joint Select Committee—whose enquiry and recommendations would lead directly to the new Theatres Act—to encompass film, television and radio. It is not hard to see why. One of the things which made life difficult for the Lord Chamberlain through the sixties was that these other media so often seemed to follow different standards to his own; it therefore became increasingly implausible for him to defend decisions to cut material that audiences could not only read in print but also hear and see on cinema screens, and even at home. Once the government had rejected Cobbold's suggestion that the enquiry should extend beyond theatre, it became more difficult to construct a case for retaining a theatre censorship mark II—one which would simply adjust how and by whom it was administered.

This concluding volume in the history of twentieth-century British theatre censorship under the Lord Chamberlain will trace the key debates and conflicts from the beginning of the decade through until September 1968, when his rule ended. A final chapter will then focus on the aftermath, looking at how the new freedom was used, and at some of the censorship battles and debates which took place in the first two or three years after his demise.

I started the first volume of this series, covering the early years of the twentieth century, with a quotation from the MP Samuel Smith, who demanded 'a stricter supervision of theatrical performances' on the grounds that 'the moral standard of a country is largely affected by the drama'. According to Smith, 'Multitudes of young men and young women form their ideas of what is right and wrong in no small degree from what they witness on the stage'.[8] Whether or not such a claim had been accurate in 1900, it would have been hard to argue in the late 1960s. It therefore has to be admitted—even if this was rarely said aloud—that probably the most obvious reason that the system of theatre censorship could be allowed to go was simply that theatre was no longer seen as likely to have much impact on society's values or on how people behaved. It was a long time since the Censors had seriously worried that watching a production of *Oedipus* might inspire audiences to go home and commit incest. Now the key debates about influence were more likely to centre on films and television programmes. It is true that staff in the Lord Chamberlain's Office continued to express concerns about direct links between the decline they identified in society's moral standards and the sorts of character, language and behaviour which contemporary playwrights seemed to favour; the issue surfaces, for example, in relation to the Royal Court Theatre production of Bond's *Saved*, with its famous on-stage killing of a baby by a group of young men:

> this scene acted vividly by well cast characters, with all the appropriate props and business and before a different type of audience, which included a proportion of the gangs that now exist, could be a direct incentive to some of the sub-humans who now associate in gangs, to perpetrate a crime of this kind.[9]

Nevertheless, if equally disturbing images are available in cinema, where they can be depicted more realistically and in close-up, did policing of theatre much matter? Again, the sixties became, amongst many other things, a decade of political protest with a necessarily international dimension; yet under censorship, the theatre was denied the freedom to discuss the most important issues of the day other than on the Lord Chamberlain's terms, and as they could be discussed in other media. As we shall see, that restriction was a fundamental reason why parliament, when it was finally given the opportunity, would vote to abolish his control.

The 1960s is sometimes characterised as a time of peace and love, but it was also about war and destruction. When it began, powerful and dangerous forces were gusting through Britain and through the world. The United States, under its newly elected President J.F. Kennedy, and the Soviet Union, under Nikita Kruschev, were locked into a space race and a nuclear arms race that threatened the very future of the human race. The howling gales of nuclear destruction probably never came closer than in 1962 when America invaded neighbouring Cuba to try and overthrow its communist President Castro, and the USSR responded by positioning nuclear bases and weapons on the island, within easy striking distance of American soil. The confrontation between the world's two super-powers never broke into direct, explicit conflict; but they fought each other in proxy wars through the sixties, most persistently and most bloodily in the Vietnam 'civil' war between the Communist North and the anti-Communist South. In Europe, meanwhile, the government of East Germany constructed the Berlin Wall; a dividing line which for nearly thirty years would separate the communist East from the capitalist West. While Britain was not directly involved in these conflicts, it allowed the Americans to site nuclear weapons on its soil (and in submarines), ready for prompt attack. In response, the Campaign for Nuclear Disarmament attracted increasing support for its not always peaceful demonstrations— the playwrights John Osborne and Robert Bolt were among those arrested at a mass protest rally in Trafalgar Square in the autumn of 1961. With a new world order, and a form of warfare which could reduce whole nations instantly to devastated battlefields, soldiers and armies lost some of their value and relevance, and in the early 1960s the British government ended the compulsory new recruitment of eighteen to twenty-one year-olds to military training, thereby abolishing a system of national service which had run throughout the previous decade. The break-up of the country's Empire was already well underway, and the 1960s would see more and more of the nation's former colonies throwing off the yoke of subjection and achieving national independence. As a former Secretary of State in the American government put it in 1962, Britain's involvement with the wider international political landscape was 'about played out'; she was rather to be pitied as a nation which had 'lost an empire and not yet found a role'.[10] Meanwhile, during his 1960 tour of Africa, the Conservative British Prime Minister, Harold Macmillan, made a controversial and highly contentious speech to the South African parliament in which he questioned the legitimacy of the apartheid government there, and the justification for continuing white minority rule. Macmillan spoke of the unstoppable 'winds of change' which were already blowing through the continent, and 'the growth of national consciousness' among subjugated races as 'a political fact' which could no longer be ignored.[11] Yet Macmillan's own government was also careful to pass a Commonwealth Immigration Act, designed to restrict the number of people from Britain's former colonies who would be entitled to take up residence in the 'motherland'.

Slightly more gentle zephyrs were blowing through the British theatrical establishment at the start of the decade, although they too brought down a few branches. Peter Hall—a young director associated with innovative experimentation and new playwrights—was appointed to run the RSC, where he committed the company to staging contemporary as well as classical work, and also to a London base at the Aldwych Theatre, alongside its Stratford home. The playwright Arnold Wesker focused on a very different priority: to establish an organisation and a venue—Centre 42— which would blow away for ever the assumption that theatre and the arts were the natural playgrounds of middle-class audiences, by encouraging and facilitating the direct involvement of broader sections of society, both as audiences and participants. Arguably, however, an even more significant theatrical signpost of the times was the way in which satire against iconic Establishment targets began to voice—and perhaps to instigate—a new mood of dissent. *Beyond the Fringe*, devised and performed by Peter Cook, Dudley Moore, Alan Bennett and Jonathan Miller, and an outstanding success at the Edinburgh Festival of 1960, quickly did as its name suggested and penetrated the theatrical mainstream. The show's willingness to mock politicians and even royalty, and its lack of respect for established values and assumptions, brought headlines and controversy, which soon took the show into London's West End. Others followed in its footsteps—notably *That Was the Week That Was* on BBC television, and the equally controversial magazine *Private Eye*—contributing to the undermining of a culture of compliance and acquiescence to authority; a culture of which the Lord Chamberlain's Office was very much part.

Yet it might be argued that the cultural and political turning point which would have the greatest influence on theatre censorship through the sixties had actually occurred in 1959, with the passing of the Obscene Publications Act. A key purpose behind this legislation had been 'to provide for the protection of literature', and the new law crucially stipulated that publication could no longer be an offence if the work in question was 'justified as being for the public good on the ground that it is in the interests of science, literature, art or learning, or of other objects of general concern'. Crucially, it also allowed that 'the opinion of experts as to the literary, artistic, scientific or other merits of an article may be admitted . . . either to establish or to negative the said ground'. These new principles had an early and a famous outing in 1960, in the successful defence of Penguin Books against a prosecution for obscenity for their publication of D.H. Lawrence's *Lady Chatterley's Lover*. While the Act made no specific mention of theatrical performance, it did apply to a film or soundtrack which could be 'justified as being for the public good on the ground that it is in the interests of drama, opera, ballet or any other art, or of literature or learning'.[12] At the very least, then, it seems inevitable that more playwrights and theatre managers would now feel they had grounds to challenge the Lord Chamberlain by arguing that what they had written or wished to represent on stage was 'for the public good', and that his policies and decisions were out of kilter with policies elsewhere. The stage was set.

CHAPTER ONE

The Inflamed Appendix (1960–1961)

Ten years ago plays used to be submitted of every sort and kind: now there seems to be nothing between the pregnant sluts at the kitchen sink and waffling morons in the Tudorbethan Lounge Hall.[1]

All we can do is try and keep the dirt from getting dirtier.[2]

The Assistant Comptroller at St James's Palace in 1961 who so generously found the time to assist a Colonel's sixth-form daughter with her essay on theatre censorship was the recently appointed and rather dashing forty-four-year-old Lieutenant Eric Charles William Mackenzie Colonel Penn. On his recent retirement from the army, Penn had been parachuted into the powerful position of Assistant Comptroller to the Lord Chamberlain, replacing Norman Gwatkin, who had been smoothly airlifted into the post of Comptroller when Sir Terence Nugent was retired to his hangar in August 1960. Nugent, in turn, was rewarded with a peerage for his thirty years of service to the Royal Family, which had included twenty-four overseeing the Lord Chamberlain's Office. The Earl of Scarbrough had been in post since 1952, and the Office still seemed to be in secure and experienced hands; even the new boy was a product of Eton and Cambridge, and the Queen and her Mother had both attended his Mayfair wedding. As one newspaper noted of Penn: 'on the social side he cannot be faulted'.[3] At St James's, the Lieutenant would become a byword for 'organisational ability' and his 'producer's eye in planning and executing ceremonial occasions';[4] he was reportedly at his best doing weddings and funerals. But Britain was changing—and so too the theatre—and Penn was about to come under attack.

Fings

The late 1950s are sometimes identified as a time when the domination of the cultural mainstream by cut-glass accents and the frivolities and anxieties of the wealthy middle-classes was challenged by writers such as

John Osborne, Arnold Wesker and Shelagh Delaney. While the reality was more complex, it is certainly true that the English Stage Company at the Royal Court Theatre and Joan Littlewood's Theatre Workshop at Stratford East's Theatre Royal did represent aspects of society which had until then been largely ignored. As Littlewood herself put it:

> In the theatre of those dear departed days when every actress had roses round the vowels, and a butler's suit was an essential part of an actor's equipment, the voice of the Cockney was one long whine of blissful servitude. No play was complete without its moronic maid or faithful batman—rich with that true cockney speech and humour learned in the drama schools.[5]

The new voices and attitudes inevitably created pressure for the Censorship, and for the theatregoers and critics of yesteryear. As one of the latter asked in despair:

> Do the modern audiences genuinely demand stage characters of the type seen only when a garden stone is kicked aside—crawling, bestial things, found in the lowest dives and in the doorways of Soho alleys, cringing, filthy characters with no morals and no loyalties. To whom prison is a second home?[6]

The question was general, but the specific play which had prompted Bill Boorne's anger and exasperation was *Fings Ain't Wot They Used To Be*, as revived by the Earl of Scarbrough's longtime adversary, Theatre Workshop.

Eric Penn had arrived at St James's a war-time hero, having been awarded the Military Cross for leading a successful and surprise preemptive night-time attack on a German machine-gun position in Italy. But it was probably a mistake to launch a similar assault against Theatre Workshop so soon after he arrived. He was not yet versed in the rules of engagement or the more subtle guerrilla tactics generally employed, and he underestimated the strength and power of his enemies. Moreover, Penn had little experience of working in the face of black propaganda from a hostile Press, large parts of which now had the Lord Chamberlain's Office well and truly in their sights. It was unfortunate too, that Penn's first sortie should come when the Lord Chamberlain himself was occupied on another front, accompanying the Queen and Prince Philip on their state visit to India and Pakistan.

Fings was a lively musical about some of the seedier elements of everyday life in London's East End, its characters including con artists, spivs, pimps, prostitutes (male and female) and corrupt policemen. The original script had been a straight play written by Frank Norman—'an old lag' who brought 'an inside knowledge of his subject', having been 'in and out of the nick, during a goodly part of his twenty-eight years'.[7] However, by the time it was licensed and first performed at the end of the fifties, *Fings* had become more or less a musical, the songs and final text having been created through the normal Theatre Workshop process of script development involving improvisation and adaptation. There had been some complaints from the Public Morality Council when the show had opened, but St James's Palace—keen to avoid confrontations and damaging publicity— had rejected claims that the show glorified criminals, maintaining that its message demonstrated that crime did not pay. This conveniently ignored the fact that while the two main gangsters do indeed decide to go straight ('Here's to life within the law/No more strife agin the law'), a police sergeant goes in precisely the opposite direction and takes over as 'guvner' of the criminal gang they are leaving.[8] The implication that there was no firm dividing line between the law and the outlaw—that cops and robbers were seemingly interchangeable—was clearly a dangerous one in terms of morality and the social order. Still, the performances in the East End of London had received relatively little public attention. The difference in 1960 was that the show transferred to the West End's Garrick Theatre— where it would eventually run for some 800 performances. This level of exposure soon led to expressions of disapproval and alarm.

One of the first voices belonged to the Countess of Swinton, the wife of a long-serving Conservative MP and a personal friend of the Lord Chamberlain. Scarbrough's reply to her in March 1960 was described by Gwatkin as 'A first class letter which can serve as a pattern for future occasions'; actually, it is also striking for the liberal principles it enumerates, not least because it appears to be a private and personal expression of views: 'I would not like to see it published', he told her.[9] Scarbrough's letter insists 'that the stage should try to be a mirror of life and particularly of contemporary life'; and given that 'some contemporary life is pretty sordid' it was 'not surprising that in these days there are a number of pretty sordid plays'. In other words, the theatre could not live in the past or hide from reality:

> There has been quite a live development in the theatre of plays about, or attempting to typify working class themes, quite often by playwrights, or with the assistance of producers, from that class. The Theatre Workshop in Stratford, London E. is an example. Several of its plays have reached the West End theatres and this is one of them.

Perhaps surprisingly, he declared that 'In principle this development in the theatre should be welcomed' and 'certainly should not be suppressed', whatever one's personal preferences:

though I cannot say that I enjoy plays of this genre that I have seen, I feel that I must be especially careful to see that a play about life in a tenement or slum has the same freedom as, say, the more agreeable farces about life in country houses and smart hotels. Again that means that the idiom has to be accepted up to a point and the environment.

Perhaps, he suggested, this new emphasis would prove to be just a phase, and life would soon go back to how it had been in the fifties: 'I do not know whether this development in the theatre is going to last', wrote Scarbrough; 'I would think it doubtful whether the play going public will find entertainment in these sort of plays for any length of time'. But the Lord Chamberlain had no power to turn back society's clock. 'It should not be expected that the theatre should ignore the trends and manners of the day and be required to retain standards unrelated to those of the others', he advised the Countess:

We cut out quite a bit, but I admit we pass much which would never have been thought of for the stage fifty years ago . . . One must take some notice of the freedom with which books, magazines, films, television, to say nothing of one's own children, discuss almost everything. It would not be fair on the theatre and certainly not politic for the censor to require quite different standards for the stage.

But others also took up the case against *Fings*. On 31 December 1960, the MP J.H. Temple passed to the Home Office a complaint from one of his constituents: 'I hope that your department will put as much pressure as possible on the Lord Chamberlain', he urged, since 'the nauseating stuff which appears on the stage and on television is one of the main causes of hooliganism and bad behaviour in our country today'. Temple confessed that he himself had never been to a performance other than *My Fair Lady*, but still felt able to tell his constituent that 'I more than agree with you that plays portraying the activities to which you refer are extremely bad for society and I cannot understand how they get sufficient support to justify their production'. The Home Office passed the buck: 'it is a matter entirely for the Lord Chamberlain and the Home Secretary has no authority to interfere with the exercise of his discretion'. Temple now wrote directly to Scarbrough, asking him 'to take note of the rising public indignation at some of the theatrical shows which are permitted to be shown on the London stage'. Penn replied carefully, echoing Scarbrough's affirmation that theatre must be allowed to 'reflect modern thought and aspirations, together with contemporary ideas on morality and politics'. The censor, said Penn, was obliged to 'exercise a very nice judgement indeed in deciding the point at which free expression becomes real incitement to crime or immorality'. He also suggested it was 'generally impossible to prove a direct connection between one of these advanced plays and a particular crime'. In part, the issue at stake was class. Whose world was depicted in the theatre, and in whose terms? The Censorship could not be seen to take sides:

> It is probably true, too, that the impact of this type of play is the greater because recently it has portrayed the life of the 'submerged fraction' of the population and has often been written by authors drawn either from the working class or from the community depicted in the play. These plays being sordid in setting and character give a greater shock to the respectable than would similar themes were they expounded in the 'Society' or 'Country House' atmosphere which once ruled in theatre.
>
> I know that Lord Scarbrough does not like the sordid type of play, but he has told me that he must be especially careful to see that a piece which deals with life in a tenement or slum has the same freedom as a more agreeable exposé of life set in a smart hotel.

This sense of fairness is important to note, as is the fact that the Office was prepared to resist pressures to be more draconian—though it does not necessarily indicate that St James's was relaxed about what was going on. Ronald Hill was asked to attend a performance of *Fings* incognito, ostensibly to check whether the actors were keeping to the licensed script, but also to get a sense of the atmosphere and audience reactions. 'I thought it badly acted', he reported; 'much of the dialogue I couldn't understand although I had read the ms., and I heard others saying that they couldn't hear'. Clearly, the accents and the language were not what West End audiences, or those who worked at the Palace, were used to. But Hill knew from experience how foolish the Censorship could be made to look if it tried to cut something which it had previously approved; after all, 'whores of even the lowest type have been depicted on the stage since *The Beggar's Opera*, and the two principal ladies here so burlesque the parts that there is nothing at all lascivious about them, nor, I should think, any inducements to weak-minded women to follow suit'. Nevertheless, he was uneasy about the apparent celebration of violence in the songs:

> Carve up!
> There's just been a
> Carve up!
> We've just seen a
> Carve up!
> In between a
> Kickin' and a slashin'

And a nickin' and a bashin'
Wot a carve up!¹⁰

The concern—as so often—was that behaviour seen on stage not only re-flected but influenced society:

> To my mind the most objectionable if not dangerous part of the whole piece
> was the 'Carve up' and the introduction of the Teddy Boys. The 'Carve
> up' from being a completely alien thing is, in stage plays, being written up
> almost into an inverted form of Knight-Errantry or Dragon Slaying and
> with the Teddy Boy accompaniment is being glamorised. In fact, the stage
> is helping knifing, razor slashing, and adolescent gangsterism to become
> accepted parts of life, which hitherto they have not been, and one has only to
> look towards America to see what this may lead to.

Hill acknowledged that 'Teddy Boys are glamorised even more in *West Side Story*', but he still felt that there was real danger here: 'I believe it is admitted that publicity and imitation have much to do with the frequency of such offences', he noted; and in the case of *Fings*, 'the sympathetic face it shows to the repulsive vices of the razor slasher and the ponce . . . could, I feel, have real effect on the feebler minded youths who totter on the brink of this sort of thing'. Though, as someone else in the Office pointed out, such people 'don't go to this sort of play'.

Hill also identified—as was to be expected with a Joan Littlewood show which had been running for a year—'that a certain amount of new matter has crept in'. Most of the changes were 'innocuous', but Hill listed some questionable additions:

> When Rosie entered and sees Red Hot she puts her hand up his bottom in
> the gesture which denotes squeezing the testicles from behind . . .
>
> The punter appears with binoculars round his neck and says 'Come and
> look at my binoculars' to which one of the whores says 'Don't be filthy' . . .
>
> Tosher when examining the bag containing Red Hot's loot, over which
> Rosie is bending in a very tight skirt which shows her precise anatomy, put
> his hand on her bottom so that one finger lay along the line of cleavage. I
> know this will be denied but I know what I saw . . .
>
> Whilst dancing . . . Posh pushed Rosie backwards against a table over
> which she half bent backwards, whilst with his legs open and hers between
> he pushed her in an unmistakeable way . . .
>
> The priest was, of course, introduced as a red-nosed reprobate . . . When
> Lil is taking the licence out of her bosom the priest looks right down it and
> she comments upon his action.

Moreover, in the view of the Assistant Secretary, the Office had been too lenient in its original decisions:

> I will stick out my neck and say that I really do not think that we should have passed the song 'The Student Ponce' even in this play. Living on the immoral earnings of a woman is in England regarded as the lowest form of activity a man can descend to, and it is always severely punished by the Courts. It is a legal offence. Here it is represented in such a way as, I should say, could be reasonably held to be a recommendation to immorality, and in my opinion it sounds worse when sung, with admiring Teddy Boys' accompaniment than it reads.[11]

But it would have been impolitic to revisit earlier decisions.

Hill knew that the Office was entitled to require Theatre Workshop to cut any alterations it had made to the licensed script. However, given that developing and altering a performance in order to keep it 'live' was fundamental to Littlewood's method, such a demand was bound to create the sort of conflict which Scarbrough would have tried to avoid—especially given the bad publicity generated for the Censorship by previous head-on encounters with this company.[12] With little experience, and probably knowing little or nothing of this history, Penn blundered in, sending an ill-judged letter to the licensee of the Garrick Theatre to warn him that an inspection had discovered 'that numerous unauthorised amendments in the allowed manuscript have been made'. These, said Penn, must all be deleted:

> Act One indecent business of Rosie putting her hand up Red Bot's bottom . . .
> The interior decorator is not to be played as a homosexual and his remark 'Excuse me dear, red plush, that's camp that is', to be omitted, as is the remark 'I've strained meself'.
> . . . the reference to the Duchess of Argyle is to be omitted.
> Tosher . . . is not to put his hand on Rose's bottom with finger aligned as he does at the moment.
> The remark 'Don't drink that stuff it will rot your drawers' is to be omitted.
> Tosher is not to push Rosie back against the table when dancing in such a manner that her legs appear through his open legs in a manner indicative of copulation.

One of Penn's stipulations was so absurd that it was a gift to his opponents: 'The builder's labourer is not to carry the plank of wood in the erotic place and at the erotic angle that he does, and the Lord Chamberlain wishes to be informed of the manner in which the plank is in future to be carried.'[13] As Scarbrough would have known, it was the kind of endorsement which, when leaked to journalists, could only make the Office look ridiculous, while providing excellent publicity for the theatre.

The press had a field day. The *Daily Express* reported that with one exception, 'all the other cuts now ordered were originally passed by the Lord Chamberlain'. Like many newspapers, they contacted members of Theatre Workshop for their story, and quoted the show's composer, Lionel Bart, describing Penn's letter as 'one of the funniest things I have read' and wishing he 'could incorporate it in the show'.[14] The *Daily Mail* went for maximum embarrassment, including a photograph of the Lord Chamberlain, and under the headline 'LORD SCARBROUGH CUTS A SHOW THAT MADE HIM LAUGH' quoting from one of the company: '"the funny thing is" said actress Miriam Karlin yesterday "the Lord Chamberlain has seen the play twice and thoroughly enjoyed it to judge by his laughter"'.[15] The *Evening Standard* went for 'CENSOR'S BLUNDER', and the response of the script's author, Frank Norman: '"Am I angry? Not a bit of it. The thing is so stupid it's laughable".' The newspaper also claimed that even though the number of complaints about *Fings* amounted to 'less than one out of every two thousand of those who have seen the show', this had been 'enough to send the Lord Chamberlain's men scurrying to the theatre'. They drew far-reaching lessons from the case:

> To apply standards suitable for drawing room comedy to a play of this kind makes nonsense of the whole system of censorship . . . Indeed the whole incident shows how out of touch the Lord Chamberlain's acolytes have become with public opinion. A quarter of a million people see a play without complaining. A dozen protest. And it is the insignificant minority which sways the judgement of the Lord Chamberlain's office . . . The latest action of the Lord Chamberlain's office is all the more regrettable since the signs were that the censorship had become more sensitive to changing trends.
>
> But if even a broad-minded system of censorship can take the scissors to *Fings Ain't Wot They Used To Be* after a year's run, many people will conclude that the system itself is at fault. The Lord Chamberlain's Office has spelled out the case not so much for a more enlightened way of administering his responsibilities but for the total abolition of this anachronistic and ridiculous form of stage censorship.[16]

To find such mockery and criticism in publications which were hardly at the politically radical end of the media was humiliating and embarrassing. Concerning, too. The new Assistant Comptroller had naively put his head much too high above the parapet, and in doing so had made not only himself but the very heart of the British Establishment into an easy target:

Lieutenant Colonel Eric Penn, a close friend of the Royal Family, has emerged as one of the Lord Chamberlain's closest blue pencil advisers on theatre censorship . . . To bring about the cuts, he corresponded with his chief who was more than 4,000 miles away in India with the Queen.

He used the special air lift of Royal Mail to and from India to discuss such tricky matters as the angle at which a builder's labourer carries a plank and the show's reference to the Duchess of Argyll.[17]

The author Richard Findlater took full advantage of the opportunity to ridicule a system he detested:

THE COLONEL KNEW BEST
And Only the Queen Can Stop Him.
. . . With a reviving death-wish the Lord Chamberlain's office has woken from its censor's nap—mistaken by optimists for the big sleep—and while its master, the Earl of Scarbrough, shepherds the Queen through Pakistan, it has made a stand for the Royal Household at home by vetoing bits of a West End musical, *Fings Ain't What They Used To Be*. For about a year this has been outraging public decency without any of the half-million unsuspecting citizens exposed to it (including the Lord Chamberlain himself) ever realising that their minds were being corrupted. This was left apparently to a far-sighted Assistant Comptroller in St James's Palace, a colonel from the Grenadiers who—though new to the job of show-censoring—clearly knows Bad Taste when he sees it and knows when it ought to be Stopped, dammit. Let nobody protest that the show has already been passed by the Lord Chamberlain's men: they can do anything they like, at any time, without anybody but the Queen being able to stop them. That is what we mean by theatrical tradition.[18]

John Jelley in the *Daily Mail* was equally scathing: 'WHO WILL RID US OF THIS STUFFY STAGE CENSORSHIP?' he asked:

At the moment Lord Scarbrough is out of the country. But his officers continue their primitive task of sniffing out the unspeakable and the unactable.

His agents, with hungry notebooks in hand, have been ensuring no shadow of modernity should soil the pure white souls of contemporary theatre-goers in his absence.

In this case, said Jelley, the interventions were 'petty and pernickety and piddling', and he asked rhetorically whether '**we really still need a Debrett nanny to wipe our mouths, and muffle our eyes, and choose our relaxations, in 1961?**' How was it, he mused, that the Lord

Chamberlain alone could 'touch pitch and not be defiled', or 'sample nastiness and not be corrupted?' He went so far as to describe Scarbrough as 'an inflamed appendix on the body politic', suggesting it was 'time he was painlessly removed by a simple operation'.[19]

It is the extent to which the Lord Chamberlain's Office had so clearly lost the support of mainstream newspapers that is really the big story here. In the *Daily Express*, Bernard Levin ('The Earl of Scarbrough is at it again') joined in the personal mockery: 'a study of some of the cuts the Lord Chamberlain has ordered in shows over the past few years makes me very worried about the kind of man who censors plays for our stage', he wrote:

> He is apt to see dirt not only where none is intended but where none is even visible to any other eye.
> He gets positively hysterical at any reference to the Royal Family.
> He foams at the mouth if somebody should dare to tease any of our beloved politicians.

In the case of *Fings*, the interventions had simply 'made him a laughing-stock and the play a certain runner for at least another two years'. Levin also targeted the new Assistant Comptroller:

> The trouble is that the official adviser has changed.
>   It used to be Brigadier Sir Norman Gwatkin. It is now Lieut.-Colonel Eric Penn, who recently succeeded the brigadier. (Anyone wondering what special qualifications the Army provides for knowing about plays should address the question to the Lord Chamberlain, not to me).
>   And while the earl is out of the country assisting at the tiger-shoots and other ceremonies in India and Pakistan, the lieutenant-colonel has clearly taken it into his head to get into the act.

Indeed, suggested Levin, it was 'the supporters of censorship who must be furious today, not its opponents', for the net effect of Penn's meddling must be to hasten the end of the Lord Chamberlain's control over theatre:

> Britain is a practical country, not a theoretical one. You cannot, if you want to get rid of the censorship of plays attack it on principle. You can only attack it in practice. And Lieut.-Colonel Penn has provided all the opponents of censorship with a stick to beat his whole office with.
>   It was Voltaire who said that his prayer was 'Lord, make mine enemies ridiculous'. The Lord Chamberlain's office is far more accommodating. It makes itself ridiculous without any divine intervention at all.[20]

Bamber Gascoigne in the *Spectator* even reproduced the whole of Penn's letter under the headline 'Protection Racket', satirising it mercilessly:

> This beautiful document should be useful to pornographers who haven't yet realised the salacious potential of official language. 'Aligned', in particular, is a word which has been seriously underworked in this field.

And like others, he argued that the effect of 'Colonel Penn's sudden swoop' would be counter-productive, because it exposed the true face of theatre censorship:

> I am quoting this letter because it reveals very clearly what our dramatic censor spends most of his time doing. Some people have managed to see him as a tireless defender of our island happiness, health and heritage, bravely facing up to and turning back the most unimaginable, indescribable, unheard of etc. bits of filth . . . But here he is suddenly revealed in his true colours, busily snipping away at harmless little jokes and gestures.

However, Gascoigne insisted that the blame could not be put on a particular individual: 'Criticism of the censor boils down to criticism of the office, rather than of the officer', he maintained; 'The whole function is ludicrous, and nobody could make it anything else'.[21] It can only have added to Penn's embarrassment that he and Gascoigne had served together in the same army brigade. Indeed, Gascoigne's father was moved to send the Assistant Comptroller a personal letter of apology:

> Dear Eric,
> I can't tell you how sorry I am to read the absolutely monstrous article in the *Spectator*—written by my son—I have told him what I think of him—I can only hope that you will forgive what I think is due to misguided exuberance of inexperienced youth—I can think of no other excuse.[22]

But most other newspapers maintained the tone of derision, often indicating that the institution headed by the Lord Chamberlain belonged to a bygone era: 'Fings ain't what they used to be except in Stable Yard, St James.'[23]

Outwardly, at least, the Office took it on the chin. Penn even attempted to buy the original of a *Daily Mail* cartoon of himself to hang in the office, though he was put off by the price ('Entertained as we all were by your admirable drawing, we feel that we would not be justified in purchasing this drawing for fifteen guineas'). But news of the disaster reached high places: '*Fings Ain't Wot They Used To Be* caused a little stir after lunch today', reported Scarbrough to Gwatkin, en route from Madras to Bombay;

'The Queen asked me if I had seen about it'. He counselled silence as the best policy, asking Gwatkin to 'Give Eric my strong support'.

In his letter to Countess Swinton, Scarbrough had explained that 'Censorship is one of those walks of life in which publicity is better avoided'. Thanks to Penn's gung-ho attitude, the Lord Chamberlain had—not for the first, and certainly not for the last time—become the story. It was not entirely Penn's fault. After all, the Office had received a number of extremely strongly-worded complaints about *Fings*, mostly from individuals whose positions commanded respect at St James's Palace. When the worst of the fuss had eventually died down, Penn tried to understand why the play had provoked such strong reactions, given that 'in terms of obscenities the script does not compare with that of the avant garde plays which we receive now-a-days'. He concluded it had as much to do with the play's form as its content, and the fact that it had been presented in a mainstream context:

1 The play is a 'musical' and is therefore seen by what one might call 'the normal theatre going public'.
2 Unlike the avant garde plays it has a comprehensible plot. This plot although almost farcical in content is accompanied by authentic detail.[24]

Meanwhile, the MP whose letter had precipitated the debacle, wrote again to the Home Office proposing that a parliamentary committee should be set up, not to dismantle the system of censorship but to give it 'stronger and more rigid directions'. In reply, Hill pointed out that technically the Lord Chamberlain already enjoyed 'completely unfettered jurisdiction over the stage if he wants to use it'. Indeed, attempts to strengthen his powers would probably be counter-productive, and 'generate an abundance of opinion against such a step'.[25]

Struggles with the Past

The willingness of much of the press to stick pins into the Lord Chamberlain or paint him as a latter-day King Canute does not mean that theatre critics or journalists necessarily relished current trends any more than he did. In a *Daily Telegraph* article of February 1961, W.A. Darlington claimed hopefully that the tide was already on the turn, and that 'constructive criticism' by sensible reviewers (such as himself) was having a 'mellowing effect' on new playwrights, encouraging them to write with less anger and greater maturity. He insisted that while some critics had 'welcomed the brass-bed-kitchen-sink drama with ecstatic cries', the more balanced ones had warned that 'kitchen sinks and Left-wing politics were likely to have only a limited appeal to the public and that class-consciousness on the stage interests only the class-conscious'. This, said Darlington, had brought the new young playwrights face to face with a paradox and a dilemma:

> Hailed at first as being 'contemporary' dramatists before all else, they now find themselves hampered by the fact that the only section of contemporary society about which they can write with sympathy or even knowledge is their own, while the audience to which they are addressing themselves consists mainly of other sections.

Those who paid to watch theatre were not politically minded, asserted Darlington, and the better dramatists had therefore decided 'to abandon the contemporary', and had 'gone back into the past for the themes of their next plays'.[26]

Reporting the following week on *Luther*, the new offering from the Royal Court by 'the daddy of the moderns'—John Osborne—the Lord Chamberlain's official Reader, Sir St Vincent Troubridge (proudly descended from Lord Nelson) extolled Darlington's critique of what he himself christened the 'dustbin dramatists'. But to his horror, he found that—at least in the case of Osborne—in retreating to the past, they took their dustbins and their 'modern lavatory complex' with them. 'These miserable creatures would much rather excrete than laugh', complained Troubridge; 'This is just naughty little smart-alec small boy John Osborne scribbling words on lavatory walls'. Troubridge disliked Osborne intensely: 'I wish him a stricture plus stoppage of the bowels.' The line that most incensed the Reader was the central protagonist's comparison of himself to 'a ripe stool in the world's straining anus'. It would have been bad enough in a modern context, but the historical setting was too much. 'This from Martin Luther, if you please.' A list of some fifteen cuts was sent to the theatre, but the days when theatre managers could be relied upon to accept such decisions and jump to attention were over. The Court's director, George Devine, came calling:

> Without in any way being personally threatening, Mr Devine said that John Osborne has taken up the attitude that he is now a playwright of such stature that no-one has a right to touch his work, and rather than alter a single line of it he will withdraw it.

Probably to Troubridge's disapproval, a compromise was reached with the theatre by his superiors, with cuts eventually applied only to 'piss', 'crap' and the 'Balls of the Medici'. Even the line which had so angered the Reader was permitted, Devine persuading the Office that the constipation was an allegory for 'the state of religious costiveness induced by the then excesses of the Roman Catholic Church', and that 'The physical phenomena resulting from the relief of constipation are applied metaphorically to the process through which Luther relieves himself of Catholicism'. One can almost hear Troubridge's snort of derision. Scarbrough was more generous—and keener to avoid unnecessary fights:

> I have said elsewhere that if one accepts the general theme of a play, one must accept the idiom or context and judge doubtful passages as to whether they fall properly within the idiom or context and do not go outrageously beyond it.
>
> Judging this play by that kind of formula, there can be no doubt that the general theme, which is historical, is fully acceptable. In addition to that I have always understood that Martin Luther was a notoriously coarse-mouthed priest. I do not, therefore, have any doubt that a good deal of coarseness is to be allowed in this play.

Not that the Royal Court was going to thank the Lord Chamberlain for his concessions. 'We still find it difficult to understand why several words are allowed to be used in Classical Theatre and not in Modern', they complained, pointing out that 'the word "piss" . . . is frequently used at the Royal Shakespeare Theatre, Stratford, and the Old Vic'. It reluctantly suggested some possible alternatives:

> For 'Convent piss' we propose 'Convent kidney juice', 'Convent widdle' or 'Convent piddle'.
> For monk's piss we suggest 'monk's widdle', 'monk's piddle', 'monk's urine'.

In addition:

> Whilst we appreciate your kindness in suggesting 'testicles' . . . we all feel that this seems smutty in comparison to the original, which was much more ambiguous, less clinical and less absurd.
> May we suggest ballocks instead?

The Office passed 'kidney juice', 'monk's urine' and 'filth', but rejected 'shit-scared', 'stool-scared' and 'bowel-scared'. The problem over the Medici was easily solved by increasing his anatomical appendages: 'Delete "Balls of the Medici"', stated the final endorsement, 'and substitute "The five balls of the Medici"'.[27] Possibly the Censors were taking the kidney juice.

Another historical play which raised some hackles in the early part of 1961 was *The Devils of Loudun*, submitted by the RSC for its new base at the Aldwych, and the first sign of the commitment by the company's

new director, Peter Hall, to his policy of staging contemporary dramatists alongside classical texts. Based on Aldous Huxley's book about a
French trial of 1623, the script was by John Whiting, who, according to
the jaundiced Troubridge, was 'accepted as a leader by most of the younger
dramatists upon the strength of four resounding and impressive flops'. Yet
Troubridge described this play as 'a tremendous affair' and, in his own
inimitable way, made the obvious connection:

> In this confused, unhappy and apprehensive age, it is perhaps natural to cast
> back to famous witchcraft trials of the past and detect in them some parallels
> with our day. This has already been done by Arthur Miller (husband of the
> mammapotent Marilyn Monroe) in his *The Crucible*.

The Reader was ready to be magnanimous: 'One appreciates that drawing-
room conversation is hardly to be expected of devils', he conceded; and
given that 'the main action relates to the supposed demonic possession of
four nuns', it was inevitable there would be 'some lewdnesses'. However,
he thought the text needed 'sorting out' in terms of 'general blasphemy'
and was worried about a lengthy torture scene. Troubridge proposed a
string of cuts, including references to 'the shaving of pubic hair', 'coition
noises', 'farting', and the suggestion that 'men kneel in church . . . because
they kneel to enter a woman'. Other lines marked by him for excision
included:

> 'Is it true that the men of your parish have got into the habit of masturbating
> with apples?'
> 'exotic liquids . . . flowed between us'
> 'Conjoined in ever varying ways dictated by my lover'
> 'we all know what the young women in these places get up to between them-
> selves'
> 'There is evidence of recent and constant intercourse of an unusual nature'.

Some elements he found implausible: 'I have yet to mistake the farting
of an incontinent woman as the voice of revelation.' The Censorship also
insisted there must be '<u>NO</u> cries of ecstasy', that Mignon was definitely
'<u>NOT</u> allowed to clutch himself behind', and that 'Grandier must <u>NOT</u> be
tortured in view of the audience'. In some cases, whole speeches or entire
pages were to be deleted.

   Whiting and the RSC accepted most of the cuts, and agreed to supply
'minute stage directions', showing how the torture scene would be played so
as to avoid giving offence or becoming too disturbing: 'The author asserts
that he is not interested in sensationalism or sadism.' But Troubridge
described the revised script as 'a singularly half-hearted attempt to comply

with the Lord Chamberlain's instructions'. New lines had been added which were themselves 'objectionable', while 'some of those ordered to be removed remain in truncated form'. Demands were made for further cuts, particularly to stage action:

> It is not permissible to show a priest in bed with a woman . . .
> The Lord Chamberlain will allow this scene only upon your undertaking that no business or properties will be introduced which would indicate that an enema was about to be administered.
> The devil's coition noises to be deleted.
> Beherit will not be allowed to effect an entry 'per anum', and the action regarding Beherit will not be allowed until stage directions are furnished for inclusion in the script to the effect that this devil effects an entry by way of some other orifice.

Furthermore, a licence could only be issued if stage directions were added specifying 'that the torture chamber is blacked out during the time the wedges are inserted and hammered home', and that 'Grandier's broken legs are not to be shown'.

Whiting's play was finally licensed and staged in a much-changed version, but the Office still received complaints from people who thought the Lord Chamberlain had been too lenient:

> I doubt if you would care for a daughter of yours to see it or to read it: it is not only unclean, but blasphemous. I came away feeling that the most necessary thing was a bath, as I have always understood that he who touches pitch is defiled, and I felt that I had been literally besmirched with pitch.

Penn was forced to defend the decision to allow even a much-adulterated version of Whiting's text largely on the grounds that it was based on actual events and a book by Huxley. 'Although these facts would not necessarily justify the piece', he wrote, 'they do go some way towards differentiating it from mere fiction'. He went on:

> The Lord Chamberlain realized that it might cause offence to some but it is not, he thinks, a blasphemous play since it represents an historical fact, and although the facts may be unpalatable to many he does not think that the play itself is a corrupting one.

It was a view, he said, which

> has been reinforced by the reports of the Lord Chamberlain's officers who saw the piece staged in London and who told him that it had been staged

objectively without any of the disproportions or exaggerations which a producer intent upon putting an obscenity on the stage might have made.[28]

Different Voices

If the past was not safe ground, then the present was equally unpalatable. Reporting on *Billy Liar* in August 1960, Troubridge identified 'a lot of nasty stuff that must come out', including 'loutish slang' and a reference to contraceptives, even though the articles weren't named ('I haven't got— you know'). Other cuts included 'frigging', 'bog off', 'randy as an old ram' and 'He gave one to a bint in Sunderland. Went through her like a dose of salts'. The Office allowed itself to be persuaded to approve references to aphrodisiac pills ('There is never the slightest question that Billy would <u>actually</u> seduce Barbara') and to 'virgo intacta' ('characteristic of her plain, direct, blunt (but not unkindly or vulgar) Northern personality'). Interestingly, there was no attempt to censor one word which had often been cut before, Troubridge noting: 'I have left all Father's "bloodies" in since this is a part of his "character".'[29] For 'character' here, we may, of course, read 'class'.

In fact, it was a feature of theatre in the early sixties that new languages and speech patterns were slowly beginning to test and enrich the British stage. In September, for example, the Royal Court submitted a sharply observed and wittily written drama by the Jamaican-born writer Barry Reckord. *You in Your Small Corner* was described by the Reader as 'A slice of life play, set in Brixton, with the slice cut rather near the knuckle'. The story focused on the life of a young Jamaican student and his white girlfriend, and 'the hopes, hates, envies, jealousies and prejudices, racial and social and class, which envelop them'. Unfortunately, from the Office's point of view, it also 'goes into their sex life in close, almost clinical, detail'. There was no doubt about the quality of the writing—but none, either, about the need to neuter it:

> although I am recommending what seems almost an inordinate number of cuts, it must be admitted that the dialogue rings true to the characters and locale. It is a great merit of this play that the characters are believable, and the play convinces—though I am afraid that it will reach the stage in a con- siderably emasculated form!

More than thirty alterations were made to Reckord's script, some of them fairly trivial, but others which significantly undermined the energy of the writing as well as the ideas. There were two lines for which the writer pleaded. The first was a provocative and rhetorical question: 'why couldn't the painters paint a virgin worried because she 'as one on her arm, one by her side and another in 'er belly'. The Censorship refused to concede: 'It is most improbable that the Lord Chamberlain would allow any reference to the Virgin as being the mother of other children.' The final version was therefore the very much less effective 'why couldn't the painters paint a virgin worried'. The other line—eventually permitted—was the aggressive and deliberately ambiguous command to 'Lay them and be top'. The Office agreed to interpret this as a political rather than a sexual exhortation— 'all the previous context refers to the social position of the Negro'—and therefore of less concern: 'although there is a dual meaning to the line . . . the emphasis is on the social position'.[30]

In the spring of 1961, the Royal Court submitted a translation of *The Blacks*. 'Jean Genet is a wild, revolutionary creature with a prison record, and a self-confessed homosexual', sneered Troubridge. 'Being a disciple and protégé of Sartre', he added, 'Genet is not particular about being understood'. By 'battling through Niagaras of speech from poetic to crazy, and leaving the dirty bits for later consideration', the Reader did his best to construct a coherent narrative for his report. He also acknowledged that Genet's texts possess 'a certain dynamism of violence which carries them along'. Nevertheless, Troubridge drew attention to a myriad of lines and actions which he believed over-stepped the boundaries: 'The dirty lines set out below would probably not shock the virtually unshockable Court theatre audience', he noted, 'but there are other considerations'. For example, 'The fact that a strangled person is apt to urinate and defecate in death is best left to the doctors'.

Most of Troubridge's specific cuts remained on the final endorsement:

Omit 'farting' and 'goat f----r'.
Omit 'My member adorned with moss' and substitute 'The join of my thighs adorned with moss'.
Omit 'I was pissing' and substitute 'letting it go' . . .
Omit 'droppings' and substitute 'excrement'.
Omit 'flowing down your black stockings'.
You are warned regarding the business of Bobo's obscene dance.
Omit 'I fart' and substitute 'break wind'.
Omit '. . . a nigger's hole' and substitute '. . . a nigger's backside'.
Omit 'unbutton' and substitute 'open up' . . .
Omit 'sperm' and substitute 'your ambrosia'.
Dies Irae chant is not to be used . . .
Omit 'military gout' and substitute 'an old military complaint'.
Omit 'high, stiff and firm' and substitute 'right up high'.

Yet it was what was unwritten but which might appear in the physical presence of a performance which concerned Troubridge the most. *The*

Blacks struck him as 'a play in which much obscene gesture might be interpolated', and he proposed that the Lord Chamberlain should inspect final rehearsals. This was an approach the Office employed only rarely, partly for sheer practical reasons—there were simply not enough staff to do it, even within London—but also for strategic reasons, as Hill now pointed out:

> The difficulties inherent in sending someone to view a play from the point of view of censoring the action are:
>
> 1) Although perhaps a particular incident could be banned, the fact that a representative has been can be used as a carte blanche cover for all later variations—i.e. 'we haven't changed anything and the censor has seen it all'.
> 2) There is nothing to cover such visits in the Act, which says that every part of a stage play must be submitted. There is a High Court diktat that 'business' is part of a play, and the proper course is to ask for complete descriptions of any equivocal action and then allow or disallow as dialogue.
> 3) . . . I was told by the Director of Public Prosecutions that if we passed degraded or obscene dialogue or plots, we must be prepared for, and would have difficulty in securing convictions against those using 'business' or 'action' which was the natural concomitant to the words.
> 4) Lastly since it is impossible for a representative to visit every play, or indeed any play produced far from London, it is inequitable to visit London plays.

Troubridge's suggestion was not taken up.[31]

Dealing with Dirt

As we know, by no means all theatrical managers and producers were opposed to censorship, or sympathetic to the new waves rippling through British theatres. In July 1961, Henry Sherek, a leading theatre impresario, gained newspaper headlines ('Filth In The West End Theatre') for speaking out at an industry lunch against a system which he said had become too tolerant. Sherek wanted to revive the campaign to institute a differential 'X' licence in the theatre, similar to the model used in cinemas, in order 'to save embarrassment to people who take children to the theatre and find they are watching a filthy play'. Sherek had had his own battles with St James's in the past, but he championed both the principle and the practice of censorship as a 'safeguard against sliminess and plays that cater for the lowest possible taste'. He now accused the Lord Chamberlain of having 'done a complete about-turn in allowing plays about ponces, queers, and homosexuals to go on', declaring that he found himself 'embarrassed at the filth he has allowed in the theatre', and appalled that it had penetrated even the commercial theatre:

> You walk down the West End and what do you see? Plays like *Fings Ain't Wot They Used To Be*, *A Taste of Honey*, and *Sparrers Can't Sing*. They all have their place in the theatre, of course. But there's too much emphasis on sexual perversions and the like today.

To help pump up the controversy, the *Daily Mail* quoted the response of Stephen Lewis, author of *Sparrers Can't Sing*: '"Who is this Henry Sherek, anyway? I'll punch him in the nose if he's implying my play's filthy".'[32] Bill Boorne, the *Evening News* theatre critic claimed that Sherek's opinions were shared by 'the majority of theatregoers', who looked for 'Sugar and sweetness: romance and glamour', and were currently 'clamouring to get in' to see *The Sound of Music*. This, insisted Bill Boorne, was what people really wanted from theatre, 'in spite of to-day's cynics and the off-beat boys and girls who really amount to so little'. But Boorne feared that Sherek's warnings had come too late, and that many people had already taken matters into their own hands by turning their backs on live theatre: 'Dare one make the almost sacrilegious comment that Joan Littlewood and her Theatre Workshop realism and sordidness helped in the end to veer many people away from the theatre?'[33]

Meanwhile, Sherek wrote to the Lord Chamberlain privately, challenging him to take a stronger line and confidently claiming he had public opinion on his side: 'If you are interested, I could send you a very large batch of letters full of general complaints about a number of the plays shown in London' he offered, 'but I don't suppose you <u>are</u> interested'. Scarbrough knew that Sherek's idea for a system of restricted licensing based on the model of films—an idea which he had himself championed in the 1950s— was effectively dead in the water, having been killed off as unfeasible by a previous Home Secretary. Whatever his personal views, there was therefore no point in engaging with these new proposals, so Sherek was reminded that 'The Lord Chamberlain is not an arbiter of taste' and that it was not within his remit 'to formulate public taste'. Nor was he concerned 'with the merits of a play'—though 'if he were, half the theatres in London would be closed'. His task was now effectively defined as trying 'to help to keep the public peace and to prevent the lowest forms of dirt'. If the theatre contained too much dirt then the fault lay with playwrights and managers who 'basically want to make money' and therefore 'give the public what they think the public will pay to go and see'. Managers—including Sherek himself—should therefore 'take the beam out of their own eyes before they start poking about for motes elsewhere', and align their money with the principles they claimed: 'Risk bankruptcy, produce good clean plays and educate your public my dear Henry', advised the Comptroller.

Sherek replied with some indignation: 'I do not like dirty plays', he insisted; 'in the great number of plays I have done since the war, I have never done a dirty one'. Indeed, on the occasion when a previous Lord Chamberlain had told him that presenting Lilian Helman's much-banned *Children's Hour* would make him 'a corrupter of youth', he had reportedly 'turned a bright purple' and withdrawn his application on the spot. The Comptroller held to his point: 'I still maintain that certain Managements know that dirt is good box office, and that is all they care about.' As for the Lord Chamberlain, he 'cannot even if he wished to do so forever travel in a horse carriage'; he was 'now in a motor car' and many people were 'trying to force him into a spaceship'. He also reiterated the principle that, if only for the sake of future historians, theatre must be 'a contemporary mirror' to its own age. If today's society was dirty, then theatre had a responsibility to reflect this:

> for the Lord Chamberlain to prevent it from putting on plays in the idiom and on hitherto esoteric subjects which are now blazoned forth in the Press, Parliament, ecclesiastical convocations and drawing rooms would be an offence against the twenty-first century and an ostrich like attitude to the 1960s.

As for the specific charge against the Lord Chamberlain's shift in policy over homosexuality, 'the decision to allow plays on one of the oldest habits in the world was not taken lightly, but after much consultation and heart searching and with, it was hoped, adequate safeguards'. Still Gwatkin's letter did acknowledge that things were becoming harder and that the Office was 'constantly being holed below the waterline'; as he admitted, he was 'beginning to wonder who one is trying to protect'.[34]

No doubt it was true—when had it not been?—that there were plenty of theatre managers who were only too ready to use sexual titillation to make a buck—or even just to retain a foothold in an industry threatened by the growth in film and television. But of course, there was much more to it than that. In 1960, the Censorship had found itself involved in a debate 'As To The Lord Chamberlain's Jurisdiction Over Ballets Africains With Dancers With Bare Bosoms'. Although there was no script as such, the manager of the Piccadilly Theatre—perhaps to cover himself or perhaps just to seek some publicity—contacted St James's in advance to warn them about this visiting international production in which 'four of the dances are performed by coloured girls who are naked above the waist'.[35] The Press got hold of the story, and the *Daily Herald* ran an article asking whether the 'Eighteen dusky beauties' would be permitted to appear: 'will the Lord Chamberlain make them cover up?'[36] Penn thought a special case could be made: 'May I suggest, in view of the proposed dances being Genuine Ritual Folk Dances, in which it is customary for the girls to be so attired, that it would be in order for them to be so performed.' He also pointed out that 'The public see a good deal of this in film, newsreels and on television and apparently without complaint as they realize that this form of dress, or rather lack of it, is both genuine and natural'. Gwatkin—for probably the first and only time—decided he would like to attend a 'dress' rehearsal, and subsequently reported that he felt 'sorry for anyone who could take . . . offence'. But wary of creating a precedent of which other managements might take advantage, the Office chose not to issue a licence but to define the performance as 'ballet', and therefore outside its jurisdiction. However, one person's Genuine Ritual Folk Dance is another person's dirt, and not everyone was so relaxed. The following year, a doctor was so appalled by witnessing African dancers on television that he wrote to Scarbrough to complain, mistakenly assuming that the Lord Chamberlain had responsibility:

> The programme came on without any warning of the indecency that we were about to view, and although as a doctor the human body comes in my view often, I have never seen it portrayed in such a sensuous and revolting manner. To show African teenage girls virtually naked except for a flimsy loin cloth struggling and writhing sensuously all around the platform was in the lowest possible taste and completely unprofitable and unnecessary. We had in our house at the time some teenagers who were viewing with us at that early hour in the evening and we were shocked and appaled [sic] that they should have been shown such things. The fact that these primitive and ignorant dances take place in countries where the people as yet know of no better way of life is absolutely no excuse for making them cheap entertainment. I would calculate that the damage done to young people who saw this programme was impossible to estimate. In these days with the dreadful decline in morals in our nation, such things can only worsen the situation and I feel very strongly that this sort of thing should be banned completely.[37]

It is typically the second half of the sixties that is often associated with sexual freedom and promiscuity, and with theatre which reflects this. However, Ann Jellicoe's breakthrough play at the Royal Court, *The Knack*, stirred up controversy in the early years of the decade. Jellicoe herself called the play 'an outrageous comedy about sex and young people', and its title was taken by critics as referring to 'seduction', 'the art of getting girls', and 'the science of clicking with a girl'.[38] The script did not go down well at St James's.

I realise that this play by Anne Jellicoe, who is aged 40 but I am told likes to think that she is still 21, is written about undergraduates for an undergraduate audience and much of the dialogue is typical of the topic of conversation of many undergraduates.

The Reader described it as 'A sniggering little undergraduate revue-sketch inflated into a solemn comedy' and 'blown up with endless, characterless verbiage and a lot of profanity'. It would, he declared, 'be even more tiresome to see than to read'. Heriot proposed a series of cuts, and the Assistant Comptroller marked several additional passages for consideration. One of the proposed cuts was Tolem's suggestion that women could be passed around between the men: 'After I had had a woman Rory can have her and, if I wish, I can have Rory's.' Bill Gaskill at the Royal Court contested the decision:

> It should be emphasised that Miss Jellicoe in no way approves of Tolem's suggestion, contained in this sequence. Nor does she want the audience to approve. She has written this sequence so that the audience will see and judge the inhumanity and selfishness of men such as Tolem. To remove the sequence would seriously weaken and damage her purpose.

The Lord Chamberlain's Office accepted it was 'not much worse than a good deal of other stuff' which was said in this 'certainly not moral play' and backed down. However, they did insist on a further fourteen cuts, including 'how many times did you have her' and what they called 'that word' from the phrase 'Women I regularly fuck'.[39] In the *Daily Mail*, Jellicoe—outed as a 'former Brownie' who 'never became a Guide'—was quoted as saying that Scarbrough had been 'pretty reasonable really'.[40]

At the same time as it was dealing with *The Knack*, the Office was simultaneously negotiating over an Edward Albee double-bill, also at the Royal Court. 'Another ripple of the nouvelle vague from America of "anti-plays" in imitation of the European school headed by Ionesco, Pinter and Simpson', wrote Heriot of *The American Dream*; 'I have not the faintest idea what this play is about'. His report on *The Death of Bessie Smith* accused Albee of writing 'as if he was perpetually frustrated in his sex-life'. A string of cuts was proposed, including 'Johnny-dos'; 'Because I used to let you get on top of me and bump your uglies'; and 'I went sticky wet'. The cuts were again challenged by the English Stage Company, and the Comptroller had a meeting with 'the author and two starry-eyed producers' to hear their case: 'they pointed out that these two plays were important works and had been received with enthusiasm in America' reported Gwatkin; 'I doubt the first remark and the second does not cut much ice with us'. He wanted to take a strong stance: 'My own inclination is to have very little mercy on them', he wrote; 'I don't see why Americans should come over here and make the English stage dirtier than it is'. Many of the arguments centred on disagreements over slang, and the difference between British and American usage; the Office reluctantly backed down on 'Johnny-dos' ('They argued that as we talk about the johnny enough it is rather straining at the gnat to wonder what went on in the johnny') but resisted other examples:

> They admitted that the word 'crap' meant shit, but was a politer form of that particular word and that in America it was a normal colloquialism and that we had allowed it. I said that as far as I knew we had never allowed it except in its meaning of the game . . .
> They pointed out that the word 'arse' is frequently used, which is true, but never in combination with 'licker' . . .
> They argued that 'tumescence' means rowdy or disturbed. I think it means 'bumpy' and that is obviously the reason why it was cut . . .

Also cut was the line 'I let people draw pleasure from my groin', over which the Office was certainly not going to back down: 'I nearly lost my temper with them over this as their argument was so fatuous', reported the Assistant Comptroller; 'I suggested that they might at least offer to alter the word "groin", but they said it was vitally important'. Even more contentious was the line 'at night the sheets of my bed are like a tent, poled centre-upward in my love for you', which the Office had also disallowed: 'They went into hysterics over this and said it was the most important part of the play and to cut it would ruin it.'[41] The Censorship refused to back down.

Lady Chatterley

The *Daily Mail* cartoon which Penn had tried to buy at the height of the controversy over *Fings* had imagined the Censorship facing the prospect of a new Lionel Bart musical adapted from *Lady Chatterley's Lover*. Though it contained no songs, it was indeed a stage adaptation of Lawrence's novel which catapulted the Office back into the next round of its fight with the Press in the autumn of 1961. The previous November, the trial against Penguin Books for publishing the novel had reached its momentous verdict that the work should not be considered obscene, and in 1961 it was republished with extensive publicity. Somewhat surprisingly, a stage version of the novel was licensed without difficulty in August 1960, for a proposed production in the heart of London's West End.[42] While contemptuous of the earnestness in both novel and play text, Heriot—in a not unintelligent report—saw no grounds for intervention:

Lawrence's message was, briefly, that sex should be taken out of the head, where it had become too cerebralised, and put back where it belongs, below the belt. Quite a useful message if he had not become obsessed by it, to the detriment of his work. The famous novel . . . is not a novel but a thesis. It is not about people, but about embodiment of ideas, and the characters have no life of their own . . . This play is a devout and pedestrian extraction of the story . . . Removed from their literary context, the persons in this play move with the unpredictable irrationality of puppets. Their conversation reads like a careful translation from a foreign language. There is a dreadful Teutonic humourlessness about the whole thing.

It will be, I am afraid, hilariously funny in production—but that, alas, was never the author's intention, as it was never his intention to write a de-liberately pornographic book. He seems to have been defeated by his lack of humour on both counts.

Heriot testified that 'There is not a word to cut', with the Comptroller en-dorsing his judgement: 'And that is extraordinary remembering the book.'[43] Of course, the reason for this was that John Hart's careful adaptation had already done the work for him.

However, in July 1961 the Arts Theatre Club announced that it was staging Hart's adaptation privately, and that some of the novel's original language (if not the action) had been restored: '**On Stage for Lady C (Four Letter Words and All)**' announced the *Daily Sketch*. The article went on:

> The beautiful blonde who is to play Lady Chatterley on the London stage next month told me yesterday: 'I have no qualms about the four-letter words which will be spoken in the play.'
>
> Smoky-eyed Jeanne Moody had just been posing for pictures with Walter Brown, who plays the gamekeeper, Mellors.
>
> She went on: 'If these words were being used as expletives it would be awful, of course. But they are used with great tenderness and sensitivity. They do not stand out in the dialogue. I doubt whether the audience will notice them.'

Meanwhile, the play's producer, Miss Wanna Paul, was quoted as saying that she hoped the production would subsequently play in the West End: 'We shall invite the Lord Chamberlain to the first night, and I hope he will allow us to transfer the play to a public theatre without deleting these con-troversial words.' [44]

The show opened at the Arts in August in a private production, and reviews were generally poor. The *Daily Telegraph* said it was 'scattered with a lot of specious philosophizing and a few four letter words', and complained that after being

> lectured from the stage on the baneful effects of the Industrial Revolution, the importance of the English heritage, the falsity of the class structure, and the full meaning of sex, we begin to wonder whether we have accidentally made our way into a revivalist chapel instead of a theatre.

The 'bedroom scene' was 'tepid', and

> The first night audience was restive and giggly throughout the opening act, watching and waiting to see if the four letter words would appear. Once they did, dropping plainly and unexcitingly from the actors' lips, it subsided into boredom, relieved only by an occasional snigger at the ineptness of some of the acting.[45]

Nevertheless, Paul duly submitted the script for licensing to see if it could go public. Heriot's opinion of it had plummeted:

> There is a kind of strawy smell of badness about the play, like an old shop-egg that makes it unpleasant to read. If Mr Hart were a cynic one could dismiss it, but he is, I am afraid, one of those terrible people, a humourless enthusiast. No one else could have produced such a ridiculous play—and the addition of the four letter words are, of course, completely unnecessary, and have a shock value, not of sexuality but of absolute unsuitability.

Meanwhile, Scarbrough received a very long, very impassioned letter from someone describing himself as 'trained in Germanic Philology', urging him to hold the line over 'fuck': 'We have enough filth in this country, without permitting more. Whilst General De Gaulle has cleaned up France, or is endeavouring to do so, our country sinks lower so that not only is it weak economically, but also morally.' Much had been made in court of the origins of the 'f' word, but the letter-writer insisted it had 'nothing to do with Anglo-Saxon', and had emerged in English as a result of 'intercourse with the Low Countries'. As for the trial of Penguin Books, the philologist was adamant that the court's decision had been misguided and misinformed:

> The decision that the word was fit for public use and for publication, was a decision of an uninstructed jury, bludgeoned into believing a falsity by an imposing array of experts . . . The Crown lost its case through its lack of

will-to-win, or through sheer ignorance and stupidity and opened a flood-
gate to a state of affairs which is appalling . . .

   Moreover, the word is definitely one that is not used in any decent society.
If a person has begun to say that he ***** his wife, then love has begun to
sicken and decay, or he is a crank, or a sadist.

Its use, he insisted, was both uncivilised and un-English:

   I have heard a great deal of swearing in miners' and other homes, but never
   the word in question. It would be regarded with horror; though perhaps, not
   today in the homes of the nouvelle vague of intellectuals and aesthetes who
   have brought this country to such a degree of baseness that a patriot feels
   that it is not worth fighting for.
      Even the pagan Romans observed certain decencies . . . Are you to allow
   on the stage, what a Roman pagan would not have allowed in public?

Penn was not going to get drawn into such debates. He politely thanked
the writer for his 'interesting and erudite letter', and concluded: 'I think
we may take it for granted that the Lord Chamberlain will not sanction the
use of the words to which you refer in a public performance.'[46]
   But of course, a stage version of *Lady Chatterley* was always going to
be about more than words. In physical terms, the private performances
had evidently been quite chaste, with one critic suggesting that Lady
Chatterley appeared to be dressed in 'heavy protective armour', and
another comparing her to an Egyptian mummy.[47] Stung by criticisms
that the production had failed to embody sexual energy between Lady
Chatterley and the gamekeeper, the Arts Theatre let it be known that
they were reworking key scenes, and that the actors would henceforth
be naked. Although this nakedness would not be visible to the audience,
since the actors would be either in the bed or draped in its sheets, there
would be a very different edge to how the scene was played, and how it
was viewed. As Paul herself later put it: 'The audience don't see much
more, but they do realise it is a real scene closer to what Lawrence meant.'[48]
This was probably little more than a cynical marketing strategy (and quite
possibly a deception) to produce more (and better) publicity. It is at least
questionable whether the performers would have found it easier to project
convincing passion if they were, indeed, naked. However, the Theatre
staged a rehearsal of the new version especially for the press, supposedly to
allow Campbell Williams, the owner and director of the Arts Theatre, to
decide if he was willing to allow it. Whether the change had much overall
effect on the production is less clear. The *Daily Telegraph*'s occasionally
excited report indicated that it was probably not enough to alter the tone or
atmosphere:

As far as Mr Brown, the gamekeeper, was concerned, yesterday's new version made no difference. He remained 'swathed in sheets' . . .

Miss Moody kept her back discreetly turned to the audience when a sheet of her pink slip lay handy. Her natural condition, however, was quite apparent.

At the end of the ten minute scene Mr Williams announced: 'It was very artistically done and in the best of taste. I see no objection to the scene being done in this way from now on.'

The reviewer concluded that although the scene was 'certainly less prudish than when I saw it on the opening night', it was 'still a bit coy and certainly less revealing than two separate scenes, involving two separate actresses, which can be viewed in Anouilh's *Beckett* at the Aldwych Theatre'.[49]

Whether or not the new staging was sufficient on its own to have much impact, it put the Lord Chamberlain's Office onto red alert, and generated some of the column inches that the theatre must have hoped for. A Conservative MP duly fulminated against the performance (which of course he had neither seen nor intended to see) and announced his intention of taking legal action. Headlines soon ratcheted up the temperature: 'M.P. Refuses to see Lady Chatterley', reported the *Yorkshire Post*; 'MP says Lady Chatterley Breaks Law' announced the *Daily Telegraph*; and the *Daily Worker* offered 'Tory Seeks To Clothe Lady C'. A spokesperson for the Arts Theatre Club invited Ray Mawby, the complaining MP for Totnes, to attend a performance: 'I guarantee he will find nothing salacious in it.' But Mawby had no intention of taking up the offer ('MP Is Not Keen On Seeing Show'—*The Scotsman*).[50] Meanwhile, Penn wrote to the Home Office, enclosing newspaper cuttings and a letter of complaint—'one of several received in this Office protesting against the fact of a naked actress having allegedly been shown in bed with a naked actor'. He pointedly reminded them that since this was a private performance 'as at present advised, the Lord Chamberlain understands that such performances are not within his jurisdiction'.[51]

What the Lord Chamberlain's Office did have to decide about was the licence application for the proposed transfer to the West End. Hill went incognito to watch it at the Arts, and noted 'the introduction of the word "cunt"—twice', and several references by Mellors to 'cold-hearted fucking'. There was no possibility of allowing these in a licensed version, not least because of the precedent they would create:

The obscene words have of course been the subject of a Court case. It was noteworthy that although passed as pure, no newspaper or periodical has chosen to publish them except the 'Spectator' (I think). The stage is a different medium from a book—and a dramatised version of a controversial book is often far removed from the intention of the original author. To allow these words would mean also having to allow them in other 'serious' plays.

Hill also recommended cutting a reference to 'maidenhair'—'which I thought was a fern'—but it was the costume and the staging in 'the ante and the post-coition scene' to which he devoted most inches: 'we have not so far as I know ever allowed two people in bed together in anything approaching an erotic scene'. He then listed the physical actions which he had witnessed but which were not detailed in the script: 'The action of this scene as depicted in the stage directions is comparatively innocuous— nothing indicative of any attempt to resume the night's exercise!' On the one hand, the notion that a script should prescribe every movement, gesture or piece of on-stage action is clearly, with most plays, a nonsense. On the other hand, to base censorship only on the spoken words and take no account of the non-verbal is equally absurd and suggests a similar failure to understand how the medium works. In Hill's view, the law was unequivocal in its requirement 'that every part of a stage play must be submitted', and that this was supported by 'a High Court diktat that "business" is part of a play'.[52] In the present case, specifying the actions was vital:

> In my opinion unless this scene is specifically and rigorously confined in the licence to the submitted stage directions, the Arts Theatre management will face us with a fait accompli—if they do so after a detailed warning on the point then if brought to Court they can be shown deliberately to have defied rather than disobeyed the censor. I feel that all that can be allowed is hayloft—not bed—no specific covering—Connie as desired in a non-diaph-anous slip and <u>no</u> action beyond that detailed.

Penn wrote to Scarbrough, confirming the list of 'objectionable words' to be cut, but again indicating that the greatest danger lay not here but in the staging of the key love scene:

> So much has been made of this scene in the Press that it is hard to believe the Arts Theatre will not endeavour to reproduce the scene on the stage . . . unless a very firm and detailed warning limiting the action is included in the licence.

Only by being specific, he urged, could they prevent the theatre from exploiting the situation:

> It is suggested that a warning should be given to cover the following:
> 1) Mellors must wear pants.

2) Connie must wear a non-transparent slip so that she is never nude from including the breasts down.

3) Limiting the action absolutely to that detailed in the stage directions now submitted.

Another head-on collision seemed inevitable: 'I remember having seen one Press report', warned Penn, 'that Miss Wanna Paul, the producer, had stated that unless they were allowed to use the four letter words and unless the hayloft scene is presented as it is at the Arts Centre, she would not attempt to produce this play in a West End theatre'.

Doubtless remembering the embarrassment over *Fings*, Scarbrough reminded his staff to check they were not cutting anything they had previously allowed. But he endorsed the Assistant Comptroller's recommendations and added the stipulation that no bed should be allowed: 'their own stage directions refer only to "straw" and that should be adhered to'. He was also adamant that he 'would not agree to the couple being a) naked and b) in a single bed'. Was this a causal slip, or was he leaving the way open for a possible future U-turn which would allow him to approve a double bed without seeming to contradict himself?

On 5 September, the Office informed Wanna Paul that a licence could be issued, subject to a series of amendments and conditions:

> The following is disallowed . . .
> The word 'cunt' twice
> The phrase 'It's thee down there and what I get when I'm inside thee and what tha gets when I'm inside thee'
> The words 'Sir John Thomas'
> The word 'Maidenhair'
> The word 'fucking' (three times)
> An assurance is required that the stage directions given in the manuscript will be implicitly followed . . .
> No bed either actual or makeshift will be allowed, the only covering being straw . . .
> Connie must never wear less than the stated script, which must be opaque, cover her breasts and be of adequate length . . .
> Mellors must be reasonably clothed, at least in pants.
> The action between Connie and Mellors must not exceed that described in the stage directions submitted . . .[53]

Of course, the contents of this letter were soon leaked to the Press. 'Now—No Bed for Lady C' announced the *Sunday Pictorial*: 'The Lord Chamberlain has said NO to Lady Chatterley. And the shock will kill her—on the West End stage.' The *Sunday Telegraph* also quoted the rather exaggerated claim by Wanna Paul that 'If we took everything out that the Lord Chamberlain told us to do we wouldn't have a play'.[54]

Lady Chatterley had only another week to run of private performances at the Arts. Wanna Paul telephoned the Lord Chamberlain's Office 'to explain to you how very innocuous it all is', and to ask them to send a representative to watch a private performance. Penn advised Scarbrough against this: 'You have always been absolutely clear in your decisions about this play and I think that no useful purpose would be served by a visit.' Scarbrough agreed: 'I think we are on a good wicket over this', he wrote, 'I will not budge an inch'. Crucially,

> no purpose at all can be served by seeing the play at the Arts Theatre. Any sign of relenting would be most impolitic, and her request can only be a propaganda device which might involve us in difficult arguments. Therefore a firm, polite refusal to attend should be returned.[55]

A month after the Arts Theatre production closed, Paul submitted for licence a revised version of the script on behalf of a company called Theatre Holdings. 'If such a poor play could get duller, this one has', reported Heriot; 'It now turns up with the offending words removed and an introductory scene which hints that Lady Chatterley is about to have an affair with a nasty Irishman called Michaelis'. He recommended allowing it, with the necessary warnings about staging and costume, and Scarbrough cautiously agreed that, subject to a 'very strong warning' being issued, 'this rubbish is reluctantly recommended for licence'. But he was not going to be outwitted:

> It is possible that attempts will be made, in order to advertise the play, to suggest that the Lord Chamberlain has relented. I think we should be ready at once to say all the Lord Chamberlain's requirements have been met in this new version.

The company was sent another detailed list of what was and was not permissible, and 'a particular warning that no lovemaking beyond that actually noted in the Stage Directions submitted will be allowed'. Nearly sixty years earlier, the Censorship had become embroiled in controversy when the Lord Chamberlain's Office refused to license Maeterlinck's *Monna Vanna* on the grounds that in one scene the heroine is supposedly naked under her cloak—even though, since she never removes the cloak, there was absolutely no reason why the actress should really have been so. Remarkably, Paul's wish to have Lady Chatterley supposedly unclothed beneath a sheet (but again unseen) produced a similar decision: 'I am to make quite plain to you, that the Lord Chamberlain will not allow

"Mellors" and "Connie" to appear to be together under a blanket in a naked condition whether this actually is or is not so.'[56] The licence was not taken up, and the public production of *Lady Chatterley* did not occur. Paul had managed to stir up some good headlines: ('Woman v. Lord Chamberlain').[57] But overall, the publicity over *Lady Chatterley* was never as hostile towards the Lord Chamberlain as it had been in relation to *Fings*. Perhaps more people were willing to accept that a play derived from such a contentious source needed controlling, and no critic had defended it as a masterpiece. Crucially, though, the Office had played its hand much more effectively, while Paul had perhaps overplayed hers in the search for publicity.

There was one final dimension to the *Lady Chatterley* case which was, in its way, a warning of conflicts to come. In May 1961, the Lord Chamberlain received an enquiry from Ted (later Lord) Willis about a proposed dramatisation of the court-case against Penguin Books 'based on an actual transcript of the trial'. Indeed, he suggested that a similar version had 'already been done on a set of long playing gramophone records'. Such an adaptation and re-creation of a real trial on the stage would have been a significant landmark. As the Assistant Comptroller pointed out in his reply, 'there are many trials which would lend themselves even more readily to dramatisation'. This fudging of boundaries between reality and acting, between fact and fiction, was something the Lord Chamberlain was determined to prevent:

> The dignity of the Courts and the universal acceptance of the decisions made therein are, it seems to Lord Scarbrough, of such unquestionable importance that he feels unable to allow on the stage anything that might detract from their status or reflect upon the proper administration of Justice . . .
>
> In the theatre with evidence compressed to suit a theme, and actors whose gestures and inflections are dramatic and not forensic, the result, with the best intentions in the world, can be no more than a caricature of the trial, reflecting the editors' views.[58]

It was an issue which would dog the Lord Chamberlain's Office in the years to come.

CHAPTER TWO

No Laughing Matter (1961–1962)

Even the most reputable managements to-day are capable of action which would, twenty years ago, have been attributed only to third rate touring companies and no reliance can be placed on anyone.

(Comptroller of the Lord Chamberlain's Office, January 1963)[1]

I think Arnold Wesker should be Lord Chamberlain.

(Harold Pinter)[2]

In August 1961, the Earl of Scarbrough was invited to chair a literary luncheon at Foyles's Bookshop, in honour of the well-known comedian and music-hall entertainer Bud Flanagan. Flanagan and his Crazy Gang had encountered plenty of censorship problems in the past, their enthusiasm for double entendres and sexual innuendo ('Cut the business where Nero pulls his helmet plume through his legs, imitating discoloured urine . . . Cut the business where a bent organ pipe becomes erect when the bride enters . . . Cut the Chinese gag . . . based on an obscene assumption about the female pudenda') bringing them into inevitable conflict. Heriot had condemned one 'alleged entertainment' by the Gang on the grounds that 'its main source of humour is not even sex but excrement and urine', and in 1960 the Lord Chamberlain had been driven to seek an assurance that a dog urinating on stage during a performance had been a one off, 'and that the possibility is minimised by giving the dogs drinks only at appropriate times'. By contrast, Norman Gwatkin, now the Comptroller, was known to have a 'penchant' for the Gang, and had been accused by his colleagues of treating them with something 'suspiciously like favouritism'.[3] Gwatkin himself admitted that 'they get away with murder, bless their hearts'—and saw a strategic reason for taking up Christine Foyle's offer: 'it would be a good, democratic gesture' which 'would show the Lord Chamberlain's appreciation . . . of an artiste who has, indeed, given pleasure to thousands'. But perhaps it was too much of a risk. 'Once you start, where can you stop?' he wondered; especially since 'you will be in the chair as

Lord Chamberlain and not as the Earl of Scarbrough, whatever anybody says'.[4] The invitation was duly refused.

Comedy and Satire

Comedy was always dodgy ground for St James's Palace. By the early sixties, the Crazy Gang had become—at least in Heriot's words—'a sad bunch of ageing low comedians too tired to do anything more than go lower'.[5] A new generation of comedians and satirists—both British and American—was now rubbing shoulders with the fading stars of the forties and fifties, and there was a much greater willingness to break some traditional social and political taboos. Leading the way was *Beyond the Fringe*, 'the seminal show that lit the blue touchpaper for the 1960s satire boom'.[6] Originally submitted for licensing in 1960 as 'the "official" revue of the Edinburgh Festival', Heriot called its script 'a tatty little pseudo-intellectual revue, full of tiny mental jokes'. He cut some 'homosexual gags', and the performers were warned more generally that they must not 'represent the bye-play of homosexuals'. But some of the sketches contained more overtly political and offensive comedy; one of the best known sketches, which dared to poke fun at the hackneyed idolising of RAF pilots in the Battle of Britain, certainly got up some noses: 'I imagine we can shortly expect a skit on Dunkirk', fumed one correspondent to the Lord Chamberlain; 'I am angry and disgusted that callow young men, who have no memory of the last war, can get away with this sort of behaviour'. The Assistant Comptroller could only agree: 'It is a regrettable trait of this country to mock its heroes', he wrote; 'Nelson who was venerated in his time and whose life was one of selfless service to the Navy, is never mentioned on the stage today except in terms of derision'. But the Office was not willing to intervene: 'The fact that "the few" are being treated in the same way is an oblique acknowledgement of their greatness, which may help perhaps to stomach affronts of those least qualified to comment.'[7] Another sketch lampooned the current Prime Minister, Harold Macmillan—something which would have been unthinkable in a public performance ten years earlier—but again, the Office did little other than tut.

Beyond the Fringe was a huge success at Edinburgh with audiences and critics, and an updated version was licensed in April 1961 for the West End transfer. John Trevelyan, from the British Board of Film Censors, attended, and then contacted Penn to question whether some of what he'd heard had really been approved, or whether 'these boys are putting in "ad lib" lines'. He cited an unsubtle example in which someone describing school floggings exclaims 'I never got an erection—I mean a reaction'. Penn seemed surprisingly relaxed:

It is not uncommon for 'ad lib' lines to be introduced from time to time, and, although certain allowances are naturally made for this practice, it does so happen that some 'ad lib' lines, such as you have described in your letter, do go, shall we say,—if you will forgive it—slightly beyond the fringe.

However, the Office did intervene in 1962 over a Peter Cook sketch about 'Labour's New Image', objecting to a reference to a tall glass 'with a frothy creamy head on top', and a caption warning that: 'if you don't vote Labour, your genitals will drop off'.[8]

But in fact, whatever the reputation of *Beyond the Fringe* for new and daring radicalism, the Censorship actually got its knickers in more of a twist over certain other revues. Troubridge, for example, was 'disgusted' by *Ssh!*, a revue submitted for performance at 'a hole-and-corner Bayswater Theatre' in October 1961:

it is what one rarely gets nowadays, a show deliberately intended to be dirty. It is a lewd, suggestive, grimy affair with no other subject for satire or humour other than double entendres on sex intimacies, perversity, or the lavatory. Many of the songs and the sketches should be cut entirely, and almost all the others need deodorizing.

The Reader was also suspicious of the revue's possible context: 'One asks oneself what sort of an audience the unknown Mr Hutchins hopes to assemble in darkest Bayswater for this salacious stuff—and even what his other activities may be.' There was much to object to:

I didn't like the suggestion on page one that one of the girls, Fred, is a Lesbian, and still less do I like it that on pages 2 and 3 there are four boys in a women's dress, one made up as a Negress, which seems to me particularly offensive.

Indeed, he specifically defined the 'incitement to copulation by a Negress' as 'offensive'. Ideally, Troubridge would have wished to reject the whole show; but he recommended a more strategic approach:

To ban entirely a revue consisting of some twenty-four numbers is always difficult for the Lord Chamberlain, but there remains the Chinese Ling-Chi, or 'Death of a thousand cuts'. If my recommendations are accepted there will be precious little dirt left to be offered in Bayswater.

Above all, it was the homosexual inferences and the 'female impersonators' that most worried the Reader. One song was 'not allowed if played by a man', and the manager was also advised 'that the footwear must be

Wellington boots and not high-laced boots'. Other cuts included gags about 'discharge in hand', 'a pansy sketch about urination', the line 'I suppose it is nice to be different', a song called 'Sea Whores' ('the whole point of this number, repeated at the end of each verse, is that mermaids do not have female genitalia'), a reference to 'enormous physique', and—some seven years before the musical *Hair* repeated the idea—a song called 'Do it Yourself' which 'seems to recommend masturbation'. Nor did Troubridge trust the theatre to implement the required cuts, suggesting that either someone 'should go down after December 11 to see what they are really playing' or that they should 'tip off the Paddington police' and ask them to check. The Office also wrote to the London County Council, as the licensing authority for the venue:

> A similar entertainment provided by a different producer and entitled *We're No Ladies* was given at this theatre in 1958, and from a report made by his Lordship's representative at the time it was the opinion that the actors therein might be homosexuals, that the occasion was one calculated to cause, and actually causing homosexuals to assemble, and that the cost and lavishness of the costumes for such a small and insignificant show was inexplicable.[9]

The Council promised to look into the matter.

It was not only the smaller venues that ran into problems over their sense of humour and their vulgarity. One West End revue which provoked trouble was *The Lord Chamberlain Regrets*; 'The title', noted Heriot, dryly, 'is tempting providence'.[10] The main conflicts centred on 'The Dark Lady of the Senates', 'a mild not very funny scene about the wife of the American President', in which 'the uncrowned Queen of the United States' appeared on roller skates. As the press put it, Scarbrough 'stepped gallantly forward yesterday to spare the blushes of America's first lady',[11] but coverage of his intervention was generally negative. For the *Evening Standard*, it showed that 'The Lord Chamberlain's men are either completely lacking in any sense of humour or are determined to work themselves out of a job'; in *Plays and Players*, an editorial mocked 'the magnificent lack of humour' shown by 'our man at St James's Palace', as well as 'the sheer Alice in Wonderland absurdity' of a 'stupid and archaic system' which meant that the offending line could be published in national newspapers but not spoken on stage. Readers were also reminded that the decision was not an exception, but part of a pattern:

> The Kennedy case, unhappily, is not an isolated incident, but merely one in a whole series of illogical and inept decisions. The fault, of course, does not lie with the Lord Chamberlain and his not-so-merry-men, but with the system itself. Theatre censorship such as ours is outdated and unnecessary,

its only effect being to make a laughing stock of our theatre as a whole. It should be abolished forthwith and forgotten as speedily as possible.

It didn't help in this case that the banned material was also broadcast in a television programme entitled *Is the Law an Ass?* introduced by the (then Labour) MP, Woodrow Wyatt. Meanwhile, the writer and future Labour MP, Gerald Kaufman, wrote to the *New Statesman* questioning why a send up of the Russian leader had escaped cutting, and the *Daily Express* helpfully pointed out that sketches about the British Royal Family and politicians had also been allowed to stand.[12]

As the title of the revue suggested, St James's Palace itself was a key subject of the revue—the link that ran through its sketches. Throughout the performance, an enlarged photograph of the appendix to a (genuine) letter from the Lord Chamberlain's Office was displayed on stage, with its list of required deletions and amendments, and the Office was provoked by this to risk making even more of a fool of itself:

> I am to point out that copyright in letters, and letter headings, remains the property of the writer. This being so permission to reproduce them is required in each instance, quite apart from the requirements of the Theatres Act.
>
>   To save you trouble I am to say that, apart from the permission originally given for one letter, no further licence to publish any of the Lord Chamberlain's letters will be granted . . .
>
>   At the end of Act One the words 'OMIT THE REST OF ACT ONE' may only be displayed on a plain piece of paper with no reference to the . . . Lord Chamberlain's office or the Lord Chamberlain's office writing paper.[13]

In response to a complaint in August 1961 that *The Lord Chamberlain Regrets* was now subjecting the National Anthem to ridicule, Gwatkin wrote sadly that 'We can but hope that contemporary public opinion will pull itself up by its own shoestrings to a position of more dignity and decency'. But public opinion showed few signs of doing so. In January 1962, Heriot was duly appalled by Spike Milligan and John Antrobus's *The Bed-Sitting Room*, a farce-cum-satire set in the aftermath of an atomic war. The Reader called it a 'tasteless, sniggering charade', which was 'as inconsequential as Mr Milligan's radio show but with all restraint removed and all his fixations on top'. Certainly some of the cuts related to fairly juvenile silliness: 'However the "Farting kit" is presented, it mustn't.' But the script also contained 'blasphemous jibes at religion and the establishment'—as when Harold Macmillan is apparently 'transformed into a parrot and eaten by his daughter and son-in-law'. It seems doubtful whether the requirement to delete the line 'have a bit more of Harold' and substitute 'have a bit more Prime Minister' would have been sufficient to preserve Macmillan's dignity. The Crazy Gang had never gone this far— or selected such political or sacred targets to poke fun at:

> The voice of Lord Home must not be recognisable nor must it be a homo-sexual voice.
> Cut the supposed extract from *Lady Chatterley* substituted for the marriage service.
> Cut the reference to the Duke of Edinburgh and the singing of the Queen . . .
> Cut Lord Fortnum pretending to be God.[14]

Improvisation and *The Premise*

It was a comedy show from New York that really hit the headlines in 1962. *The Premise*—'A singularly unfunny "politically conscious" American off-beat revue'—was submitted in July for London's Comedy Theatre.[15] Several sketches were based around more or less improbable confrontations between the USA and the Soviet Union, and although many of the targets were relatively soft, four scenarios were refused licences outright, while others also required quite significant amendments. In one of the banned scenes, the segregationist Governor of the Southern State of Dixieland dies of a heart attack and discovers, to his horror, that God is black. The satire was doubtless directed against George Wallace, who in 1962 was elected with the support of the Klu Klux Klan to be Governor of the State of Alabama, and whose inaugural speech in January 1963 would culminate in his promise of 'Segregation now, segregation tomorrow, segregation forever'.[16] The decision to ban the scene in Britain was no less inherently racist: 'This sketch must come out since the Deity appears as a negro.' It was also widely reported in the press, along with the story that the Comptroller at St James's Palace had asked William Donaldson, the company's manager, to write a letter of apology to the Lord Chamberlain. The *Daily Mail* reported Donaldson's response that 'I certainly will not apologise either to Sir Norman Gwatkin or the Lord Chamberlain', who were 'merely servants of the Queen'. Rather, 'if a discourtesy has been committed by me it is only fitting that I should write to the Queen herself'. In any case, Donaldson added, 'the only people the sketch could possibly offend are negro-haters'. And he asked: 'Are those the kind of people the Lord Chamberlain is trying to protect?'[17]

In another sketch—which still reads well (and might give as much offence today as it did in the early sixties), a star-struck God, speaking with a 'vaudeville German accent', trades tricks unsuccessfully with a showbiz magician who has just arrived at the pearly gates. God is immediately impressed ('No kiddin'? You was a magician?') and childlike in his delight when the magician produces eggs and American flags from thin air ('those was the best tricks I ever saw . . .'); meanwhile, God's own tricks with lightning and thunder seem corny and old hat ('Well, I don't got the technique that you got').[18] But the most contentious element in *The Premise* for the British censorship was actually a series of scenes featuring J.F. Kennedy and his family. Even though the mockery was relatively mild, Scarbrough banned on principle the depiction of the current American President. Embarrassingly for St James's Palace, however, the company promptly contacted the White House and secured a telegram stating that Kennedy himself had no objection to the sketches, which 'the President has seen performed in Washington'. This story quickly found its way into the British newspapers. 'I have been besieged with phone calls this afternoon from the *Daily Sketch* and *Express* about the disallowed portions of *The Premise*', reported Hill; 'I told them I didn't know anything about it and that the only people who did know were on duty and not available'. He added: 'The *Express* man was quite pleasant but the *Sketch* woman not so good!' The Censorship was once again exposed, but Scarbrough judged it would look even worse to backtrack, and the ban remained.

In fact, the company had managed to pull a bit of a fast one, and a couple of weeks later Scarbrough received an apology from David Ormsby-Gore, the British Ambassador to the United States, on behalf of the President:

> I was staying the weekend with him when that ridiculous row blew up over the script of the new revue coming on in London. I explained to him the rule that you applied against the inclusion of any item ridiculing the Head of a Friendly State. He said that he fully understood and in any case would not dream of intervening in a matter which was entirely for Britain to decide herself. He then telephoned the White House and made the most tremendous row, as neither he nor Mrs Kennedy had been consulted before the telegram had been sent to the producers in London . . . He was extremely apologetic about any trouble the incident had caused you and he was furious that the impression had been given that he was interfering in a decision which was entirely one for you to make.

Whatever the truth of this, the damage had been done—though Scarbrough diplomatically reassured the Ambassador 'that the incident did not cause me any trouble', and even claimed that the effect had been to underline his authority:

> I maintain a rule about ridiculing Heads of State, principally because some of them—dictators from the Middle East and others—believe that censorship of plays reflects Government policy and get huffy if they are guyed in

revues. It is therefore useful to fall back on this rule, and the publicity given to it in the case of President and Mrs Kennedy has strengthened my hand for the future. In addition, I think there are a good many people in this country who do not think it is polite to laugh at Heads of State and who would resent The Queen being ridiculed abroad. Finally, by maintaining this rule, I keep at arm's length the efforts which a few less reputable producers constantly— not unsuccessfully—make to raise a laugh about The Queen. For all these reasons, the rule has its uses.

Then a new row over *The Premise* developed when the Lord Chamberlain received a complaint that the show included live improvisation by the actors in response to audience suggestions:

> One of the scenes from *The Premise* to which I took exception, was an improvisation of a scene from the film 'Psycho', a member of the audience called out for a sordid ending of the scene, another was when a member of the cast asked for an object to do a scene with, this time somebody called 'birth control', a scene was done to this and the so called joke was that it didn't work.
>
> I really do feel that this improvisation is dangerous, you just never know what is going to be said.[19]

Given that the title page of the script included the word 'IMPROVISED' in capital letters, someone at St James's must have noticed this element of the show earlier. Moreover, a few days before it opened, *The Times* had published an article about it headlined 'Theatre Experiment in Art of Improvisation' which even referred to 'audience participation' and the 'prospective tangles with the Lord Chamberlain' concerning the lack of a fixed script, which would need to be 'sorted out' before the show could open.[20] Reviewing the show subsequently, Kenneth Tynan wrote in his *Observer* column that he had originally 'refused to believe that they improvised, basing my incredulity on the fact that the Lord Chamberlain forbids impromptus'; however, he was now convinced that 'when the cast invite the audience to suggest themes for improvisation, they do indeed make up what follows as they go along'. He described it, approvingly, as 'spoken jazz'.[21]

The Office could no longer ignore the situation, and the Comptroller demanded an explanation from the theatre manager and the company.

> In view of the admission by certain actors that they improvise every night, I must ask you to forward immediately any explanation you may be able to offer. In the meantime, you will please take steps to ensure that the play is performed in exact accordance with the licensed manuscript.

The company was unapologetic:

> This revue is based on the technique of improvisation built up by the cast
> during two years work together. All the sketches in the show have at one
> time been improvised on the spot in front of an audience. Exactly what is
> improvised and what is not is very difficult to explain in a letter.

For the Lord Chamberlain, this was a clear admission of guilt, and ten
days later the man behind the show, the American playwright and director
Theodore Flicker, wrote again to try and legitimise their practice more fully:

> In an effort to aid you in creating a principle whereby your office is not
> placed in a position of banning from the United Kingdom the legitimate
> art form of improvisational theatre, I shall define improvisational theatre for
> you.

Flicker summarised the historical tradition of the form, accepting 'that the
same rules of decency and morality apply to improvisational theatre as to
any other public form of expression'. In fact, rather than claiming it as a
legitimate practice which should be open to all, he endeavoured to make a
special—but hardly plausible—case for his company:

> I think it would be fair for your office to say that unless actors were
> specifically trained by a recognised authority in improvisation and that
> unless a specific theatre piece were designed specifically for improvisation
> that they could not do it.[22]

Flicker was subsequently quoted as having said that 'To explain to army
officers how improvisation takes place is one of the most humiliating experiences of my life'.[23]

There had been previous requests to permit improvisation in performance, but none had been granted. The problem for Scarbrough now was
that it was already occurring—and had been every night since *The Premise*
had been licensed. Moreover, the public knew that this was the case. But
Flicker's proposal to limit the practice was unworkable, and to allow the
show to continue would effectively establish a precedent of live improvisation which must ultimately kill off the entire system of censorship 'since
anything could be interpolated and the answer would be that it was an
improvisation'.

Hill was dispatched to watch *The Premise*, and reported that what he
had seen was 'absolutely harmless', and therefore 'one of the worst possible
cases on which to base a prosecution'. However, he had no doubt that
it was technically illegal under the 1843 Theatres Act, or that 'once we

condone it we deprive ourselves of much of our control over the theatre which we cannot afterwards regain'. Trying to deal with the situation now was 'probably the nicest exercise in administration that could possibly be posed'. The fact was that 'For the first time, certainly in contemporary times, improvisations have gone unchecked on the English stage and this has already been noted by the theatrical world'. Moreover, 'If we threaten without prosecuting, we merely incite the public to go and see the show and to form an erroneous opinion that we are crazy in wishing to ban it'. It was the future implications which made the case so significant:

> Imitators will surely follow . . . Some of the imitations will be of the present high class, others will not—some will be pure, some will be obscene or otherwise unacceptable to us—but provided they are done on only one evening as allegedly improvisations, we shall be powerless to control them.

Indeed, astute managers would soon realise that 'sketches of which we were likely to disapprove could be kept out of submitted manuscripts and inserted afterwards as improvisations'.

There were three possible responses:

1) To do nothing which may involve us in condoning a breach of the law.
2) What would probably have been done as a matter of course in the past, and that is to give fair warning and then prosecute . . .
3) To warn the licensee, who has not been consulted yet, and the producers that in our opinion they are breaking the law.[24]

Rather than standing alone, the Lord Chamberlain sent a private and personal letter to Henry Brooke at the Home Office, warning him 'It may be necessary in the course of the next few weeks to take measures in defence of the Censorship which could be embarrassing to anyone defending the Institution'. Scarbrough was by now counting the days to his own retirement, but said he was keen to resolve this issue before handing over to his successor. 'I am doing my best to find a solution', he told Brooke, 'but it is doubtful whether one can be found without rendering the Censorship of Plays practically impossible'.[25] He also wrote to his incoming successor, Lord Cobbold, to tell him 'I will try and dispose of the "improvisation" problem before I leave: but it is a tricky one and I cannot be certain I shall be able to'.[26] As Scarbrough told the Home Office, he had no wish to expose himself by prosecuting those involved in *The Premise*: 'the Lord Chamberlain feels some sympathy for them, and is reluctant to use his powers under the Theatres Act unless it is clearly proved to him that improvisation is illegal'.[27] He even suggested that his decision to issue a licence had been based on a principle 'As the entertainment revives an art form extant in Italy four hundred years ago the Lord Chamberlain has overlooked the breach of The Theatres Act'.[28] In effect, he was seeking to take advantage of the situation and pressurise the government into acknowledging that there were problems with the whole issue of theatre censorship which needed to be addressed.

But the government was still reluctant to take on the issue, preferring another fudge. On 3 January 1963, Scarbrough wrote a 'strictly confidential' internal memorandum for the file, detailing a private meeting he had held with the Home Secretary:

> He hoped very much that it would be possible to find some sensible way of admitting genuine improvisation and felt that that would be in accordance with the tradition in which successive Lord Chamberlains had used common sense rather than pedantry to get over recurring problems.

The question, then, was 'Can genuine improvisation be admitted, with a fair chance that it will not lead to great abuse?' Following Fricker's suggestion, two possibilities were now outlined. One was to grant the freedom only 'to a recognised school of acting where training in improvisation is given'; the other was to demand that the theatre manager or company promise 'to refrain from introducing matter which would otherwise be disallowed'. But since such promises could not necessarily be trusted, might it be possible to require that a financial bond be signed as a guarantee? A dubious Hill produced a draft for what such a bond might look like:

> Know all men by these present that I recognise that I owe unto the Lord Chamberlain Her Majesties Household the sum of five hundred pounds, to be paid only if I introduce into such improvisation as I perform any reference at all to the royal family, any invidious reference to any living person or person recently dead, anything likely to cause a breach of the peace, anything indecent, anything blasphemous.

The Assistant Secretary doubted this would be workable in practice, since all the terms were open to dispute and there could be no guarantee that the Lord Chamberlain's definitions would be accepted in court: 'the actor's view of what is indecent is as good in the face of the law as the Lord Chamberlain's', he pointed out; 'There is not any statute which says that any man's opinion is in law better than any other man's opinion, even when the parties are say the Lord Chamberlain and Mr Bernard Levin'. Clearly, such a system could work only if the Office defined its terms and boundaries much more precisely and in advance. And even if this were possible, it would represent a fundamental shift, carrying its own significant dangers:

How foolish we should be held out to be when we published, as we should have to publish, our list of prohibitions since these prohibitions would have to be absolute ones and not subject to consideration, and absolute prohibition is the most repulsive form of censorship. We have never so promulgated a code, the offence at law has always been the presenting of something <u>not previously allowed</u> by the Lord Chamberlain, contrary to section 15 of the Theatres Act.

Nor was that the only issue: 'Who enters into the Bond or undertaking?' asked Hill; 'it would be administratively impossible to require all actors to enter into Bonds for the observance of the Lord Chamberlain's conditions'; nor would they necessarily have the funds available to support the pledge since 'most of them are men of straw'.

Hill concluded that the task he had been set was all but impossible. 'I find great difficulty in drafting a letter in conformity with the Lord Chamberlain's instructions', he wrote. He was certainly unconvinced that caveats would solve the problem:

> If the Lord Chamberlain concedes the principle of improvisation in my opinion he cannot limit its application in any degree. He could not allow five minutes improvisation and forbid ten minutes improvisation, nor could he allow one type of improvisation and forbid another.
>
>   Nor could he limit his decision to specified individuals. It would be too invidious to compare school a) with school b) or to ordain that a self-trained improvisateur of the calibre of Emlyn Williams cannot perform, when some callow actor with six months training at school was allowed to do so.
>
>   In fact the principle would have to be universally conceded.

To Hill, the law was clear as it was and should be observed. He took advice from two independent legal sources, who both confirmed that any use of improvisation on stage would be a technical breach of the 1843 Theatres Act. Hill drew a parallel with the situation over private theatre clubs, which had emerged from a willingness by previous Lords Chamberlain to bend the law, and had then developed into a practice which fundamentally undermined and threatened his control and authority. 'The point to be made is that it is not possible to apply the law in any fashion to suit convenience of the time.'[29]

A few days later, Penn noted that 'the Lord Chamberlain has seen and accepted these views', and conceded that he was not going to be able to solve the issue. 'Very fortunately the play folded up before a final and difficult decision had to be made.' The immediate problem had gone away, but the key thing was for the censors to try and prevent it becoming a precedent. The Comptroller wrote a private memorandum to the three official readers, Heriot, Troubridge and Coles:

> What is important now is to ensure that nothing similar happens in future.
>
> To further this, a letter stressing that improvisation is illegal has been sent to the producer and licensee of the theatre concerned in case they try it on again, and to the West End Theatres Managers Association, for information.
>
> It is essential that any possibility of 'improvisation' should be very carefully watched for in any script submitted for examination and killed before birth. We have just skidded round one difficult corner and we may not be so lucky should there be another one.[30]

Matters of Breeding

Even without the issue of improvisation, Scarbrough's last year in office was never going to be a relaxed one. Keen to avoid confrontations and publicity, Scarbrough was often surprisingly tolerant, frequently approving material which his Readers had recommended refusing. Even so, there were plenty of more or less trivial things which he could not bring himself to license. In January 1962, a 'strong warning' was issued to Stratford's Memorial Theatre that 'the vomiting must not be too realistic' in Elaine Dundy's *My Place*, and that 'the stains of vomit must not be visible'.[31] From *Zoo Story* by Edward Albee ('The first play by a bogus American writer') all references to an erection were cut.[32] A surprising endorsement on another script stipulated 'Omit "Behold, thy redeemer cometh". Substitute "And who's fooling with the dimmers?"'—the original line having been ruled 'blasphemous when said by a man to his mistress'.[33] In the same month, Peter Ustinov was taken aback to find the Lord Chamberlain had banned the line 'she was never very small' from his most recent play. 'Is obesity censorable?' asked Ustinov; 'If so, am I still permitted on the stage in person?' The licence was issued only when he agreed to change 'small' to 'thin'.[34] In April, it was the Royal Court and Samuel Beckett, with *Happy Days*, as the Office objected to 'stuck up to her diddies in the bleeding ground', 'castrated male swine', 'sadness after intimate sexual intercourse' and 'for Christ's sake'. The Court's Artistic Director, George Devine, declared himself 'puzzled' and requested 'some sort of lead as to the Lord Chamberlain's thinking'. As he explained: 'in view of Mr. Beckett's great distinction in the world of letters I do find it difficult to approach him without having some sort of an idea of what the problems are'. 'S. Beckett is not as important as he may think', scoffed the Assistant Comptroller, but Scarbrough backed down, ruling that everything other than 'Christ' could be passed. To placate his Reader he added that 'We need not endorse Mr. Devine's opinion of Mr. Beckett'.[35]

In February 1962, the Royal Court submitted *The Blood of the Bambergs* —John Osborne's latest assault on the Establishment. The narrative was centred on a Royal Wedding and—ominously—was billed as the first part of a trilogy with the collective title 'Plays For England'. Troubridge also drew attention to the play's 'many wisecracks at the expense of the Lord Chamberlain's Office', and summed it up as 'a vitriolic attack on Monarchy and Royalty'. Indeed, the Queen's sister is shown, having to make a choice for husband 'between Prince William, a pleasant, wet young man who drives cars too fast, and Prince Henry, who is a homosexual'. She opts for William, but when he is killed in a car crash on the eve of the wedding, the State secretly substitutes a drunken, Australian press photographer. The Reader thought this was 'Clearly intended to involve and reflect upon Princess Margaret and the Earl of Snowdon'. Another journalist is shot by the Comptroller of the Lord Chamberlain's Office (Colonel Taft), 'showing, I suppose, the ruthlessness of courtiers in defence of royal secrets', and the play ends with the crowd wildly cheering and celebrating the Royal Wedding, 'the implication of the author's attitude seeming to be "you are here cheering a fraud—as all Royalty is"'. Apart from his general distaste, Troubridge foresaw a very particular threat: 'If this play is licensed, and I hope it will not be, then . . . Colonel Taft must not be made up to resemble Sir Norman Gwatkin—just the kind of joke which would delight John Osborne.'

Scarbrough opted to cut rather than ban, and while this was partly a strategic decision to avoid publicity or confrontations, the principle of liberal tolerance he stated also deserves to be recognised, though we might also note that it is crucially predicated on an assumption that the performance could do no real damage:

> Since the beginning of recorded history it has been a recognised function of the dramatist to criticise and satirise contemporary life, and this function should not be denied unless the satire is beyond all endurance and the effect likely to be dangerous.
>
> We may not like Mr Osborne's denigration of Royalty, but it is not beyond endurance.
>
> Nor can this play be classed as dangerous to the Monarchy. There have been much more vicious lampoons of Royalty in the past, and at the present time British Royalty can survive satire of this kind without anxiety, even though it probably will find some response in some quarters.
>
> There are much deeper feelings about the Monarchy among British people than Mr Osborne appears to recognise. They do not need the assistance of the extreme step of suppressing stage criticism, and in these days of multi-publicity attempts at such suppression do not succeed, but are liable to give greater impetus to it.

In any case, Osborne was already well known 'for his expressed views on "England"', and as a 'gossip columnist' with a private life of which many disapproved. 'These are factors which diminish to some extent the damage which he may do.' Indeed, Scarbrough also observed that 'It may be bad policy—and no service to the Royal Family—to appear too touchy on allusions to Royalty'. Nevertheless, the cuts did require that there must be no impersonations of living persons, no uniforms resembling those of the British Services, and no resemblance to the British national anthem 'in notation or rhythm'. In other words, audiences must be assured that this was not really Britain we were seeing.[36]

Sensitivity to depictions of Royalty remained high on Scarbrough's agenda. In March he cut 'Royalty'd marry anything these days' from a Theatre Workshop production,[37] and in June, *Fit to Print* had an entire scene removed because there was 'no reason why the Queen or a Lady Member of the Royal Family should be introduced'.[38] The singing of the National Anthem was also excised from *The Bed Sitting Room*—possibly for fear of what the parrot might do to it—and in December, a reporter from the *Daily Express* informed the Office about a revue with a female impersonator 'who was made up to represent the Queen and who said "I wish you all a merry Christmas" in imitation of Her Majesty'. The Office had already expunged the Queen Mother and Prince Charles from the show, but when Hill went to watch it he discovered that the Censors had been tricked:

> I have no hesitation in saying that a representation of the Queen was included . . . The script reads 'Enter the anonymous lady wearing a mask covering face who says "And a merry Christmas to you all"'. I recommend that the producer be required at once to adhere to the script and warned that the anonymous lady must (a) wear a mask and (b) not resemble any known person.
>
> It was suggested to me that possibly Queen Victoria might be substituted. I said I thought the Lord Chamberlain would reject this since Queen Victoria had been allowed to be impersonated only in historical plays.[39]

A sketch in *The Lord Chamberlain Regrets* was even more shocking: 'The most serious thing in this piece is the fact that they have chosen an actress as near in size as possible to The Queen and put her in a very small hat such as The Queen affects on public occasions', reported Hill; 'The Actress stands quite still and I think there was a sense throughout the audience of who was intended'. Worse, the sketch involved this character bestowing the Royal Colours, with unexpected effects: 'the authors have made a woman strike a man's sexual organs and in such a way that the act is deliberate', complained a member of the public; 'In case this is not offensive enough the woman is made to appear as the Queen'. Hill went to see it and agreed that it was a dubious moment:

> The Ensign is sideways on to the audience so that the exact point of placing the Colour is hidden, from most of the audience anyway. The bulls-eye could therefore be the stomach, although precious few of the audience I imagine mistook the intended target area.

Though it could have been worse: 'The cry of anguish was not falsetto.' The company resisted changing the scene: 'The interview was stormy', reported Gwatkin; 'They claim that the sketch is one of the great moments in that beastly production, and I am afraid that we may well have some scenes thrown by this disgruntled mob, in the press'. Scarbrough remained adamant that the Colours should be presented only by someone 'bearing no resemblance to <u>any</u> member of the Royal Family'.[40]

One play about a queen which was particularly tricky for the Censorship to deal with was 'a tasteless affair' submitted in November 1962 by the Library Theatre in Scarborough, under the title *Send us Victorias*. This featured a talking effigy of Queen Victoria in a wax museum, and a lecturer who discusses with his audience the history of haemophilia in European Royal Families: 'Through listening to him they learn that Queen Victoria passed haemophilia to the Russian Royal House which led to the Soviet regime', explained Heriot; 'This does not appear to be true'. Either way, the discussion must be suppressed: 'We have already rejected fantasies much less repellent than the present one.' Once again, Scarbrough decided the best approach to take with 'such a small and insignificant play' was not to disallow it but to 'kill it by cuts'. A blanket requirement was issued 'that no reference to haemophilia will be made'—though the Office particularly disliked someone telling Victoria 'your son was a bleeder'. Unfortunately, the press got hold of the story, and a lecturer in the Department of Zoology and Comparative Anatomy at St Bartholomew's Medical College sent the Lord Chamberlain a three-page table tracing the 'distribution of haemophilia among Queen Victoria's descendants', and confirming that although 'there is no haemophilia in the British Royal Family of today', it had indeed spread from Victoria's son, Leopold, into the royal households of Russia and Spain. Forced onto the back foot, Penn sought to reassure him that it was not historical or medical fact which had been the issue, but the 'objectionable' references to a Sovereign who was 'part of the very recent history of this country'.[41]

However, writers were increasingly starting to see British monarchs as fair game, and to contest the class-bias inherent at St James's Palace. In 1962, David Turner—a scriptwriter for *The Archers*—accused the Lord Chamberlain of political and cultural bias in some of the cuts he was told to make to the script of *Semi-Detached*—a play which would later reach the West End with Laurence Olivier in the main part. The removal of certain expressions revealed 'class prejudice on the part of the Lord Chamberlain's reader', and Turner strongly objected to the deletion of a reference to the tradition of immorality in British monarchs: 'I am asked directly to suppress what I believe to be a political truth. I feel that this is an unjust demand within our State.' The Office backed down. 'Charles II, James II, George II . . . weren't models of rectitude where the ladies were concerned.' But they refused to concede over some of the language—and it was this which provoked Turner:

> If a definition of obscenity is a term which is repulsive to hear and gives an emotional feeling of indecency, then in the working class areas of the Midlands the words 'pregnant' and 'conceived' have this effect and must be considered to be obscene. To the working class family, they have a dehumanised, alien and clinical flavour which produces a mood of abhorrence. The lower classes use homely euphemisms in order to escape the harshness and, to them, crudity of the terms. Hence, they use phrases like 'pudding club', 'clicked', 'bun in the oven' and 'cake in the stove'.

Turner also complained about inconsistencies in the Lord Chamberlain's practice: 'The term "bun in the oven" is apparently permissible in a play of social realism (*Taste of Honey* . . .) but is impermissible in a satirical comedy. Here I feel literary criticism is being applied.'[42]

The Office was not persuaded to make further concessions over Turner's play, nor later in the year when Oscar Lewenstein argued for 'clap cold' as 'a common expression in the North, with no indecent meaning' for the Blackpool run of Keith Waterhouse and Willis Hall's *All Things Bright and Beautiful*. 'This may be so. But a southern audience will have other ideas.' However, when this production reached London later in the year, it was actually the set which generated controversy and complaints.

> According to the 'Daily Mail' there is, at the Phoenix Theatre a play in which a working lavatory is part of the scenery . . . This is to me offensive and obscene, objectionable and obnoxious and repellent and shows a disastrous falling away from ordinary standards of decent propriety.

Kitchen sinks were bad enough, but a toilet? 'I fear I agree with the complainant', wrote Hill, 'and assume we pass these things only to enable the stage to have enough rope to hang itself'. Yet it was not feasible to intervene, since Scarbrough had overruled his Readers in allowing references in the dialogue to the smell of a lavatory: 'As the DPP said, if we allow the dialogue we must expect and cannot complain of, concomitant scenery and action.' There was no real response the Office could make to such objections 'except to say that we don't censor bad taste', noted Hill; 'but in other aspects we do, so that argument is manifestly untrue'. Penn informed the complainant that the Lord Chamberlain 'feels it is not his province to do more than protect the community from what will actively corrupt or debase', and tried to put the blame on modern tastes: 'It is the humour of the times to give ostentatious display to those aspects of life which in other days were the subject of decent reticence', he wrote; while this was not 'a pleasant or a nice play', it was 'typical of the times in which we live, however much we deplore them'.[43]

At the end of March, Troubridge officially retired from his role of Reader—though he would continue reporting for another three years—and was replaced by Maurice Coles. It fell to the new Reader to report on yet another Osborne/Royal Court play, *Under Plain Cover*, which showed a brother and sister living together as a married couple:

> I have read and re-read this play a number of times, in an endeavour to give the author the benefit of the doubt, but my first impression remains unshakable. It is that this play is a study in sexual perversion—what is more, the study is a detailed one which gains in force rather than loses from being largely suggestive, except in the final stages of the play.

Apart from the 'distasteful atmosphere of perversion' which dominated the sexual games of the central characters, Coles drew attention to 'a lengthy discussion lasting nine pages of the script on the subject of women's knickers, which explores practically every possible aspect of the subject usually associated more with schoolboys' dirty stories'. He recommended outright refusal, but by now Penn and Gwatkin were more in tune with Scarbrough's light touch approach: 'I don't suppose we boggle at a little tedious incest', wrote the Comptroller; 'I wonder what abnormality Osborne's bleary eyes will light on next'. He was contemptuous of the playwright's advocates: 'I am sure that a lot of people will swoon with delight at this latest Osborne effluent'; but he judged that no-one was likely to be corrupted by it: 'I should think that the morals of anyone who pretends to understand what this play is on about will already be beyond contamination', he sneered; 'And the remainder will ride the storm unsullied'. Lines cut included 'all references to the Royal Family', while a reference to someone sleeping with the bride and the groom was changed to being on 'intimate terms' with them, but overall the amendments were relatively minor. Certainly, the not yet dead Public Morality Council 'expressed much perplexity' that the script had been passed for public performance at all, 'having regard to the sex perversions and abnormalities it portrays' as well as the 'vulgar and disgusting dissertations on various articles of female underwear'. Gwatkin was more concerned that the new reader had been overruled; 'As we have gone right in the "face" of the Examiner's recommendation I think you might, perhaps, write him a private letter?' he suggested to Penn; 'We don't want to discourage him'. The Assistant Comptroller duly sent Coles a confidential letter to boost his confidence:

> the method by which you draw attention to <u>any</u> part of the script, or business, to which exception might possibly be taken is most certainly a very great help to the Lord Chamberlain and to myself and I hope, please, you will continue to do this. This may mean that a certain amount of what you draw attention to is 'allowed by the Lord Chamberlain'; but it makes it much easier and far better for us if you draw attention to everything which you think might be tricky.[44]

In July, the Office chose not to intervene over *The Voice of Shem*, Stratford East's adaptation of part of *Finnegan's Wake*. 'I have no doubt that the text simply seethes with sexual and scatological references', wrote Heriot; 'but if they have not leapt to my eye, I swear they will not sound on the ears of a Stratford audience'.[45] A licence was also finally issued for Anthony Shaffer's play about the Nazis, *The Savage Parade*, which had been refused fifteen months earlier on the grounds that it might have prejudiced Eichmann's trial in Israel. By now, Eichmann had been executed, though Heriot still thought it was 'a bit soon' to allow it. In fact, the original Reader's report had suggested the play might 'well be offensive to the "friendly" Israeli government', particularly 'accusations that Jews torture prisoners' and 'the author's final observations that the Israeli's eye-for-an-eye revenge philosophy is no better morally than the Nazi "shove-them-in-the-gas-chamber" genocide and that the Jews would be capable of the same excesses given an opportunity'. Troubridge had even proposed that it was 'more an anti-Semite than anti-Nazi play'. Moreover, many European countries—including Britain—had experienced an unpleasant wave of anti-Jewish demonstrations at the start of the sixties, so the issue was a live one. Scarbrough worried that the play 'may be so offensive to the Israeli Government as to damage friendly relations' and 'whether these suggestions, coming so soon after the end of the Eichmann trial might give rise to racial disturbances'. He consulted the Foreign Office, which, as always, declined to share the responsibility, beyond suggesting that some passages might indeed 'merit the Lord Chamberlain's careful consideration'.[46] Scarbrough, doubtless deciding it was better not to draw unnecessary attention to the issue, signed the licence without imposing any endorsements.

Homosexuality—shifting the rules

Scarbrough had fought through most of the 1950s to keep explicit references to homosexuality out of the theatre, before eventually capitulating and letting it be known that the supposedly blanket ban was to be removed, with plays being considered individually on their merits, rather than on principle. However, he had tried to maintain a ban on 'innuendoes or jokes', on 'embraces between males' and 'embarrassing displays by male prostitutes', as well as on anything he considered 'violently pro-homosexuality'; perhaps most problematically of all, he had also decreed that he would 'not allow a homosexual character to be included if there was no need for such an inclusion'.[47] These criteria, and the general level of tolerance towards the no-longer-forbidden-subject, were tested several times in the early sixties. In March 1960, *Look on Tempests* had opened at London's Comedy Theatre, with Vanessa Redgrave as the wife trying to come to terms with her (off-stage) husband's betrayal. The play's treatment of the subject was discreet and more or less innocuous, but Hannen Swaffer's report in the *People* appeared under the headline: 'Censor Abdicates'. According to Swaffer, 'By licensing *Look On Tempests* . . . the Lord Chamberlain has made almost unnecessary his continuance in the office of chief censor of the stage'.[48] A few months later, however, an extensive list of cuts was imposed on a new version of the 1957 play *Compulsion*. 'A Censor's Axe Falls Seventy Times' was the headline in the *Daily Sketch*, while the *Daily Mail* ('The Censor Hacks at Murder Play') reported that 'American producer Clement Scott-Gilbert and his director Glen Farmer were baffled by the decision' and 'prepared to battle with the censor'. The newspaper quoted their responses:

> The idea that the Lord Chamberlain no longer objects to serious plays involving homosexuality would appear to be a myth, said Mr Farmer.
> Said Mr Scott-Gilbert: 'I just cannot understand it. We submitted this play because the subject was no longer taboo.'
> But the Lord Chamberlain has made the most amazing cuts. I shall have to sit up all night re-writing it in time for the opening.[49]

Moreover, for all its political satire, the only cuts made to the script of *Beyond the Fringe* related to comic depictions of homosexuals. In one, 'two males, described as "dreadful queens" impersonate the rugged manly figures of a cigarette advertisement'. The Reader commented: 'I don't think the time is yet ripe for homosexual gags of this kind.' The other was a scene in a public lavatory, approved only in return for a guarantee 'that all homosexual gestures and business will be omitted and the piece played as between two aesthetic young men', and that 'the word "darling" be omitted where it occurs as being a feminine endearment'.[50]

In January 1962, the Office removed a lesbian character from a play by Aberdeen students set in a nuclear fallout shelter: 'Her vice is not essential to the main thesis', wrote Heriot, knowledgeably; 'she is only there because the author has read *Huis Clos*'.[51] In February, Troubridge agonised about 'the advocacy of homosexuality' in Kieran Tunney's *A House of Glass*, and recommended outright refusal. 'I feel we have not yet got quite as far as this' he wrote, for while 'it does come under the Lord Chamberlain's memorandum as a sincere and serious work on the subject', it was 'both too intensive and too specific'. The overall perspective of the play was also highly questionable:

> Above all there is a theme, put forward by a psychiatrist as the mouth piece of the author, and this is definite advocacy of certain homosexual relationships. This theme is that, while those who came to these practices in youth or puberty, through a corruption from a man or woman, can be cured by psychiatry, those in whom homosexuality is congenital, cannot be so cured, and should be allowed and encouraged to establish a quasi-marital relationship with another man, to relieve them both from the squalidity, danger of blackmail, etc. of promiscuity with male prostitutes.

What clinched it for Troubridge in this case was the epilogue, which leapt into the future to show the failure of a marriage into which the protagonist has entered in a doomed attempt to cure himself. Five years on, we see him 'contemplating his descent into the underworld of queer's clubs as soon as his wife has staggered to bed'. Not everyone at St James's agreed with the Reader's judgement. 'If you are going to allow plays on homosexuals, then this is a serious play on the subject, and within the terms of the L.C.'s dictum must be allowed', wrote Hill; 'There is nothing in the action described anywhere to cause anxiety, the whole thing is decently done physically'. Though he did object to a line suggesting that 'Two of our greatest Generals in the last war were as queer as coots but it didn't stop them from winning battles'. Hill acknowledged, too, the hypocrisy in the Office's current policy: 'I should not have thought we were sufficiently advanced as to allow descriptions of homo-sexuals physical love affairs. This ought to come out (which of course shows the falseness of the stand on this particular subject!).' On the other hand, Gwatkin read the text as no more than 'a mild plea to let the incurables live their own lives', and Scarbrough agreed it would be inappropriate to ban it:

> I expect it will arouse controversy, but nevertheless it should be passed (a) because having given notice that serious plays on the subject will be allowed

it would be pusillanimous to retract when the first really serious work comes along, and (b) because some good may come of free discussion of the subject on the stage, now that there is free discussion in all other mediums.

However, he insisted on specific cuts: 'I see no reason . . . why, to make his case, the author should be permitted to implicate definite sections of people—e.g. Lords, Commons, Generals and Court Circles.'[52]

In July, Coles recommended extensive cuts to *Escape from Eden*, whose author, Graeme Campbell, was described by the Reader as 'a third-rate Tennessee Williams'. Set in New Zealand, it contained what Coles called 'the usual Williams assembly of tortured, twisted, sex-ridden (and homosexual) characters, in a festering, enclosed family community in a remote corner'. Again, it was the homosexual elements which worried him most: 'There is much in this play which I feel certain will have to be deleted since it comes under the category of "embraces between males or practical demonstrations of love".' Coles also cited 'homosexual passages' which 'if taken in isolation, may seem innocuous, but acquire an altogether different significance when considered in the light of the development of the relationship between Sebastian and Barrie'. These included stage directions indicating that Barrie 'blushes and moves nervously away' when Sebastian puts an arm round his shoulder, and another which referred to his hands trembling. Coles also drew attention to a long section in the second act:

> There is so much in these fifteen pages which requires consideration that it is impossible to list everything. This is the 'love scene' between Seb and Barrie: I say 'love scene' advisedly because it is just that. You will see exactly what I mean if you read it several times, and then transpose it in your mind, reading Seb's lines as if spoken by a girl to a boy she is in love with . . . How much is cut depends on how far you are prepared to allow an author to go in a situation like this.

Scarbrough was actually prepared to allow the author to go quite a long way, cutting only the more explicit lines such as an unambiguous plea by Sebastian to Barrie to 'Let me go to bed with you. Please. Please', and Barrie's admission to having 'been with men sometimes'.[53] In some respects, then, *Escape from Eden* can be seen as a breakthrough play.

Challenging the System

The year 1962 was a popular time for new versions of Brecht. In January, Troubridge was irritated when *The Caucasian Chalk Circle* was submitted by the Old Vic: 'It is rather pitiful that direct Communist propaganda should be produced by the Company (under the Patronage of the Queen) which will be the nucleus of our future National Theatre.'[54] In May, Coles had struggled with *The Jungle of the Cities*, submitted for Stratford East:

> I cannot pretend that I was able to make head or tail of this play, though I presume that the title has some significance. Also, since this is Brecht, I assume that the play has to do with the struggle between capitalism and communism: but . . . who represents which I am unable to say.[55]

In October, Heriot observed that on re-reading *The Good Woman of Setzuan* 'one begins to see how specious the author's reasoning is and how dishonest his manipulation of the story to make it fit his ideological framework'.[56] In November, he reported on *The Rise and Fall of the City of Mahagonny*, originally submitted for Sadler's Wells but then switched to the Royal Shakespeare Theatre at Stratford:

> It all seems as simple as a temperance tract—but then, I believe that Brecht is simple and that his reputation has been inflated by the ignorant young of this generation and that very soon his nauseous blend of sanctimonious communism and elementary humanism will meet the oblivion it deserves.

But the cuts were relatively minor. 'We've pissed whiskey'—'surely a unique line in the history of opera'—was duly changed to 'spewed', while 'shit heap' became 'cesspit'.[57] *Baal* ('gross, revolting and ugly') required more extensive blue pencilling for its mixing together of religion, sex and excrement. The Reader was revolted by its hero's appetites: 'satiating himself deeply in carnal pleasures, taking and throwing aside women indiscriminately; and despite his revolting ugliness, having no lack of bedmates'. Again, Heriot predicted the playwright's demise: 'Brecht is a fashion just now, but already some critics are beginning to suspect that he's been grossly over-praised and that his philosophy is bogus.'[58]

In December 1962, the Labour MP Dingle Foot introduced a bill to the House of Commons which proposed acting on the recommendations of the 1909 Joint Select Committee of Enquiry into stage censorship by making it optional rather than compulsory to submit a play for licence. Foot said it was 'astonishing that we had put up with this essentially silly form of restriction for two-and-a-quarter centuries', and that 'we should put a stop to it now'; in his view, it was 'fantastic that playgoers in London should not be able to watch scenes which they could witness on the stage in Washington, New York, or in most parts of the Commonwealth', and he ended by quoting Bernard Shaw's dictum in the preface to *Mrs Warren's Profession*:

all censorship exists to prevent anyone from challenging current conceptions and existing institutions. All progress is initiated by challenging current conceptions . . . Consequently the first condition of progress is the removal of censorship.[59]

But the bill was opposed by MPs concerned about 'the brothel type of play', and defeated by 134 votes to 77. Six years later, 'the audacious Mr Foot' would play a significant role as Attorney General in the Labour Government's abolition of theatre censorship by the Lord Chamberlain. Even in 1962, the Press reported that in refusing to accept Foot's case 'Parliament stands almost alone'.[60]

Earlier in the year, Professor Harry Street of Manchester University's Law Department had sent the Lord Chamberlain a draft extract from his forthcoming book about civil liberties in contemporary Britain. Street invited the Lord Chamberlain to correct any factual errors, promising anonymity in return for any further information or insights. Street was a respected and distinguished academic, a former visiting professor at Harvard. Sensing the potential significance of his book, Gwatkin wrote a detailed seven-page reply which was fulsome—not to say sycophantic—in praising the author's research and analysis:

> If I may say so without presumption I find it difficult to believe that any-one, not a Member of this Office, should have been able to give such a just explanation of its attitudes, and your interpretation of some aspects of The Theatres Act I have read with real benefit to myself.
>
> Normally here, where we are the target for the prejudiced and sensational writer, we do not comment upon what is submitted to us with regard to the censorship; nor do we offer any defence of it. But in your case I feel that, for such a balanced paper, we ought to do what we can to help.

Doubtless the Comptroller hoped to exert some influence on Street's text, and his questioning of the legitimacy of established authority. Having suggested some slight amendments to the author's empirical account, Gwatkin sought to engage with his libertarian criticisms at a more profound level:

> I assume we both agree that the basic problem is a simple one—complete liberty always engenders some excesses, are these excesses in any particular case sufficiently severe to warrant control, and how do you control the controller?

Speaking 'from our knowledge of the excesses which can arise in theatre', Gwatkin challenged Street's call for liberty by asking him a series of current questions:

1) . . . should an author, with the whole of fiction open to him, batten on the sufferings of persons involved in some real life drama? . . .
2) Can the law contemplate:
   a) The dramatisation of *causes célèbres* with the Judge, Council, Defendants and so on impersonated, the evidence condensed or wrongly emphasised in the interests of a dramatic theme, or to make propaganda for some pet theory of the Author, such as the abolition of capital punishment; even to the suggestion that there has been a miscarriage of justice? . . .
3) Should there be not even the slightest curb upon the current flood of mockery and denigration of all aspects of authority, The Monarchy, Government, Religion, Officers of the Services, Police and so on?

Street's text had pointed out that references to politicians were often disallowed, even if they were inoffensive. 'Would anyone ever really be interested in producing an inoffensive play about a politician?' queried the Comptroller, and he made explicit a position which was usually more hidden:

The sort of thing that we might get might be something of the order of a play entitled 'Suez' with Anthony Eden and his colleagues impersonated, the whole written by one of the well-known Left Wing playwrights and staged at The Royal Court Theatre. Under the present regime a play expounding all the political principles involved would probably be passed provided the setting was Saxonia and Pharoahstan and the characters were general ones. But there is surely a case for avoiding the attribution of fictional words and actions to living individuals which must be the case in a play of political descriptions where Cabinet Meetings and Lobbyings and so on would have to be described.

Street had also queried whether, even if one accepted the need for theatre censorship, 'a man whose main function is Court Ceremonial is likely to have the appropriate background experience for the task'. Gwatkin responded forcefully:

This is the one place where I will make some defence of the Lord Chamberlain . . . If you will think for a moment I am sure you will agree that Lord Chamberlains in history have never been merely concerned with Court Ceremonial—Shrewsbury, Holles, Newcastle, the Duke of Devonshire,

Breadalbane, Viscount Sidney and so on . . . We in the Office may be submerged in Ceremonial, Protocol, Precedence and other archaisms but the Lord Chamberlain most certainly is not.

Gwatkin told Street that his reply was written 'rather unguardedly' and that his comments were 'more for your cogitation than for actual quotations'. He concluded: 'For obvious reasons I have marked this letter "Confidential" and I should prefer after you have taken any notes from it that you want, that it should be destroyed.' Still, Gwatkin hoped that his comments would 'be used to modify your own speculations'.[61] But while Street did make some alterations in the light of points raised, his published text set theatre censorship within a broader context of contemporary legal freedoms and control, and remained unequivocal in its conclusions and recommendations. Crucially, Street recognised that the real impact of theatre censorship was invisible and impossible to measure: 'What is incalculable is how many worthwhile controversial plays about politics, the Crown, and the Church the British theatre would have had, if dramatists had not known that plays on such themes would be banned.' It was an anachronism: 'How does one justify censorship of plays on the stage, if there is no legal censorship by an outside body in respect of television and radio?' As for the potential influence of theatre on real life behaviour, Street agreed that anything which prevented crime would be in the public interest; however, 'not many of the matters which the Lord Chamberlain prohibits would be criminal'. Rather, he wrote, 'The Lord Chamberlain avoids injuring people's feelings and wounding their susceptibilities and protects institutions such as the monarchy, the Church, the armed forces, and the police, to an extent to which the law could not possibly go'. In Street's judgement, there was 'no adequate reason for compulsory censorship', or even for 'maintaining the present machinery, on . . . an optional basis'. If, despite this, theatre censorship was allowed to continue, then its basis should be fundamentally altered, since it was placed 'in the hands of the Lord Chamberlain, not in consequence of a carefully thought-out decision of policy, but only through a historical accident'. Moreover, the extent of his authority was surely indefensible since even Judges were not given comparable 'unlimited discretion' to decide whether an act was criminal. Street therefore recommended that, as a minimum, the grounds on which a play might be refused a licence should be defined, and that the procedure for dealing with plays should be judicialized, with a censor accountable either to parliament or through the courts.[62]

Fighting Back

Increasingly beleaguered, attacked and embarrassed from all sides, the Lord Chamberlain's Office considered trying to seize the initiative. If only more people understood what the Censorship was up against, they would surely be more supportive. In response to a Mr Haw from Huddersfield who accused the Lord Chamberlain of being generally 'against freedom of speech and thought', the Comptroller sent him a copy of Scarbrough's current entry in *Who's Who*, his accompanying letter mixing a studied and exaggerated politeness with a carefully sharpened knife:

> On reflection, you may feel it strange that, with such experience, Lord Scarbrough should forbid stage pieces of complete inoffensiveness; and possibly there may be other explanations than those immediately apparent to you.
>
> Again, I would not for one moment controvert your honest opinion upon the future necessity for censorship. It is based, I am sure, on consideration of all aspects of the case.

With a well-practised tone of withering and patronising courtesy, the Comptroller carefully explained that

> Any censorship must, of course, confine freedom of thought and speech and is justifiable only as a preventative or deterrent of licence.
>
> Where we differ, I should say, is upon the danger of licence and, to assess that, quite a lot of experience and facts are necessary.

He also appended a list of unacceptable words garnered, he claimed, from a recently admired play. One can sense Gwatkin's quiet pleasure in directing such a list to the correspondent:

> CUNT
> FUCK
> BALLS
> MY ARSE IS MADE OF LEATHER
> HARDCOCK
> ARSEHOLE
> CRAP RIDDEN
> WOG SHIT
> SHIT SODDEN
> SHITTING BRICKS
> THE WOMAN WOULD USE YOUR BALLS FOR EAR-RINGS.[63]

Meanwhile, senior staff discussed what practical steps they could take which might help to restore the institution's reputation. Recent policy had been to keep out of the public eye whenever possible, but now St James's needed some good publicity to counter the stream of press mockery. Even when rejecting a request from the *Daily Mail* for an interview with Scarbrough in 1961, Penn had acknowledged that there was much to be gained from keeping the media onside; 'any large organization or Office of importance requires skilful Press relations if it is not to be subject to Press snipings and thereby to be presented to the public in a disadvantageous manner'. Regrettably, the Office lacked the resources to act on this, and the Assistant Comptroller had reluctantly concluded that it was safer not to get involved:

> If we were to start any discussion with the Press and tried to 'put over' the Lord Chamberlain's task as censor, the stream of questions, even on the smallest points, would be continual and endless. This would indeed require a separate and skilful Press-minded staff.
>
> We could not have that on financial grounds alone.
>
> In these circumstances it is better to say nothing and to have no dealings with any of the Press, however annoying and unjustified their resultant pin-pricks may be.[64]

But they were looking for opportunities.

In August 1962, it was announced that Scarbrough would retire the following January, to be succeeded by Lord Cobbold, the former governor of the Bank of England. The *Observer* published an article on the 'Censor's New Tolerance' which was surprisingly sympathetic to the current regime, and gently critical of his detractors: 'Lord Scarbrough, has become a good deal more liberal since 1958', declared John Ardagh, 'yet his censorship functions are still denounced as an outrageous despotic anachronism by nearly all playwrights, critics, actors and progressive theatre managers'. Ardagh had evidently been granted an unofficial interview with someone at Stable Yard—probably Hill—and he was ready to sing the Office's song: 'The staff conceive it as their job to protect the ordinary, decent family from being embarrassed at the theatre', he dutifully reported, 'and to "keep a step or two ahead of public opinion"'. It was, he insisted, 'very rare now that a play is banned outright'. Though it is doubtful whether all of the details Ardagh shared with his readers had been intended for publication: 'Borderline cases dealing with the Royal Family are sometimes seen by the Queen Mother', he wrote, 'who is said to be concerned to keep skits on Prince Charles off the stage'.

According to Ardagh, even amongst those who opposed censorship on principle 'the present system, responsible only to the Crown, is thought by many to be at least preferable to the kind of Government or police interference that exists, say, in France'. He quoted two well-known objectors to censorship—Jonathan Miller and Michael Codron—who had supposedly admitted that present practices and policies were 'mostly innocuous, sensible and even helpful', and were 'better than dealing with a lot of prudes'. Even John Osborne was said to be 'well aware of his lordship's growing tolerance'. The key message was that, for whatever reason, fundamental shifts in attitude and practice had taken place, and deserved to be recognised:

> Constant pummelling from critics, Press and theatre people, changes in public opinion, fear of looking ridiculous, and the simplicity of evading bans or cuts by resorting to club theatres, have all contributed to the Lord Chamberlain's change of policy.

This was probably better publicity for Scarbrough than he might have expected from the *Observer*—even if some of the language was rather revealing in terms of class bias and expectations:

> The Lord Chamberlain's staff are not in fact as priggish and out-of-touch as they might appear to the outside world or to an incensed modern play-wright who has never met them. Although there is no final appeal against their verdict . . . in practice, under the new, more liberal regime, playwrights or managers are allowed to come along and negotiate the changes. They are greeted with courtesy and generally with great reasonableness, and if they come with a set of alternative proposals and a confident, well-bred manner, they can often win a good many concessions.[65]

Still, for St James's Palace, this article was a step in the right direction, and Penn drew up a strategy for instigating a charm offensive through the media by offering the prize of an interview with the Lord Chamberlain himself:

1 Aim
  To explain to the widest possible audience the task of the Lord Chamberlain concerning Plays of the Stage.

2 Method
  We wish this article to have the widest possible circulation and therefore we hope that it may be published in:
  National Press
  Provincial Press
  General Magazines
  Specialist Magazines

The author chosen would 'receive every assistance from the Lord Chamberlain's Office', and would be required to submit the article to them for approval (or censorship) before publication. But there were important decisions to make—not least who should be given the opportunity to write such an article:

> There appear to be three alternatives:
> i   A person of standing, with literary ability, connected with the theatre:
> Actor
> Producer
> Manager
> ii   A skilful and reliable journalist . . .
> iii A writer of distinction, with no connection with the Press or the Theatre.

Then there was the question of which newspaper to go for. The *News of the World* enjoyed the widest circulation, but would the *Sunday Times* or the *Observer* be more appropriate? The crucial factor, said Gwatkin, was 'what category of the public we wish to reach'. There were other issues to resolve: 'Are we to say, when asked, if we have helped the author to write his article', he wondered? And how should they respond to subsequent requests for information and interviews? Would it be best to 'adopt our customary silence' or should the Lord Chamberlain give regular press conferences?

The Office also knew that shifting public perceptions would not be easy:

> However it is presented, an article on the Censorship will be anatomised by the enemies of the Office, parts will be lifted from their true context and used against it, whilst examples of the Censor's own actions in apparent contradiction of his policy will be used to make him seem ridiculous.
> This must all be accepted.

But it was worth fighting for. 'When the dust of battle settles it will be worth looking again at the salient facts', wrote Hill; 'The reasons why the Lord Chamberlain is Censor, what he tries to do, and what he has to deal with'. He had no doubt that the task remained important. In a society where 'venereal disease in adolescents is increasing, as is the disease acquired from homo-sexual sources, and where violence is a commonplace', the theatre's potential to relieve or to exacerbate contemporary problems might be unclear, but it was still significant. 'How far the stage would contribute to this scene were it not for its control cannot be estimated.'

Following parliament's rejection of Dingle Foot's bill, Hill contacted the Home Office:

> When we were speaking the other day I told you that so many tendentious reports about the Lord Chamberlain and the Censorship were published that we had given some slight thought to publishing a counter blast.
>
> Whether we shall or not I do not know, especially as I feel it would be quite useless to put anything out unless the press would print the actual obscenities that have to be disallowed. I did, however, go so far as to knock together a certain number of facts which, after a good deal of polishing, might have served the purpose and I enclose a copy herewith in case you find it either amusing or of use.[66]

On the same day, Scarbrough also wrote to the Home Secretary, Henry Brooke.

> When we had a word at the Diplomatic Party about a month ago we agreed, I think, that it might be useful if I came along and had a talk with you on the subject of the Censorship of Plays. The fact that this subject was aired yesterday in the House of Commons makes me feel that I would like to have such an opportunity. Would you therefore please suggest when you would find it convenient.

Although Foot's bill had been comfortably defeated and further parliamentary debate was not imminent, it was surely only a question of time before the issue resurfaced. Given the unique position of the Lord Chamberlain in relation to the royal household, there was a real fear that mockery of him and his Office could encourage criticism of the reigning monarch. Yet Scarbrough also wanted to be sure the government appreciated that no effective alternative to the present system would be easily achieved:

> Did it not exist, Censorship could be administered only by:
>
> i)   The propagation of a set of rules, which, in use, would be inflexible and impractical.
> ii) An elaborate and costly system of inspection to ensure that such rules were obeyed.[67]

Brooke and Scarbrough met for discussions shortly afterwards, though the idea that the Lord Chamberlain should actively try to turn the tables on his attackers seems not to have found much favour:

> He had read the notes I had made for Lord Cobbold and said that he and one or two of his advisers, to whom he had shown them, agreed with every word. In particular he felt absolutely convinced that it was no use for the Lord

Chamberlain to try and answer his critics. Much the best policy he thought was the one we had pursued of not getting involved in arguments. He went on to say that he could see no workable alternative to the Lord Chamberlain as Censor. He also felt that however vocal the criticism was directed at the Lord Chamberlain and not at the Queen's household, and he did not feel that the Queen herself was in any danger of becoming involved. I pointed out that if the Lord Chamberlain passed things which were regarded as particularly outrageous it might react adversely on the Queen, on the ground that it had been done by one of her Household; he admitted that but thought that it had never yet become a serious problem.

The message from the Home Secretary and the government seemed to be that he should take it on the chin and keep smiling—at least for now:

He realised that it must often be very irritating and uncomfortable but he was quite convinced that a great deal of sound opinion was in favour of continuing the Lord Chamberlain as Censor, and they felt it was in good hands. If it ever arose that sound people began to have misgivings then he agreed that a different question would arise.

There was one other person whose views mattered:

He asked if the Queen had any particular views upon this and I said that she had never definitely told me that she thought it ought to be out of the hands of the Lord Chamberlain, though I felt that she was sorry that it gave rise to much criticism. The Home Secretary said that of course if the Queen definitely wanted the system changed the government of the day would have to consider it seriously. I told him that there was no question of that at the moment.[68]

Lord Cobbold was due to take over as Lord Chamberlain in early 1963, and while Scarbrough was doing his best to reach some sort of resolution to the problem of improvisation, there were other challenges to the last. Bill Naughton's *All in Good Time* focused on the always tricky subject of male impotence. The dialogue was uncomfortably direct, and once again, the Reader linked this to the social background of the characters: 'Both families are working class, so the subject is discussed from every possible angle in language which is often crude.' 'It is not obscene', ruled Scarbrough; 'I think the present generation can take it quite easily'.[69] Reporting on John Arden's *The Workhouse Donkey*—'sprawling, shapeless, verbose'—Coles complained that the playwright 'relies over much on lewdness for laughs'. And he drew particular attention to a scene 'which may be acceptable in a strip club . . . but not in a stage play'.[70] It took pages of cuts, six months of argument, negotiation, re-writing and careful checking before the script could be licensed. Even in the summer of 1963, 'get stuffed' had to be changed to 'get knotted', and 'I knocked them yeller gels' to 'I kissed them yeller gals'.

Troubridge was equally disparaging about an adaptation, *Stephen D*: 'James Joyce has been the idol of the "progressive" highbrows for thirty years', he sneered. 'But I must admit that to me he is still the big foul-mouthed phoney and purveyor of Hibernian jibber-jabber.' He admitted that the text contained 'fewer ruderies' than he had expected, and that censoring Joyce was always 'a little dodgy because of his wide reclamé', but a number of cuts were imposed on grounds of blasphemy: 'The Lord Chamberlain is very averse to the invocation of the Deity in any expletory form.'[71] Much more extensive alterations were demanded in Tennessee Williams's new play, *The Night of the Iguana*. 'None of the characters in a Williams play will ever achieve any kind of mental or moral sanity', advised Coles, who declared himself 'sickened by Williams's obsession with sexuality, masturbation and excrement'.[72] It would take two years for a compromise to be reached and for Williams's play to be publicly performed.

Then in the final days of his watch, Scarbrough had to deal with a text which was judged to be virtually beyond amendment, written by one of the wittiest—and least deferential—of the coming generation of young British playwrights. Heriot described Peter Barnes's *Clap Hands Here Comes Charlie* as 'a worthless, scatological play' and its submission 'an impertinence'. Although the central character, an anarchic street-musician and tramp called Charlie Ketchum, is hanged for his crimes and sent to hell, his supposed vices are redesignated as virtues and he is transferred to Heaven. Heriot had no doubts: 'This is a definitely corrupting play, since we are asked to admire and sympathise with a stinking, dirty, liar, thief, fornicator, blasphemer and murderer who (sharing the author's point of view) is against any form of culture or organised society.' He listed some of the offensive transgressions:

> The text is riddled with bad language. There is a scene where Charlie sits on a lavatory seat with his trousers down and soliloquises. The trial scene includes the putting on of the black cap and the judge's final words, interrupted by indecent expressions by Charlie. In the death cell there is a blasphemous interview with the prison clergyman and a baptism in urine from a chamber-pot. No detail about hanging is omitted—and treated in a farcical manner. Excrement is mentioned on every possible occasion.

Scarbrough confirmed his Reader's recommendation, and the manager who had sent in the play was informed that the Lord Chamberlain was 'surprised that you should have submitted this play in its present form'. He was informed he would need to remove 'many obscene passages' before it could even be reconsidered, and that it would be necessary 'for several scenes to be omitted or drastically altered'.[73] If the Office hoped this would shame Donald Albery then they were wrong; indeed, Heriot reported that the producer had 'impertinently pursued me to my home', where he tried (in vain) to convince the Reader of the play's literary and intellectual merits.[74]

In February 1963, Lord Cobbold took the helm. As Scarbrough packed his bags, it was reported in the Press ('TV Scraps Jokes Curb on Comics') that the BBC was officially abandoning a long-standing policy to ensure its comedy was at all times 'clean and untainted'. The policy had been embedded in a booklet which had specifically outlawed all 'references to religion, royalty, politicians and sex in its light entertainment TV programmes', as well as imposing an 'absolute ban on jokes about lavatories, effeminacy in men, immorality, honeymoon couples, chamber maids, fig leaves, prostitution, ladies underwear, lodgers and commercial travellers', and even 'jokes derogatory to political institutions and Acts of Parliament'. The pioneering and successful Saturday night satire *That Was the Week That Was*—itself a child of *Beyond the Fringe*—had made its name on its willingness to break taboos, mocking (and milking) some of the Establishment's most sacred cows. A policy dreamed up in 1951 could hardly survive, but the BBC's decision was interpreted by the Lord Chamberlain's Office as depressing evidence that they were effectively capitulating and 'abandoning censorship'.[75] Scarbrough knew perfectly well that the days of the theatrical status quo were numbered, and he informed Cobbold of his discussions with the Home Office: 'I thought it worthwhile to implant in that office the seed that some day there should be a change.'[76] It would come on Cobbold's watch.

CHAPTER THREE

Pleasuring the Lord Chamberlain (1963)

Censorship has always selected Art as its principle enemy and rightly, for Art . . . helps to disintegrate, it breaks up the pattern of life and puts it together in another shape which may turn out to be harrowing . . . or even apparently anarchic.

Censorship, on the other hand, is unifying, adhesive, soothing, the plaster of all those authorities intent on holding society together . . . Our best allies against censorship now are the young.

(John Osborne)[1]

If a work of art depends on obscenity then it isn't one

(Assistant Comptroller)[2]

In a recent article assessing the historical significance of 1963, the *Spectator* and *Daily Telegraph* columnist Christopher Booker (at the time a left-wing satirist for *Private Eye* and *That Was the Week That Was*) describes it not only as 'a watershed year' but 'the year old England died'. For Booker, it is 'the moment when the "old order", which had for so long seemed to be at the core of our national identity, finally crumbled, giving way to the very different kind of country that in many respects we still live in today'.[3] The key political event of the year which both marked and accelerated this shift was the scandal involving John Profumo, a minister at the War Office and a rising star in the Conservative Party. Profumo—who was married to a successful actress (and who, as it happens, had been involved in the world of amateur theatre)—was forced to admit he had had an affair with a woman who had also been sleeping with a military official (and probably a spy) from the Soviet Embassy, compromising national security at a time when Britain and the USA were locked into an East/West war which was in danger of changing from cold to very hot. When Profumo came clean and resigned in June it was a devastating political and moral embarrassment for the Conservative Party, further exacerbated by the fact that he had spent months denying the affair, and lying to the House of Commons. According to Booker, the result of this scandal was that 'all the swelling tide of scorn and resentment for age, tradition and authority, all the poisonous fantasy of limitless corruption and decay into which it had ripened, were finally unleashed in their full fury', as the exposure 'was seized on with glee as a shadowy indictment of Britain's entire ruling order'.[4] As the *Daily Mirror* had demanded under the headline 'The Big Lie', 'What the hell is going on in this country?'[5] Although the Prime Minister, Harold Macmillan, resisted immediate calls for his own resignation, this followed before the end of the year—ostensibly on health grounds. In a move which was hardly likely to be seen as progressive, the Party replaced him with Sir Alec Douglas-Home, an aristocrat and an Earl. In terms of its political leadership, power seemed to have moved from an old England to an even older one. But although they held on until the following year's general election, the Tories under Home, and the values they seemed to embody, were irrevocably damaged and increasingly irrelevant.

Enter Lord Cobbold

The Lord Chamberlain who took up the reins from Scarbrough in January 1963 was still very much part of the 'Old England'. Lord Cameron Fromanteel 'Kim' Cobbold had served as Governor of the Bank of England from 1949 until 1961, and had a reputation for dignity, efficiency, and authority. He was known as a man who could keep secrets and act with discretion. Indeed, he would eventually be remembered for being 'always the Governor, even when shaving and wearing nothing but his pyjama trousers'.[6] Despite these qualities, he made an unfortunate start to his time as Lord Chamberlain when, caught off guard, he unwisely told a journalist that 'my yardstick for judging a play will be a simple one—just whether I enjoy it'.[7] Cobbold soon regretted his much-cited comment—'It was one of those London Airport interviews where a microphone is pushed in front of your face at six in the morning when you've just taken on a job and flown across the Atlantic'—and was keen to retract it: 'One's personal likes and dislikes are obviously not relevant in the least for censorship purposes: in fact one has to make a positive effort to push them out of one's mind.'[8] But for once he had been caught with his pyjamas down, and his off-the-cuff remark was a gift to the anti-censorship lobby.

Cobbold may have been part of an old order, but he knew it would have to adapt in order to survive. In a private memorandum, he described the censorship of which he was in charge as 'an obvious nonsense' and predicted that his position was one which 'five or ten years later, nobody in their senses would take on'. Moreover, he was 'strongly influenced' by his awareness of the potential impact which attacks on the Censorship might have even higher up the social ladder:

although we ran it from St James's and not from Buckingham Palace, and though we did our best to maintain that it was quite a different function, there was increasing danger that it would reflect on the Monarch and give ammunition to criticisms that the Palace was stuffy and out-of-date.

In Cobbold's own words, he 'started nosing around with Ministers and officials to see what could be done'.[9] However, the new Lord Chamberlain was prepared to play a long game, and in the meantime to maintain a similar course to that of his predecessor, relying heavily on the experience of his staff, and avoiding conflicts and publicity as much as possible.

However, Cobbold did bring in some new approaches. Traditionally, the Office had inspected live performances only rarely—not least for practical reasons—and usually in response to complaints. Within a few weeks of Cobbold's arrival, Penn sent round an internal memorandum with a more pro-active policy:

PLAYS TO BE OFFICIALLY INSPECTED—INCOGNITO

The Lord Chamberlain wishes plays that we consider to contain doubtful or tricky dialogue or action, about which we think we may receive complaints either about what is contained in the script or may be extended cunningly by the producers or actors, to be officially inspected—incognito—on the third night after they are first produced in London.

Would Mr Heriot, Mr Hill and Miss Fisher please keep a careful eye on any such plays and let me know when they think such a situation is about to arise.[10]

The fact that the policy was only really at all feasible within London, and therefore implied a differential approach, could not be helped. Whether his staff were prepared to give up very many evenings to act as unpaid performance spies is surely doubtful. Cobbold also instituted a more organised approach to documenting the cuts he imposed—throwing an interesting light on the gaps he must have discovered in the existing procedures:

The Lord Chamberlain wishes to keep a check of the cuts that are made in stage plays.

He would accordingly like a copy of the Appendix of each letter we send to the person submitting a play, in which any cuts are required.[11]

This tightening up seems to have been provoked by one of the first challenges Cobbold had to negotiate—complaints about a revised version of the Milligan/Antrobus satirical farce, *The Bed-Sitting Room*. This script had been submitted by Bernard Miles before Scarbrough's retirement—

along with a request for the restoration of some previously disallowed material:

> We would like to plead for the word crapp, which is a well-established English proper name. One of the Crapps even has the courage to put his name in the telephone directory . . . We telephoned Mr Crapp and he is deeply hurt that anyone should take exception to his name, which was also his mother's.

Miles did his best to appeal to the official sense of humour:

> We plead permission for me to bring the authors to your Office to read and illustrate these particular passages. We would beg that the whole staff be assembled, and I think we could guarantee to raise many an innocent laugh—and perhaps gain a reversal of your ruling . . . I feel sure that if his Lordship could meet the two authors he would agree that they are both good men, full of warm and generous impulse towards humanity, and that their aim is simply to relieve Man's intolerable burden through the safety valve of laughter.

But the staff were not amused: 'This is disingenuous', wrote someone in the margin; 'There is no question of using a proper name but of using a slang expression for excrement'. As for Miles's suggestion of a comic demonstration, Scarbrough was unenthusiastic. 'Unnecessary', he wrote; 'try and put him off'. Some twenty-five cuts were duly imposed, including representations of the Prime Minister, references to the Royal Family, a clockwork Virgin Mary whistling the Twist, and a Priest describing 'Lady Chatterley's Lover' as 'the good book'.

Even so, Cobbold soon received complaints about the performance, some of them from important people. These included the Dutch Ambassador, the Countess of Dartmouth and the Honourable Mrs Stonor, who had watched it in the company of Graham Greene. She (and supposedly Greene) had been appalled by the insults directed at Christianity and the Catholic Church, while the 'brilliance of the conception and production' was less a compensation than 'an added peril' because of the appeal it made to 'the young intellectual community' who witnessed it: 'The Theatre last night was playing to capacity, and the performance was rewarded with much applause.' Penn went to see the show, and reported six deviations from the licensed script, all containing 'an element of blasphemy'. Cobbold issued a no-nonsense but carefully vague threat to the management:

> I am anxious to maintain my predecessor's helpful and co-operative attitude to responsible managements. But co-operation is a two-way traffic. It is only

fair to add that if I form the opinion that anybody is not playing ball, I shall do my best to tie them up as tightly as possible, which will be very tiresome for all concerned.

But it was the decision to check the performance at all that was of most significance: 'This episode strengthens my view that, whenever we feel that a play is near the edge and that a twist of action might send it over the edge, we should get somebody from here to see it', noted Cobbold; 'This would very much strengthen our position'. And when *The Bed-Sitting Room* transferred to the Duke of York's Theatre, he duly arranged for another secret inspection.[12]

Unfinished Business

Cobbold soon came up against some other unresolved issues—not least the question of improvisation. In April 1963, Heriot reported that *Looking for the Action*—a new American revue 'funnier than most, and entirely free from offence'—included a sketch called 'Press Conference' featuring the Russian President, Nikita Krushchev, and his interpreter. As part of this, members of the audience were invited to pose questions 'which are answered on the spur of the moment'. The result was 'unlikely to be obscene', but the Reader warned that 'it might involve lèse majesté'; and as he added, 'in any case improvisation is frowned on'. When Penn advised the management that the scene required a script, the company responded by submitting 'ten stock answers together with 26 sample questions to which these answers are given'. They also claimed that 'if a question is unsuitable, the actor in question says simply, "next question, please" or carries out some mime without any words which makes it quite clear that he is unable to answer the question'. Rather surprisingly, the Office approved this, but a secret inspection revealed that neither the questions nor the answers in performance 'bore any resemblance to those cited'. They included:

'When are you coming to England?'
'I will return to England when the next Communist Government is there—in five or six months time.'

'Is your interpreter's beard necessary?'
'Perhaps.'

'Where do you get your shoes made?'
'Mrs Krushchev makes them.'

The mole also noted that the sketch had been 'introduced with a reference to the Lord Chamberlain (at which members of the audience hissed)'. It was clear that the case had 'all the possibilities on a smaller scale of *The Premise*', but when the company was advised that improvisation was illegal, the sketch was apparently dropped.[13]

There were also some scripts on which the files had not yet been closed. Oscar Lewenstein had submitted a revised version of Brecht's *Baal* at the end of January, for George Devine's production with Peter O'Toole; 'The piece has had a lot of alteration', reported Heriot, 'possibly because the original was too near to German to be other than jaw-breaking to say'. Further cuts and negotiations had occurred, but the 'bogus piece of Teutonic pretentiousness' had eventually been approved. However, in March 1963 the Public Morality Council wrote to the Lord Chamberlain to express its view that: 'Having regard to the seductions and near blasphemies which seem to form most of the play it was a matter of some perplexity to the committee that such a play should have been granted a licence.' But the Council's never-changing stance carried little weight or respect at St James's Palace. 'Oh! my!', wrote a senior member of the Lord Chamberlain's staff in the margin of their letter. In April, however, Lady Cynthia Tuker from Falmouth also wrote to Scarbrough 'to protest against this play ever having been licensed' for the British stage:

> Although realising that to-day increasing latitude is given to plays which would once not have been tolerated, I and my friends, who were of a considerably younger age than myself, were astounded that such a performance should be permitted on the London stage. Both by word and by implication it descended to depths that I have not before witnessed in a public performance. We left the theatre in disgust during the third scene . . .
> It is scarcely surprising that we have the problem of difficult young people when such shows as *Baal* are not merely staged but advertised as literary masterpieces.

Penn explained that because Brecht was 'a dramatist of international repute', a ban 'would arouse far more excitement and interest than would the fact of its presentation'. He also pointed out that 'the audience attracted to Brecht is likely to be a somewhat specialised one', and insisted that the Lord Chamberlain had taken a calculated decision:

> Despite the unpleasant nature of some incidents involved, he decided that the cumulative action was artificial in effect; and that the squalor in which the piece is embedded is a further element in repelling the audience from, rather than inciting them to, immorality.[14]

After six months of negotiation and rewriting, John Arden's *Workhouse Donkey* was finally licensed in June 1963, but Tennessee Williams's *The Night of the Iguana* proved even tougher. Two weeks after Cobbold's enthronement, he received a letter from the playwright's American agent saying she was 'dismayed by the real lack of understanding the Lord Chamberlain's office is showing concerning one of Williams's finest plays', and drawing attention to the fact that in America it had been 'received by many critics as Williams's greatest play of self-transcendance' [sic], and was about to open in several European countries. While the playwright might consider revising individual words, some of the offending material 'cannot be changed without completely altering what Mr Williams means this play to be about':

> It is because so many critics and so many audiences felt so deeply about *Iguana* that I am more than unusually shocked by the many points the Lord Chamberlain's letter indicates must be changed before the play can be produced in London . . .
>
> It seems unbelievable to me that a play which has left other audiences so touched can be found objectionable.

Cobbold hid behind his predecessor: 'As it was dealt with by Lord Scarbrough, I prefer to stand on the decisions which he took.' In April, Lewenstein submitted eight revisions proposed by Williams, but indicated that in respect of three further changes which the Censorship had demanded, the playwright was 'still very unhappy'. 'I couldn't really care!' commented Heriot in the margin. With neither side prepared to back down, the play remained unlicensed and unperformable until 1965.[15]

In 1961, the film director Anthony Asquith had used his presidential address at a conference of the Association of Cinematograph, Television and Allied Technicians to demand greater uniformity of censorship policy across films, television and stage, so that 'one does not have to rush from one medium to another to see what the other one has forbidden us to see'.[16] Building a united front with television was another item on Cobbold's agenda when he arrived, but the attempt met considerable reluctance, as Penn reported: 'An enquiry on our behalf resulted in an almost rude statement from the BBC that they did not wish to cooperate with us in any way whatsoever.' Indeed, television companies were unwilling even to divulge their broadcasting plans in advance: 'The only possible way of ascertaining whether these plays are to appear is to examine the "Radio Times" and "TV Times"', explained Penn; and 'even that is really not very helpful, since without checking the actual transmission nobody will know whether the version is an expurgated one or not'. He also pointed out that standardisation would not necessarily be straightforward, since television was 'an entirely different medium, and the effect is often widely different from that obtained on the stage'. He therefore advised Cobbold that 'in the majority of cases the fact that a play has appeared on television does not affect the issue so far as we are concerned'.

The Home Office was still clear that the Lord Chamberlain should not engage in public debate about censorship—however provoking some of the attacks and criticisms might be. In March, however, Hill was offered a chance by the *Daily Telegraph* to promote the Censors' side of the story in return for supplying some good titbits—'I wish I could persuade you to send me all the examples you might have met of "try-ons".' Hill told the paper that 'the Lord Chamberlain's policy has always been not to enter the lists', and the offer was turned down.[17] But in an effort to try and rescue the Censorship, Cobbold was ready to reverse tradition, and Gwatkin agreed in May that the Assistant Comptroller would 'discuss the principles of stage censorship, "off the record"' with Lionel Crane of the *Sunday Mirror*. '"Interviews" as such are, I am sure, out', wrote Gwatkin to Penn; but 'if a stuffy attitude is maintained I think it does more harm in the end and tends to make the censorship an even worse joke than it is at the moment'. Sadly for them, the resulting story appeared under the headline 'This charming chap is doing a damn silly job', alongside a distinctly unflattering photograph of Cobbold, and a caption asking 'Do we really need someone to decide what is too saucy for us to see or hear?'[18] So far so bad.

The following month Cobbold refused an invitation from Associated Television Ltd to be interviewed by John Freeman alongside Joan Littlewood and Roy Jenkins in a programme to be called 'The Censors'. Although John Trevelyan of the British Board of Film Censors also refused, their silence led to further accusations and even outrage in the press: 'Why did these two officials shrink from the public gaze and reject the opportunity to justify their existence?' asked an editorial in the *Daily Mirror*; 'Are they too unsure of themselves? Is their position so unutterably weak that they have no defence which would stand up to intelligent cross-examination?' Certainly, the idea of a cut and thrust debate, or a possibly hostile interrogation, was far from Cobbold's mind as he explored the possibility of a newspaper interview on his own terms. But the *Daily Mirror* thought 'the two most powerful censors in the country' had shot themselves in their respective feet: 'Perhaps by force of habit these wielders of the gag and muzzle have gagged themselves.'[19]

Ghosts from History

One of the first new scripts to raise difficult political questions for Cobbold was *Night Conspirators*, a play set in contemporary Germany in which a neo-Nazi revival culminates in an elderly Hitler re-emerging from hiding to take power. It was the work of Robert Muller, the journalist, theatre critic and screenwriter who had himself fled from Germany to Britain in 1938, and the script and its central premise inevitably carried a certain power.

ADAM: You will address my father as my Fuhrer . . . Speak to them father.

HITLER: [*Trying to speak, eyes flashing*] I . . . I . . .

ADAM: Speak to them father, you are in power.

HITLER: [*Haltingly*] I . . . assume . . . the responsibilities you . . . have . . . vested . . . in . . . me . . .

ADAM: Speak to them! Speak to them!

HITLER: [*becoming increasingly self-possessed*] I am ready . . . ready to speak for myself—and—to act! You have done your duty by . . . the fatherland!

VON MARKHEIM: The same voice! . . .

HITLER: [*addressing the audience*] . . . sixteen years of shame, of humiliation, to be wiped out . . .

[*From now on his voice rises in a crescendo of hysteria. The music grows in volume*] I demand the obedience of every German man, woman and child. I demand discipline, I demand sacrifice . . .

ARCHBISHOP: A miracle!

VON SCHLITZ: The same voice!

[*The sound of sirens is heard in the distance*] . . .

HITLER: [*ranting*] I pledge my life to the restoration of Germany's rightful place among the nations! Our enemies shall tremble before our regained strength. I renounce all treaties entered into by the corrupt and treacherous Bonn Republic—I renounce our dependence on NATO and the United Nations! I renounce all limitations placed on our defences!

[*Onto the main salon's back wall are now projected filmed images of soldiers and storm troopers marching, of cheering masses at the Nuremberg rallies. Loudspeakers placed in the auditorium ring with 'Sieg Heils'. The music continues*]

HITLER: I shall forge the fatherland's might into an invincible instrument of our destiny! No-one shall stand in our way! All who defy us, will be destroyed . . .[20]

Night Conspirators had first been seen on ITV's 'Armchair Theatre' the previous May, with an introduction which sought to persuade the audience that what they were watching was actually a secretly filmed documentary report rather than a work of fiction.[21] Now Troubridge queried how the 'very touchy' Germans might react:

> There might well be a diplomatic protest at the licensing of this, and as such high matters are beyond the purview of an Examiner, I suggest strongly that the Western Department of the Foreign Office should be asked to give the play a quick read for possible diplomatic offence . . .
>
> First of all the Lord Chamberlain will decide whether he considers a vocal and successful Hitler to be a permissible stage figure nowadays. If, as some people (including Sir Ivone Kirkpatrick in his Memoirs) consider, there is a real danger of a neo-nazi movement, then I incline to think this play might be a timely warning . . .
>
> More important to my mind is the danger of giving diplomatic offence by representing leading West German soldiers, business men and clerics as all crypto-nazis.

Cobbold did consult the Foreign Office, but chose to avoid the publicity which rejection so often guaranteed:

> It seems to me legitimate comment and I do not think it very profound. Refusal of licence might easily attract more headlines than the play itself; nor do I see objection to presentation of Hitler on the stage.[22]

The script was licensed with only minor alterations.

No significant political objections were raised either to *Oh! What a Lovely War*, the Theatre Workshop script which arrived within a few days of *Night Conspirators*. Gerry Raffles, the company manager, had contacted the Office in advance to check whether there would be any objections in principle to either the 'impersonation' of General Haig in the First World War or to 'an out and out attack'. In response, Hill had advised cautiously that although there was no automatic ban on the representation of a real person, 'where it was someone recently dead, the Lord Chamberlain would almost certainly ask for the family to be consulted'. He added— probably following a steer from higher up—that 'the views of the family would be given weight, but would not necessarily be conclusive'. That, in itself, marked a significant shift in policy. When the actual script for this 'shapeless, lumpy documentary' arrived at the beginning of March, Heriot was anxious about the criticisms of Haig, and also the suggestion that the English had been the first side to use chlorine gas. However, he 'had a word with the comptroller who tells me that there is nothing libellous about this, since it is all in the history books'. As a result, the licence was issued with fairly minimal alterations of language.

Oh! What a Lovely War opened at Stratford East in March, and transferred to Wyndham's Theatre in June 1963. More than fifty years on, it is hard to judge the play's contemporary political impact, but it clearly chimed with the mood of a generation ready to challenge the values and attitudes handed down by an establishment now exposed as hypocritical and incompetent, and, as Booker puts it, 'increasingly scornful of all those traditional values and assumptions which had been losing their grip'.[23] Some—including Littlewood's former partner and co-founder of Theatre Workshop, Ewan MacColl—suggested the piece was too comfortable and lacking in political bite; that its songs were cheerfully tuneful and reassuring rather than challenging or subversive. The transfer to the West End—and the show's commercial success there—increased the suspicions and mistrust of those who followed MacColl's line. But it is clear from the angry letters of protest sent to the Lord Chamberlain that many people saw it differently: 'It attacks everything that is sacred and decent, as you must know. It is not entertainment (it is too dull for that), it's propaganda. Has no-one got the guts to take a stand . . . I call upon you either to exercise your functions or resign.' Again:

> Ostensibly it is a play against war and against the armed services of this country . . . but the real motive of the play obviously is not simply anti-war but anti-god. It is an all-out attack upon our Christian faith . . . In a country which is still officially Christian, where Her Majesty the Queen is Defender of the Faith, it seems to me utterly outrageous that such a production should be permitted on the London stage. What a picture of our country to give to those who come to our theatre from abroad at this time of year, and what a misbegotten philosophy to feed to the hundreds of younger people of our own country who appear to flock to this kind of thing.

Or:

> I had the greatest difficulty in restraining myself, from my four shilling seat in the gallery, from creating a disturbance so disgusted and horrified was I. Like Colonel Hore-Ruthven I wonder how the censor could have passed this play, but presumably by an oversight it was not read.

What is also striking is that *Oh! What a Lovely War* was recognised not only as a play about the past, but as 'dangerous anti-British propaganda' which had a very contemporary message:

Mr Raymond Fletcher, Lord Grey of Fallodon and others are quoted, clearly with the object of making people believe that deterrents do not deter. If a majority of the people in democracies like ours and America's could be brought to believe this, both of us would abandon—or weaken on—the deterrent and be at the mercy of Russia. Those who try to bring this about, whether Communists or not, are the most deadly enemies of our country.

The widespread positive critical reception the play enjoyed also infuriated those who saw it as a left-wing falsification of history: 'The disturbing thing is that all the newspapers praised the play and not one of them discerned its anti-british [sic] flavour and intention.' Nor was it just the press:

Mr A J P Taylor, a fellow and tutor in modern history at Magdalen College, Oxford, gave a lecture, in which he said that this play gave a better account of the 1914 war and its origins than any history had yet done, and concluded that the cause of that war was the deterrent and that our own deterrent would contribute to bringing on a third war. All this was reported at some length in 'The Times' . . . Mr A J P Taylor is known to be a Communist or a near Communist, and it should never be forgotten that, however useful or distinguished a Communist may be, he is a member of a sect which is pledged to ruin our country.

In responding to such complaints, the Office accepted that the play had 'a purpose of propaganda as well as entertainment', but indicated that although they were out of sympathy with many of the views it carried, it was not their role to suppress it:

The Lord Chamberlain does not consider it his duty to forbid the expression on the stage of controversial opinions and arguments even though they may be distasteful to many people . . .
  The Lord Chamberlain naturally has his own opinions . . . nevertheless, in this country it is permissible to expound almost any opinion in a persuasive manner, provided it is not an incitement to crime, indecency or violence. It could never be a part of the Play Censor's duty to suppress free speech within these limits . . . he does not consider it his duty to forbid the expression on the stage of opinions which it would be legal to publish in other ways: he does try to ensure that such plays are represented with reasonable regard to contemporary standards of behaviour, and they do not needlessly give cause for offence.[24]

Penn added that 'where strongly controversial views are expressed, there is always anger on the part of those who disagree'. This might seem 'unfortunate'; however, he explained, 'it is felt to be incompatible with the nature of the censorship as it exists here so to soften strong opinion on the stage as to make it universally acceptable'.

Too Much Reality

Of course, those who thought *Oh! What a Lovely War* was not political or aggressive enough might have pointed at the very fact that it had been licensed—not to say absorbed by West End culture and middle-class audiences—as evidence of its lack of real challenge. Certainly it would be wrong to assume that political censorship was over. In July 1963, a month after Profumo's confession and resignation speech in the House of Commons, a Mr Alan sought advice on his plans for a possible piece of what we would now call 'verbatim theatre'. He wanted to know 'whether a dramatisation of the Profumo affair in which actors spoke only the "lines" first uttered in either Parliament or the Courts would in any way transgress the rules laid down by your office'. Penn's reply on behalf of the Lord Chamberlain made it perfectly clear that such a piece would not be licensed, and was therefore not worth writing:

> He has asked me to tell you that he has come to the conclusion that it would not be in the public interest for the proceedings of Parliament and of a contemporary court case to be enacted in dramatic form; even though the dialogue consisted entirely of authentic extracts therefrom.[25]

In fact, it was another documentary drama which stirred up the most arguments. When Rolf Hochhuth's *The Representative* was submitted by the RSC in April 1963, it had already 'caused a lot of commotion' in the author's native Germany, and productions in several other countries were also planned. Heriot wrote the initial report:

> This play is a violent indictment of Pope Pius XII, and tacitly, of Christianity itself, that the former made no overt gesture to prevent the wholesale massacre of Jews by Hitler . . . Many English Catholics believed that he was pro-German since he was an excellent German scholar and surrounded himself with many high-ranking officers in the Nazi command.
> The play itself, immensely long, is horrifying in the way that the official film of Belsen is horrifying—that is, the mind shudders to be reminded that all this is fact.

Cobbold summed up the text as 'a criticism of the supine attitude of the church in Germany towards Nazi atrocities and in particular an indictment of Pope Pius XII who is alleged to have taken no stand against these atrocities and almost to have connived at them'. He noted, too, that 'the play has given rise to violent and heated discussion in political and religious circles in Germany', and even to accusations 'that Hitler had led the war against the Soviet Union as the Pope's crusader'.

Heriot had initially recommended that the script could be licensed 'with some excisions', but that advice should be sought from Mons. Gerald O'Hara, the Pope's Apostolic Delegate to Great Britain, who had worked closely with Pius. Not surprisingly, O'Hara was strongly against allowing it: 'The play is indeed even more objectionable than I first thought', he wrote, and he drew attention to specific parts 'which I find particularly unjust, indefensible and inexcusable'. He added:

> I am sure that it will interest the Lord Chamberlain to know that more than one community of Jews, after the War, sought an audience with Pope Pius XII in order to express gratitude for all that he did for the people of their race during the Nazi-Fascist regime.

There was no easy way to deal with this play, and Cobbold wrote to both the Home and the Foreign Office:

> I find this an extremely difficult decision. It has been produced and run successfully in Germany and I gather it is likely to be produced in the United States of America. It would therefore in some ways look stupid to ban or cut it here and, as is so often the case, this might even stir up the whole controversy more than if I gave a Licence. On the other hand, the play would undoubtedly give great offence to many people and I cannot help feeling that Pius XII is, only five years after his death, more of a contemporary character than a historical figure.

As usual, government departments were wary of taking any responsibility: 'It seems to me very evenly balanced, and I am afraid you must be prepared for criticism whatever decision you take', said the Home Secretary, rather unhelpfully. Though he did add that 'On a narrow balance, I would myself be disposed to refuse the licence on the grounds that the play deals with the actions of a person who has died very recently, and that it would unquestionably give offence to large numbers of Her Majesty's subjects'. In the end, Cobbold decided that an absolute ban might be counter-productive:

> The Lord Chamberlain feels that, by disallowing in this country a play which has been produced in Germany and is likely to be produced elsewhere, he would not in fact be helping to protect the greatly respected memory of His late Holiness.

It is well known that a ban by the Lord Chamberlain immediately ensures the maximum of publicity. The Lord Chamberlain feels that, in all the circumstances, a ban in this country only would be more likely to exacerbate than to quieten controversy.

A better strategy was to negotiate on details of what could and could not be allowed. Specifically, 'the "Armaments Scene"' was to be 'cut in its entirety' because it suggested that the Vatican's 'alleged acquiescence in the Nazi treatment of the Jews' was due to their 'thriving financial interests in the armaments industry'. 'This', decided Cobbold, 'had no basis in fact and therefore was not acceptable'.

Defending themselves against complaints that they had agreed even in principle to issue a licence for Hochhuth's text, Penn insisted the decision 'in no way implies support or agreement for its theme'; rather, he suggested, it was better for the accusations against the Catholic Church to be aired, 'since suppression gives rise to false assumptions of sinister and secret influences at work'. He also pointed out that 'numerous excisions' were being required. A further discussion centred on the RSC's wish to end the performance by projecting authentic and disturbing film sequences drawn from official archives and footage taken by members of the Nazi SS. Having viewed this material, Heriot advised strongly against allowing the more graphic sequences:

> The following omissions must be made:
> 1) A vague, unfocused shot, apparently in slow motion, of a naked woman running . . .
> 2) All close-ups of the naked male and female half-skeletons, in particular all those where the ghastly putrescence can almost be smelt and where the pudenda of both sexes are accentuated by emaciation.
> 3) Shots of corpses being unloaded from a lorry.
> 4) A shot of a female body being tipped into the communal pit.
> A distant shot of a bull-dozer at work on an amorphous heap of bodies might be permitted, also the view of the bull-dozer pushing earth over the heaps of bodies and the communal burial service.

Certainly it could have been argued that the inclusion of such explicit shots was unnecessary and verging on the pornographic and exploitative—though the assumption about where and how the images should properly be used is obviously debatable.

> To permit these scenes I have mentioned would be to outrage the audience. These dreadful pictures properly belong to official records and could only blunt the edge of the author's indignation. There are enough pictures of the

<u>living</u> dead behind barbed wire (which I consider permissible) to point the pity and horror of the situation.[26]

A licence for *The Representative* was finally issued in September, with a number of endorsements and a guarantee that the programme would include a special supplement with articles contributed by the editor of the *Catholic Herald* and the present Pope to provide a contrasting perspective to that of the play. Although theatres lacked the legal power of cinemas to limit the age of audiences, the RSC also agreed to forbid entrance to juveniles. Later in the year, the Parisian production was regularly interrupted by members of the audience invading the stage and being ejected. London never quite matched that.

Teenage Sex

A much older German play had also landed on Cobbold's desk soon after his arrival at St James's Palace. One of the loopholes in the Theatres Act was that performances on Sundays were presumed to be exempt from licensing, and in April 1963 the ESC gave two Sunday night performances at the Royal Court of Wedekind's *Spring Awakening*, a play first published in the 1890s, and staged in Germany in 1906, but which had never been permitted in Britain. At the invitation of the theatre, Penn and the former Comptroller Lord Nugent attended a Sunday showing. The text had not yet been formally resubmitted but Penn identified five specific pieces of business which would require amending before a licence could be issued: first, a girl being beaten by a boy ('on this occasion done inoffensively but will require tying up'); second, a boy sitting on a lavatory with a photograph of a girl between his legs ('possible that an element of masturbation may be introduced here'); third, a boy lying on top of a girl and kissing her ('it would appear that they were going to have intercourse here after the curtain was lowered'); fourth 'a very homosexual scene' in which two boys are seen 'embracing and literally kissing each other' ('as far as Lord Nugent and I could make out this had nothing to do with the Play whatsoever'); and last, a 'mass masturbation' by a group of boys with their backs to the audience ('accompanied by the most unattractive noises'). Penn considered that if these specific elements were dealt with then it would be possible to give approval; however, when the script was sent in shortly afterwards, Coles saw it differently:

> This is one of the most loathsome and depraved plays I have ever read. It is concerned with the turgid sexual fantasies and experiments of the awakening adolescent instincts of provincial German schoolchildren in the 1890s. It is a sick, diseased unhealthy play with no redeeming features whatsoever.

> The talk—and action—is concerned with masturbation, homosexualism, copulation, sexual aberration and sadism . . . unending discussion of the more disgusting aspects of sex.[27]

In the event, it would be another two years before a version of the script was finally deemed acceptable for licensing. Perhaps this is not surprising, considering that in May 1963 the Office also cut 'merde' from a new translation of *Miss Julie*, along with the line 'Oh, she's got her monthly coming on, and then she always acts strange'.[28]

Another Royal Court play about the lives and attitudes of adolescents—but this time set in contemporary Britain—also ran into trouble in the summer of 1963. *Skyvers* was written by the Jamaican born playwright Barry Reckord, and its story focused on

> a group of sixteen year old boys in a State Comprehensive School . . . depicted as vicious, arrogant, foul-mouthed, dirty-minded, ignorant, uneducated beasts, already well on the way to Approved Schools and Borstals, violent towards their school masters and each other and brutally sexual towards their girl friends.

The swearing and the contemporary street and sexual language may have been both authentic and vivid, but it went way too far for the Censorship. 'Is it possible to complain about mss submitted with the "ultimate four-lettered word"?' enquired Cobbold of his Assistant Comptroller; 'They know we would never pass it and I don't see why Miss Fisher should have to read and type it over and over again'. The Reader was similarly unimpressed. 'The list of recommended cuts or deletions is a very long one', wrote Coles, 'and contains more foul language (including the ultimate in four-lettered words) than I can remember seeing in any other play'. Apart from expletives, lines cut included:

> Did Elen make a noise when you done 'er?
> Yeah. (*a nasty snigger*). She went squeak, squeak, like a little rat . . .
>
> She's an easy feel but a hard lay.
>
> Look, if you don't shut your 'ole, I'll poke you.
>
> Your lulu's gonna split and all the boys in town's gonna 'ave a bit of it.
>
> There's a whole in my Liza, dear bucket, dear bucket.

Such language is clearly provocative and unpleasant in what it reveals about the misogynistic attitudes of the characters, but to remove it deprived the text of its richness. George Devine, the artistic director of the Royal Court, wrote an article for the programme under the title 'Stage Censorship', objecting to recent decisions in relation to both *Skyvers* and *Spring Awakening*:

> The issue is a very simple one. Should the public be allowed to choose for itself in matters of taste (because that is the fundamental issue), or should it have its tastes controlled for it? There is really nothing more to it than that.

He pointed out the inequity built into the system:

> By joining a Club, (if you had a guinea), you could have seen Wedekind's play as he wrote it. You could have seen Reckord's play as he wrote it. In other words, provided you pay for the privilege, you may see the original work. But if you are un-privileged, you must see a version of the play which an appointed official decides is in good taste.

And he defended the legitimacy of the writers' approach:

> Wedekind . . . wrote certain scenes to be shocking in order to promote the argument and dramatic shape of his play. . . Should the public, by the judgement of an official of good taste, be prevented from seeing the play as the dramatist conceived it?
>   Reckord, a new writer of acknowledged seriousness, gave his characters certain so-called obscene words to speak because the speaking of them by them was not only characteristic but promoted the dramatic argument. By seeing the play without these words, removed in the interests of good taste, the public is seeing a watered-down version. Is this right?

Devine proposed a 'new' solution; namely that theatres such as the Royal Court could be granted special permission to present plays sanctioned with an 'X' certificate, which would 'warn the public that things were being said or done in that production which might be considered in bad taste', and that apart from references to the Royal Family—which would remain taboo—it would be up to theatres to take the risk.[29] But as Penn pointed out to Devine, such a strategy could not be introduced without new legislation, which would necessitate extended parliamentary debate.

It was another school-based play which caused more indignation and embarrassment at St James's Palace than any other script submitted in 1963—albeit a very different kind of school from the one featured in *Skyvers*. David Benedictus's *Fourth of June* was also an exploration of adolescent sexuality, based on the author's own novel and, at least to some extent, on his own experiences. Its setting was another bastion of the 'old England' now under attack—a public school. And not just any old public school, but the one which had produced not only Harold Macmillan (the resigning Prime Minister) and his predecessor (Anthony Eden) but also Macmillan's replacement (Sir Alec Douglas-Home), as well as a remarkably high percentage of Conservative cabinet ministers. Not to mention most of the senior staff at St James's Palace. In effect, if not in intent, then, the play exposed another pillar of British society as pretty much a den of iniquity and corruption. Coles reported on the script in November 1963:

> It presents a picture of life at Eton College with the majority of boys shown as dirty-minded, or perverted, or womanisers, or sadists. The Headmaster is depicted as a Machiavellian opportunist, and the Housemaster as a well-meaning but ineffective idealist, completely out of touch with the boys. The Bishop (diocese unnamed) is shown as a peeping Tom, a sensualist and a perverter of small boys, while the Captain of the House is a sadist and a homosexual who tries to seduce his fag. There is not one likeable character in the play.

The narrative focused primarily on Scarfe, a former grammar school boy, and therefore an outsider, 'who is bullied, ridiculed and finally flogged by the Captain of the House into a state of paralysis'. Scarfe commits suicide, and although the House Captain is punished with expulsion, others who are equally guilty are allowed to go free 'because they have influential parents'.

The novel had caused considerable controversy two years earlier, so the stage version was bound to be equally contentious. 'This play makes me very angry', wrote Penn to the Lord Chamberlain; 'That is presumably its object'. But Gwatkin's perspective is particularly revealing: 'The Public School is probably England's best secret weapon', he wrote; 'However, if mothers really knew what went on at Public Schools I think these institutions would die out very quickly'. Reassuringly—or not—he added that 'only a minute percentage of boys suffer permanently', while 'a gigantic majority battle through successfully and they are all the better for the experience'. So why should writers focus on the negative examples? 'All schools have their ups and downs and it seems grossly unfair to single out one particular school for faults which are common to all.' Moreover, warned Gwatkin, if the play were staged as currently written, 'the Eton authorities could sue for libel and slander, including the Lord Chamberlain with the author in their action'. He believed that at the very least they should 'make the school anonymous' and that it was the Office's responsibility to 'cut the script mercilessly'. But he recognised they would be entering onto dangerous ground:

Prejudice in some quarters against Eton as Eton being what it is, it is sure to be said that this treatment is ordered by Etonians to rescue Eton regardless of the fact that any similar play about another named school would be dealt with in the same way; but I am afraid that that has to be faced.

Cobbold also had another problem: 'This play presents a special difficulty to me because of my interest as a fellow of Eton', he wrote; 'It is the sort of problem that a minister of the Crown would, I think, normally ask a colleague to decide for him'. But in this case, nobody else could take the responsibility. Cobbold therefore took it upon himself to consult privately with the current Provost of Eton, saying he 'would gladly consider any representations which he cared to make on behalf of the Eton authorities'. However, they decided together that it was already too late to try and disguise the school, and that it would therefore 'not be in the best interest of Eton for the Lord Chamberlain to insist on the play being amended'. Better to cut and license:

> in view of the publicity already given to the book on which this play is based and the certainty that the play would be known to be directed against Eton . . . an attempt to avoid identification with Eton would be more likely to damage Eton's interests by attracting more publicity and notoriety.

Some fifty changes were demanded to dialogue and action, and a revised script was submitted in January 1964 which was duly licensed after further small amendments. Hill went to watch this version in performance, and was 'glad to report that the Producer had adhered implicitly to the Lord Chamberlain's instructions' and that he 'could find nothing in the manner of production that called for any adverse comment'. Specifically:

> There was no suggestion of going for each other's flies in the fight.
> There was no physical application of the cane to Scarfe's anatomy—in fact the beating scene as such did not exist. Scarfe stood at the front of a darkened stage explaining his feelings, whilst symbolic swishes could be heard from further back.
> The reference we had passed to contraceptives in the tuck shop was omitted.
> The seduction (attempted) of Bigby was acted in an unexceptionable manner, no gestures at all.

Yet Hill encountered a strange and disturbing experience:

> I was alone, and was mildly surprised to note that I was flanked on each side by an elderly unaccompanied gentleman. Suddenly at the commencement of the beating scene when Defries was handling the cane lovingly and it looked

as though Scarfe was about to receive a public flogging, I became aware that both my companions were literally panting with suppressed excitement.

This confirmed Hill's fear 'that plays that hover on the verge of the perverse draw not only the normal audience, but those whose perversions are being exhibited'. Fortunately 'the gentlemen were disappointed on this occasion', he reported, strangely adding that 'the remainder of the performance gave rise to no more pants'. 'What an odd expression' wrote Gwatkin beside the last three words.[30]

Abortion, Artificial Insemination, and the Fashionable Rut

Another play of sexual awakening which opened in June 1963 after a period of wrangling was Bill Naughton's *Alfie*, best known now through the 1966 film version starring Michael Caine. The playscript had first been submitted just before Cobbold's arrival, and Coles had expressed his distaste: 'This play is well in the fashionable rut of sordid realism—the more sordid the better.' There was a multitude of specific lines and phrases to which the Reader had objected, but he drew particular attention to the scene involving an on-stage abortion 'complete with groans and cries of pain, which I cannot think can be allowed'. The producer, Bernard Miles, wrote to ask whether 'In view of the fact that this play was presented on the Third Programme and received a magnificent press, may I bring the Author . . . along to discuss the matter with you in person?' A meeting with Penn and Hill took place the following week:

> It was explained to the visitors that it was accepted by The Lord Chamberlain that the play was a moral rather than an immoral one, and that it was realised that the basic facts of life were nowadays discussed freely in any company; but that in our opinion some of the clinical and practical detail in the play was of such a disgusting nature in the literal sense of the word that it was felt that to sanction it would give a precedent for action and properties of a vividness which could end by blunting the sensibilities of and indeed brutalising the audience.

Miles seems to have accepted most of the cuts 'without question'. The abortion scene proved more problematic, but the basis of an agreement for rewriting was achieved:

> Instead of going behind the screen, Mr. Smith has to leave the stage.
> There must not be any jingle of instruments.
> Lily's short cry is to be omitted.
> Mr. Smith scrubbing away is not to be seen or heard.

However, after discussing this with Cobbold, Penn warned Miles that the Lord Chamberlain was 'still disturbed about the possible effect of this scene' and was 'not prepared to give an unqualified assurance' that the changes would be enough to save it. He also advised him that 'any additional modification which will make less minute the physical representation of the preparation for and consequences of the abortion, will advance your chances of acceptance'.

In mid-May a revised version was submitted with the abortion duly shifted off-stage, and following further negotiations and cuts a licence was finally issued in early June. Again, Hill was dispatched (incognito) to view an early performance at the Mermaid, and reported that in general, 'for these days, there was nothing to which real objection could be taken'. However, he identified in some detail one piece of business to which he certainly did take objection:

Alfie and Ruby caress each other running their hands over each other's bottoms and hips, but Alfie puts his hand over Ruby's breast and squeezes it. In each case (three times) she is in a house-coat and 'undies' and on the third occasion, (she is a big bosomed woman, half her breast is showing over her undies), he puts his hand over her mostly bare breast and squeezes it.

The year 1963 was famously, according to Philip Larkin, when sexual intercourse began.[31] Booker, too, suggests the nation was by now 'enjoying a full-scale "permissive revolution"'.[32] Even Hill realised that the Lord Chamberlain's treatment of breasts might need updating. As he noted— perhaps after checking with Miss Fisher, who kept the records—'We have in our straight-laced past always forbidden breast squeezing'. But where could you draw the line? 'If you admit even a short squeeze you lose complete control', he wrote, anxiously; 'lengthened squeezes, other actions, and greater degrees of breast nudity then follow and short of seeing every performance it is impossible to decide what is really impermissible and what is mildly objectionable'.

Heriot decided he would like to see the show too, and he then met with Hill to thrash out a joint position. Their conclusion was that the traditional St James's Palace breast policy should be upheld:

I have telephoned to Bernard Miles this morning and explained the Lord Chamberlain's rule that breasts may not be touched.

I explained that the reason for this is the difficulty of establishing a dividing line between brushing gently against the bosom and gripping them.

Bernard Miles said that he appreciated this and he will have any touching or handling of the breasts of Ruby immediately stopped.

> I accepted his suggestion that Alfie could outline the shape of Ruby's bosom with the hand at a safe distance away.

The Lord Chamberlain's interventions did not prevent protests against the staging of *Alfie* from those trying desperately to hold back the times. 'I fail to see how we can instil any high moral standards in our young people when plays of this nature are presented for public showing'; 'It seems such a pity that the great capital city of London should have such exhibitions going on, apparently with official approval'; 'I cannot imagine it being allowed on any stage anywhere else in the world'; 'The tragic part was that there were several coloured people in the audience, and what they thought of us goodness only knows'. The Public Morality Council also notified the Lord Chamberlain that its 'plays committee' had subjected the production to 'severe criticism', but the Office still had no time for their views. 'They make these occasional sallies', Gwatkin advised Cobbold, 'to wheedle subscriptions from gullible old ladies'. Cobbold put the Council firmly in its place:

> The present production (after considerable cuts and alterations at my request) seemed to me to justify a licence. I think, if I may say so without disrespect to your Committee, that the attitude of responsible critics and of the general theatre-going public towards the production confirms my judgement.

The tone was not lost on Gwatkin: 'I particularly like this last sentence', he noted; 'I hope they will appreciate his word "responsible"'. But the Council's president took issue:

> I suggest that the claims of 'broad-mindedness' should not be accorded too ready an acceptance by your Lordship. Broad-mindedness, in fact, is generally a euphemism for departures from what are generally regarded as decencies of life . . . the line must be drawn between decency and indecency and my Committee feels strongly that in much modern entertainment (so called) that line is receding dangerously.[33]

In its day-to-day practice, the Censorship continued to tread and negotiate an indiscernible line, so that decisions were often bound to appear as almost arbitrary. In June, they made extensive cuts to such 'silly obscenities and Joycian distortions' as 'shittle', 'buggerer', and 'buggerglass' in Bristol University's version of *Ubu*. 'I cannot conceal my astonishment that so Jonsonian a word as "bugger" should be considered theatrically taboo', wrote George Brandt, the translator and producer.[34] In July, the Press reported that *Figuro in the Night*, Sean O'Casey's 'tilt at the hypocritical and narrow-minded morality of Irish life', had been returned from St James's 'so blue pencilled' that the director had decided it was no longer practical to include it in the Irish Comedy Festival planned for Stratford East.[35] In August, it was the turn of a Cambridge University production of Henry Miller's *Just Wild About Harry* to be presented at the Edinburgh Festival alongside the Footlights Revue. Miller's play was to be directed by the young Stephen Frears, with a cast of then unknowns, including Michael Pennington, Richard Eyre, John Shrapnel and Eric Idle. To Coles, it was no more than 'a squalid and degrading play, reeking of sex and violence, plus that peculiarly American brand of sentimentality which turns the stomach of many English people—including myself'. Among the twenty or so words and phrases excluded were 'go fuck a duck', 'take a leak', 'get yourself a new bladder', 'scared shitless', 'in rut', 'getting your end in', 'old futzer', and 'pig's arse'. The Office also insisted that the company should 'Cut drastically or omit altogether a detailed medical description of the technique and possible consequences of an abortion'; however, a member of the company phoned the Lord Chamberlain from Edinburgh to explain that the dialogue relating to the abortion was deliberately absurd, consisting of medical terms strung randomly together: 'They consulted a Doctor (who was with him when he phoned) and made quite certain that it really was all nonsense.'[36] According to Eric Idle's account, cuts were also made following complaints by the Edinburgh Watch Committee, and another phone call—this time to Henry Miller in America—who gave permission for the production to go ahead with the revised script. Unfortunately, Idle recalls that the first night was a disaster, with the revolving set toppling forwards 'like a pack of cards' towards the front rows, and sending the London theatre critics scurrying for safety; 'all save one, the world-famous critic Harold Hobson, who was stuck in his wheelchair as the set collapsed into the seats all around him'. According to Idle, the play was not performed again.[37]

The first play actually to be rejected by Cobbold in its entirety and as beyond revision was 'A nasty sniggering American comedy' about artificial insemination. Submitted by Emile Littler in October 1963, Heriot called *The Wayward Stork* 'one of the most tasteless affairs I have read', suggesting that 'If all these medical goings-on are illegal in this country I would be delighted to recommend the withholding of a licence'. Although out and out refusals were still to be avoided wherever possible, Penn agreed it would be 'a very tricky one' to license:

a) The medical profession on both sides of the Atlantic are automatically brought into disrepute.
b) As described, the artificial insemination of Julia is completely illegal as it is carried out without her consent.

c) In practice the donor is never known and in this play the donor is identified.

Heriot consulted his own doctor for advice, and Penn took the script to a senior consultant at the Middlesex Hospital. The latter was certain the play would provoke resentment within the medical profession:

> For a doctor to inseminate a woman without her consent is obviously illegal and I am quite sure that if such an action were brought against a doctor in this country he would certainly be struck off the register and I should imagine get a pretty heavy prison sentence . . . from the general public relations point of view, I cannot think of anything more damaging to the reputation of the profession than to suggest that any member of it would enter into a really serious subject such as artificial insemination in this musical comedy atmosphere.

The consultant even warned it had the potential to 'damage the relationship between the public and the profession'—though he added that he had 'more faith in the commonsense of the British public than to worry about it'. But the licence was refused.[38]

Who's Afraid of St James's Palace?

Another American play which became the focus of a longer and more intense struggle in 1963 was Edward Albee's *Who's Afraid of Virginia Woolf?*, first submitted by Donald Albery in April of that year. 'If we are to believe American novels and plays, the Groves of Academe resound with the hyena-shrieks of the unhappily married', observed Heriot. He found the play, 'interminable but powerful', recognising its strength as drama: 'The odd thing is that with all its nastiness the play grips; it is marvellous theatre.' While the Reader acknowledged it as 'a remarkable play', the constant slang and casual swearing went beyond what the British stage was used to. He recommended over fifty changes to words and phrases including 'hump', 'clip joints', 'Jesus money', 'frigging', 'crap', and 'personal screwing machine'. He was also concerned about the seduction scene and the use of the 'Dies Irae'. The Office knew Albery as an old and wily adversary, and Heriot was adamant that they should stand firm against his strategies: 'the quality of the play is unimpaired by these omissions in spite of anything Mr. Albery will say', he insisted, 'and he undoubtedly will try to persuade us that this is untouchable Literature with a capital "L"'.

Albery's intention was to import the production from America, where it was already running. In May, he and the American producer, a Mr Wilder, came to St James's, where Penn told them he accepted it was 'not designedly or in effect a corrupting play', and that Albery was 'a man of the highest reputation'. Then battle commenced:

> The following points were made by the visitors:
> This play is the most important one produced on Broadway for some years . . .
> The play is acceptable to the Americans, it is in their own idiom, and the Lord Chamberlain should be prepared to view it through American eyes . . .
> It was pointed out that as the play is to be seen by English people it is felt that it must be assessed by English and not United States standards.
> The producer is most reluctant to make any changes at all. He made all the now conventional statements about language of this kind being essential for the characterisation; integrity of presentation; need not to be hypocritical and so on.
> It was pointed out that the Lord Chamberlain had to have regard to the gradual debasement of the stage which followed the introduction of obscenities into plays.

By the end of the meeting, the Office had made some concessions. 'Screw' was to be allowed when it meant 'buzz off', 'but not when it is a euphemism for "f—k".' The sexual encounters between Nik and Martha involving hands inside dresses and between legs were to be 'portrayed inoffensively' and 'limited to normal embracing'. There was a lengthy debate about 'bugger', which Penn identified as 'a transitional word', carrying two distinct meanings: '(a) originally and sometimes now "sodomite"; (b) a vulgar term of either endearment or opprobrium without the implication of (a).' For the moment, they decided it remained 'still too unpleasant for general use'. As for the 'Dies Irae', the producer assured them this was 'not irreverent' and that there had been no complaints in New York. Penn agreed that it would not 'wound any except the most highly susceptible of religious feelings', and after checking with Cobbold, he confirmed they would 'allow the extracts from the Roman Catholic Requiem Mass . . . on the understanding that they are portrayed in a gentlemanly manner'.

Although a long list of cuts remained, Albery had won some significant concessions. He could also afford to bide his time, since the production was not yet ready to cross the Atlantic. In September, the author himself accompanied Albery to St James's Palace with a list of some proposed alternatives. For 'personal screwing machine' he substituted 'personal propagating machine', while 'mount her like a goddam dog' was replaced by 'use her like a goddam dog'. Albee argued successfully for 'humps' but lost out on 'ball' and 'scrotum'. He tried to convince Penn to back down more generally on the cuts to slang and swearing:

> Mr. Albee pointed out that each time the word 'JESUS', 'CHRIST' and 'BUGGER' were included in the MS they had been put in, not to shock, but because they were the definite language that would be used by the characters portrayed in this play . . . I suggested that Mr. Albee should review the situation and consider which of the Jesuses and Christs he thought were the most important.

The Office was not disposed to be sympathetic 'Mr. Albery is at his usual games', wrote Heriot; 'He is the "greediest" impresario in London and I really think this office cannot be too firm with him'. Gwatkin agreed that he had got 'away with too much as it is'.

Albee submitted further alterations, and requested again that his use of Christ and Jesus should 'stand unaltered for the reason that their use is not intended as a profanation but rather as a necessary indication of the natures of the characters'. His claim was disputed by Heriot: 'These are all used (or nearly all) as expletives—which cannot surely indicate character?' This was a nice point, and Hill advised Cobbold that 'Heriot's statement that blasphemy does not paint character is not I think completely correct'. However, he thought the Reader had made the right recommendation for the wrong reasons:

> We have hitherto prohibited 'Christ' or 'Jesus' as expletives—the variations once allowed are many, and the principle is one that, if allowed here, would I think have to be extended to all serious plays, since there is nothing to justify particular exemption from the rule for this play.

Cobbold agreed, but Albery wrote again in January 1964, to say there were 'three occasions where the author considers it of the greatest importance he should be able to retain the use of the word "Christ"'; Penn asked him to specify where these occurred, but warned him that 'Blasphemy has not hitherto been allowed on the stage, and it is unlikely that the Lord Chamberlain will feel that this principle is greatly affected by the number of times the name of the Saviour is involved'. Whether it was Albee or Albery who then had a moment of inspiration is not clear, but their next move was in effect checkmate against the Lord Chamberlain. How could the Office possibly object to the words 'cheese us', now proposed as a substitution throughout the text in place of 'Jesus'? Cobbold did refuse 'Cheese God', as well as 'Cries sake'; but the Office had been outmanoeuvred. When the production opened in early 1964, Hill went to inspect it; 'Martha exits with the word "cheese us"', he reported, 'which in this context sounds exactly as one would imagine an American female would say "Jesus"'.[39] The Office could only hope that other playwrights and managers would not pick up the same trick.

*   *   *

By the end of 1963, suggests Booker, '"Old England" was dead'.[40] In December, Vincent Troubridge really did die, and Coles was reported to be suffering a nervous breakdown. 'It will be a nuisance', wrote the Comptroller of this last, aware of the implications for Charles Heriot's workload as the only fit Reader. 'Have a word with Charles about it', he suggested to Penn, 'not forgetting that Charles's wife is also subject to this trouble'.[41] There were more problems on the horizon. In a prosecution which Hill thought could prove 'an embarrassment to us', the Metropolitan Police had recently insisted that a performance by a Soho striptease artist in Soho counted as 'dramatic entertainment' and therefore required a theatre licence. 'Traditionally', Hill explained, the Lord Chamberlain issued his licence only for performances which involved 'a plot or consecutive train of thought and action, plus physical actions, but not necessarily speech':

> By contrast, the Lord Chamberlain would not feel that a single performer, removing her clothes slowly in an erotic manner, was performing more than a series of physical actions, which could be held to be artistic, or inartistic, decent or indecent, but not dramatic.

The last thing the Office wanted was to enlarge its field of responsibility:

> Generally speaking, the Lord Chamberlain works these days in very difficult conditions, and is anxious not only that it should not be thought that he is attempting to extend his jurisdiction, but also that his jurisdiction should not, in fact, be extended.

Remarkably, Hill also advised the police that drawing a dividing line between what was and what was not the Lord Chamberlain's responsibility had no firm legal backing or status and was 'perhaps no more than an office convention' or 'custom'.[42]

The improvisation problem had not gone away, either. Already, John Roberts of the RSC had been in touch with the Office about proposed performances in the Aldwych's World Theatre season the following April to be given by the Peppino de Filippo Company, 'prime exponents of the art of the old Italian *commedia dell'arte*'. Roberts had been informed that improvisation was illegal, and had promised to supply a script in advance. 'Whether this will, in fact, be done I don't know', wrote Hill, 'and I fear that the improvisations would be vast—albeit in Italian which will help'.[43]

Most ominously of all, in a climate where challenging tradition was becoming de rigueur, the Lord Chamberlain's word and even his threats no longer carried the weight of yesteryear. Hill's inspection of *Who's Afraid of Virginia Woolf?* in early1964 discovered that the Office's endorsements were not being fully observed. 'No attention whatever has been paid to the requirement deleting slipping a hand between Nick's legs', reported the secretary; moreover, in what Hill called 'absolute defiance of the Lord Chamberlain', some of the words they had specifically disallowed had been retained. He had no doubt that the producer was very deliberately thumbing his nose at them. 'The Lord Chamberlain is beginning to be defied', wrote Hill, 'even by West-End managers, who once upon a time might argue, but never went beyond that'. Yet even though Albery was 'blatantly ignoring the Lord Chamberlain', and there was surely 'material here for a prosecution', Hill advised that they were probably powerless to do anything about it; 'we should not have a good "moral" case', he wrote; 'And in view of the times I would counsel doing nothing'. The implications were worrying:

> Donald Albery when he was here said he thought the time had come, as he put it, 'for a manager to do what he wanted, even if it meant going to prison for it', and he also suggested that the best way to deal with plays was for the producer to tell the Lord Chamberlain one thing—to save the Lord Chamberlain's face—and then do what he wished to do in his own interests.

As Hill acknowledged: 'These precepts appear to have been put into practice.'[44]

CHAPTER FOUR

Some S. I will not Eat (1964)

The Lord Chamberlain is, and has for some time, been on the defensive. Why then does he exist at all? Partly, of course, because his office is one of those historic relics that are so well entrenched into our national life that they need such intolerable ingenuity and energy to remove that it is hardly worth the effort: but partly . . . because people feel that a token barrier must be left in case something really dreadful should be perpetrated one day.

(John Arden)[1]

I had a talk with the Queen on August 6th about theatre censorship. I told her about the campaign which the Aldwych were running, which she thought rather tiresome . . .

(The Lord Chamberlain)[2]

When Harold Wilson's Labour Party came to power in the autumn of 1964, it marked a rejection by the electorate of the privilege and tradition associated with the old order. Wilson was a grammar-school boy from the West Riding of Yorkshire, and appeared to represent the possibility of a new world—or at least, of change and widespread reform of the old one. The theatre was never going to be high on Wilson's list of priorities, but it was unlikely to survive untouched. A few months earlier, an article in *Queen* had commented that 'The best-kept secret about censorship in Britain 1964 is that there is so much of it',[3] and Lord Willis—himself a playwright—had recently asked the Home Office Minister, Lord Derwent, 'whether he is aware that this country is the only country in the world where we have this father figure as the dictator of what goes onto our stages?'[4] Moreover, the Lord Chamberlain was all but ready to jump—or allow himself to be pushed. Two months before Wilson entered Downing Street, Cobbold noted in a private memorandum that he had talked to the Queen about theatre censorship, and had conveyed his concerns to her: 'I said that I was bothered from time to time that some of the criticism of the LC office might reflect on the Crown', he noted; 'She thought this came mainly from the critics, who were not much good anyway, and did not think it much mattered if the palace were occasionally charged for being a bit sticky'. But acknowledging the risk that his position 'may become increasingly difficult to hold, particularly with the growth of television', Her Majesty had endorsed Cobbold's position: 'She agrees with my general view that the time may come fairly soon when a general enquiry (e.g. by Royal Commission) may be appropriate on the whole subject, and cover theatre, cinema, television and literature.'[5]

Peter Hall and the RSC

Cobbold had clearly been goaded into raising the topic with the Queen partly by recent clashes with the Royal Shakespeare Company; he knew that if the RSC—heavily subsidised by the Arts Council and government as it was, and bearers through their very name of the monarch's official seal—complained that intervention by the chief servant in the Royal household was preventing them from fulfilling the function entrusted to them by the House of Commons, there was the potential for a constitutional confrontation, which would inevitably be talked up in a hostile press.

St James's Palace had already been involved in skirmishes around the work of Peter Hall and the RSC. In the autumn of 1963, for example, Cobbold received a complaint from the Vice President of the British Drama League about the 'really disgusting production' of *The Tempest*, which was being 'performed as a pantomime' at Stratford's Memorial Theatre. 'What I could not stand', wrote Mrs Whitworth, 'was Caliban "attending to nature" on the stage'. Although only plays written after the 1737 legislation required licensing, technically the Theatres Act also gave the Lord Chamberlain the right to stop any performance 'in the interests of good manners, decorum or the public peace'. But to do so here would have made him even more of a laughing stock. 'We have rarely, if ever, used this section, and to do so in this present instance would be a great mistake since every newspaper in the country would insist that the Lord Chamberlain was now censoring Shakespeare's plays', advised Hill; 'I would suggest we tell her politely, but not quite truthfully, that there is nothing we can do'.[6] Mrs Whitworth was advised to take it up with the Warwickshire Police, and this particular Caliban seems to have escaped being locked up.

Things would get much worse in 1964. In February, the RSC presented an anthology of short extracts at the Aldwych Theatre—its London base— under the title *The Rebel*, made up from poems, prose passages, and songs voicing 'the eternal battle between constituted authority and the man who says No'.[7]

Curse the blasted, jelly-boned swines, the slimy, the belly-wriggling invertebrates, the miserable sodding rutters, the flaming sods, the snivelling, dribbling, dithering, palsied, pulse-less lot that make up England today. They've got the white of egg in their veins and their spunk is that watery it's a marvel they can breed.[8]

D.H. Lawrence's diatribe and conjuration had originally been directed at a slightly different (if not unconnected) fading order, but the inclusion of this passage was aimed straight at Cobbold and the world he represented. Not that the Censorship was prepared to allow 'spunk' on the stage. Heriot dismissed the content—'An anthology of alleged "rebellious" literature assembled with not very much research and no taste by whoever Patrick Garland may be'; and he had little time for the form—'Three long Acts of being read to is not my idea of entertainment'. He duly marked specific words and phrases for deletion, as well as the 'conceited impertinence' of an article whose author was 'the unspeakable Muggeridge' and this 'very nasty' and 'particularly revolting example of Lawrence's hysteria'. But the main conflict centred on the inclusion of a poem by e.e. cummings, 'I Sing of Olaf', and in particular the lines 'I will not kiss your f.ing flag' and 'There is some s. I will not eat'. The RSC pointed out that this very poem had been read from the stage of the Royal Court during its recent Poetry Festival, as well as on BBC television, and as part of a Sunday night performance at their own Stratford theatre. The Lord Chamberlain stuck to his guns, but the inevitable mockery he attracted for doing so was no doubt enhanced by the RSC's solution; not only was the poem printed in the programme, but when the actor on stage reached the contentious lines he paused to allow the houselights to be turned on and the audience to read the lines silently to themselves.[9] 'Some s. I will not eat', was Peter Hall's message to the Palace.

Meanwhile, a company within the RSC had been working intermittently on Jean Genet's *The Screens*. In November 1963 the Lord Chamberlain's Office had dismissed the script as 'entirely worthless', describing it as an 'enormous, sprawling, vaguely symbolic play by a self-confessed criminal and pervert' who was 'preoccupied with anal eroticism'. 'I do not pretend to understand the play', confessed Heriot; but he had encountered Genet's work before, and knew what he didn't like: 'He has regressed into surrealism and a portentous style (even allowing for the bad translation) that becomes empty bombast whenever he gets really serious.' Significantly, the Reader claimed that the Algerian context meant that the play was 'regarded as being too dangerous, politically, to be performed in France'; and he identified well over fifty cuts which would be required before a licence could be considered in Britain. At the start of 1964, the RSC set up an 'experimental outpost' under the direction of Peter Brook and Charles Marowitz, based at LAMDA and committed to exploring Artaudian ideas to create a 'theatre of cruelty'. A public performance given by this group in

January included extracts from Genet's play, and another one in February also incorporated 'a comic recital of the censor's list of cuts' which had been imposed on the text.

In April, the group invited Cobbold to watch a rehearsal of the first twelve scenes of Genet's play. Despite some confusion ('no one told me that it wasn't at the Aldwych!!') Hill managed to attend and reported back. 'The acting was stylized and declamatory throughout and the "business" made little impact on me', he observed; but much of it had proved not as bad as the censorship had feared: 'The buttoning of the flies which occurred on one or two occasions was reasonably done, i.e. buttoning of the top two buttons, not of the more suggestive ones in the middle.' But while Hill admitted that he 'did not detect any pictorial obscenities', the general language and content still caused concern:

333333

> The action is laid in Algeria and the author sets out to establish the degraded morals, manners and spiritual life of the native population . . . the action is liberally sprinkled with 'f– – k', 'pissing', 'shit', one woman announces she will 'go take a piss' and very evidently does so . . .

Then there were the politics: 'A fierce and very biased denunciation of French attitudes in Algeria—so biased that I imagine that it would expose some of the actors to martyrdom if it were played anywhere in France where the "colons" have been settled.' Moreover, Hill had no doubt that 'its attraction for some will be the fact that they will ally British colonists in Rhodesia or Kenya with the French in Algeria'. On top of this was the 'open and sadistic enjoyment of filth and cruelty on the part of the author', which greatly worried the Lord Chamberlain's secretary:

> Genet's almost loving descriptions of the man murdering his mother, the personal enjoyment one can sense that he feels in relating the rape and blinding of a white French girl by an Arab, show a foulness of mind which in other days would have made the man a social outcast and his work unacceptable.

Hill's conclusion was that *The Screens* 'merits no sympathetic treatment', and he offered his overall assessment:

> Looking at the play as dispassionately as I am able, I cannot feel that it can do any good, and the only consideration for the Lord Chamberlain is the assessment of the amount of harm it will cause:
> a) It will give some offence to the French.
> b) It will introduce the audience to conceptions of filth and cruelty which, if they do not discuss them, must have some degrading influence.

c) The play is not a trumpet call for justice and freedom, it seems to me rather to be an attempt by the author to relegate all the nobler aspirations of man to the sewage farm which apparently bounds his horizons.

He therefore confirmed Heriot's view that the licence should be withheld unless there were drastic alterations, and was convinced that if the public realised the contents of the script then most would support the Censorship:

I have read the suggested deletions and I think that they are the least that could be enforced. If this means the abandonment of the play I would feel the fact a matter more for satisfaction than regret. I would feel that the Lord Chamberlain would be justified in meeting the usual campaign of calumny that would result, by sending a list of his cuts, without comment, to some popular paper such as the 'Daily Mail', which used to have the public weal as one of its motives.

Moreover, it was vital to make a stand now, since 'the remaining unacted scenes of this play are even worse than those in the first instalment, and concessions here would be used as levers for extorting more later'. For Hill, Genet's play typified what the Office was now up against:

The play is one more example of the pressure being brought on the Lord Chamberlain to abandon all the conventions of decency in favour of dramatic needs. The reason always advanced is that of the man who, accused of burglary, defended himself by pronouncing all property to be theft. In the same way the producer will say what are conventions—or come to that what is decency, pornography, obscenity, blasphemy. One of the problems of our time is that we have to find the definition.[10]

A few days after Hill had watched the rehearsal of *The Screens*, the RSC notified the Lord Chamberlain of its intention to revive Beckett's *Endgame* and Pinter's *The Birthday Party*, and queried whether the original restrictions still applied. Penn replied that all the cuts remained in force. In the case of *Endgame*, this meant that 'pee', 'balls', 'arses' and 'swine' (as applied to God) were excluded, and in that of *The Birthday Party*, a passage referring to the Lord's Prayer ('Thy Kingdom come, Thy Wimbledon') and the lines 'you pierced the holes' and 'you hammered in the nails'. While not extensive, such cuts were irksome, and when the RSC included the details in its Newsletter, one member wrote to Cobbold mocking him over his religious sensitivity in relation to *Endgame*:

If you suppress a fact it's usually because it's true and damaging . . . Are we to take it that some infallible proof of the non-existence of God has reached your ears, and you feel at all costs that the news must not be broadcast to the general public?

Is it on the other hand simple piety—a fear of an implacable Jehova's thunderbolts and whirlwinds . . .

Penn's reply matched the letter for irony, claiming that the Office was more in touch with majority opinion:

It is good of you to analyse the motives that may have moved the Lord Chamberlain to excise the phrase mentioned . . .

The disallowance may seem derisory to very sophisticated persons, but to less subtle and simpler members of society, who find the phrase abhorrent, the action is completely justified.

The Lord Chamberlain today makes so many allowances in favour of 'adult' Theatre goers that he feels that some slight consideration for the feelings of those not comprised in this description ought not to be resented.

In June, representatives of the RSC came to negotiate.

They asked whether '. . . balls . . .' in the sense of having made a muck up of something could be allowed. They did not particularly press for this request. They particularly asked that they might be allowed the word '. . . pee . . .'. The alternative is '. . . piss . . .' and we also discussed '. . . piddle . . .' I am wondering just how offensive the word '. . . pee . . .' is now.
p.37. '. . . bastard . . .' . . . is spoken by an atheist . . . Is 'swine' . . . in actual fact not just as bad?

Cobbold was not in the giving vein:

BALLS—NO
PEE, PISS, PIDDLE—NO
BASTARD—NO

There was one more request:

p.54. They asked for '. . . arses . . .'
I said that in all probability this would be allowed. (As it is known, we do now allow '. . . arses . . .' in this context)

The RSC had struck gold. 'ARSES—ALLOW', ruled Cobbold, and the RSC wrote to thank him and to pass on the fact that the playwright was 'grateful for the restoration of "arses"'.[11]

Meanwhile, the RSC opened another home-grown play—David

Rudkin's *Afore Night Come*—but only after much private and public wrangling with the Office. Set among a group of fruit pickers in the Midlands, the play has a disturbing and unsettling atmosphere throughout, and the climax is the brutal killing and beheading of an Irish tramp by fellow workers. 'It is a play of menace, ending in murder: murder unpunished, undiscovered, and almost without remorse', reported Coles. The Censorship stipulated that 'the killing must be semi-hidden from the audience' and that 'there must be no severance of the head', and the RSC responded by announcing they would cancel the performance entirely: 'we cannot continue with the production, since such an alteration would turn a superficial killing into a back-alley murder and a climactic experience into a flash of sadism'. This was probably a tactical manoeuvre rather than a real threat, designed to put pressure on Cobbold, who knew full well how the press would react if they were fed the story.

As well as the violence, there were also problems over the language in Rudkin's play. Much of the dialogue was broadly realistic and colloquial, and the refusal to allow words such as 'bugger', 'sod', 'Christ' and 'fuck' led to a long list of required changes. In March 1964, John Roberts and Clifford Williams from the RSC came to discuss the play with Penn and Hill:

> They agreed with the required alterations in principle except for the references to the words 'bugger' and 'sod'.
>
> They claim that these two words are such an integral part of the language of the setting of the Play that they wish to make a special plea to the Lord Chamberlain . . . John Roberts asked whether it would be possible for the Lord Chamberlain now to consider these two words in accordance with the sense in which they were used, for instance the word 'bugger'; to disallow it when it was used in the active sense and to allow it when it was used just as an expression. This would be in the same way as we now regard 'frig', 'piss' and 'crap'.

This request was rejected ('Never with my co-operation!'), but the Office eventually accepted not only 'squite', 'bastard' and 'cocked up' instead of 'sod', 'sodding' and 'buggered up', but even 'firk', 'firkin', 'firkers', 'firkle' and 'firk-all'. 'It seems to me that it really is half way to "fuck" and I do not know what you will feel about it', wrote Penn to Cobbold, and the decision to allow them is difficult to account for. Especially since they refused to allow 'knackers' as a substitute for 'bollocks'. 'This is a sly move to get past us. We allow "knackers" when they mean "bones" but not what they mean here', wrote Penn. As for the head, the RSC had to accept that the murder would be

'Masked' from the audience by three actors and that the severing of the murdered man's head then takes place not only 'up stage' of a tree but also with a screen of large boxes hiding it from the audience.[12]

The RSC made sure that its dissatisfaction was public knowledge. When the play opened at the Aldwych the programme contained an article attacking the censorship, while the press also gave voice to their grievances:

> The Lord Chamberlain, 59 year old Lord Cobbold, originally suggested 34 cuts and now still insists upon 25 deletions from the printed text. The words he finds unspeakable are not those many reasonable adults would find unprintable—they are usually bloody, hell, Christ and Jesus. They do not affect the theme of Mr Rudkin's powerful and serious work. But the Royal Shakespeare Company feels that such obsessive snipping and scissoring robs the language of the plays' Black Country yokels of its rough and realistic vitality.

Readers were also reminded that the RSC's problems over censorship were not confined to this single production:

> This is not its first clash with the Lord Chamberlain whose aim, it suspects, is to protect the theatre-going public from any contact with the realities of modern day life . . . Peter Hall points out that the same Christs which are forbidden in *Afore Night Come* occur freely in *Henry V.*[13]

The 'Dirty Plays' Controversy

At the end of July, the RSC's continuing experiments with an Artaudian theatre of cruelty led to the submission for licence of Peter Weiss's *Marat Sade*. 'The author must be a devoted disciple of Brecht and goes one better than his master', wrote Heriot; the script, he said, was 'written in doggerel verse', with characters who 'talk and behave . . . like the simpler cartoons in *Pravda*', so that 'one almost sees the top-hatted capitalists riding the sweating workers and holding fat money-bags clearly marked with sterling and dollar signs'. The action, meanwhile, was 'dismally slow' and 'held up by the stylised madness of the actors' which amounted to little more than 'a wonderful excuse for bad acting!' Heriot drew attention to some of the stage business which appeared in the script:

> We must have full details of the business of guillotining the priests . . .
> Duperret must not put his hand under Charlotte's dress . . .
> We must have full details of the copulation mime . . .

This last was replaced by an action 'in which the patients mime rocking boats', with an added requirement that it must contain 'no sexual connotation'. Textual alterations included changing 'they think about nothing but screwing but we are the ones who get screwed' to the rather less direct 'they don't give a damn what they're doing/but we are the ones who get done'. As for the violence, the RSC promised that it would be 'suggested in a stylised way' and that it was 'not intended to make the execution in any way realistic'.[14]

However, it was RSC's production of a French play which stirred up the most headlines in the summer of 1964. Roger Vitrac's *Victor* was a 'surrealist comedy' derived from *Ubu Roi*, and, in Heriot's words 'a heavy handed satire on (inevitably) the bourgeoisie'. The Reader admitted: 'my rising nausea prevents me from offering a detached opinion', but he referred disparagingly to its 'brutal parodies', and 'usual obscenities', and said it had 'enough blasphemies to be entirely <u>a la mode</u>'. Most of these could have been dealt with in the usual way, but there was one particular problem. *Victor* featured a 'mysterious woman visitor . . . who farts continuously', and this was clearly beyond the pale. 'Cut "Who goes pop, pop, pop all the time" . . . "I'd like you to fart for me" . . . "She went phut, phut, phut all the time" . . . "You can have a belly ache without needing to do biggies".' Having failed to persuade the Lord Chamberlain to allow 'the continuous "farting" of an actress', the RSC then came up with an imaginative alternative: each time the character supposedly broke wind, a musician would play the opening bars of Beethoven's fifth symphony on a tuba. It would have been hard to find grounds for refusing this substitution, but Hill could smell danger: 'It was according to the author incontinence of wind', he spluttered; 'the Lord Chamberlain <u>appears</u> to have made it incontinence of Beethoven's fifth symphony.' Would the Office get any credit? Would they heck: 'instead of the Lord Chamberlain's leniency in not banning the whole scene as it deserves being praised, he will be held up to ridicule as the discoverer of a farcical disease'. Hill was right, and the only thing the Office could do was to ask the RSC to make it clear in any public statements that the tuba idea had not emanated from St James's Palace: 'It is frequently and erroneously suggested that alternatives are put forward by this Office.'

The press still had a field day—it was the summer season, after all— and, as ever, the Office got it in the neck from both directions. On the one hand they looked silly for intervening, on the other they looked weak and put upon. One producer, Jack Minster, of Minster Productions Ltd, wrote to express his disgust at the level things had reached, and to ask the Lord Chamberlain to 'retard the growing license to authors and managements that in recent years you have been encouraged to extend'. According to Minster, 'the London Theatre is suffering badly from a number of plays

which have offended public taste, and driven away audiences in thousands',
and he even suggested that 'there is little more now short of the actual
sexual act left to be done on the English Stage'. Minster had himself
clashed regularly with the Lord Chamberlain over his own productions,
but now it had all gone too far:

> I have had cause in the past to question the consistency of your depart-
> ment and when I remember that the word 'copulation' was excised from the
> script of a play by Hugh and Margaret Williams and that now you are being
> pleaded with over the inclusion of a woman breaking wind in a proposed
> production of *Victor* at the Aldwych Theatre, the mind boggles.

Penn sent him the standard reply: 'The Lord Chamberlain cannot
himself establish standards of behaviour for the community; he can only
try to see that the Theatre of the day is related to contemporary views of
propriety, whilst forbidding the demonstrably obscene or immoral.' He
also invited Minster to come and discuss any cases of injustice he felt he
had suffered: 'if you feel yourself aggrieved over any particular decision it
is always possible to have it reviewed'. Minster was not appeased. Nor did
he accept the Lord Chamberlain's refusal of responsibility:

> While it is comforting that we can come and talk to your office about a
> script, it is not consoling to hear from you that the demonstrated farting
> of a woman on the stage is, in the opinion of the Lord Chamberlain, in
> line with contemporary views of propriety. The Lord Chamberlain may
> believe, modestly, that he cannot establish standards of behaviour for the
> community—but in fact, in passing tastelessness in plays, this is exactly
> what he is doing, and thus do standards become formed or deformed.

Minster's own views on gender were hardly in tune with the changing
times: 'In licensing plays containing matters such as that in *Victor*, women
are diminished and are further deprived of respect, already something
almost vanished.' He even advanced a theory that the whole thing was 'a
homosexual reprisal'.

Other voices were also raised against *Victor*, with one correspondent
declaring he was 'shocked and besmirched that such unamusing depravity
should be allowed a performance'.[15] And what must to us seem like a trivial
and absurd case quickly sparked off a profound groundswell of resentment
from critics and producers who were fundamentally opposed to the
direction in which theatre—and, doubtless, society—were travelling. The
fault-lines are interesting. W.A. Darlington—the long-standing theatre
critic for the *Daily Telegraph*—no doubt had the RSC's Oxbridge-educated
Peter Hall and Peter Brook in his sights when he complained about 'the

intelligentsia cordon' guarding London theatres; the manager at Windsor's Theatre Royal voiced similar objections to the fact that intellectuals now enjoyed 'a concentration of power sufficient to jeopardise the play-going pleasures of the vast majority', and that 'those who instinctively seek an emotional rather than an intellectual experience in the theatre . . . have been ruthlessly torn to shreds and trampled under foot'.

Hill was eager to take the lesson: 'it shows that we ought not to accept as gospel all the intellectual arguments we have to listen to from the avant-garde', he wrote, 'always unkempt gentlemen who besiege us every time we cut "f-----"'.[16] Meanwhile, the theatre correspondent of the *Evening News* widened the debate with a sweeping attack not only on the RSC, but also on Brecht, Beckett and the 'weirdies' who 'leave audiences baffled and bewildered', and whose work could survive only within the subsidised sector, because of its lack of appeal to general audiences. This did not stop him from simultaneously denouncing those theatres in the West End which were now promoting plays such as Joe Orton's *Entertaining Mr Sloane*, even though their success **did** depend on ticket-sales:

Five years ago this 'comedy' would never have been put on outside a club theatre where it began.

Now Sir Bronson Albery (Uppingham and Balliol College, Oxford), son of that famous actress Mary Moore, agrees to it going into his theatre.

As I watched him in his box, with Lady Albery, I wondered what he thought of the way the theatre was going . . .[17]

Now it was not only the RSC, but also the avant-garde and the principle of subsidy which were all under fire, as sections of the commercial theatre industry joined in the attack on 'the salacious fare being presented on a number of stages in the West End'.[18] One of the most publicised assaults came from the veteran impresario Emile Littler, who, while himself a member of the RSC's executive committee, announced publicly that he had 'disassociated myself' from 'the programmes of dirt plays at the Aldwych'. In what Peter Hall called an 'unethical attack', Littler told journalists that the 'Plays now being presented in this season do not belong to the Royal Shakespeare Company' and that 'we are ruining our Stratford image' and 'depleting our funds' by offering plays to the public 'which they simply have no desire to see'.[19] Suddenly the press was full of angry and mocking claims and counter-claims. One correspondent in *The Times* rehearsed the link between what was happening in theatres and in society: 'Is it any wonder that crime and violence are rampant in our land?' she asked; 'The debasement of morals calls loudly for a voice to adjust these things—or are we as a nation struck dumb with the results, or do we not care?' British society was on the slippery slope, and sliding down fast: 'Coloured races no longer respect us and teenagers are in revolt for lack of example.'[20] Even the Chair of the RSC Governors, Sir Fordham Flower, admitted that the current Aldwych season was 'now popularly known as "The Dirt Plays"'.[21]

Meanwhile, the RSC—frustrated by the process of wrangling and persuasion required to secure licences—was planning a new tactic. At the start of August, they contacted St James's to enquire about the feasibility of 'from time to time' changing the Aldwych Theatre into a private club 'in order to present plays which would not be subject to the Lord Chamberlain's licence'. Such a revival of the Watergate/Comedy strategy of the mid-fifties would again seriously threaten the ability of the Lord Chamberlain to continue as censor, as Hill, a veteran of those confrontations, well knew. In his—probably accurate—view, the move by the RSC was a deliberate attempt, 'engineered by Peter Hall', to create a 'head-on collision with the Censor'. And, as Hill explained, it was Cobbold who was likely to be damaged by the impact:

> The Aldwych Theatre authorities have asked whether (as a means of defeating the Censorship) they can operate the Theatre each alternative half week as a Private and as a Public Theatre.
>
> This recreates an effort made in 1956 when the Theatre had its last cause célèbre—the disallowance of themes of homosexuality, and which led to the establishment of the Comedy Theatre as a Private Theatre . . .
>
> To have a situation in which all issues banned in a play are produced under the Lord Chamberlain's nose on a flimsy pretext, and as I believe, in an illegal manner, will bring the Office into such contempt that it must either resolve the issue by giving way completely, as it did over homosexuality, and accepting Peter Hall as immune from control; or I should think must be completely non-co-operative, if indeed it does not take preventative action.

For the benefit of newer staff at St James's—including Cobbold—Hill summarised the history of private theatres, and explained the continuing uncertainty of their status, due to the policies of successive Lords Chamberlain who had turned blind eyes to the practice of granting them a freedom of control to which the law probably did not entitle them:

> What vested rights have accumulated over the Lord Chamberlain's years of inaction I cannot assess . . . The Home Office legal adviser gave it as his opinion in 1939 that a performance would not be genuinely private if admission was so general, owing to the terms of membership or size of the society that the performance should be considered a public one.

The RSC was not playing the game.

Theatre clubs until recently have always been genuinely private in intent if not in legality, catering for people who took special trouble to join and providing amenities. They were normally never open for public performances and formed a distinct contrast to public theatres. Their presence is understood and they have not been regarded as a defiance of the Censor. The takeover of a large commercial theatre, with the transparent device of what amounts to paying five shillings to be put on a mailing list, and with the avowed and sole objective of beating the Censor is alien to the whole spirit of the tacit understanding in the theatre that has endured on this matter for fifty years or more.

Unless they could head it off, the RSC's action might be the thin end of a substantial wedge: 'Close followers of a successful Aldwych debut would be the Chichester Theatre, The Old Vic and the Mermaid', warned Hill. Nor did he think the idea of a venue alternating a private and public status on a nightly basis was feasible. He therefore recommended that, as on previous occasions when their backs had been forced against this particular wall, the best riposte would be to warn the RSC that the Office's response to any such move would be to instigate a legal test to determine once and for all whether the freedom and tolerance traditionally allowed to private clubs was a legal right, or whether the law actually required that performances in clubs should be subject to the same system of approval as everywhere else. 'My own opinion would be to see someone from the theatre and not to put anything in writing.' The hope was that the RSC would blink first and the Office would not have to follow through a threat which could only stir up even more antipathy against them.

> We should of course get a very bad Press in which it would be asserted that without question the Lord Chamberlain in the approved dictatorial fashion was attempting to close down all those organs of freedom, Private Theatres. There could be all kinds of derivative action in consequence, and it is for consideration whether this would be worse than allowing the establishment of not one but several establishments for publicly defeating and thus ridiculing the Censor.

Cobbold accepted the suggestion and indicated that rather than back down he was ready, if necessary, to detonate the charge:

> My present view about the Aldwych idea is that though the private theatre is a useful safety-valve on a small scale, this would bring it onto a scale which I could not properly disregard without becoming, as Lord Scarbrough puts it, 'a silent observer of the evasion of the law' on a scale large enough to become a public scandal or make the law ridiculous.

He instructed the Comptroller to 'make discouraging noises' to the RSC, and two days later, on 14 August, Penn reported that he had done just that in a telephone conversation with Michael Hallifax, the RSC's manager. Hallifax had told him that 'there is no particular play in mind at the moment for which they would ask to turn the Aldwych theatre into a theatre club'; but Penn said he had asked Hallifax to look into the principle 'in order to prevent a head on clash between them and ourselves'.[22] It was this potential clash which provoked Cobbold into mentioning his problems over the Aldwych to the Queen.

In the autumn, the RSC launched a new occasional newspaper for its members under the title *Flourish*, with a column written by John Arden under the provocative headline: 'How many schoolgirls has the Censor raped?' Arden's point was the—perhaps slightly spurious one—that 'since the censor subjects himself to all the words in every script' it was illogical to imagine there was any risk in allowing others a similar access. 'I can see no reason whatever for the retention of any censorship at all', declared Arden; 'it is high time we were allowed to do our own selection of what we want to hear and see'. But of course the whole rationale for a specific theatre censorship had always been that reading words silently and alone was a very different experience from seeing and hearing them in performance. Arden, however, was confident that 'the forces of freedom are moving so strongly that in a few years there will be no words not allowed', and that the next stage would be the gradual removal of restrictions on visual images and actions.

Problems with Reality

While the RSC had been the major tormentor of the Lord Chamberlain's Office through 1964, it was not the only one. In January, the Office had been forced into an embarrassing retreat over *Hang Down Your Head and Die*, a script written by David Wright and submitted by Oxford University Experimental Theatre Club. Reminiscent in style of *Oh! What a Lovely War*, Heriot found it a 'deplorable affair' that barely counted as theatre:

> This is a fanatical outcry against capital punishment, whose proper function would be a pamphlet, not an alleged entertainment of the stage. The author has dug every possible piece of relevant and irrelevant material concerning hanging . . . all this has been flung together as a spoken documentary set in a circus.

He recommended a number of changes, particularly where the script referred to real life characters and events. Certainly, there must be no representation of executions or of recognisable executioners:

Cut all representations of the Rosenbergs double executions . . . Cut the 'actuality' of Hanratty and the slides of child suicides . . . Omit the quotation from the death sentence. Omit the pseudo-folk ballad about the murder of Rowe in 1963 . . . there must be no representation of the execution . . . the slide of Haigh in the condemned cell should come out . . .

However, at a time when arguments over capital punishment were in the public eye (the Labour government would suspend it for five years in 1965) this experimental drama was actively championed by two members of the House of Lords, Lord Willis and Lord Gardiner, and an MP, Kenneth Robinson, who put substantial and effective pressure on Cobbold to treat the play as an exception. Most unusually, Penn eventually informed the playwright that the Lord Chamberlain had 'reviewed his previous decisions in the light of the further arguments now presented to him', and would require only minor amendments. In other words, he had been forced to back down—on grounds which were barely plausible and had no real precedent:

> The play *Hang Down Your Head and Die* appears to be a vehicle for anti-capital punishment propaganda and not an entertainment.
>
> It has for this reason been dealt with by the Lord Chamberlain much more leniently than would have been the case had it been a work of entertainment.

Interestingly, however, they did make a stipulation about the acting style. 'The quotations may be quoted by actors who do not impersonate the authors', stated the endorsement. In other words, there should be a gap between the performer and the 'real' person whose words they spoke. Brecht, rather than Stanislavsky.

Opponents of the censorship were keen to press home their victory and mark the case as a model for the future, as Lord Gardiner's subsequent and rather patronising letter to Cobbold shows:

> In view of the great success of *Hang Down Your Head And Die*, and the absence of any criticism of the inclusion of the parts which you originally felt should be censored, I hope that you will feel that your revision as a result of the approach we made to you was fully justified.

In reply, Cobbold insisted that 'particular experience in one case cannot necessarily be applied in others'.[23] Touché.

The fashion for a style which mixed the factual with the fantastic—placing historical events and real people within a vehicle such as a Pierrot show or a circus—continued to cause hesitations and nervousness at

St James's Palace. In February, two enquiring writers were, as the Office put it, 'discouraged from embarking' on writing a musical featuring Lilly Langtry and Edward VII:

> King Edward VII is so recent in history that although a factual play upon his life and times might be considered, the possibility of the Lord Chamberlain agreeing to any musical fantasy, in which His late Majesty appeared is so remote as not to be worth your consideration.[24]

A similar enquiry the following month met with a similar response: 'it is most unlikely that the Lord Chamberlain would agree to the impersonation of King Edward VII in any fantastic or burlesque form, or even I might say in a musical'.[25] And the Lord Chamberlain's Comptroller also successfully headed off a play about another abdication, featuring the Duke and Duchess of Windsor: 'I think it is only fair for me to tell you that it would be very unlikely indeed that the Lord Chamberlain would allow a Play on this topic at the present time, or for a very long time to come.'[26]

There were problems, too, over a different aspect of the real in March, when Theatre Workshop submitted *A Kayf Up West*—a sort of follow up to *Fings Ain't Wot They Used To Be*, written by the same author, and (at least metaphorically) from the inside. 'Mr. Norman is a self-confessed criminal', reported Heriot, 'a sort of milk-and-water Genet'. This latest offering was 'worthless and bogus', but the Reader also noted with irritation that performances had been publicly advertised even before the script had been submitted for examination—'a further example of the insolence that has always characterised Mr. Raffles' dealings with this Office'. The main problems in the play centred around the character of Vivian, an unemployed actor and a male prostitute: 'We can't very well cut the character out entirely', wrote Heriot, 'but I have made some effort to reduce the flagrancy of his performance'. As part of this, he marked 'all references to him as "she" or "her" or "that bitch"', along with 'any other feminine appellation'. The final endorsement imposed further cuts, including:

> Omit 'queen', substitute 'queer'
> Omit 'poof', substitute 'scrubber'
> Omit 'so camp', substitute 'good looking'
> Omit 'stuff it up my Harris', substitute 'where do you think I'd keep it'
> Omit 'dig that arse', no substitute.[27]

Foreign Masters

In April came a challenge of another sort when Claude Astley, of the Translators' Association, and Michael Meyer, a translator of Scandinavian plays, tried to persuade Cobbold to exempt classical foreign plays from normal restrictions. They argued for the principle 'That where the works of an accepted Master are concerned, and where the translator is one of known quality and integrity, the Lord Chamberlain should put no impediment at all in the way of a correct translation'. The Office could hardly concede: 'it would be impossible to give particular exemptions without exposing the Office to charges of partiality which would force further concessions', they ruled. In any case, 'We have never dealt in theories but always empirically'. As Penn told Meyer, there was no acceptable way of fixing the status of an individual writer or translator: 'The matter is not so much one of being unable to establish the position of the topmost, as the utter impossibility of convincing anyone that he does not belong in that category'. Meyer's reply noted sarcastically 'that his Lordship knows of no measure which would enable him to decide that *Hedda Gabbler*, *The Master Builder* and *Miss Julie* are "the works of an acknowledged foreign master"'. His tone did not go down well: 'This is sheer unadulterated rudeness', wrote the Assistant Comptroller in the margin.[28]

However, Kenneth Tynan argued on similar lines when he visited St James's Palace in his role as Literary Director of the National Theatre to discuss a possible production of Wedekind's much-banned *Spring Awakening*. Because of its status, he argued the National should be automatically free of obligations to the Lord Chamberlain:

[He] advanced the point that The National Theatre was in some aspects almost that branch of the Government devoted to Drama and that it was increasingly regarded as such abroad, where a National Theatre production was becoming accepted as the conferring of the British diploma of merit upon the play . . . Thus, when the Lord Chamberlain required cuts in this major work of a foreign dramatist of note, it was likely to be interpreted in that country either as an official slur on that country's good name—or to cause bewilderment—one branch of the British Government lauding the work, another branch condemning it.

This was an ingenious argument—but impossible to give in to:

The force of Mr. Tynan's remarks was admitted, and it was agreed that dramatically his case might be excellent. It must be remembered, however, that the Lord Chamberlain could not base his rulings entirely upon what was good dramatically; but must give heed to other considerations—what was good morally, for example.[29]

Realistically, there was no likelihood that the Office could have backed down from its responsibility towards translated texts, since the concern was not with the quality or the accuracy of the translation, but (in theory at least) whether they would have permitted it in an English play. Wedekind, Büchner and Strindberg were amongst the 'classical' European dramatists whose works continued to be very carefully watched and susceptible to cuts. As for the Greeks—and especially Aristophanes—they could be as much of a handful as any contemporary playwright; though Hill clung to the comforting belief that it was only the ignorance and decadence of twentieth-century Britain that insisted on rendering these plays in vulgar ways: 'When originally written these Greek comedies such as *The Lysistrata*, depended mainly upon their political or social satire', he insisted. It was unfortunate—if typical—that contemporary productions chose to dwell on 'the indelicacies' and to include 'every other possible indecency' they could invent—'such as when the Spartan colonel in *The Lysistrata* hobbled onto the stage bow-legged to show his balls were painfully full of sperm not having had a woman for a month'.[30]

Indecencies at Home

Of course, too many of the plays written by the younger generation of British and American playwrights might also have been described as 'full of sperm'. In late May, *Entertaining Mr Sloane*—a 'really unattractive Play . . . involving an element of homosexuality'—parked its indelicacies firmly on the Lord Chamberlain's desk. Cobbold did his best to look the other way, dismissing Joe Orton's first offering as 'very uninteresting', while acknowledging that its 'Business' would 'need careful watching'. Having already been staged privately at the Arts Theatre, Orton's play was now set to transfer to the heart of the West End, provided it could be licensed. 'There is no attempt to deal with the subject of homosexuality in a serious manner', complained Coles. The Office cut a dozen or so words and phrases and issued strict instructions about the stage action:

> You are particularly warned that any movements implying or simulating copulation have not been allowed and furthermore, that such actions in such a context have been described in Judges *obiter dictum* given in the High Court of Justice as 'obscene'.[31]

But perhaps the striking thing is that so much of Orton's script survived unscathed; and by the time the complaints flooded in it was too late to scathe it.

There was fairly gentle tinkering, too, with *Inadmissible Evidence*—the latest submission by one of St James's least favourite playwrights:

John Osborne spends a sizeable part of his time in this play indulging his retarded adolescent preoccupation with dirty-minded sex, which any normal person of his age would have grown out of years ago, but which has always been evident in his plays.[32]

Some specific sexual references were cut, including direct references to menstruation and periods, but the record here went to Peter Terson's *The Mighty Reservoy*—'A dreary mixture of simple symbolism and the two four-letter words'—which suffered almost a hundred cuts to the dialogue. The first Act alone had to lose sixteen shits, eight Christs, seven buggers, five Jesuses, a fuck, a fucking, a frigging and a pair of cunts.[33]

James Saunders's *A Scent of Flowers*—which would win for its author the *Evening Standard* award for Most Promising Playwright—told the story of a young woman who becomes sexually obsessed with, in turn, her stepbrother, her uncle, a priest and a married man, before finally committing suicide. Heriot called it 'fashionably blasphemous and heartless' in its depiction of a world in which 'love and faith and honesty do not exist' and he proposed that 'the author must be a very unhappy man indeed'. However, it was the religious setting which caused most concern:

The action takes place before the High Altar of a Catholic Church. We cannot allow a frivolous representation of a Crucifix . . . the Office Of The Dead is intoned by a priest who is the undertaker who is Death. I don't much like this as it is background to the often indecent conversation of the other characters.

Hill agreed: 'At the risk of being thought unduly biased, I find this mockery of what goes on in a Church offensive', and it was decided that the religious context and imagery should be watered down:

The Lord Chamberlain does not allow the representation of a High Altar on the stage . . . Zoe must not genuflect . . . The Lord Chamberlain disallows the Office of the Dead being intoned by the Priest.[34]

In J.P. Donleavy's *A Singular Man*, the main stumbling block was a scene in which a man and a woman are seen in bed together. 'We have had couples in bed before but only in farces—and this is a sexual fantasy not a farce.' It made no difference that they were supposedly man and wife: 'I don't think we can permit Sally to leap into her husband's bed', wrote Heriot; 'She apparently undresses and seduces him under the sheet'. The dialogue was indeed fairly explicit:

Smith: What are these Shirl?
Shirl: Feel them.
Smith: Wow.
Shirl; Feel this.
Smith: What is this Shirl?
Shirl; This is what I want you to feel.
Smith: I'd be a fool to feel it.
Shirl: Be a fool and feel it.

Other lines cut from Shirl's seduction included 'It's up. Enter me', 'don't slip out it's a year since you were in', 'Take it off it rubs me', 'Kiss my bazanna', and 'You were so nice when you were a car. Drive you bastard'. But even with these—and more—gone, there still remained the issue of the bed. Donleavy proposed playing the scene in darkness, and suggested this would render it unobjectionable. The Lord Chamberlain's Office did not agree:

> I am to say that it has been decided that it is not possible to allow a scene in which a man and a woman copulate in the presence of the audience; whether they are seen to do so, or whether the dialogue makes it plain that that is what they are doing.

The Assistant Comptroller had his own suggestion: 'There might be more chance of a version of this scene being acceptable if the participants were sitting up in bed and not under the bed clothes', he proposed. A revised script was approved only when accompanied by 'a positive requirement in the Licence to the effect that the action on the bed must not be indicative in any way of intercourse'.

Donleavy's play opened at the Comedy Theatre in early October, but one of Cobbold's secret inspections soon discovered that the Lord Chamberlain's requirements for the scene had been 'considerably disregarded', and that 'Smith and Shirl got under the bedclothes' and turned what could have been innocent dialogue into something more explicit. Hill said he would 'dearly like to give the pair of prevaricators we saw a lesson', but he persuaded the manager of the theatre—'a very decent chap'—to do the dirty work, allowing the Office to avoid the limelight:

> I told him that the producer was doing what he had been forbidden to do, and which he had given the Lord Chamberlain a written assurance he would not do. I said I was sure the Lord Chamberlain would not allow himself to be disregarded in this way and I told Mr Gurney that if he would take a friendly hint he would see the producer first thing on Friday morning and

ensure that the Licence requirements were observed, so that when the Lord
Chamberlain's remonstrance was received he would be in a position to say
that he had already acted on his own volition.[35]

Honouring the Dead

The autumn of 1964 saw a momentous change in government in Britain—
with the election of Harold Wilson marking the end of a period of
Conservative rule that dated back to 1951, and bringing with it the promise
of significant social reforms. It also saw a much less radical changing of
the guard at St James's Palace, with Gwatkin retiring, Penn stepping up to
replace him as Comptroller, and Johnnie Johnston, a retiring Commanding
Officer of the 1st Battalion Grenadier Guards, taking over as assistant to
Penn. Ifan Kyrle Fletcher had already been appointed as a replacement
Reader for Troubridge, and now Maurice Coles—who had been suffering
from ill-health—was more or less summarily dismissed. Hoping for an
increase in his rate of pay, Coles had pointed out that with an annual
income of only £250 for reading plays it was 'obviously necessary, in the
absence of private means, for an Examiner to have another job'. But rather
than having the effect he had hoped for, he was promptly instructed to
resign because he was not able 'to fulfil the requirement' or 'devote the time
necessary' to his duties at St James's. 'I think he was a little disappointed at
the prospect of not continuing as an Examiner', noted the Comptroller; 'I
tried to emphasise, as politely as possible, that this was a decision and not a
matter for further discussion'.[36]

It is a mistake to assume that no-one involved in censoring plays had any
real interest in theatre; this was probably true of most Lords Chamberlain,
and perhaps of their Comptrollers and Assistant Comptrollers; but it was
not generally the case with the Readers. Troubridge, for instance, had been
president of the Stage Society and had a real knowledge of some areas of
theatre history, while Ifan Fletcher was actually the founder and first editor
of *Theatre Notebook*, founder and ex-chairman of the Society for Theatre
Research, and founder and ex-president of the International Federation for
Theatre Research. Even Charles Heriot, who had by now been a Reader
for almost thirty years, had previously worked with Lewis Casson on a
production of *Macbeth*, and spent three years acting in repertory and the
West End, including a year with the Lena Ashwell players. Coles's new
replacement, Tim Harward, also brought with him a genuine interest
in certain kinds of theatre. Indeed, he had an Arts degree from Dublin,
had lectured on twentieth-century drama at Oxford University and was
actively engaged in research at the University of Sussex. While Fletcher
and Heriot were both approaching sixty, Harward was only 33—the same
generation as John Osborne. Crucially for his new appointment, he had

private means to support him, and he impressed Cobbold and Johnston at interview:

> From what we saw of him yesterday morning the Lord Chamberlain and I both feel that he is the sort of person we want. He appears to have a good knowledge of drama, is interested to be a Reader and I should think has quite a good brain.[37]

As we shall see, his erudition often shines through in his reports.

If the election of the Labour government is seen to mark the ending of an era in post-war British history, it may be more than coincidence that three of the plays which caused most aggravation at St James's Palace in the final months of 1964 centred in different ways on decay, death and dying bodies. At the start of December, Kenneth Tynan and Laurence Olivier submitted Charles Wood's *Dingo* for the National Theatre—a savage and in some ways still shocking attack on myths about the heroism of British and American forces during the Second World War. Reporting on it was one of Tim Harward's first assignments during a probationary period which preceded his full appointment:

> This is a difficult and provocative parody/satire in the classic anti-Establishment manner. It is a bitter, pungent attack on war and heroism. The original title—'I Don't Hold With Heroes'—is a perfect précis of the play, and the action leads inexorably to the final lines: 'What were we fighting for?' The mood recalls *Oh What a Lovely War*, and the dialogue, the stilted, enigmatic prose of Samuel Beckett.

Even Winston Churchill did not escape the aggressive satire, and Harward (who had himself been invalided out of the forces) acknowledged the play's power and theatricality: 'Heavy and often brutal and gruesome imagery are all used to convey the author's message', he wrote; 'meaning is conveyed more by emotion and polemic than through reason or logic'. Wood's play was also 'a highly stylised symbolist presentation in which the dead mingle with the living', its characters 'deployed like marionettes to demonstrate the author's argument'. But as well as demonstrating his theatrical understanding, Harward had also to prove himself politically, and this he did: 'The point of view is highly loaded and negative', he advised; 'it is a systematic devaluation of the conventional military values of the Second W.W., together with a mechanical induction of the chain of responsibility for the war itself'. More specifically, 'There are ironic references to King George VI; a merciless caricature of F M Lord Montgomery, and by implication of RSM Lord, Grenadier Guards.'

The new Assistant Comptroller liked the report, and hated the script.

'May I please have your advice on what I think is a perfectly dreadful play', Johnston asked Hill: 'I would like to advise the LC not to license, but I dare say this is not possible.' The secretary took it every bit as seriously; in his view this was about more than just contesting the past, its history and its values; it was equally about the present:

> it falls into the pattern of the 'avant-garde' of this country which now secures such disproportionate publicity for its efforts to undermine in every way the nation's will to resist. The ghastly effects of propaganda of this sort were seen in the abject surrender of France to the Germans, and the effects could be just as serious here.

Harward had compiled a three-page list of 'suspect words or phrases'. Hill added this, picking up in particular the juxtaposition of sexual imagery with instruments of war, including

> an obvious analogy between a gun with a split trail and a breach and a girl with her two legs open . . . a disgusting comparison of breach block grease and female exudations with a comparison between a man's penis and the closed fist with which in some pieces the cartridge case is rammed home into the breach.

There was, too, the explicit violence:

> Are we to make any comment about the burning soldier screaming in his tank which goes on for three pages . . . The action . . . with the incinerated corpse of Chalky is pretty disgusting. This should be specially brought to the Lord Chamberlain's notice. I think that the only decision must be either to allow it or to forbid it—it is fairly impossible to lay down degrees of verisimilitude with the incinerated corpse being used as a ventriloquist's dummy.

Hill's sentiments were fully echoed by Johnston:

> This is a terrible play with a sinister theme and dreadful dialogue . . . I am not at all happy about the representation of Chalky. Presumably it will be a dummy of an incinerated corpse, but to look like one it is bound to be a fairly disgusting sight. If it is cut out, it removes quite an important part of the plot, and we may be accused of trying to hide the horrors of war etc.

The Office knew that such interventions were merely tinkering around the edges, yet to ban it completely was difficult: 'in the contemporary scene I feel myself it is impracticable to ban the present play entirely, as it ought to be'. There were other ways to skin a cat. On 16 December, Johnston wrote to Tynan: 'The Lord Chamberlain asks me to say that he finds some difficulty over this play and would welcome an informal talk with Sir Laurence Olivier about it.' It was late January 1965 before the meeting took place and, as it happened, Churchill had died earlier that month and been accorded the most grand and respectful of state funerals. Indeed, some of the notes made by the Lord Chamberlain's staff in relation to *Dingo* are written on the back of papers detailing instructions for the funeral, which took place in the same week as Cobbold met with Olivier and Tynan. Perhaps more pertinently, Olivier had been the solemn voice of Churchill, employed in television coverage of his funeral. The meeting about *Dingo* between the Lord Chamberlain's Office and the National Theatre did not reach a definite conclusion: 'It was decided that Sir Laurence and Mr Tynan would consult further with the author' and in due course would 'resubmit it with the words and phrases that are so obviously unacceptable having being deleted'. But although it is not clear who made the decision, the National never did resubmit, and it would be 1967 before the script resurfaced.[38] One up for Lord Cobbold.

A very different but equally disturbing use of a corpse occured in Joe Orton's new farce. Writing in early December, Ifan Fletcher dismissed *Loot* as 'a mixture of filth and blasphemy', and although he listed specific details for exclusion ('offensive reference to homosexuality . . . filthy dialogue . . . reference to flagellation . . . reference to a voyeur watching homosexuals'), he found 'the whole atmosphere of the play repellent' and recommended that a licence should be refused. Johnston agreed: 'I do not think it is farcical enough as to be so slapstick that you might consider giving it one.' He was particularly disturbed by the use of a dead body within comedy: 'Even if a dummy is used for the corpse, I am not happy at the thought of it.' Heriot, however, had seen it all before, and was a little more generous: 'The point seems to me to be that the macabre element isn't all that important (the <u>Grand Guignol</u> season at the Little Theatre— during the 14–18 War went much further in horrific action on stage).' He, too, declared himself offended by 'the shocking bad taste with which it is presented', but recommended that it could be passed 'if certain scenes are re-written', and specifically provided that the corpse was 'obviously a dummy' and kept its clothes on. He also wanted to disallow the false eye.

At the start of January 1965, Michael Codron, the producer, discussed the cuts with the play's director, Peter Wood, and with Orton himself, and began negotiations: 'we would like to assume that it is possible to retain some of the undressing', he began, suggesting that he should come to St James's and 'explain to you in person how this can be decorously effected'; in addition, he wrote:

we would also be most anxious to retain the false eye business as we feel that with all possible source of offence removed the business of the false eye must surely strike audiences as a reducto ad absurdum of all police enquiry—which, in effect, is what the play is aiming to do: satirise, by the nature of farce, all detective plays.

Cobbold gave in over the eye, but not the undressing, and when the production opened Johnston was sent on an undercover mission to check that all the Office's stipulations were being fully observed. Generally, he found it 'pretty dreary' and 'not good entertainment', since it 'drags interminably'. He thought the actors—even though they were 'good theatre names'—generally performed poorly, and suspected that 'this may well be because most of them were not enamoured of the subject'. As for the comedy: 'It is a brand of sick humour which probably goes down quite well with certain sections of the public particularly those who like to be shocked . . . in some unusual way.' However, 'I was glad to see that none of the disallowances had crept in and all the stage directions and restrictions imposed by us were carefully carried out'. Although a few liberties were being taken, there was nothing which need cause the Office real concern: 'There is a certain amount of improvisation and dialogue alteration, all of it, as far as I was concerned, quite innocuous, except perhaps that an imaginary firm who make glass eyes do so for Royalty.' And the Assistant Comptroller confidently predicted that 'If it gets to the West End at all I should be very surprised if it runs for more than a few weeks'.[39]

But perhaps the cruellest and the most overtly political satire to be seen in late 1964 was John Wells and Claude Cockburn's *Listen to the Knocking Bird*, licensed a month before the General Election for Nottingham Playhouse. The focus was on the state of contemporary Britain and its increasing decay, and the leaders of the two main parties—Harold Wilson and Sir Alec Douglas Home—appeared under markedly thin disguises. While the Wilson figure doesn't escape mockery, the script was particularly vicious about Home—not least on a personal level:

— I say, I say, I say . . . What is the difference between an ordinary skeleton and Sir Alec Douglas Home?
— I don't know, what is the difference between an ordinary skeleton and Sir Alec Douglas Home?
— Well an ordinary skeleton is buried in the earth and tends to smell extremely unpleasant.
— And Sir Alec?
— He's still walking around.

It wasn't the suggestion that the Prime Minister looked like a skeleton (which everyone knew he did) that worried the Censors; rather 'the reference here is that Sir Alec is a skeleton <u>who stinks</u>', noted Hill; 'I would cut the lines "tends to smell extremely unpleasant"'. Other current and recent members of the Cabinet were also the butt of fairly unsubtle humour: in one sketch, Home demonstrates a new washing machine designed for cleaning dirty linen in private—'this underwear belonged to a former Minister of War, a Mr Profumo'—as well as a carpet sweeper with the same name as the Home Secretary because it 'whisks anything swiftly under the carpet'. The script was essentially an attack on an establishment on the point of terminal collapse, while Wilson and the Labour Party are satirised for believing they can patch up a structure which is actually past repair and requires tearing down. This is physically represented on-stage by a set clearly intended to embody the state of the nation—a heavy and ornate castle, with turrets and pinnacles, and the silhouettes of statues representing Justice and Freedom, which visibly crumbles through the evening (a sort of pre-echo of Stephen Daldry's iconic collapsing house in Priestley's *An Inspector Calls*, thirty years later). The set for Wells and Cockburn's play is first seen illuminated by garish neon lights flashing up slogans such as 'MONEY', 'SEX', 'FLESH', 'KICKS' and 'GIGGLES', and is then revealed to be a brothel, presided over by Britannia as the madame—'a fat, prim woman, with a prim suburban accent'. She—and her associates—are in denial about the real state of their home:

> The Kingdom of old England
> Stood since the earth was made
> The roof may be unstable
> The walls may be decayed
> But while the flag is flying
> The scarlet bandsmen play
> The country's not yet dying
> And everything's o.k. . . . .[40]

Heriot called the piece—not unreasonably—'A heavy-handed political satire', though even he admitted that it contained 'funny lines'—some of them 'too close to the truth to be permitted'. Johnston asked for guidance: 'As this is my first political satire I should like advice on what we let through.' Hill's recommendations reflect a Censorship in slow retreat, giving up ground only with reluctance:

> The principle I would adopt here is to allow all political matter and reference
> to such personal characteristics as would be depicted say in a cartoon. But

the attribution of personal defects I would not allow, especially as most of them are legally slanderous.

 We normally do not allow the impersonation of living people on the stage. The policy has been dented somewhat at times but I think that it ought to be preserved since once we allow it we shall be in constant trouble; and apart from the inequity of subjecting living people to insult of this kind without the possibility of answer, we shall be exposing ourselves . . . to action for slander . . . In a political sketch of this kind, which is mainly symbolic I see no harm in the characters being Alec and Harold, and even to the use of a pipe, but I would lay down the firmest prohibition upon any real impersonation in the way of make-up and dress.

In the end, much though the Office disliked some of the specific references as well as the general tone, most of what it disallowed was on grounds of vulgarity rather than politics ('Mr Ephraim Sodbucket . . . Mr Randy McPhallus . . . stuffed my crypt with her broken glass . . . dry rot in her fundament . . . reference to the Queen . . .').[41]

 At the end of *Listen to the Knocking Bird,* the whores—Veronica Frobisher-Greenslade, Lavinia Harcourt-Smythe, Rosamund Ch*mber-L*ine and Chloe Ponsonby-Hackett—sit silent and alone in the ruined building that represents Britain. Then in what could almost be taken— fifteen years before she was elected to undo the sixties and turn the nation back to the fifties—as a premonition of Margaret Thatcher, Britannia launches into a monologue against the reformers and the critics who want to change things. She speaks 'in a strange, semi-tragic monotone, her eyes flickering about as if she had gone mad'.

 BRITANNIA: You get on my nerves you lot do . . . All of you . . . Natter natter natter. Moan moan moan. Misery bloody misery. I tell you if I have any more grumbling or discontent there'll be trouble . . . any more hooliganism and smutty talk . . . any more rowdiness or outbreaks of satire . . . any more nasty carping, destructive criticism . . . and by God I'll horsewhip the lot of you . . . my patience is exhausted. Took me a lot to build this place up . . . Slaved and slaved for every penny . . . and now it's mine. It's my house! (*she stamps her foot and a certain amount of plaster falls . . .*) My castle . . . Happy here I am. We're all happy. And you're trying to muck it up. I know you are. And I know why too . . . Because you're jealous . . . You envy me my happiness and my security and you're trying to destroy it . . . Hooligan. That's what you are. Bleeding Hooligan. Well I won't stand for it any longer. You hear me. I'm going to make you suffer. I'm going to teach you a lesson you won't forget in a hurry, let me tell you . . . Teach you to be satisfied with what you've got in life. Teach you to be content. Like me . . . (*A big drum roll begins. Britannia staggers about the stage, working herself up into a frenzy . . . singing in a terrible cracked voice*) Rule Britannia (*she cracks whip*) Britannia rules the waves (*she cracks it again, almost losing her balance*) Flog the juvenile delinquents . . . bring back slaves . . . (*she staggers so badly that she seems on the verge of falling off or through the ruins*) A million Express Readers can't be wrong! . . . The time has come to get tough. (*She slows down, glaring round like a lunatic*) Blast the lily-livered psychiatrists. There's only one place for these long-haired rebels . . . The gas chamber! Let the weak go to the wall, I say. Let them go to the wall!!!

The problem for Britannia, as Chloe points out to her, is that, 'the wall's fallen down'.[42] At the end of 1964, it seemed to have very nearly done so.

CHAPTER FIVE

Blows for Freedom (1965)

It has been the practice of successive Lord Chamberlains to raise no question about productions at theatre clubs, on the grounds that they fulfilled a useful theatrical function, met the needs of a special category of theatre goers and, so long as they remained on a small scale, gave rise to little or no public controversy . . . The present Lord Chamberlain takes the same view and would much prefer to see the present practice about theatre clubs continue. He feels however that if the theatre club idea were developed so that it became a matter of public controversy and there was a danger of the law being brought into contempt, he might easily be forced as the person responsible for enforcing the Theatres Act, to test the law to ascertain whether in fact the Act could be evaded in this way. His present view is that a clarification of the point would be likely to result in much stricter control of Private Theatre Clubs.[1]

Despite the force of Pinter's argument and the physical impossibility of stuffing a mangle up an arse I'm not too happy about this one.[2]

On 6 January 1965, in a story headlined 'Osborne will pip the Censor', the *Sun* newspaper told its readers that 'The Lord Chamberlain is being made to look an ass again'.[3] This time, the issue was the Royal Court Theatre's plan to evade a ban on *A Patriot for Me* by turning itself into a private club, supposedly exempt from official censorship. Osborne's new play focused on espionage and blackmail in the Austro-Hungarian Empire of the late nineteenth and early twentieth century, with a Jewish, homosexual spy as the main character; it was, in particular, the long scene set at a 'drag ball' which lay at the heart of the censorship conflict.

A Patriot for Me

Osborne's play had originally been submitted in August 1964, and had inevitably been met with contempt:

This is a serious but not a good play about homosexuality but though we have had plays on the subject which have received a licence, Mr Osborne's overweening conceit and blatant anti-authoritarianism causes him to write in a deliberately provocative way. He almost never misses a chance to be offensive.

Heriot listed many specific and essential cuts, but recommended a complete refusal:

If the Company wish to try again then the whole of Acts 2 and 3 must be drastically revised with the ball left out and the inverted eroticism toned down. The present text seems to be a perfect example of a piece which might corrupt, since it reveals nearly all the details of the homosexual life usually left blank even in the newspaper reports.[4]

Hill agreed: 'to give the devil his due the dialogue reads well', he conceded; but 'a semi-naked man in bed with his boyfriend', who was also likely to be 'pretty undressed', seemed to put the play well beyond what the Earl of Scarbrough had envisaged in his famous 1958 minute which supposedly brought to an end the automatic ban on all signs of homosexuality; *Patriot* sought to introduce 'physical embraces between men which the Lord Chamberlain thought should be positively forbidden (where do we go if we start!)'. But Hill predicted worse trouble: 'This play looks to me like the Pansies' Charter of Freedom and is bound to be a cause célèbre.' He pointed out that the Office must box clever in what it wrote to the Royal Court, remembering that it would be bound to turn up in print:

One plea I would make is that if we disallow this piece we don't hand ourselves over bound hand and foot to these people, but instead of our usual letter, when sending the deletions accompany them with a letter saying briefly what the LC is banning—the Pansies' Ball and why—because of proselytising and corrupting. Then if they must quote us, some little in our defence will come out.

On 10 September, the Royal Court was informed that there were scenes 'which the Lord Chamberlain feels unable to license on the grounds that they exploit homosexuality in a manner that may tend to have corrupting influence'. Specifically, 'He cannot allow such scenes as a homo-sexual ball at which some of the men are dressed as women (including one who portrays Lady Godiva dressed in a gold lamé jockey strap); and others in which men embrace each other and are seen in bed together'. St James's official line was that their concerns related only to 'scenes involving intimate love-making between men', which were 'conducive to immorality'; but despite Hill's best intentions, and much to the irritation of the Censors, the press were soon reporting simply that the whole play was banned: 'Even now they bowdlerise in Osborne's favour!'

Two months earlier, the RSC had proposed turning the Aldwych into a private club in order to perform uncut versions of new plays. Now, six days after the General Election had swept away so much of the old order, the Royal Court repeated the threat:

> As you know, the Lord Chamberlain has not agreed to license the performance of this play without certain fairly drastic excisions.
>
> Mr John Osborne does not wish to make these excisions as he feels it would damage his work in a way he is not prepared to accept . . .
>
> The state of the law being what it is, we can only think of closing this theatre to the public for the period of its desired presentation—say six to eight weeks—and offering it to members of the English Stage Society during that period . . .

Cobbold discussed the situation with Lord Nugent, the former Comptroller of the Lord Chamberlain's Office, and decided to hold to the same line as before—to warn the theatre that if they went ahead he would seek legal advice to test whether Theatre Clubs really did have the right to be exempted from his control, and to point out what was certainly true, namely, that this could lead to the complete outlawing of all private theatres. Hill was convinced this was a winning strategy: 'we have a first class legal case to the best of my belief, and if we show ourself confident of the outcome, these people may decide it is not worth the trouble'. But he feared the story would not end there:

> they may decide to strike a blow for freedom. We could win our case—we might then have to apply stricter rules—there might be so much theatrical and press outcry as opposed to public, as to cause the Government to bring in new legislation.

Cobbold, too, knew that the final battle was approaching, and that placing the case in the hands of lawyers would effectively mean that 'either theatre clubs would be found to be illegal or his powers of censorship would go'. In November, Devine visited St James's Palace and was presented with a statement 'which he read carefully', warning him about the likely outcome of the action the Royal Court was proposing to take. 'The Lord Chamberlain would much regret this', he was informed, 'but it would probably be an unavoidable consequence'. Hill reported that Devine's next step would be to 'discuss the matter further with the Council of the

English Stage Company', but that he had 'seemed fairly certain that they will wish to go ahead with their plan'.[5]

The Homecoming

Meanwhile, Harold Pinter's new play, *The Homecoming*, had also arrived in the Lord Chamberlain's in tray. It was submitted by the RSC at the end of 1964, and—by contrast with Osborne's play—was greeted with some enthusiasm by the new Reader, Ifan Fletcher: 'The motives of the characters are subtly revealed behind the words they speak', he wrote; 'The dialogue is brilliantly clever'. The Assistant Comptroller saw it rather differently: 'This is a typical Aldwych play—rather nauseating.' He recommended a licence only 'with reluctance' and because he thought it wouldn't matter much: 'It is the end of the play which is the most objectionable—the last twenty pages', he suggested; 'I feel that by then only those who are unlikely to be offended will be left in the theatre!' While Fletcher could not see 'any purpose in trying to make cuts', he was overruled, and the RSC was required to submit alternatives for 'sod', 'sodding', 'Christ', 'bollocks', 'poke', 'bugger' and the injunction to 'stuff this iron mangle up your arse'. They were also advised that 'the dance must not be unduly erotic'. Pinter himself came to St James's to plead for the mangle, and the fact that he came across as being 'reasonable in his approach' evoked a level of sympathy: 'His difficulty is that he has to show a character with a veneer of charity and kindness which breaks very decisively the moment any strain is put upon it', reported Hill; 'Thus he helps an old lady to move a mangle, but the moment the task becomes in a slight degree onerous he washes his hands of the affair in terms of calculated brutality and cruelty that allows no appeal'. What could a poor boy do?

> Mr. Pinter says that after searching his mind diligently he just cannot find an effective substitute: to detract from this climax, which is designed to illuminate the whole character, will certainly spoil the long speech in which it occurs, and in Mr. Pinter's view the whole scene. The point is further made that since the whole remark is a fantastic one, it can have no obscene connotation.

Hill and Johnston conceded that 'From the dramatic point of view it is really not possible to contest Mr. Pinter's statement'. However, that alone was not sufficient. 'The issue, as was explained to him, was whether in the interests of the admitted dramatic requirement of the play, the Lord Chamberlain could so depart from accepted standards of decent speech as to allow what was asked.'

As regards 'Christ', Pinter and the RSC held a trump card, since in the case of *The Caretaker* the Office had previously failed to intervene over the line 'Christ I must have been under a false impression'. The playwright had another card up his sleeve:

> It was pointed out by Mr. Pinter that in this context the stage directions required the word to be spoken softly by a character under great stress, indeed according to Mr. Pinter the softer, the more effective, even to the point of its being mouthed rather than enunciated. This use according to Mr. Pinter is not discernibly different from invocation, and is certainly and demonstrably not an expletive.

Cobbold conceded, although according to Peter Hall—who directed the production—in reality 'Christ' was spoken anything but quietly in performance.[6] Doubtless Pinter's own acting skills had come in useful in his meeting with the Lord Chamberlain's staff. And in the end, although they were more concerned about the destination of the mangle, they decided it was not worth fighting about: 'in a play of this sort, you might have to let it go'.[7] And Cobbold did.

Spring Awakening

In February 1965, Wedekind's *Spring Awakening* resurfaced when the English Stage Company announced its intention to stage it. Kenneth Tynan, who would soon become notorious as the first person to use the word 'fuck' on (live) television, was also encouraging The National Theatre, whose controversial and provocative literary manager he was, to stage 'this beautiful and delicate play', but provided 'it can be done in full'. This was not something the Lord Chamberlain's Office was prepared to countenance: 'German Expressionism is dead. And it never was beautiful and delicate.' They therefore agreed to 'stand firm against any attempt to put back the bad language and orgiastic bad behaviour in this play', and hold to the list of cuts stipulated in 1963. The literary agents who represented the text agreed 'to urge The National Theatre to accept all but one of the cuts and recommendations'. The sticking point was the scene depicting adolescent homosexuality, which they said was written 'with such delicacy and taste' that they could not understand the objection to it: 'I am particularly amazed at this scene with its charm and innocence being disallowed.' Someone at St James's Palace questioned in the margin: 'Is homosexuality ever charming and innocent except to homosexuals?'[8]

By 1965, the National had evidently shelved its plan, and the Royal Court asked the Censorship to reconsider the existing endorsements: 'anything in it which, taken out of context might appear unwarranted or merely distasteful, can be fully justified by reference to the author's moral and artistic purpose', they claimed, while 'the omission of any of these is liable to damage the integrity of its conception and realisation'. Johnston was unconvinced. 'The letter is full of the usual specious arguments', he insisted, advising Cobbold against any significant relaxation. He also suspected that the theatre was calling the Censorship's bluff and had its next move already worked out: 'I guess that this is a try-on and they are expecting this answer; in which case they will put on this play in the same manner as the Osborne one.' But the Court did not want to follow the private club strategy if they could avoid it, and in February, Desmond O'Donovan—the putative director of the proposed production—had another go at making a case for licensing: 'I feel that I have not made certain things about the play clear enough', he wrote:

> We are, as I am sure you will understand concerned with presenting a serious work of art to the public with as much honesty and conviction as we can muster and I am afraid that to cut it radically will be to destroy it. It is, as I have said before, a play which has been very delicately composed.

O'Donovan pointed out that the Prussian government had revoked its ban on the play more than fifty years previously, in 1912. Why, he reasonably asked, was there still such a problem in Britain about presenting things just because they might be considered morally reprehensible?

> Surely it cannot be believed that the presentation of a vicious action in a moral context is necessarily vicious or corrupting. The whole of drama is a history of plays in which a horrifying action is seen and felt by the audience in the right way because of its juxtaposition to the rest of the play. The putting out of Gloucester's eyes in *King Lear* is far more disturbing to the sensibilities of an audience than anything in *Spring Awakening*.

In any case, 'The Royal Court audience is not great in number and is made up of people who do not generally go to the theatre for sensation', and even if they did, 'a person looking for cheapness will not find it in *Spring Awakening*'.

Hill remained strongly against concessions: 'I think the Lord Chamberlain for a public audience could not go further than he has done', he declared; 'especially as in these days the play is particularly unnecessary as a warning to Parents not to rule by the rod'. Indeed, there was 'a real possibility of corrupting the young', while the simulation of masturbation—'unequivocally an indecent action'—would mean that very few boundaries would remain: 'one has only to say if men, why not women, to prove the point'. Cobbold remained firm, and the theatre had to accept all the Lord Chamberlain's strictures:

Omit 'penis' . . . Omit 'vagina' . . . Omit entire scene (2:7) . . . Omit the direction 'He kisses him on the mouth. Ernst responds'. (There will be no kissing, embracing or caressing between the two boys involved) . . . Wendla must not in any circumstances remove any clothing before or while she is being beaten and the skirt only is to be hit. The beating up at the end of this scene must not be too sadistic.[9]

A year later, permission was sought to reinstate the disallowed sections of Wedekind's text for a production at Cambridge University. 'I would like to point out that the play is to be performed to a large University audience in a University town, an audience of intelligent adults', begged its student director; 'I don't believe there is an audience in England less likely to take harm from being exposed to things on the stage which are frank in their presentation of sexual behaviour'. Once again, Hill advised against backing down:

> I would not make the slightest concession on the masturbation scene . . . on NO account would I personally recommend allowing two boys to kiss and caress each other. Lord Scarbrough said he would never allow physical love making between homosexuals . . . Like nudity—it must be all or nothing . . . If it is once allowed then the degree will be out of our control.

Hill was also adamant that there was no case for considering students as a special case—far from it:

> Especially with a young and often erratic University audience, the establishment of homosexuality as an ideal world of the purest love (which is what homosexuals maintain their perversion to be) is proselytising in its most dangerous form.

A few minor concessions were agreed by Cobbold in relation to heterosexuality, but the ban remained on 'the masturbation scene' and on same sex contact: 'I am to confirm that the Lord Chamberlain will not allow any kissing, embracing or caressing between the two boys.'[10]

Going Clubbing

In early 1965, both the ESC at the Royal Court and the RSC at the Aldwych seemed ready to go ahead and challenge the power of the Censorship by turning their theatres temporarily into private clubs, following the model of the Watergate and Comedy Theatres in the previous decade. 'We are faced once again with this situation in an aggravated form', Hill noted. The aim of the RSC was 'to stage disallowed plays (conventionally speaking of the vilest description) as part of their repertory', and the Royal Court 'to stage what appears to be an extremely corrupting play in defiance of the Lord Chamberlain's Ban'. As Hill put it, 'Both Companies are dedicated to policies to which no Censor could possibly subscribe', and were now 'reaching a point where they will openly defy the Lord Chamberlain'. Indeed, in the case of the Royal Court its Artistic Director 'has openly said to us that he is not concerned with the Theatres Act and knows none of its provisions'. Hill blamed it partly on the 1959 Obscene Publications Act, which had 'thrown open the door to all who wish to publish indecencies in the guise of literature', thus acting as 'an incentive and justification for similar stage freedom'. But he considered the broader problem to be 'The cult of "Anti-Establishment" . . . and the non-acceptance of the conventional virtues'—a cult being promoted by 'young radical TV controversialists'. Given this, he feared that if the RSC and the Royal Court were to go ahead with their plans they would 'receive tremendous publicity and professional support' which would be hard to resist. Still, Hill recommended that the Office should press ahead with legal action, whatever the consequences, and even though there was no guarantee the prosecution would succeed. But *A Patriot for Me* was 'such an unpleasant play that we shall probably not get a better case on which to proceed for a long time'. It was inevitable that 'The Lord Chamberlain will be held up to obloquy in the Press and the TV. He will be pilloried as the epitome of all that is defensive of out-moded thought, backward-looking, and dictatorial'. Nor would the action frighten their opponents: 'The Royal Court attitude towards the law is an arrogant one; there is the possibility that a fine of one hundred pounds or so would have no effect, and that one of them would elect martyrdom for contempt of court as a protest.' Moreover, warned Hill, it was 'highly possible that a successful prosecution will give such a political lead to the now powerful "avant-gardistes" as will lead to the repeal of the Theatres Act'. Still, the issue could no longer be ducked:

> Failure to act now would mean that we cannot act in future. The problem fortunately concerns a play which whilst dramatically good, is so corrupting, that if it secures public acceptance, there will be little point in stage censorship for many years to come.

The only alternative was to

> admit public defeat at the hands of the Aldwych and Royal Court for the purpose of keeping the Censorship in being, albeit as an authority which will become rapidly more and more disregarded, and forced to make more and more abject concessions.

The Assistant Comptroller passed Hill's paper on to Cobbold, warning him that 'we may soon be faced with a Censorship crisis'. In response, Cobbold recorded his own position—partly for the benefit of Frank Soskice, the recently appointed Home Secretary—in what amounted to a 'back me or sack me' statement:

> If I thought that this was just a single instance which would fade out, I might on balance be prepared to live with it. But I am fairly sure that, in the present atmosphere, if the Royal Court get away with it, others, particularly the Aldwych, will follow.
>
> I think this would bring the law into disrepute and is a position which . . . I could not properly tolerate.
>
> Questions of law and of public policy are involved. I should not wish to take any action against theatre clubs unless advised by the Law Officers that the legal position is sound, and I should be reluctant to do so without the support of the Home Secretary. But my present feeling is that, if the Law Officers are doubtful or if the Home Secretary feels that action would be against the public interest, I should have to ask for the whole position of theatre censorship to be reviewed.

The following day, Cobbold sounded out Soskice in person:

> I called on the Home Secretary yesterday for a general talk about Censorship. I said that I wanted to do two things. First, to have a general gossip on a 'thinking aloud' basis about censorship and the future, and secondly, to seek his advice on a specific problem regarding theatre clubs.

As part of that 'gossip', Cobbold let it be known that he 'continued to find it difficult to form a very clear view as to whether some form of stage censorship was right or wrong', and admitted that 'if none existed I should certainly hesitate to introduce one'. On the other hand, 'there were clearly difficulties in doing away entirely with a censorship which had lasted for a long time'. He explained that his own approach during his two years in office had been 'to follow and perhaps extend the practice of my predecessor in moving towards more liberality, in accordance with what seemed to be the requirements of general public opinion'. However:

> The whole picture has probably become more difficult in the last few years, partly because of organised opposition (on perfectly sincere grounds) by such people as the Royal Shakespeare Company and partly because of the increase in television plays where different standards are, and probably must be, used.

In conclusion, Cobbold told Soskice that he 'thought that we could probably jog along for a few years with intermittent troubles, but I had some doubt in my own mind whether on the long view the present position was reasonably tenable'.

Perhaps surprisingly, the response of the Labour Home Secretary was, at best, cautious, and probably indistinguishable from that of his Conservative predecessors:

> The Home Secretary said that he appreciated the points which I made; his personal feeling however was that in practice the present arrangement worked well and that although there were screams from time to time, the majority of public opinion thought it a good thing to have some form of censorship. He thought that the arrangement by which it was in the hands of the holder of an ancient Household Office was the sort of illogicality which the British Public on the whole liked rather than disliked. He felt convinced that any attempt to review the subject would give rise to every sort of lobbying and pressure groups, and he feared that the end result would be a stricter and less acceptable form of censorship. He is therefore strongly in favour of letting things lie unless and until there is a marked swing in public opinion.

Cobbold had also talked about the current stand-off over theatre clubs, and Soskice indicated that he was 'disposed to agree' that the strategy being mooted by the Royal Court and the RSC should be challenged, 'rather than passively to allow your authority to be undermined'. That left as the next question whether Norman Skelhorn, the Director of Public Prosecutions (DPP), would be willing to proceed with a prosecution. On 6 April, Johnston contacted him with what amounted to a formal deposition:

> You will have seen the correspondence which has passed recently between the Lord Chamberlain and the Home Secretary upon the question of theatre clubs. From it you will have gathered that, whilst Lord Cobbold has no wish to extend his area of authority in the theatre, there are now powerful forces which threaten to erode it in important aspects.
>
> The quality of the plays which those concerned wish to put before the public by this means is in the Lord Chamberlain's view so degraded as to constitute another and very strong reason for setting, in the general interest, a positive limit on their activities.
>
> Lord Cobbold much hopes accordingly that it will be possible, should the situation envisaged become an actuality, for you to undertake proceedings on his behalf.

Johnston and Hill followed this up with a positive meeting at which

> The Director professed himself very ready to help, and considered that an
> evasion of the Theatres Act as described, that is by the gross expansion of
> an existing club, or the formation of a club for the express purpose of defeat-
> ing the censor, would be a suitable occasion to call upon the services of his
> Department.

Specifically, Skelhorn recommended that 'the case must rest upon the
public performance for payment of an unlicensed play', and his plan
was to wait until such a play had opened in its 'private' production, and
then to gather detailed evidence about how the club system operated in
practice, in order to be able to challenge in court whether the performance
really had been private. The only effective way to collect evidence would
be to penetrate the membership of the private club by means of a secret
informer. 'Are you going to get one of your friends to join up', enquired
Penn of Johnston. 'Yes', the Assistant Comptroller replied; 'I have asked a
chum who is a resident of Chelsea. He's lunching with me next Monday'.

Following that meeting, Johnston wrote to his new secret agent to
confirm he was 'willing to help us in our plan to have knowledge of the
theatre club activities of the Royal Court Theatre', and that St James's
Palace would pay for his subscription. But the spy had had second thoughts:

> Dear Johnny,
> Thank you so much for my excellent lunch on Monday. It was great fun and
> I enjoyed catching up on all the news.
> I got your letter this evening and have decided I don't wish to proceed
> with the scheme any further. It's so much against my nature . . . and I am not
> sufficiently convinced that I want to be acting in a police role to wish to go
> ahead . . . I will of course remain one hundred percent secure on everything
> you have told me.

Luckily, for the Assistant Comptroller, he was more successful with his
second choice—a bachelor acquaintance who lived in Sloane Avenue and
was willing to carry out 'a small favour of a confidential nature' by taking
out club membership at the Royal Court and passing on useful information. The final piece of the plan was in place.

In early May, George Devine sent Penn the press statement shortly
to be released by the ESC, indicating that because Osborne's play
'cannot be reconciled with the requirements of the Lord Chamberlain', it
would be staged for members only. The statement sought to underplay and
normalise the disagreement:

The English Stage Society is most anxious to make it clear that it is not entering into any controversial action or dispute with the Lord Chamberlain's Office. It is simply exercising its proper function as a private play producing Society of nine years standing to present a play to its members only.

Penn forwarded this to the Director of Public Prosecutions. 'As soon as it does commence we can start to be active', he replied.[11]

The production of *Patriot* opened at the end of June, accompanied by a programme which went to great lengths to insist on the historical and factual basis of the drama and the central character. Not that this would have made any difference to the Lord Chamberlain. At the start of July, Johnston sent the DPP a copy of a press advertisement for the production which suggested that membership was open to anyone, had no process of nomination or seconding, and conferred no rights on the holder beyond being able to buy tickets for private performances. In effect, he suggested, the fee amounted to no more than 'direct payment for admission to the theatre to see a Stage Play'. To point out the contrast, Johnston also attached a joining prospectus for the New Arts Theatre club; this, he thought, demonstrated the 'mere pretence' of the ESC, whose scheme was 'so capable of being widespread and general as to render the Royal Court Theatre a place of public resort'. He also advised the DPP that some of the Lord Chamberlain's staff had become Associate Members of the ESC 'without any enquiry having been made as to their antecedents'; if it could be shown that the Royal Court was not operating properly as a club, then there was a possibility that its transgression could be dealt with without undermining the status of theatre clubs in general.

On 9 July, Cobbold met with Skelhorn and told him the Office was faced by 'something of a dilemma'. He had no doubt that the Royal Court's strategy was 'a subterfuge' and that their presentation of Osborne's play was 'so near to a public performance as to be indistinguishable'. He also knew that if it was not challenged now 'it would be extremely difficult at a later date to object to so-called "club" performances'. On the other hand, he had 'no desire to wage war on theatre clubs' or 'appear to be "taking it out" of the Royal Court out of spite'. Cobbold didn't say so, but it was probably the inevitable publicity and press condemnation which was causing him to hesitate. What he sought, then, was a middle way, somewhere between ignoring and prosecuting:

We had been wondering whether there was any possibility of the Director of Public Prosecutions making enquiries and, if he felt it appropriate, issuing some form of warning which would put people on notice that any further slide away from genuine theatre clubs was risky.

But this was a route Skelhorn was not willing to take; if the law was being broken then 'it would be improper', he said, 'not to take action'. In the light of this response, Cobbold decided to sit on the fence and leave the decision on whether or not to prosecute up to the DPP and the Attorney General: 'If the Director decides to take action it will involve publicity', he noted; 'The Queen should perhaps be aware'.

A few days later, the situation was complicated still further when Lord Goodman, the Chair of the Arts Council, and an opponent of stage censorship, wrote to George Devine to say he was 'perfectly willing to express to Lord Cobbold my opinion of the absurdity of permitting a play, which is represented as not being available to the public, to be seen by a vast horde of people through the contrivance of paying a shilling or two for club membership'. He was equally forthright in expressing his own view that Osborne's play should not be significantly censored: 'I think there are a few lines which could reasonably be excised, but otherwise in these days its exhibition to the public seems to me to be in key with current notions.' Although Goodman was careful to state that he was voicing a personal opinion, his position catapulted the Arts Council into more or less direct conflict with the Lord Chamberlain—a potential danger which St James's Palace had long worried about. With various versions of events appearing in the Press, Skelhorn told Cobbold that the Attorney General and the Law Officers agreed that 'the way in which this play has been presented at the Royal Court Theatre constitutes a "public performance" and that a prosecution under section 15 of the Theatres Act 1843 would stand a good chance of success'. Despite this, he explained, they were now 'strongly of the opinion that it would be inexpedient to institute such a prosecution in connection with the performance of this play', given it had 'attracted a great deal of public interest and a good deal of support'. Evidently, the government had no more desire than Cobbold to face the antagonism and mockery of the press. This must have been a blow to Cobbold, but whatever his real thoughts, he remained diplomatic, and expressed his 'considerable sympathy with the view taken by the Law Officers that in all the circumstances it would be inexpedient to institute a prosecution in this case'. However, he also advised them that he would 'take similar action if there should be a more flagrant case of this nature in the future'. Hill was less sanguine about the decision:

Had the Attorney General said it was politically inexpedient to prosecute there could have been no objection. But
1. He says there is a clear breach of the Law.
2. That because some people like the play and it has been running for a month, there should be no prosecution. This despite the fact that the

play is adjudged by the Lord Chamberlain to be corrupting and unfit for performance.

3. This seems to me to be a quite outspoken statement of lack of faith in the Censor's decisions and is I think the most complete official disapproval of this Office that I have seen.

The Lord Chamberlain had sought the government's backing. In fact, he had been backed further into a corner.

The immediate issue now facing St James's was whether to hold up the white flag and license Osborne's script, or to hold to their judgement: 'It is noteworthy that all of us in this office—all in different spheres of society feel the same about this play' wrote Hill to Penn, 'and that the Police Officer deputed to visit it—himself a theatre goer of experience felt a definite note of corruption underneath the skill of the production and acting'. Lord Goodman wrote to Cobbold to argue the opposite case: 'The author has not exploited the sexual perversion of his principal character, but used it only for the purpose of depicting the dilemma of a homosexual', he insisted; 'I cannot imagine that anyone who sees the play would regard it as presenting homosexuality in an attractive light'. For Goodman, there was an even more important principle to observe; Osborne's play had 'an important topicality at this moment of time when the whole issue of the position of the homosexual in society is under discussion'; it was therefore 'wrong that a play that has a point of view that might influence opinions and viewpoints on the question should not be available for public performance'. Historically, of course, it was precisely the fear that theatre might influence public opinion which had worried Lords Chamberlain.

Goodman also took up another cudgel. Censorship procedure was in theory based on the written text rather than the production. Goodman—inevitably speaking with the weight of the Arts Council behind him—challenged the plausibility of such an approach:

> I remain of the view that you cannot fairly judge this play from the text if the result of reading it alone was to leave you with the conclusion that it is not fit for public presentation. The impression created by reading a play derives from the impact of a personal imagination on a printed text. Even with readers as experienced and cultured as I know you employ, there must be subjective features which make it infinitely preferable to see the play if there is a performance available.

A key justification for the Lord Chamberlain's method had always been that a script, once licensed, could be staged in different ways without the need to resubmit it. Goodman threw doubt onto the relevance of this argument:

I appreciate that there are many productions where the point which you make about a licence operating 'in rem' for all performances is valid: but, in connection with this play, which is a long and historical discursive one, it is, I think, fanciful to suppose that any management is likely to put it on for the purpose of enhancing its pornographic possibilities.

Goodman also queried Cobbold's insistence that each play must be judged in isolation:

I think in assessing questions of this sort, it is proper to take into account the previous record and reputation of the author. Obviously this cannot be conclusive, but with an author like John Osborne, whose works are always serious in purpose and free from any suggestion that they have any obscene or pornographic intention, I should have thought that this factor would weigh heavily in assessing the situation.

Meanwhile, the ESC was still seeking a licence in order to transfer their production and were keen for Cobbold to send someone to inspect it. They were probably unaware that Johnston had already attended secretly—as the guest of a friend—and was still strongly against allowing it. The ESC pointed out that no critics had described the play as 'obscene or corrupting', that they had received no complaints from audiences, and that its public supporters ranged from Lord Goodman to John Betjeman. They were also ready to compromise and negotiate further. Penn resisted the company's 'pestering' of him to go to a performance for as long as he could, but eventually decided he had no choice: 'What is my reason for saying no?' Having watched it, Penn conceded that *Patriot* was 'well written, well acted, cleverly constructed and produced with great skill'. Also, that it was 'a serious play about homosexuality'. However, he still had no doubt it was a 'blatant portrayal of the way of life of homosexuals', in which 'the dialogue, acting and form of production (clothes etc.) have all been devised to give homosexuals pleasure of seeing their way of life depicted on the stage'. For these reasons it was 'not at all to my liking', and his opinion remained unchanged: 'I do not think that the tolerance of homosexuality in this country has yet reached the point where this Play, in its present form, is suitable for public performance.' Heriot backed him up fully:

The very fact that the homosexual scenes, especially the 'drag' ball, are presented in the best terms would certainly attract all the perverts in London and might even persuade the young and ignorant that such a life might not be so bad, after all. It is thus a corrupting play and as such unsuitable for general representation. Think of possible amateur performances in the future!

Hill agreed that 'the homosexual ball will give a homosexual thrill to homosexuals or near homosexuals', and insisted that some of the actions 'appear to indicate an attitude of positive gloating'. He suspected that an ulterior motive was at work:

> One should never forget that according to the BMA report on homosexuality and prostitution, the percentage of homo-sexuals in the theatrical profession is far larger than the national average, and that a universal need of such characters is justification for their habits.[12]

It was 'ludicrous to suggest' that Osborne's play was intended to expose the characters and their way of life to criticism and condemnation. And even if it was well-intentioned, 'to accept that intimate displays of the methods and activities of homosexuals are a necessity for illustrating the pathos of their human situation would be to open up the most unwelcome prospects'.

While the Lord Chamberlain had not come out of the confrontation particularly well, neither had the Theatre. Unable to secure a licence, the production closed without the West End transfer the management had neded to cover their financial investment. Indeed, the ESC and Royal Court claimed to have lost fifteen thousand pounds on the production.

Sex Uncovered

Sex was everywhere in 1965. 'There seems no doubt that authors and managements are investigating how far they can take their audiences in subjects and treatment which have hitherto not been considered suitable for public performance', commented the Reader in his report on *Little Malcolm and his Struggle against the Eunuchs*. David Halliwell's play featured a political party calling themselves the 'Dynamic Erection', and the Reader warned that 'Spoken by scruffy art students the expression is likely to cause considerable ribald laughter'. The party duly became 'Dynamic Insurrection'.[13] In the case of David Mercer's *Ride a Cock Horse*, the very title was 'indelicate' and 'an impropriety'—though the Censors reluctantly acknowledged it was probably uncuttable, 'coming as it does from a nursery rhyme'. However, for all that Mercer's play was 'certainly a serious piece of work', Fletcher, who was now starting to recognise the lie of the land, suggested that the content and the language required considerable intervention: 'It is so obsessively concerned with the sexual relationship, that its effect on its potential audiences must be open to considerable conjecture.' Heriot was more direct: 'This play seems to be written by a man who has just discovered sex', he wrote contemptuously, 'but not the duality of sex'. It certainly couldn't be licensed as submitted: 'we should think of the respectable women in the audience most of whom don't care for menstrual and obstetric references'. To the Assistant Comptroller, it was 'a vile play from which anyone of any sensitivity ought to walk out'; however, given the collapse in public taste there was insufficient reason to ban it entirely: 'The play is not a direct inducement to vice since few will want to emulate any of the characters.' A list of over thirty cuts was sent out and Johnston also wrote to the Chief Constable of Nottinghamshire to ask him to have the play checked when it opened at the Theatre Royal:

> The play is not one that commends itself in any degree to the Lord Chamberlain as will be seen from the long list of deletions which have been required, and the subject holds such possibilities for stage action that it is desired to ensure from the inception both that his Lordship's requirements are being observed, and that the play is being staged in a reasonable manner.[14]

Arguably, one of Cobbold's most significant decisions in 1965 was to approve the script of Frank Marcus's *The Killing of Sister George* without any changes. Fletcher's report of 18 March signalled his doubts at 'the atmosphere of lesbianism which runs right through it', and highlighted two particular scenes 'deriving directly from the masochistic attitude of Alice, the "slave" character of the relationship', in which she eats the butt of the other character's cigar, and drinks her bathwater. Heriot pointed out 'that all the characters are lesbians, living in a private world as well-defined and as populous as, say, the perverts in Osborne's *A Patriot for Me*'. With the Lord Chamberlain's Office under siege, it is not hard to understand Heriot's sense of near paranoia:

> This leads me to suggest, I hope without fantasy, that the present play may well be a trap for the Lord Chamberlain. Three of the four characters in the play are going to a 'drag' ball. It is clear that this occasion is entirely lesbian . . . Now, if the Lord Chamberlain licenses this play, I can easily imagine the cries of righteous indignation in some quarters that a play clearly about lesbians is permitted while a play not entirely about perverts is not.

Yet there were 'almost no individual lines to which exception could be taken' and 'nothing really in the action'. And although the characters are shown cross-dressed for the party, the party itself occurs offstage. 'I am not convinced that a licence should be withheld', wrote Johnston; 'On the other hand it may be dangerous to let through a play with this theme'.[15] Cobbold chose to risk the possible 'indignation' of the Royal Court, and accusations of inconsistency, by licensing it without cuts. What made the case of *The Killing of Sister George* particularly significant was that despite—or because of—its theme, it was immediately staged in the West End, won the London Theatre Critics' award for the best play of 1965, and was recommended by *Plays and Players* for several months as 'the best play in town'.[16]

Of course, it was the form and the discretion of Marcus's play which made it acceptable both to the Lord Chamberlain and to West End mainstream audiences, and Cobbold took a very different view of Charles Dyer's *Staircase*, which focused on the relationship between two elderly homosexual hairdressers living together in the East End of London. Dyer's script was submitted in the autumn of 1965 with an unapologetic letter from the playwright: '*Staircase* is written with honesty and truth upon homosexuality and how it affects the lives of two old men.' Heriot decided—with no real basis—that the characters were 'probably non-practising'; they were rather 'timid, facetious, gentle' and showed 'a real affection for each other'. But he concluded that 'in view of *A Patriot For Me* and the narrow shave of *The Killing of Sister George* I am inclined to suggest that this piece is not recommended for licence'. Johnston was 'in two minds as to what recommendation to make' to the Lord Chamberlain: 'I think it is a poor play (and the author from his letter seems ghastly), but then you are not an arbiter of taste.' He acknowledged that it was 'a serious treatment of homosexuality' within a comic narrative, and leaving aside the fact that 'the two men address each other in terms of affection' there was 'hardly any offensive action' to worry about. The arguments on either side were finely balanced:

> If you grant it a licence, subject to cuts, I feel you will be accused of allowing a homosexual play that is comedy and almost farce whereas you banned *A Patriot* which was serious, historical and depicted the disastrous effect on a man's career as a result of his homosexuality.
>
> On the other hand if you refuse this play a licence, people I am sure will accuse you of being unnecessarily stuffy.

In early October, a list of cuts for *Staircase* was sent out. The most contentious and the most problematic moment was a stage direction: 'Harry cradles Charlie in his lap, stroking his head and rocking him backwards and forwards.' For the time being, the decision was left pending as the planned production was abandoned. But the following year, the RSC took the play up, and negotiated compromises on some of the cuts. Not, however, on this direction, and to secure the licence they had to guarantee that 'there is no action of this nature, here or elsewhere'. Only in 1967 did a 'moving letter from the author' which argued that 'The deletion of this stage direction robs my Play of an important moment of humanity' persuade the Lord Chamberlain to let it through:

Although one of the Characters is suspected of being homosexual, it has no bearing upon this moment of Mercy: one human-being is comforting another at a time of fright and distress . . . During the War, I saw men in moments of fear, hug their comrades and say 'Don't fret. Don't fret'. I did not pause to wonder if such men were homosexual. It had no bearing on the situation. It was a moment of life between people. And in *Staircase*, I have re-created this moment . . .[17]

A Fright at the Opera

Sex reached even the Royal Opera House. In the summer of 1965, the Lord Chamberlain's Office received a surprising request from the Assistant General Administrator there, John Tooley, in relation to a forthcoming production. Schoenberg's *Moses and Aaron* was to receive its premiere, directed by the censors' old adversary Peter Hall, and the planned staging of the finale involved dancing around a Golden Calf in what quickly became known as 'the orgy scene':

> I am writing to ask for your guidance on the problem of nudity on the stage. I appreciate that, as a general rule, nudity is not allowed but there do seem to me to be exceptions, more particularly if the skin is of dark colour. For instance, I believe that when African dancers have appeared here no objection has been raised to them dancing with uncovered tops. If this is the case, would you agree to allow us to use two dancers on the stage with bare tops, but suitably coloured, in our forthcoming production of *Moses and Aaron*.

Regrettably, the precise details of the Office's reply are unknown: 'I telephoned Mr Tooley today and told him what guiding rules we use about nudity, and the particular difference of black breasts and ballet!'[18]

When the script for the opera was submitted, Heriot was dismissive: 'Apart from the gigantic Golden Calf orgy there is little spectacle—which is perhaps why Mr Peter Brooke [sic], the present producer has engaged a whole zoo of camels, horses, sheep and goats.' The Reader also claimed that 'protests from the chorus have been received that they refuse to appear on stage "in two bandages"'; he therefore recommended that before granting a licence, 'some warning should be uttered about the appearance of naked virgins and the mutual strip-tease as the frenzied Israelites disport themselves'. The management of the R.O.H. was duly reminded of the need to wear briefs and brassieres, and that 'the naked youth' must be 'adequately clothed'. Tooley tried again:

> I have been asked by Peter Hall . . . if he could be allowed to have two nude women on the stage for a very brief moment. He has no intention of making their appearance a central feature of this scene, but very much as a throwaway idea They would simulate two dead girls who would be brought on stage in a crowd, which would momentarily part to reveal them and immediately reassemble to hide them again.

Perhaps ill-advisedly, or perhaps deliberately, Tooley added a further detail which was bound to arouse the Censors' interest: 'I think you should also know that in the orgy scene it is proposed that a few men will wear phalluses and that there will be some erotic movement.' But he reassured them that

> The use of phalluses has been suggested by Peter Hall, not again as a central feature of this scene but very much in the way they would have been used in the period in which the action takes place and as being preferable to simulated copulation.

It is hard not to wonder whether the Opera House was hoping for a conflict with the Lord Chamberlain, and the publicity this would generate. 'We are fully aware that we are approaching dangerous ground', wrote Tooley, 'if we are not already there'.

Either way, Hall's idea did not go down well. 'No, no, and no!' wrote someone on the letter—underlining the final 'no' four times; 'This is unheard of—and a bad sign that Mr Hall is making a spectacle of a work he is afraid will otherwise be a failure'. Penn reminded the Opera House of the 'general prohibition of indecencies in dance, dress and gesture on the stage', and informed them that

> In consequence, the Lord Chamberlain wishes me to say that he is not prepared to allow two nude women to be brought onto the stage, nor is he prepared to allow men to wear phalluses, or indulge in erotic movements whether simulative of copulation or otherwise.[19]

Meanwhile, reports appeared in the press claiming that the company had recruited a group of extra dancers—'some sexy bombshells' who more usually plied their trade in the clubs of Soho—to take on the roles of extra virgins.[20]

Johnston attended the official opening of Schoenberg's opera to check if the requirements had been observed. But probably the last thing the Office wanted was to find itself embroiled in battles with the Royal Opera House as well as with the Royal Shakespeare Company and the Royal Court, and the Assistant Comptroller was keen to find reasons not to intervene over an opera which he thought was 'brilliantly staged and very spectacular'. Anyway, there was 'so much individual action by such a large cast that it was difficult to see everything', and although there was 'a general effect of some nudity', he thought that 'on the whole it was discreetly done'. Johnston couldn't help noticing 'a few bare bosoms', but he was gratified that 'none were "flapping"'. As for the male organs, 'No phalluses were worn, but some men did carry one above their heads and wave about some long coloured objects'. At one point, he noted, 'There were a number of writhing couples embracing amorously who, as the scene unfolded, became semi-nude', and who remained on stage 'sprawled about in abandoned positions'. Fortunately, although 'Peter Hall went as far as he could go to depict depravity', the audience was not 'shocked to the extent that they minded'. As further evidence, Johnston pointed to the *Daily Mail* review (headline—'An Orgy But NOT Erotic') which confirmed that the production's 'sexual excess' and 'simulated copulation' were made 'as realistic as public decency permits', but could be excused because they were 'a demonstration of the depravity to which men and women can surrender when they exchange God for gods of their own making'.[21] Johnston's summing up for *Moses and Aaron* was therefore that 'By and large it was alright, but only just!' The Assistant Comptroller also did his best to put down a marker to head off any future attempts to cite Schoenberg's opera as a precedent: 'The orgy scene, played as it was, would not in my opinion be permissible in a stage play, but does not seem out of place in an operatic setting of this sort.'[22]

Meeting the Press

In the spring of 1965, Cobbold took an unprecedented step. Under sustained attack from the Royal Court and from much of the press, and in an attempt to break the pattern, he agreed to give a personal interview to the *Sunday Times*. In March, the newspaper's editor wrote to Cobbold:

> The idea that we should carry a tape-recorded interview with you, on the subject of censorship, still seems to me an excellent one. As you say, it is desirable that it should take place, and appear, when there is no immediate controversy taking place—that is, as soon as possible.

He proposed the veteran theatre reviewer J.W. Lambert as the person best suited to conduct the interview, and sought to reassure Cobbold over any doubts he might have:

> Although he will I hope put some pointed questions to you, as well as those enabling you to say what you have in mind, it is no part of our intention to

set out to pillory your office. We could let you see most of the questions in advance.[23]

The interview took place almost immediately, and was published on 11 April. Generally speaking, it was respectful and decorous, allowing Cobbold to present his approach as moderate and balanced. Indeed, some questions might almost have been written so as to allow him to argue his case effectively.

> Q: I believe that once a play has been licensed . . . it is available for production anywhere. This could open up alarming possibilities, which I suppose you have to bear in mind?
> A: Yes, indeed, very much so . . . we are dealing with highly reputable managements, highly competent producers, who come to us and say, quite properly and quite accurately, that they can put on a certain scene without giving the slightest offence to anybody. I accept that as absolutely true; but the same scene as produced by a less competent management with a quite different production might result in something very undesirable indeed . . .

Other questions did the work for him:

> Q: In the case of sex, I suppose as far as subject matter is concerned you wouldn't necessarily bar anything so long as it was acceptably handled at its own level? A serious play, or a farce, about an illegitimate child might be inoffensive, for example, and so might a serious play about venereal disease, but hardly a farce about venereal disease?
> A: I think that's about right.

The interview mostly kept away from specifics, and, with the exception of *The Representative*—'the single play that has given me the most preoccupation'—made no mention of individual texts. Where contentious issues were touched on, the follow-up question was generally not asked:

> Q: Would your Office take a different view of physical contact between homosexuals and physical contact between a man and a woman?
> A: To some extent a different view.

Cobbold freely admitted that 'If one were starting from scratch in 1965 I don't think one would invent this particular set-up', and that 'the whole question of censorship has entered a new phase with the growth of drama on radio and television'. However, he was at pains to project an image of untroubled confidence in the continuing practicality and effectiveness of the system:

It might well be that in due course it would be a good thing to have a comprehensive look at censorship in all these media. But I feel myself that that
might perhaps be more productive in a few years' time, when there has been
longer experience on the television side.

He was also careful to keep hidden any sense of conflict:

Most of the managements have been in touch with the people in my office
for years and are on very good terms with them. They write in, and they
come in, and explain and ask for reconsideration; and of course one is always
ready to look at any arguments that are put up . . . So there's a good deal of
give and take on this. And very often we arrive at an arrangement which is
perfectly proper and suits everyone concerned.

He made it sound rather like good, friendly sport—or a gentleman's club:

There is a bit of gamesmanship in all this. Some managements, not all, put
in a number of four-letter words and other things that they know perfectly
well will be cut out, possibly in the hope that we will cut them out and leave
one or two border-line things in.[24]

The Home Secretary responded approvingly. 'I found it most interesting reading', wrote Soskice, 'and, if I may say so, thought you put
forward your views, with which as you know I am in full agreement, very
clearly indeed'. Cobbold also received a letter of support from Geoffrey
Dearmer:

I was an examiner of plays from 1936–1958, and I venture to write to say
how very much I appreciated your interview in a recent Sunday newspaper.
    This is surely the first time in history that the Lord Chamberlain has
come out of his shell and defended the Censorship. My senior colleague at
the time, until his retirement, Henry Game, wrote to me a week or so ago to
say how well you had done it. I most heartily agree, and the fact that it was
done at all is what matters.[25]

For an institution with the roots and traditions of the Lord Chamberlain's
Office, to give an official newspaper interview had indeed been a
revolutionary departure—though it was doubtful whether such a bland
and affable discussion would weigh much against the negative publicity
and coverage the Office continued to receive. But potentially, a precedent
had been established—though it was not going to be open house. In June,
the Office refused a request from *Newsweek*, and in September it turned
down a television interview for a late night arts broadcast: 'Too small a

programme . . . nothing much to be gained.' It would be 'a different matter' if the request had come from 'something big like *Panorama*'.[26]

Saved

The play most often credited with precipitating the end of the Lord Chamberlain's reign as Censor is Edward Bond's *Saved*, submitted by the Royal Court in the summer of 1965 while the arguments over Osborne's *A Patriot for Me* were still at their height. Heriot was utterly contemptuous:

> A revolting amateur play by one of those dramatists who write as it comes to them out of a heightened image of their experience. It is about a bunch of brainless, ape-like yobs with so little individuality that it is difficult to distinguish between them . . .
>
> The writing is vile and the language and conception worse. Whether this could ever be considered a work of art is a matter of opinion; but it does seem that the taste of Messrs Devine and Richardson has gone rancid—though with all the public money at their disposal, I don't suppose anybody cares.

As for characters, Pam was 'a brainless slut' with 'sluttish parents', Len had a 'moronic intellect', and all the rest were 'moral imbeciles'. The Reader was also dismissive of Bond's ability to construct characters: 'They . . . behave in an unreal way, not because what they do is false but that their motivation is not sufficiently indicated.' Heriot was fully aware of the need to avoid absolute bans where possible, and, in spite of his loathing for the play, his initial report proposed that a licence could in principle be issued; however, this was to be dependent on the theatre agreeing to make more than fifty changes, including the 'gratuitously salacious' three-page section in which Len repairs Mary's stocking while she is wearing it, and the whole of the nine-page scene in which a baby is stoned to death in its pram.[27]

Bill Gaskill, the Court's director, had 'some doubts about the extremes of violence' himself, but he was committed to staging Bond's play. Even before submitting it to the Lord Chamberlain, he sought advice from his predecessor, George Devine, who carried the scars from years of battles with St James's, and had a pretty clear sense of how the Office was likely to play it, and the games of 'give and take' the Court would need to indulge in. The violence, he realised, would 'automatically disturb the reader', and Devine annotated the script, marking everything he judged 'likely to meet with objections', and recommending they should 'cut all the words we *know* will not be passed' before sending it in; 'a few less bloodies would help', wrote Devine, and Bond should be ready to 'swallow pride and reinvent'. In the case of the baby scene, he predicted it was 'the scatological bits' which would cause the problems; 'Worse kinds of violence' might be approved, 'but references to shit and piss will never pass'. As for the scene with the stocking, they might 'get away with . . . it' by trusting the actors and making the actual text less explicit: 'Often things are *said*, which don't always need to be *said*', he observed, shrewdly, of Bond's text.[28] Devine's recommendations were premised on the assumption that the main priority was 'to get the play on with a licence'. This may not necessarily have been the case. 'The shorter the list of dubious passages and *obvious* disallowances . . . the better chances you have', wrote Devine, but his advice was effectively ignored and at the end of June an unaltered text was submitted to St James's.

Following Heriot's initial response, Bond's script was passed around— and beyond—the Office, eventually reaching Tim Nugent, the former Comptroller. 'I have read this revolting play which certainly ought not to be shown on any stage', wrote Nugent to Penn; 'the scene of the killing of the baby is the most revolting I have ever read'. He had little doubt this was 'filth for filth's sake'. Yet he agreed with Heriot's judgement:

> I would therefore recommend banning it except for one consideration and that is this: I believe the Lord Chamberlain when he bans a play in its entirety normally does so because the 'theme' of the play offends . . . In this play the 'theme' . . . of hopelessness fecklessness and the complete amorality which springs from them has been done before e.g. *The Entertainer* and others of Osborne's plays. It is mostly the <u>examples</u> of hopelessness etc. which are so disgusting.

The best strategy, he suggested, would be to offer a licence 'with the many and absolutely necessary cuts that Charles Heriot suggests', and which were 'tantamount to banning the play' from public performance, without doing so explicitly. 'Devine will merely put it on when the Court is a Theatre Club whether it is banned or not and I cannot conceive how he can put it on commercially with the cuts that the Lord Chamberlain will insist upon.' In strategic terms, the Royal Court would have been outflanked:

> Another point occurs to me which you may think too fanciful. If the play is banned could not Devine tone it down considerably and then put it on at his Theatre Club as an example of the Lord Chamberlain's prudishness. Whereas if the play is not banned but merely cut to ribbons he couldn't bring off this childish score off the Lord Chamberlain.

Penn agreed that banning the play outright 'may give Devine the greater advantage'.[29]

At the end of July a list of forty specific cuts, along with the 'baby' scene and the 'stocking mending' scene, was sent to the theatre. A few days later, William Gaskill and his Associate Director, Iain Cuthbertson, came to St James's to talk with Johnston. They had asked Bond not to attend, on the grounds that he 'might have been angered or provoked and this might have increased the Assistant Comptroller's intransigence'—though Bond himself later claimed he was more inclined to laugh at the antics of the Lord Chamberlain's Office:

> I could not have been angry. The Assistant Comptroller's office is in a corner of St James's Palace. Outside a busby sentry marches by the window. The Assistant Comptroller is by profession and appearance a guards colonel. He thinks *sod* corrupts . . . So it would have appealed to my sense of the comic to sit before him and swap unacceptable buggers for acceptable bastards. I would have kept as calm as he did.[30]

Supposedly, Bond had actually prepared 'the customary list of alternatives' for most of the disallowed words and passages; however to cut 'the two most essential scenes', or to see them 'emasculated beyond theatrical viability', was a different matter. According to the Assistant Comptroller's minutes, it was on these that the meeting concentrated:

> They have yet to talk to the author about the baby scene, and they wanted to know how much of this scene would have to be changed for it to be acceptable. Without committing you precisely, I explained it was impossible to give an opinion on something that was not yet in existence, but I said it was unlikely that you would agree to the death of the baby on stage <u>by any means</u> or any violent action leading up to the death, other than perhaps the pram being pushed about between them . . .
>
>   They think they will have difficulty getting the author to modify the baby scene . . . they consider the baby's death essential to the plot, so I suggested this could be done off stage.
>
>   We shall hear more from them when they have seen the author. If an impasse is reached, they will put this on as a club performance.[31]

Johnston had suggested requiring that the murder of the baby was unseen by the audience, but 'described by an eye witness after it had happened'. It was a plausible idea, but such a shift would have destroyed Bond's stated intentions:

> Clearly, violence and sex are critical problems for some people. They cause a lot of suffering, and because of this a dramatist has a moral duty to deal with them and a moral duty to deal with them as effectively as he can. In the

theatre this means that violence and sex must be *represented* in some way. It is a technical necessity. It is not sufficient to talk about the subject . . . because this is ineffective on the stage. It is bad theatre. It obscures and diminishes the problem.[32]

Gaskill and Cuthbertson had asked Johnston during their meeting at St James's Palace whether the Office had given thought to banning the play outright. 'I replied that you had considered doing so, but as a result of considering various opinions you had decided against this', wrote the Assistant Comptroller. Bond would subsequently also express surprise that *Saved* had not simply been rejected *in toto*, identifying two probable motives. First, he suspected that the censors 'probably did not want to appear to be interfering too much in the English Stage Company's work', given some of the recent clashes; but he also read it as a telling indication of their growing ineffectiveness:

> Probably they believe themselves to be no longer just in a weak position logically, culturally and morally—that, after all, need not have immediate practical consequences—but now also in a weak position politically. If the Labour government majority were larger, theatre censorship would probably be stopped. For this reason they probably want to be as quiet and accommodating as their provoking job will let them be.

In some respects, mockery—even sympathy—was now more appropriate than bitterness and resentment: 'being banned has not angered me at all', claimed Bond; on the other hand, he knew that the shadow cast by St James's Palace was a long one, preventing dramatists from dealing effectively or directly with issues of sex and violence.

> It follows that either the dramatist must use trivial subjects, or at least not two of the most important contemporary subjects; or, if he deals with them, that he must deal with them in a technically incompetent, and consequently (in view of their importance) dishonest way. In effect, you cannot have an honest and culturally virile theatre as long as you have a censor.

Ultimately, theatre censorship was

> not concerned with individual acts of corruption or shock, but with something more amorphous: keeping up the moral tone, keeping the party clean, not in front of the servants, what the eye doesn't see, setting a good example. Perhaps the censors think the theatre should put up a good front for the foreigners. But it is too late for that.

Moreover, he said, their decisions were 'dictated by the lowest standards in society', which presumed everyone was motivated by greed and self-interest:

> No doubt some people would exploit sex and violence if they could, but certainly The English Stage Company, The National Theatre and The Royal Shakespeare Company would not. Yet censorship must act as if they would, and consequently it is as dangerously retarding to society as it is unjust to writers.

Bond argued that because of censorship, British theatre had become 'a second-rate art'. His powerful onslaught concluded with echoes and restatements of many of the arguments hurled by opponents and victims of theatre censorship over the last sixty years:

> The damage done by censorship isn't limited to banning words, sentences, scenes or even occasionally plays. It does other, less publicised damage. It is a shadow that falls across the whole business of writing a play. While he writes, the dramatist must always wonder whether the censors will pass what he is writing, whether he is free to say what he is saying. They are arbitrary (they will allow something in one play and ban it in another) and unreasonable (no reasonable person would ban *sod*) so that the dramatist must always guess . . . This does not trouble the second-rate dramatist—but if a dramatist starts to probe and analyse it becomes an insidious influence and he finds himself writing not for the truth, not even for his audience, but for the censor. That is why even our best plays are disappointing. They are disfigured by the censor even before they are submitted to him. They wilt in the bad climate.

He concluded: 'We get the plays the censors will allow us to have.'[33]

Compromise over *Saved* was unlikely, and in September the Royal Court duly announced that the theatre would be turned into a club in order to present the original uncut version to members only. Johnston informed the Director of Public Prosecutions, but Skelhorn was reluctant to become involved. In fact, he proved hard to contact, having more important things even than stage censorship to deal with: 'As he is generally prosecuting for rape or murder he is sometimes difficult to get.' Hill thought the decision not to take legal action over *A Patriot for Me* had only made things harder now:

> I think it is useless to do anything unless the Director is prepared to take action either by warning the Company that their present procedure is, in our opinion, illegal; or by staging a prosecution.

If a prosecution is decided upon then we gather evidence.

If a warning is decided upon, then we make use of the facts gathered for *A Patriot*.

Or we do nothing as in the case of *A Patriot* and accept one more hole in the Theatres Act.[34]

Cobbold wrote to the DPP. Although his mask of diplomatic politeness did not completely slip, his frustration at what he saw as the lack of support over *Patriot* was apparent, and he made it clear that this time he expected something different. The important thing was to get in early, rather than wait until it became 'inexpedient' to intervene because of the level of critical and public support a play might generate: 'At the risk of impertinence I still wonder whether some form of investigation and warning might not serve to mark the point of principle and hold the line', wrote Cobbold. And he dropped another strong hint that, unless he received stronger backing, then his own position would quickly become untenable—and that the government would have to deal with the consequences:

What does concern me is that if the move away from genuine theatre clubs to disguised public performance is allowed to go unchallenged, it is bound to spread and, as I see it, to bring the Law into disrepute. I think that any Lord Chamberlain would find difficulties in attempting to administer the present Theatres Act indefinitely if it became clear that it could be flouted with impunity.

But Skelhorn still insisted there was nothing he could do until after the play had been presented, and advised that the Lord Chamberlain should make sure someone from the Office went 'to witness a performance at the first opportunity' so they could begin to gather the details and proof they would need in court.

Other evidence which I would have to consider and which you no doubt will be able to provide will be the terms upon which admission is obtained, to what extent the Society might be considered to be a bona fide theatre club, their advertising or other invitations to membership.

Six days later, the DPP's Office informed Cobbold that they were consulting with the Attorney-General. But once again, Cobbold's own preferred option had been rebuffed:

I have again considered your suggestion whether some form of warning might be suitably given. I feel, however, that it is undesirable to do this where those responsible are plainly contending that the production of the play in the way which they are proposing does not constitute any offence under the Act. The response to such a warning would I feel inevitably be a reply that they do not agree that they are committing any offence and in effect to challenge us to prosecute. Unless, therefore, we follow it up with a prosecution the warning would only serve to indicate a weakness and uncertainty on our part as to the legal position.

Meanwhile, the ever-vigilant Ronald Hill had noticed that the production of *Saved* was being promoted in the current issue of the *London Theatre Guide* without any indication that admission would be restricted to members of the Royal Court Theatre Club. He passed the advertisement on to the DPP, who suggested they should see if tickets were indeed available to buy through an agency. But then Hill spotted another advertisement which threatened to blow the grounds for prosecution out of the water. On 17 October 1965, an advertisement appeared in the *Sunday Times* for Paul Raymond's Revuebar. Alongside a picture of a bunny girl, ran the following copy:

> 'HEY! I'VE GOT A PROPOSITION FOR YOU'
> I'm Bunny Susan from the Raymond Revuebar. And I have fixed a special deal with Paul Raymond which means you can become a member for LIFE for only £2. And even more! You get a free ticket to see the Strip-Tease Spectacular in the club's own theatre.[35]

Evidently, all you had to do to become a life member was to sign a coupon printed under the advertisement and post it back personally to Bunny Susan with the requisite cash. Hill quickly realised that if this was occurring at Raymond's Revuebar—and its performances accepted as legitimately 'private'—it would be impossible for a court of law to decide that the Club performances at the Royal Court were any different. Hill forwarded Bunny Susan's offer to Johnston: 'I feel that any case brought against the Royal Court might be much weakened were Counsel to point to the fact that the GLC were apparently unconcerned at the activities of the Raymond Revuebar', he wrote. The only hope was that Bunny Susan and her boss were themselves likely to be called to account; sadly, 'an enquiry on my part at a low level of the GLC gave the impression that no action was contemplated by them'.[36]

Saved was due to open on 3 November. On 2 November, Hill wrote a confidential note to one of his spies inside the Royal Court:

> This is the play that I would very much like you to see . . . If you would be kind enough to let us have your views as to the suitability or otherwise of this play being performed before the public, I should be most grateful. What

you have to tell us will be treated in strict confidence and will not be referred to outside here. I know also that you in your turn will keep this matter to yourself.

I will also see that you are refunded for the cost of two tickets.

Hill himself secretly took out membership of the English Stage Society, disguising himself under the address of his rowing club since he feared that his work and home address were 'equally well known'.[37] He attended the performance, and his lengthy and detailed report included information about gaining entrance as well as about the production.

At the box office I asked for a stall and was asked if I was a member, I said 'yes' and was asked if I had a ticket. I again said 'yes' and produced my wallet and started to produce the ticket at which the box office lady did not look, so I did not complete the manoeuvre. The box office lady said 'I'm sorry to have to ask you'.

In contradiction of the regulations governing private clubs, the Lord Chamberlain's secretary had also been allowed to buy a glass of light ale at the bar without proving his membership.

Hill's account of the evening paid attention, too, to the audience: 'The auditorium was two thirds full and . . . well dressed and affluent: far removed from the characters on the stage', he testified. As for the performance, the stoning scene was 'almost the ultimate in degradation', and 'quite horrible, even when so badly played that one could not really believe there was a live baby in the perambulator'. He accepted that 'At the Royal Court it is unlikely that anyone got more than a sadistic thrill from the scene'. But that was no reason to justify public performances:

acted vividly by well cast characters, with all the appropriate props and business and before a different type of audience, which included a proportion of the gangs that now exist, could be a direct incentive to some of the sub-humans who now associate in gangs, to perpetrate a crime of this kind.

On 8 November, the DPP thanked Johnston for the information about Bunny Susan, and informed the Lord Chamberlain that no decision had been made about a possible prosecution of the Royal Court. He also reminded him that there was 'no action that can be taken without our obtaining the requisite evidence to establish a contravention of the Act', though he mentioned that a disguised police officer had been allowed in without becoming a member. Two weeks later, Cobbold and Johnston attended a critical meeting at the Home Office at which it became evident how seriously the situation was being taken:

The Home Secretary described why the decision which now faced the Law Officers as to whether a prosecution should be brought against the Royal Court Management in connection with *Saved* had caused Ministers to consider the form of censorship itself.

This was what Cobbold—and Scarbrough before him—had long been waiting for, and he now presented the Government with an ultimatum:

> Should the Law Officers decide—as they had earlier that year—that though the play broke the law it was not in the public interest to prosecute, then he could not say too strongly that he would feel it his duty somehow to represent to Parliament that it was impossible for him to carry out his duties as theatre censor under the Theatres Act, 1843.

The Home Secretary duly confirmed that he was considering setting up an official enquiry into the future of theatre censorship, and Cobbold greeted the proposal enthusiastically. In his view, he said, the Theatres Act was out of date, and he requested that if and when such an enquiry was publicly announced it should be 'made clear how much he welcomed [it] and that the decision to set one up had been made with his full and unreserved agreement'. He also insisted that it 'should be handled in such a way that The Crown should not in any way whatsoever be thought to be implicated'.[38] These points were all accepted. However, there was less agreement when the Lord Chamberlain expressed his conviction that any enquiry should not concentrate on theatre alone, but also explore the censorship of film and television.

Two weeks later, Cobbold was informed that the Attorney General had decided to go ahead with proceedings against the ESC for contravention of the Theatres Act, and at the start of 1966 summonses were issued against Gaskill, as artistic director, and also the licensee of the theatre and the company secretary for presenting an unlicensed play. The defendants were advised by their counsel, John Gower, to plead 'not guilty', and to gather witnesses 'with as much standing in the community as possible' to defend the significance of the play and the Court.[39] The first hearing at Marlborough Street Court took place on 14 February, when 'theatre people crowded the court'; the case was adjourned until 3 March, with the hearing completed and judgement given at the start of April. In addition to Hill, two police officers (a Detective Sergeant from the Flying Squad and a Chief Inspector who had seen *Saved* five times) all gave evidence that they had been able to obtain tickets, buy drinks, and even return to the theatre for the second half of the performance after going to a pub during the interval, all without having to prove that they were members. The defence counsel did his best with Hill over his testimony that the box office had not asked to see his membership card:

'I do not want to be insulting but you were not generally accustomed to having people treat you as a liar.'

He replied: 'No sir.'

Mr Gower said: 'It was therefore not much of a surprise to you that the lady took your word for it.'

Gower also sought to establish the merits and cultural importance of the Royal Court and the English Stage Company, with Sir Laurence Olivier—whose letter championing Bond's play had already been published in the press—famously among those appearing as witnesses to insist that the ESC had for the last decade 'without any question in the minds of anyone in my profession, been of the most extraordinarily vital value' as 'a work-shop for the dramatist'.[40]

Everyone—including the magistrate—was well aware that historically, theatre clubs had not been prosecuted or faced such a rigorous checking procedure. But the Lord Chamberlain and the DPP also knew that the government's Law Officers had previously advised (although few other people were aware of this) that there were no legal grounds for making a distinction between public and private theatres; in other words, that it was only a convention and tradition—with no legal basis—that greater freedoms should be allowed to club performances. And yet, most of the debate in court centred on whether or not the Royal Court and the ESC had properly observed the legislation so as to guarantee that the performances of *Saved* had genuinely been available only to private members of a proper theatre club. Both the prosecution and the defence agreed that there could be no offence if the proper conditions had been met. The prosecution's case was therefore based on the claim 'that the society was not a *bona fide* theatre club'.[41]

It seems somehow appropriate that the court case against the ESC was concluded—and judgement handed down—on 1 April. By coincidence, this was also the day after Harold Wilson's government had won its second general election and been returned with a vastly increased majority for a further term of office. The authority this gave the Labour Party made it highly likely that more social reforms—including legislation on censorship—would be introduced and enacted in the near future. For the moment, however, the magistrate, Leo Gradwell, found that the law had indeed been broken with the performances of *Saved*. The Lord Chamberlain had won, and the ESC and the Royal Court had lost. As Hill explained later:

Our case was based upon the fact that the alleged private theatre club, the English Stage Society, was little more than a façade. During the course of the case it was proven that the Society relied almost entirely upon the officials and staff of the English Theatre Company, that the committee of the Society was self-elected and self-perpetuating; that the finances of the Society, although kept in separate accounts were in fact operated as an extension of the Theatre Company finances. It was shown that copies of the rules were never sent to members, that there was no system of election or discrimination of choice of members, that there was nothing in common between members except the wish to see plays and no system of proposing and seconding.

However, the sentences were relatively slight. The ESC was fined just 50 guineas in costs, and the three individual defendants discharged for a year. This was not the victory St James's had wanted. The magistrate even accepted not only 'that everybody connected with the stage society was "perfectly splendid"', but, more pertinently, 'that the society was as careful as they could reasonably be expected to be'. But potentially most crucial in terms of its implications was Gradwell's conclusion that the 1843 Theatres Act provided for no distinction to be made between public and private performances. 'In his opinion everybody who showed for hire a play that had not passed the censor was liable under the Act.'[42] It was a decision which chimed with previous recommendations by the Law Officers, and although Cobbold thought it would 'probably achieve the result of discouraging similar activities in the future', by effectively removing the safety valve of 'private' performances it also ensured that the pressure on the Censorship would only increase. The Lord Chamberlain's hopes were now tied to the proposed Joint Select Committee of Enquiry As he told the DPP, after the case of *Saved* was over: 'I am hopeful that something may emerge which will ease the difficulties.'[43]

CHAPTER SIX

Going Wild (1965–1966)

I should very much like to come and have a gossip about it with you as soon as you are settled in.

(Letter from Lord Cobbold to Roy Jenkins, the new Home Secretary).[1]

Bible Stories

'We have only one blanket prohibition today, and that is a refusal to allow the impersonation of Christ or the deity on the stage', wrote Hill in the autumn of 1965. As he acknowledged, this prohibition was hard to justify 'since it affects all plays reverent or irreverent', and seemed ridiculous when 'the Lord Chamberlain does not use powers he possesses to forbid the acting of miracle, mystery and morality plays written before 1843'. However, responding to an embarrassing public controversy over the refusal to license a 'pro-Christian' play by a first-year Oxford undergraduate, he did his best:

> Christ is a supernatural being and any impersonation by a human person must be inadequate in greater or lesser degree . . .
>
> The personal human characteristics attributed to Christ will vary with the beliefs of the author; they will not necessarily be in accord with the Scriptures . . .
>
> They must greatly disturb beliefs, and may not in principle benefit the cause of religion . . .
>
> Where the plays are a source of profit, there is the likelihood of other than religious motives being involved, and a greater possibility of distortion to meet 'popular' requirements. The Christian Religion is after all supposed to be a truth established on revealed facts, and not a subject for fiction . . .
>
> In the Commercial Theatre it is quite possible for actors of blemished life to be caste [sic] for the role of Christ, again to the distress of the religious (one actor in the past for instance was prosecuted for living on the immoral earnings of a woman).[2]

But in *The Times*, Professor Neville Coghill declared it 'a preposterous nonsensical idea to prevent Jesus appearing on the stage, seeing that this was one of the great experiences of the Middle Ages all over Europe'.[3]

A couple of months earlier, the Office had clashed with a Presbyterian minister seeking to connect Christianity with a younger audience by transposing the New Testament story to a contemporary setting. Heriot described *A Man Dies* as

> a vulgar gimmicky attempt to present the life of Christ in modern teenage terms. The characters wear modern dress; Christ jives with His disciples; Pharaoh is interviewed by reporters, the innocents are machine-gunned with slides of Sharpeville shown . . . The Romans are Hitler and his minions (on accompanying slides); the crucifixion is accompanied by a slide of the hydrogen bomb; Peter smokes a cigarette when denying his Lord; Stephen is beaten up by leather-jacketed yobs and the Lord's Prayer is re-written for the kind of audience expected.[4]

This play had already been staged in a church—where it required no licence because it was considered as an act of worship rather than a stage play presented for hire—and extracts had been shown on (commercial) television; but Cobbold was advised there was no precedent for issuing a licence for such a play. Ewan Hooper, one of its two co-authors, pointed out that it had already been presented by church organisations all over the world. It was understandable, he agreed, that putting Christ on stage would 'cause his Lordship to hesitate', but he offered an ingenious—not to say Brechtian—perspective:

> At the first performance of this play we felt a similar concern and wrote a programme note pointing out that the actors were not in any sense 'being' Christ or his disciples, they were 'standing where the historical characters stood' and showing us their actions, no more.

Cobbold enlisted the support of the Archbishop of Canterbury. 'Although I recognise that the intention of the authors is good and that the play is not written in any irreverent spirit, I believe it is right to maintain the practice of not allowing the portrayal of Christ', he wrote. 'I should feel fortified in this view if I knew that it had your blessing.' The Archbishop endorsed his position, and the licence was refused. However, when the play was shown on television for a second time—as one of the best religious television programmes of the last year—the Lord Chamberlain received another set of unwelcome headlines: 'On Your Screen: The Play the Chamberlain Banned' shouted the *Daily Sketch*.[5] The *Daily Express* highlighted the absurdity that this 'rock and roll passion play' could be broadcast on television, but 'cannot be seen by a few thousand theatre-goers', and urged the Prime Minister to act: 'In the past Mr Wilson has expressed doubts about the system of stage censorship. He should not stop at words. He should introduce a measure that will remove for all time the Lord Chamberlain's dead hand from the theatre.'[6] Indeed, there were so many protests that the Home Secretary asked Cobbold for an explanation. Hill did his best to argue that television was 'a more remote and ethereal medium than the living stage', so that 'impersonations of the Deity will be generally acceptable'. He also explained that some people would be offended by an actor making money out of impersonating Christ on the commercial stage, and pointed out that performances in a consecrated building were exempt from censorship; 'The fact that the subject is thus made financially unattractive ensures that it is reserved to those whose motives are completely altruistic'.[7] But he probably knew the argument was tenuous, and with religious issues starting to dominate the censorship agenda, Cobbold needed a way out. In May 1966, following discussions with the Archbishop of Canterbury, and with at least the tacit support of many other church leaders, it was announced that the automatic ban on the portrayal of Christ was to be rescinded. 'Regard will still be paid to the advice of the joint parliamentary commission of 1909 that stage plays should not do violence to the sentiment of religious reverence', promised the Lord Chamberlain. But another plank had gone.[8]

No Facts Please, We're British

In the autumn of 1965 the RSC submitted sections of a script dramatising the 1926 General Strike, written and compiled by Clive Barker and David Wright, and 'served up', as Heriot put it, 'with all the Brechtian trimmings possible'. The performance was to incorporate 'slides, film, popular ballads, sub-titles—placards, addresses to the audience, commentators, and long chunks of "interpreted" speeches duller than Hansard'. Heriot disliked it intensely:

> Whatever else it is, the General Strike is an absorbing piece of social history. The authors of this interminable documentary have made it insufferably dull, with a highly coloured Boss versus Worker slant, like a cartoon in the Daily Worker.

Inevitably, it also raised a number of political and biographical questions. In one scene, 'the police baton <u>all</u> the strikers to the ground'—and Heriot objected: 'Even though this is probably a stylised mime, I think it is false to represent the police yet again as totally brutal.' Then there was the question of whether to allow negative representations of real people. 'I suppose

every man's political actions look quite different to his friends and opponents', wrote Hill, philosophically. He thought that the dead were probably
fair game, but for the living it was a different matter: 'As Lord Reith and
Lord Citrine are still alive I should insist on their permission before allowing their impersonation.' The script also made use of 'the disembodied
voice of George V accompanied by a slide or film'; and it ended with what
Heriot termed 'a frivolous comment from George V'; namely, 'That was a
rotten way to run a revolution. I could have done it better myself'. Clearly,
the authors were making an ironic observation that it is those who already
have power who understand how to take it: 'Everyone knows the first thing
to do is to shoot the bobbies.' Hill had no doubt this was unacceptable, as
'an attempt to involve the Sovereign in politics'. Anyway, 'We do not allow
the Sovereign to be represented until the immediate family at any rate are
dead'.

Johnston and Hill interviewed the RSC's Literary Manager, Jeremy
Brooks.

> They are very anxious to retain the two small scenes . . . He asserts that the
> words spoken by the disembodied voice are actually words used by the King,
> and I have asked him to produce documentary evidence. However strong his
> arguments appear to be, I gave him no indication that you would allow the
> portrayal of so recent a Sovereign.

The company also promised that 'the batoning of the crowd by the police
will be carried out entirely as a stylised movement', but the Office was not
prepared to back down over the issue of the King:

> The Lord Chamberlain has carefully considered your request to retain the
> photographic images and the speeches of King George V and he appreciates
> that you have gone to great trouble to ensure that the words spoken by the
> 'disembodied voice' are words actually used by the King, but he is of the
> opinion that he cannot allow the portrayal in any form of so recent a Sover-
> eign.[9]

In the event, the RSC abandoned its planned production for other reasons,
and the project does not appear to have been ever revived.

Strike was not the only documentary script submitted by the RSC
in 1965. The previous November, they had sounded Hill out about a
dramatisation of the American judicial trial of the senior nuclear physicist
Robert Oppenheimer, known by some as the father of the nuclear bomb.
Oppenheimer had subsequently been accused of having Communist
affiliations and, humiliatingly, had had his security clearance revoked. The
RSC promised that 'nothing essential' had been added or omitted, and

that 'every effort has been made to give a faithful interpretation of what happened without altered emphasis'. But there were two areas of principle for the Censorship. The first was the 'impersonation' of living people: 'The play could certainly not be allowed without a legal check that no libellous statements were involved', wrote Hill; 'We should be breaking a strict rule that living persons are not represented on the stage, and the ramifications of that decision would be many and difficult'. However, 'much more important' was the fact that permitting 'a dramatic representation of an actual trial of recent date' would establish a precedent. 'Many would obviously jump at an opening', worried the Office, and all sorts of cases would surely follow: 'Ludovic Kennedy with all the latest murder trials, Lord Willis with Profumo-Ward-Keeler and so on.'

In June 1965, the RSC formally submitted Heiner Kipphardt's *In the Matter of J. Robert Oppenheimer*, with an accompanying letter:

> We realize the difficulties the play may raise in its depiction of living characters, both for us in terms of presentation, and for your office. What we would like to emphasize is the completely DOCUMENTARY nature of the script. It is our intention that no word of dialogue should be included in the production which was not actually spoken by the individuals concerned at the Atomic Energy Commission Security Board held in April, 1954. To this end, we are at present checking the script minutely against the official transcript of those proceedings, and if we discover any inaccuracies or re-wordings, we will be deleting them from the script.

They pointed out that the play had already been staged 'in nine major European cities', with 'eleven further productions pending', including one in America; moreover, their own stage production was being mounted 'in conjunction with the British Broadcasting Corporation', who would be 'recording our production during the final stages of rehearsal, and transmitting it on the same night that we open in the theatre'.

Johnston focused on what he perceived as the naïvety of these claims: 'The point is made by the Aldwych that the script of the play is an accurate transcript of the proceedings—may be, but is it humanly possible to faithfully recreate what actually happened?' He endorsed Heriot's view that the script should be turned down, but was 'a little worried as to what will happen if a licence is refused'. There were problems either way:

> there may be quite an outcry over this country taking a different view to America and various European countries. On the other hand if a licence is granted, this might open the flood gates in another direction and there will be a mass of plays depicting trial scenes involving living people—e.g. the Ward/Profumo case.

Cobbold wrote a personal and confidential letter to David Bruce, the US Ambassador in London: 'I apologise for involving you in these strange troubles!' he began.

> Our normal rule is not to allow living persons to be represented on the stage, certainly not 'in an invidious manner'.
>
> On top of this I should normally be reluctant to allow a recent trial in the British Courts of Justice to be re-enacted on the stage with the obvious possibilities for twists of emphasis which might be introduced.
>
> On the first point, I am considering the possibility of finding out whether Oppenheimer would object and on what grounds—that of course would be for the Aldwych people to ascertain.
>
> But on the second point I should much welcome any view which you felt able to give me. The play has been produced in several Continental countries and at first sight it may seem silly to make a fuss here. If it had already been produced in the Unites States without repercussions, it would certainly seem silly to be 'plus royaliste que le roi'.

Bruce discussed the case with the Legal Adviser of the State Department in Washington, and suggested to Cobbold that the American administration was fairly relaxed:

> the Adviser told me that since the hearing was not before a Court of Justice he thinks there is no parallel with the re-enaction of a trial in the British Courts of Justice. He has also consulted with a member of the present American Atomic Energy Commission who shares his view. People therefore think there is no objection that could validly be made by the American Government to the licensing of this play.

However, he added a crucial qualification: 'the Legal Adviser thinks it important that the Aldwych Theatre authors carry out exactly their undertaking to use in dialogue only the words actually spoken by the individuals concerned at the Atomic Energy Commission Security Board hearing held in April 1954'. This absolute requirement was passed on to the RSC, and despite the previous assurances of authenticity, it put the cat among the pigeons. In August, they informed the Lord Chamberlain they were postponing the production:

> In the process of checking the documentary accuracy of the script against the actual transcript of the proceedings of the Atomic Energy Commission Security Board, we have discovered that there are several radical differences between them on matters of fact.

In the light of this, we are now undertaking a major revision of the text, to bring it into line with the facts of the transcript.[10]

It would be more than twelve months before the Office heard from the RSC again about Robert Oppenheimer.

You Couldn't Make it Up

At least documentary dramas had scripts to inspect. In August 1965, Hill received a telephone call from the *Sunday Times* asking why the Lord Chamberlain was permitting live improvisations to take place nightly at the Comedy Theatre within an American revue—*The Star Spangled Jack Show*. Hill went to the next performance and confirmed that 'from half to two thirds of the show has deliberately not been submitted to the Lord Chamberlain'.[11] The *Sunday Times* did its best to stir up trouble:

> An interesting situation seems to be developing between the Lord Chamberlain, the theatre censor, and the Second City Company of Chicago.
>
> Michael White, who is putting up the show, says that the company are not going to pay any attention to any ruling of the Lord Chamberlain.
>
> 'Improvisation', he says firmly, 'is a part of the theatre. I didn't bring it up with the Lord Chamberlain in the first place because I knew he'd object. In any case what can he do about it?'[12]

What indeed. White's primary aim in talking to the press was doubtless to generate publicity for his show, and the licensee of the Comedy Theatre, a solicitor called Wingate, contacted Hill the next day:

> He produced a letter from Michael White in which the latter informed Mr Wingate that he proposed to have a row with the Lord Chamberlain and hoped Mr Wingate would not mind . . . Mr Wingate said he would see Mr White and tell him he must stop the improvisations or he would close the show.

While the Lord Chamberlain could hardly ignore the provocation, a direct confrontation might have been counter-productive: 'I said I hardly thought such drastic action was necessary', Hill told Johnston. But the story was leaked, and the *Daily Mail* rang St James's to say that they had heard that the Lord Chamberlain was going to close the show if the improvising continued. 'I told the reporter that that was not so', said Hill, 'but that I could offer no other comment'. Instead, the Office sent White a letter by recorded delivery, (to ensure he could not deny receiving it) which listed the unlicensed items they had discovered during their inspection, and alerted him to the 'substantial penalties' to which he would be liable if the practice continued: 'each day upon which all or any of these unapproved items is acted for hire will constitute an aggravation of the offence of continued transgression'.

Once again, St James's Palace became the focus for media interrogation and speculation, with not only the national press, but also *Private Eye* and the BBC seeking interviews and comments. Having achieved his aim, Michael White now submitted a new batch of fifteen sketches for the show. Meanwhile, an assistant in the Lord Chamberlain's Office—David Buchanan—visited a performance and enjoyed it. 'There was no improvisation', he noted, and 'nothing really objectionable'.[13] But White was not finished yet. Buchanan had mentioned that the auditorium had only been half-full, and White needed more press coverage. On 31 August, the *Daily Mail* carried a headline 'Show Goes On With Two Banned Items'.[14] 'I don't know what you think', wrote Hill to Johnston, 'but he is obviously looking for a fight'. The Office decided to call White's bluff:

> We have already got such a very good case against him that I wonder whether we ought not to collect all the evidence we can, so that if we want to slap him down and the LC should agree, we should have such a case as would not only teach them something, but be a warning to others.

Wingate, meanwhile, again promised to close the show down unless White could demonstrate that everything in it had official approval. The Office was extremely appreciative of Wingate's stance, which had even earned the Censorship some positive (if unwarranted) publicity:

> As the result of Mr Wingate's strong action Mr White has been put to great inconvenience. Mr Wingate's threatened closures have been attributed to the Lord Chamberlain, and both the Press and certain producers now believe that the Lord Chamberlain cannot be lightly threatened, although in fact we have as yet taken no action. But for Mr Wingate the Lord Chamberlain would have had the choice of taking legal proceedings or being publicly exposed as ineffectual.

Hill was confident the Office now enjoyed the upper hand:

> Mr White has endeavoured to force a show-down on this matter, but made the mistake of confusing the issue by including some 15 other unlicensed items . . . He could be proceeded against on something like 34 counts, of which only two would relate to improvisation, and the result of which would be:

i) to make the point about improvisation in the least possible offensive way

ii) put Mr White to such expense as to make him think twice before challenging the Lord Chamberlain again . . .

The Secretary said they could either issue a 'written reprimand' or invite White to St James's 'to discover what his silly vendetta is all about; and to attempt to conciliate him to avoid a recurrence'. But he added a note of caution: 'Mr White seems to be both vindictive and a man with a mission. He will learn by his mistakes this time, and will confront us again with the improvisation issue in terms that we cannot dodge.' It was Hill's view that 'the current circumstances present the best opportunity for action we are ever likely to have'.

Cobbold was less eager to go for the jugular, doubtless fearing that the Office would still end up on the losing side. He thanked Wingate for his assistance, and asked whether he thought they should prosecute White or just send him a nasty letter. Strangely, Wingate never replied—a message came that he had broken his leg and gone away. Five weeks later, Johnston informed White that the Lord Chamberlain was not going to prosecute, but also issued a warning: 'He expects however, that in any future production with which you may be concerned, the provisions of the Theatres Act 1843, will be meticulously observed.' Some chance. The fact is that White ('originally Weiss', as Hill gratuitously observed) had effectively cooked a snook at the Lord Chamberlain.[15] And it is hard not to question whose corner Wingate had really been fighting.

On the same day that the Lord Chamberlain's Office told White there would be no prosecution for improvisation, they also received an enquiry from William Gaskill and the Royal Court about their plan to mount 'a special entertainment for children over the Christmas season', under the title *Clowning*.

We would very much like to present Keith Johnston's lecture demonstration as a children's show this Christmas, but we realise that it would be impossible to submit a complete script, which would be a wholly accurate description of such a performance. Could you let us know what your own feelings about such an entertainment would be and what steps we should take to present such a performance for your approval? We would be very glad to arrange a typical demonstration for you to see, or could supply a script of the basic framework.

Gaskill cited the honourable heritage of *commedia dell'arte*, adding that 'As much of our studio work here is devoted to improvisation, it would seem a pity if this cannot find some public outlet'.

Clearly, the show sounded harmless—and it would be hard to imagine more damaging publicity for the Office than to be cast as a bunch of Scrooges blocking an educational Christmas clowning show for children. But 'Humbug' Hill never dropped his guard: 'The history of the stage contains more than one example of dodging the law by giving stage plays disguised as lectures, classes, tea-parties etc.', he warned; 'We should beware of being beguiled in the same way'. Christmas might be Christmas, but principles were principles. And the Royal Court was the Royal Court:

> We should remember, however much we wish to help
> a) That these people NEVER PLAY FAIR
> b) A concession means to them no more than a lever to extract more concessions.

And to be fair to Hill, he was probably right to be suspicious that the theatre would, at the very least, be hoping to muddy the waters and go on to cite this show as a precedent. The Office asked Gaskill to supply more information, and the Royal Court provided 'a detailed description' and again offered a demonstration. Johnston thanked them for their 'quite absorbing lecture on Clown and Mask Work', which 'seems to me to contain the ingredients for an acceptable "copy" within the meaning of the Theatres Act'. He continued:

> As you know, whether we wish to or not, we are precluded from allowing completely unfettered improvisation, since no copy can be submitted beforehand. Such illegal improvisation would be exemplified by the actors working out a situation based on a spontaneous phrase from the audience.

The good news for the theatre was that 'Your "lectures" are not in this character'. On the other hand, some hurdles still remained, for the 'script' referred to 'audience exercises' and 'audience participation', as well as 'exercises for clowns', without detailing what these might be.

> The Lord Chamberlain wishes to put as little restraint as possible upon what seems to be an admirable entertainment and the one definite prohibition we should legally need to make would be upon the working up of unforeseeable situations produced by the audience. I do not know whether 'clowns answer questions put to them by the audience' is designed to fall into this category, but if it is it would be the one thing which I fear would have to be disallowed. If on the other hand the questions invited are true questions designed to elucidate some aspect of the lecture, then they would not be a part of the entertainment.

In early December, the Royal Court submitted further material and Heriot wrote the required Reader's Report. Doubtless the fear of newspaper cartoons loomed large, and the Office had to perform one of its tricky balancing acts:

> I have discussed it with Mr Hill, and we agree that a license can be given on the skeleton supplied, provided that there is no 'audience inception'. That is, that the audience shall not be permitted to suggest subjects for improvisation or mime other than from those in the script or from a 'controlled setting' . . .
>
> I do not suppose that, in a work for children, we shall have any trouble. But it should be made plain that any licence permitted is given without prejudice and does not constitute a precedent for other entertainments of this nature.[16]

A licence was issued and a kind of mini-Rubicon had finally been crossed.

Meanwhile, canny producers and managers had cottoned on to the fact that a threat to flout the censorship guaranteed them newspaper coverage, and with the Lord Chamberlain lacking the will or the authority to carry out prosecutions, an intention to abandon the script or improvise on stage was no longer necessarily something to keep hidden, but rather something to shout about. In November 1965, Hill reported in relation to Theatre Workshop's new musical that

> The 'Sun' newspaper was on the telephone to say that Lionel Bart has held a large Press Conference over *Twang!*, to say that he expects trouble from the Lord Chamberlain as the script he is going to use bears little resemblance to what he has sent to the Lord Chamberlain, especially as the characters will 'ad lib' most of their parts.[17]

The *Daily Mirror* said Bart had told them that 'unless the Lord Chamberlain's psychic he can't possibly know what's going on', and that the only way he could find out would be 'to set up a bed in the auditorium'.[18] A *Daily Sketch* headline announced *Twang* as 'THE SHOW THEY MAKE UP AS THEY GO ALONG', quoting Bart's claim that 'Two Thirds of it is ad-libbed and anything can happen'.[19] In an even more direct challenge, Bart also informed the *Guardian* that there would be 'constant changes' to the script during the show's run and that he expected this to 'cause trouble',[20] and he openly discussed the practice of ad-libbing in a radio interview on 'Today'.[21] It was—at least in part—desperate publicity for a musical facing a host of problems—but it was also damaging publicity for the Lord Chamberlain, whose will was apparently being flouted with impunity.

In December, Michael White squared up to the Lord Chamberlain's

Office again. The previous year, in what Heriot referred to as 'some freak of mis-casting', Spike Milligan—'a radio and television low comedian with a well-defined following'—had appeared in the title role in *Son of Oblomov*, a play (loosely) derived from a novel by the nineteenth-century Russian writer Ivan Goncharov. Depending on which account you read, Milligan was either ad-libbing from the start because 'His total lack of ability to learn his lines and to act made him gag his way through the piece' or began doing so after the original text proved less than effective. White advised Hill that 'Spike Milligan does not and will not keep to the script', and that 'Depending on his mood and that of the audience he [was] liable to address remarks to stage hands, individual members of the audience etc. in the manner of a comedian of a Variety Show'. Johnston knew full well that this was a contravention of the Theatres Act, but in an effort to avoid another confrontation, suggested that *Oblomov* 'does not fall into the category of a controversial play' and did his best to turn a blind eye.

White had assured Johnston that there was 'never anything improper or that causes offence' in Milligan's performance, but in December 1965, a clergyman complained to St James's about offensive innuendos and interactions with the audience. Johnston promised 'to remind the producer of his responsibilities', and promptly warned White that 'the dialogue in which Mr Milligan invites members of the audience to tell him whether they have "done it together before they were married" is objectionable', and would not have been permitted if it had been in the submitted script. White saw no need to apologise—far from it: 'I would like to observe that I have heard the joke which you mention as objectionable in at least ten music-halls up and down the country and I have never noticed anyone objecting.' However, he did submit an updated script, as he had promised to do nearly a year earlier. 'It is astonishing that even Milligan fans should laugh at this dismally unfunny wrecking of a classical Russian comedy', lamented Heriot; 'I understand that Milligan was too stupid or too conceited to learn his part and that, finding that his nauseous fooling went down with the audience who came to see him (and not the play), the piece was transformed after a very short time into the thing it is'. Possibly Heriot was not aware—though Cobbold would surely have been—that the Queen had chosen to celebrate her 39th birthday by attending a performance of *Oblomov*, and then having dinner with the comedian of whom he was so contemptuous.[22] Heriot had also attended a performance, and found the style not to his taste: 'Milligan', he said, 'hogs the show' and 'crashes every emotional scene with a facetious remark or gesture'. In early 1966, Penn wrote again to the management with a reminder that improvisation was not allowed. No-one at St James's expected this to have any effect, but, as even Hill admitted: 'I do not think we can do more.'[23]

The Government Inspectors

In December 1965, Roy Jenkins, whose determination and commitment to social reform would prove crucial over the next couple of years, took over as Home Secretary, and at the start of January, Cobbold met the Prime Minister to update him over recent discussions. Cobbold told Wilson that he did not advocate the complete removal of pre-censorship:

> I said that, as a result of three years experience, I had come (a little regretfully) to the conclusion that some form of censorship ought to be maintained. If it were only a question of obscenity, I should be a little inclined to drop censorship and leave the Theatre to find its own level—though this would be unwelcome to managements and would open the field to the local watch committees. But I thought that there would be dangers of the avant-garde theatre going wild on subjects like religion, attacks on royal family and personalities, in a way which would be unacceptable to public opinion.[24]

His preferred solution was to 'unload' his duties and responsibility 'on to a Board of Censors on the lines of the British Board of Film Censors',[25] and to do so with almost immediate effect. He even proposed that he himself should speak with 'the Queen's authority' in the forthcoming House of Lords debate. And in order to allow the government to defer legislation until a select committee had had the chance to explore different options, he suggested setting up a temporary board to take the reins in the meantime. 'The Prime Minister thought these ideas worth pursuing', reported Cobbold, 'and encouraged me to discuss the subject with the new Home Secretary'.[26] However, when Wilson sought wider advice, the Lord Chancellor pointed out that a Board would be no more acceptable to the opponents of censorship than the Lord Chamberlain. 'What the Lord Chancellor actually said', noted his secretary, 'was "Over my dead body"'.[27]

On 26 January 1966, the Home Affairs Committee accepted in principle the plan to set up a Joint Select Committee to investigate theatre censorship, and agreed that this could be formally proposed during the House of Lords debate scheduled for 17 February. BBC2 promptly invited St James's Palace to contribute to a late night symposium:

> They feel there will be a terrible gap if the Lord Chamberlain's Office is not represented by a spokesman, or alternatively if he will not receive one of their reporters to give your point of view.
>
> In their usual artless way, they say they are concerned only to air the facts before the public, that anyone coming will be lightly treated and they do not intend to 'knock' anyone.

But Cobbold declined the invitation, as he did a request from Auberon Waugh for an interview in the *Daily Mirror*.[28] For the moment, he preferred to keep his powder dry.

Hill provided Cobbold with a detailed briefing document for the House of Lords debate. 'The Act works upon the principle of confiding to the Lord Chamberlain's discretion the assessment of what could cause serious offence or do harm to the community', he wrote; and while conceding that the holder of the office was 'not a man of the theatre', and had 'no ability to judge the quality of a play that is superior to that possessed by any moderately cultured playgoer', there was no hint of apology or doubt in the position he staked out:

i   He is always a man of much administrative experience coming to the Office after a career elsewhere.
ii   As a member of the Royal Household he is politically neutral.
iii He has easy access to the highest sources of advice—religious, social, medical and political.
iv   He has many other duties which keep him in contact with the outside world.
v   He has social, financial and official status sufficient to enable him to withstand the pressures to which the Office of Censor will always (and properly) be exposed.

Moreover,

As the decision rests on one man it can be swift, varied to suit the circumstances, and it is possible to argue a case with little formality.

As for the opposition, it was rooted in the fact that his status and function were out of kilter with the spirit of the times: 'The Lord Chamberlain is an autocrat in an increasingly democratic world', Hill admitted; 'With the rise of the cult of "anti-Establishmentism" especially amongst playwrights, the Lord Chamberlain provides a ready-made stock target'. But he pointed out that in terms of the general public, 'more reproach him for what he allows, than for his prohibitions'.

Hill also provided ammunition to try and demonstrate why censorship was still essential, citing recent examples of 'indecent' material on which he had had to act:

Meals on Wheels—an actor going through the motions of exposing his private parts to an actress.
Saved—a gang of youths take the napkin off a baby, spit on its sexual organ, rub its face in its own excrement and stone it to death.

The Screens—Foreign Legionnaires break wind in the face of a dying
lieutenant . . .
The Mighty Reservoy—'shit' or derivations twenty-five times, 'cunt' twice,
'fucking' or derivations thirteen times . . . 'pissed' seven times, 'bollocks'
one, 'shithouse' one, 'sod' one.

Genet's *The Balcony* was cited as reflecting the 'increasing desire to use
Religious analogies to illustrate some dramatic and unusually indecent
situation', while Osborne's *Inadmissible Evidence* and Wedekind's *Spring
Awakening* were 'calculated to conduce to crime or vice'. Hill—always
ready to turn defence into attack—even proposed the introduction of a
new category which he believed required policing—'Denigration of the
Administration of Justice'. Here, it was specifically the documentary genre
which he wished to target:

> There is an apparent tendency for politically minded playwrights to adopt
> recent Court Cases of note and, using the actual participants and evidence,
> so to tailor the proceedings by cutting and re-distribution of emphasis, as to
> fit the facts to their theories. These theories are always that there has been a
> gross failure of justice.

And Hill concluded his gung-ho defence by criticising the 'increasing
numbers of plays which have grossly flouted all the accepted canons of
decency in language or incident'. In this case, subsidy was to blame:

> It is noteworthy that the plays emanate almost entirely from managements
> in receipt of large sums of public money, and not from managements which
> need to rely entirely upon public support. The complete rejection of these
> plays would involve the restriction of views and principles doubtless sincerely
> held and is difficult; their acceptance is correspondingly difficult bearing in
> mind the concept publicly stated by Mr Peter Hall, the doyen of this class
> of producer 'if somebody wants to write a currupting play [sic]—whether
> sexual or political he must by democratic principle be allowed to do it'.[29]

On the 17 February, the motion was proposed in the House of Lords
by Lord Annan 'that a Joint Committee of both Houses be appointed to
review the law and practice relating to the censorship of stage plays'.[30] A
leader column in *The Times* the previous day had suggested that 'Lord
Annan should have an easy time of it', since 'The British arrangements for
censoring the theatre are wide open to criticism'. However, the newspaper
recognised that reaching an agreement and setting new principles would
be infinitely harder; 'Easy to demolish in argument the censorship may
be, yet anything but easy to abolish in practice'.[31] Still, there was never any

real doubt that the proposal to set up an investigation would be approved, although the Lords debate went on for five hours. Some speakers, including Cobbold, favoured a wider brief, which would look at theatre alongside television and cinema. Whatever their views on the principle of stage censorship, everyone was very polite about Cobbold and his predecessors, casting the Lord Chamberlain more as a victim in need of rescue than as an oppressor. 'Theirs is a very difficult and often unpleasant task', explained Annan, insisting it was 'universally acknowledged that the present Lord Chamberlain . . . and his predecessor . . . have been models of courtesy and kindliness and conciliation towards authors and producers of plays'. But he also listed examples of playwrights and companies whose work had recently been interfered with, notably Osborne, Beckett, the National Theatre and the RSC, as well as the Berliner Ensemble, who had been 'astonished when they were ordered to change the text of two of the Brecht plays they were performing in German'.

Given that the motion had the support of both Lord Cobbold and his predecessor, the Earl of Scarbrough, it would have been hard to oppose it. But there was no consensus that abolition would be either an inevitable or a desirable outcome. Scarbrough was quite clear that it was not 'practical politics to abolish it entirely'. For one thing, there was 'quick money to be made from obscenity, from indecency and from representation of cruelty', and censorship was necessary to prevent people being 'lured' by this. Yet because the Censor was inevitably going to be involved in public controversy, the Earl thought it 'questionable whether it is really good for his position as head of the Sovereign's Household'. Cobbold himself spoke near the end of the debate. There were, he said, 'two main questions'— namely: 'should there be a theatre censorship; and if so, who should do it?' He echoed Scarbrough's argument about the inadvisability of 'the association of the censorship with the crown', and was unequivocal that some form of censorship must be sustained. Its 'basic philosophy', he insisted, 'centres on the conception of preventing offence to individuals, to sections of the community or to the community at large'. If it were simply obscenity he would 'be inclined to take the risk' of total abolition. But there were more important issues—'particularly violence, religious questions and the offensive treatment of personalities'—and the role of the censor was to represent and embody general contemporary attitudes:

> In the present state of public opinion I do not think it would be generally acceptable, or indeed in the best interests of the theatre, that extreme violence, sadism and the more horrific types of crime should be allowed on the stage . . . one can acceptably go some way further in these directions on the screen. In the theatre, with its more human and direct relationship between player and audience, the limit of acceptability is reached a good

deal sooner. Similarly, I believe that public opinion as a whole would not at the present time favour complete freedom in the treatment of Christianity on the stage, or offensive representation of living personalities, from the Royal Family and foreign Heads of State downwards.[32]

The proposal for an Enquiry was finally approved on 24 May 1966, and the Joint Select Committee sat formally for the first time on 26 July. It would meet a total of sixteen times, concluding nearly a year later in June 1967. Cobbold couldn't get out fast enough. Two days after the Committee's first meeting, he sent a 'Personal and Confidential' letter to the Home Secretary, again proposing that while the enquiry was taking place his own powers should be delegated 'to an appropriate body', operating either under the Arts Council or through the Board of Film Censors. (Though to be on the safe side, he wished to reserve 'a right of veto only in cases which involve the Monarchy or overseas Heads of State'). His suggestion was politely turned down. 'I am afraid that, attractive though the idea may be of using this interval for experimenting in delegation, the law simply will not allow it. I have checked this with our legal adviser who has confirmed that the 1843 Act gives you no power to do this.'[33] Reluctantly then, Cobbold had to Carry on Censoring while democracy took its course. As we shall see, the final two and a half years of his reign show few signs of much slackening of intent.

CHAPTER SEVEN

Getting Tough (1966)

Suppose the law remains unchanged—something else is changing all the time—and that's the kind of play which the Lord Chamberlain bans, and later, licenses . . . Some plays he licenses today deal with subjects which in 1909 would have seemed, even to opponents of the censorship, quite inconceivable on the stage. And if he retains his powers of censorship, and goes on getting more and more broadminded as the years go by, and if the plays which he bans today—such as *A Patriot for Me* and *Saved*—are licensed by him in the years to come, I wonder what sort of plays will be left for him to ban. What could they possibly be about?[1]

An apparent anomaly in the Theatres Act, to which opponents of theatre censorship had frequently drawn attention, was the fact that it applied only to plays written after 1737. In February 1966, the press got wind of a student production of *The Lucky Chance* by the Restoration playwright Aphra Behn, whom Hill dismissed as 'a pornographic novelist of the eighteenth century'. The point, of course, was that as a seventeenth-century play, this required no licence, and Hill had to fend off queries from journalists: 'I have told the *Manchester Daily Mail* that the propriety of young children appearing in such a play is a matter for the County Council under the Children and Young Person's Act 1952.' Behn's play was being staged at Durham University, and Hill expressed a general unease about the potential danger of classical plays from more decadent ages falling into the hands of contemporary provocateurs: 'If we want an example of "harm" done by plays I think it is to be found in this sort of backwash from the Royal Court, which induces the young at universities to rake over sexual muck-heaps of history.' Moreover, it was a practice which seemed to be growing:

There is already a theatre at Oxford specialising in this sort of revival, at Cambridge the ADC were proposing in an Elizabethan drama recently to have the actual semblance of copulation on the stage etc etc—the disease spreads apparently to Durham University and so on.[2]

Although technically the Lord Chamberlain did have the right to close down any production, in reality there was little the Office could do to curtail the trend.

One of the first contentious new plays in 1966 was David Pinner's 'extremely disturbing' *Dickon*, a play about a man dying of cancer in which 'the audience is spared nothing'; the Reader, Ifan Fletcher, reported that its subject was 'death obsession', and it culminated in the on-stage death of the central character after his son 'mixes morphine and feeds it to his father like gruel'. Even more distressing was the following scene, in which the family strip and wash the body; Fletcher worried in particular about a stage direction indicating that 'all the white stuff that Dickon pumped into dad comes spouting out of his dead mouth'. The play, he said, had 'a morbidity which is positively Jacobean', and he likened it to 'a modern version of a horror drama by Webster'. The Reader had no doubt it was a serious and well-written piece; 'What is more difficult to consider is the effect of this play upon its audiences'. He recommended it should be licensed only if the climactic death scene was omitted: 'I think it is not unreasonable to consider the effect of this play on children who might be taken to see it.' Heriot was more antagonistic, calling it 'a play by an ignorant poet', who was unaware that 'dead bodies cannot regurgitate'. Certainly, 'The washing of the dead body is a miserable business in real life and could only be offensive to adults in the audience'. The script was licensed only after extensive cuts which significantly undermined its structure and cohesion.[3]

Dylan, a biographical play by the American playwright Sidney Michaels about the last years of Dylan Thomas, had been staged on Broadway two years earlier, when Alec Guinness had won a Toni award for his performance. This cut no ice at St James's Palace, and extensive cuts were made since 'the actions which are required from the actor playing Dylan are likely to give offence to reasonable people'. Lines rejected included 'You've got a poker up your arse', 'I'm gonna squeeze your boobs (*pinches her breasts*) Squeak! Squeak!', and 'Miss Stuart, your tits are couplets'. Fletcher suspected the author's motives:

> This play seems to me to be aiming at a dirty-minded audience and is far from the category of some of the socially difficult avant-garde works now being written. With these, I feel there should be as much tolerance as possible. I see no reason why tolerance should be extended to this play.[4]

Heriot was even more cynical: 'There is still a lot of money to be made out of dead Dylan Thomas', he noted; 'a Welsh poet vastly over-praised, whose drunkenness, pettishness and general bad manners are essential elements in the present fashionable "anti-hero"'.[5]

At the start of February, Michael White submitted a revised version of Allan Sillitoe's stage adaptation of his own novel *Saturday Night and Sunday Morning*, which had first been staged in 1964. 'The plot and general sordidness remain the same', wrote Heriot; but he also noticed some changes: 'In the original the abortion took place off-stage. Here it appears to be on-stage behind a screen. This will not do.' He was also suspicious about the use of dialect; 'I have a feeling that all these "beggars" in the text will slide into "boggers"'. He therefore recommended that the production should be inspected in performance, which Hill reluctantly did ('I will only say that I do suffer for my country') when it reached London. He duly discovered that not only was the abortion taking place on stage, but 'beggar', 'buggered', 'sod' and 'Christ' were all incorporated within the dialogue—though none of these had been approved in the script. With both the trial of the Royal Court over *Saved* and the House of Lords debate on theatre censorship scheduled to take place in the next couple of weeks, it was a delicate moment. Was it better to turn a blind eye and avoid publicity, or to demonstrate that censorship was both necessary and effective? Would the Lord Chamberlain appear justified or petty for intervening, sensible or weak if he let it go? Hill chose not to comment during his visit:

> I came to the conclusion it would be best not to speak to the Manager but to review matters on Monday. There was obviously nothing so terrible as to warrant my taking action that could at once result in a furore and Mr White appealing to the Press for the advertising fillip his play obviously needs.

The instances where the production had transgressed and broken the law were not particularly shocking: 'The "buggers" and "sods" were mechanical evasions of our requirements', wrote Hill, and 'the audience expressed no resentment'. Even the abortion had been screened by a clothes horse covered in blankets, and by steam from the gas oven, so that 'I did not find it too bad'. In fact, 'the most unpleasant scene was the beating up', in which audiences see 'the battered Arthur crawling to the footlights to be sick and ejecting some liquid with a violent swish', his face 'a mask of blood'. What particularly disturbed Hill was his 'feeling that the author was really interested' in this violence, and the fact that 'some of the more vicious pieces were greeted with interested one might almost say appreciative laughter'.

Hill and Johnston therefore met with Michael White, along with the producer and a solicitor. They wished to show themselves as accommodating and even magnanimous, but also to demonstrate that the system was effective in uncovering breaches of the law, and capable of enforcing it where necessary. Johnston announced that the Lord Chamberlain was prepared to reverse his original verdict and allow the abortion scene to take

place on stage, but only after full directions for the staging had been submitted. On the language, he insisted that alternatives must be submitted
for the 'obscenities', and that for now all such words 'were to be removed
from that evening's performance whether or not appropriate substitutions
had been evolved'. The Office decided to make 'a double check' by seeing
the show again, since 'The Ld. Ch. wants to get tough with the people
concerned with this play'. Two days after the trial of *Saved*, and the night
before the House of Lords debate, Johnston therefore went to watch 'this
vulgar and dreary play' and ensure that the Lord Chamberlain's rulings
were not being ignored. 'The film was better and I enjoyed it more', he
observed. But at least he was able to report 'that all the beggars, buggers
and boggers have been removed', and 'that all our requirements have been
met with'.[6]

In the same month, the Office censored the sound of a woman in
childbirth from Bill Owen and Tony Russell's musical *The Match Girls*:
'I suggest screaming is disallowed, but that you would accept moaning',
wrote Hill, and Cobbold agreed.[7] In April, they objected to a flogging scene
in Bolivar Le France's *Make the Drums Talk*, 'A lurid melodrama set in the
West Indies in the Seventeenth Century'. The incident was clearly intended
to expose the cruelty and injustice of those in power, but this seems only to
have added to the Office's distaste: 'the argument is tilted always in favour
of the slaves', complained the Reader, and the Lord Chamberlain issued
'a strong warning that the flogging itself must be minimised as far as
possible'.[8] Meanwhile, in the case of 'a surprisingly dull play about Burke
and Hare', the Censorship decreed that 'Burke cannot be allowed to drop
with an audible crack as his neck breaks',[9] while restrictions on an Oxford
University production of Aristophanes' *The Frogs* included:

> Dionysus must not break wind . . .
> The business of soiling himself and wiping himself down cannot be per-
> mitted . . .
> Cut 'except, maybe, a good strong emission' . . .
> Cut 'I'm coming' . . .
> The prostitute must not be naked.[10]

In the case of an Exeter University revue, they warned 'that Adam and
Eve must be adequately clothed, and that the love making must not be too
erotic', while for *Pink Jesus* at the Jeanetta Cochrane Theatre the thirty
excisions included 'all reference to Durex'.[11] In April, the cuts in a new
version of *Lysistrata* included 'I'm so stiff I can hardly walk', and warnings
that 'the men must not walk as if with a painful erection'.[12] In May, they
disallowed 'get stuffed' in an Oxford Playhouse production of Labiche's
Italian Straw Hat,[13] while a licence was issued for an adaptation of *Tristram*

Shandy only 'on the understanding that . . . "Mr Walter Shandy sits up in bed" is portrayed as stated and without any suggestion that he is on top of his wife'.[14] In June, the script of a farce called *Adam's Apple* contained a number of directions which the Office insisted on qualifying:

> The stage direction 'Adam and Eve are revealed theatrically naked in all-over flesh coloured tights', is allowed only on condition that Adam wears an appropriate nether garment and that Eve's tights are completely opaque.
>
> The stage direction 'The attentions of James become more and more devoted', is allowed only on condition that massage is limited to the back above the waist.[15]

Royal Scandals

The script Hill had drafted for Lord Cobbold to draw on in the House of Lords debate, explicitly stated that the Lord Chamberlain had 'no interest in the continuance of the Censorship except in so far as is necessary to protect the Queen and the Royal Family'. Moreover, his list of examples of the shocking submissions with which the Office had recently had to deal included the representation of the Queen as one of the seven deadly sins in Charles Marowitz's production of Marlowe's *Dr Faustus*—the Queen was cast as Sloth, and her fellow-sins included Stalin, Mao Tse Tung and President de Gaulle—and 'Mockery of Prince Charles for failing to pass his eleven plus examination'.[16] The Lord Chamberlain's royal protection extended beyond those currently alive, and one of the most problematic plays submitted in January 1966 was based on some rather dubious goings-on of the 1890s which implicated the then Prince of Wales and future King, Edward VII. *The Scandal At Tranby Croft* did not specifically claim to be a documentary drama, but it was based on historical research and centred around a court trial, with characters stepping between the witness box in the present and the past events they were describing. The primary villain was Sir William Gordon-Cumming, who had been accused by his fellow players of cheating at baccarat—itself an illegal gambling game. The Prince had been acting as banker, and although the accusations against Gordon-Cumming were dropped in return for a signed promise that he would never play cards again, he subsequently brought a court case against his accusers, in which his solicitor cross-examined the Prince of Wales. Gordon-Cumming eventually lost the case, but doubts were raised as to whether it had been conducted fairly, and the Prince of Wales was subjected to embarrassing public criticisms.

Jack Russell's drama painted Gordon-Cumming 'as a maniacal brute, whose desire to cheat in the presence of the Prince of Wales was a kind of perverted ambition'. He was also shown as a sexual predator and rapist, sharing 'Don Juan's ambition to seduce every possible type of woman'. One of the lines the Office insisted on cutting was the declaration 'The violation is bloody and she often ends up better off than when she started'. However, according to Heriot, 'The overall impression is one of overweening pride, brutality and appalling vulgarity', with 'not one member of the house-party . . . given any redeeming features'. Although the Prince of Wales was a relatively minor dramatic character, the play clearly drew attention to the decadent and hedonistic (not to say illegal) lifestyle in which the future King had participated. The Censorship also automatically stipulated the removal of probably authentic verses which had been sung against the Prince of Wales—'They are typical of certain contemporary lampoons, but they don't add anything to the thesis'—along with one of his speeches.

At the end of February, the Management informed the Office that the script was being revised 'especially to make the character of Sir William Gordon-Cumming seem less nasty'. Specifically, they had removed 'all references to his sleeping with chambermaids, and possibly with Mrs Lycett-Greene'. Johnston promised that the Lord Chamberlain was willing to issue a licence 'subject to all business relating to Sir William Gordon-Cumming going to bed with housemaids, and references to him as a fornicator being removed'. The revised script was also shown to Gordon-Cumming's daughter, who thanked Cobbold for his courtesy, and admitted that—although she didn't much like the play ('I still hope that perhaps no-one will finance it')—it was 'blatantly on Papa's side'. Meanwhile, Cobbold wrote to the current Queen's private secretary:

> You may wish to inform The Queen that the Lord Chamberlain has licensed a play entitled 'The Scandal At Tranby Croft' which will shortly be performed at the Theatre Royal, Brighton.
>
> This will be the first play, licensed by the Lord Chamberlain, in which King Edward VII is represented on the stage.
>
> The Queen may recall that in 1962 the Lord Chamberlain discussed this question and Her Majesty said she had no objections to plays concerning King Edward VII now being allowed in principle.[17]

Of course, we can be pretty sure that any play which had explicitly attacked or criticised him—or even one that had been too nasty about his friends—would have been refused a licence, even seventy years after the events had occurred.

Sexual Revolutions

In the summer of 1966, the Labour MP Leo Abse introduced to parliament a private members' bill which would, when it was passed the following year, decriminalise private homosexual acts between consenting males above the age of 21. The debates and campaigns which occurred before this significant (if flawed) Act became law were sometimes vitriolic. Abse did not enjoy the official backing of Ministers or his Party, and later claimed to have been 'sent shit through the post on an almost daily basis'; he also had to grit his teeth to win over MPs by persuading them they should feel sorry for 'faulty males'.[18] For its part, St James's Palace continued to become as hot as ever under its collective collar about the idea of representing or directly alluding to homosexuality on the stage.

In May, Sir Laurence Olivier informed St James's Palace that he wished to give public performances of *A Patriot for Me* at the National Theatre. Hill acknowledged that 'Sir Laurence Olivier is a brilliant actor', but found some of his views on theatre distinctly suspect; 'he is also an avowed supporter of the Royal Court Theatre and swore recently on oath that *Saved* was a brilliant and moral play'. Hill was adamant the ban on Osborne's most controversial drama should remain: 'the two male love-making scenes will excite interest and curiosity, or sadistic pleasure', he predicted; and he warned that 'a proportion of any audience always views the play subjectively and whether from inclination or weakness of mind, enjoys the vicious incidents at their own value and out of context of the piece'. In particular, the effect of THAT SCENE still worried him the most:

> The transvestite ball is not essential to the action, but only to the atmosphere of the piece and by presenting homo-sexuals in their most attractive guise—dressed as pretty women, will to some degree cause the congregation of homo-sexuals and *provide means whereby the vice may be acquired* [my emphasis].

Equally important was the risk of setting a precedent. It was easier to try and maintain an absolute rule than to allow uncertainty and variation to creep in. 'Nudity has been effectively controlled by forbidding <u>any</u> movement unclothed', argued Hill: 'Similarly in my view male love-making must either be utterly excluded, or it must be accepted that in a short time males will make sexual advances to males on the stage with the same freedom that men and women now do.' This, said Hill, was 'the goal of the homo-sexual'—namely, 'that he be accepted as normal'. Therein lay the danger of *A Patriot for Me*. 'The homosexual suffers no lack of advocates today, and assistance from the stage is unnecessary.' Olivier was informed that the Lord Chamberlain 'cannot and will not license the play as it stands'.[19]

By contrast, the Office licensed *The Failure*—'to be produced by something called Teenage Theatre'—without objection, even though the story

centred on a boy who has been expelled from school after being discovered
in bed with a younger pupil. What saved it was the fact that the act had
occurred before the play begins, and that the focus is on the repentance
of the expelled boy who explains to his father 'that his homosexual lapse
was merely an experiment'.[20] Altogether a different case was Christopher
Hampton's *When Did You Last See My Mother*, described by Heriot as 'a
dreadful little amateur drama' submitted for performance at a small venue
in Oxford, where Hampton was a second year undergraduate. Hill agreed
that it was 'dreary' and 'rather tiresome', and that the story of 'two grubby
undergraduates . . . obsessed with sex and smut' and possessed of 'homosexual leanings' demanded intervention. He also wanted to go further than
simply cutting the script:

> I have no evidence, merely a strong suspicion that this little theatre at Head-
> ington is not under the surveillance of the University authorities and I there-
> fore suggest that this piece should be watched to prevent its unspeakable
> little author from getting away with anything.

Johnston was inclined 'in this enlightened age, and in a play of this sort',
to be less draconian, but Cobbold sided with Heriot, and a long list of cuts
was sent out.[21] Nearly fifty years later, Hampton recalls the experience:

> I vividly remember the whole correspondence and negotiation with them—I
> seem to remember the very first word of the play (Crap!) was disallowed.
> The notepaper was the thickest cream vellum and the letter hilariously
> began 'I am desired by the Lord Chamberlain . . .' They demanded 40 or
> so cuts, I protested; and to and fro we went, until, on the very day of the
> first performance, the authorisation to do the play finally arrived. I was
> sufficiently anxious there might be some interruption of the play to go on
> stage (I was acting in the play) with the authorisation in my pocket.[22]

Even with all the cuts, the Censors had overlooked something which
would later embarrass them: 'What they failed to notice', recalls Hampton,
'was the stage direction in which a wrestling match culminates in a kiss'.
This was 'fortunate, since the play would hardly have made sense without'.
However, in the summer of 1966, the play received a Sunday performance
at the Royal Court, before being taken up for a three-week run at the
Comedy Theatre, where it was reviewed in the *Daily Telegraph* under the
headline 'Playwright's Precocious Talent'. Darlington identified Hampton
as a young playwright of real potential, but one sentence in his review
leapt off the page at St James's Palace: 'No doubt as time goes on he will
cease to shock the squeamish, as for instance by bringing down his final
curtain on a pair of young homosexuals locked in an embrace'.[23] A quick

check now revealed that in issuing the licence the implications of a stage direction stating that the two men 'simultaneously hug each other' had been overlooked—much to the horror of the Lord Chamberlain's secretary: 'What we have thus allowed is two homo-sexuals loving each other in public', he frothed; 'This is now the next step forwards accomplished, and we shall for ever more have this play cited as the example for allowing loving scenes between homo-sexuals'. What to do? 'We haven't a leg left to stand on unless we invoke S.14', wrote Hill; 'My own feeling is that someone (other than me) ought to see this play and if the embrace is a loving one then we <u>should</u> invoke S.14 and cut it'.

Section 14, to which Hill referred, was that part of the 1843 Theatres Act which had rarely been used, but which gave the Lord Chamberlain the right to intervene in relation to any performance of any play (even one written before the Theatres Act had come into force) if he thought it liable to cause a breach of the peace. But the Assistant Comptroller opted for a more diplomatic route, contacting the managers of the theatre and the company performing, who assured him that the newspaper had got it wrong: 'Mr Bevin watched carefully last night's performance, and confirms that before the final curtain there is no more than a spontaneous hug between the two young men.' Could Darlington have been referring to a different curtain? wondered the Lord Chamberlain's Office—such as the one at the interval when 'the two men have a fight . . . during which one pins the other down'. But this, the manager assured them, was 'wrestling not embracing'. 'What a relief!' wrote Johnston; adding that 'we must remember Mr "D" was wrong', since 'he will surely be quoted'.[24] Had they checked with the reviewer—or sent one of their own staff to watch a performance—they would presumably have discovered that it was not Mr 'D' who was in error. Easier, perhaps, not to know.

That was not quite the end of the affair. A year later, when he was negotiating with the Censorship about 'a peck on the cheek' in Simon Gray's *Wise Child*—('the Lord Chamberlain does not allow pecking on the cheek between two men')—the producer Michael Codron insisted 'that the Lord Chamberlain had allowed him to have two actors kissing on the lips in the play *When did You Last See My Mother* at the Comedy'. And to the horror of the Comptroller, this was confirmed by the Reader. Not that the Office backed down: 'I told Codron that he could have no kissing or pecking.'[25]

Something even worse than homosexuality provoked the ire of St James's Palace in the summer of 1966, in Bamber Gascoigne's *Leda Had a Little Swan*. Gascoigne was known to both the Comptroller and the Assistant Comptroller, who had been senior officers in the First Battalion Grenadier Guards, the regiment in which Gascoigne had served as a second lieutenant during his National Service. Moreover, Gascoigne's father was a personal

friend of the Assistant Comptroller, so there had been almost a sense of
betrayal when Bamber, having recently graduated from Eton College and
Cambridge University, published an article attacking theatre censorship.[26]
In addition to achieving fame as the first presenter of the television show
'University Challenge', Gascoigne had also written a book on twentieth-
century drama, and now his first play was scheduled for performance at
the Jeanetta Cochrane Theatre.[27] Heriot was enraged by the script:

> Mr Gascoigne, it will be remembered, was the critic whose father apologised
> to the Lord Chamberlain for his son's impertinences in the *Spectator*. He
> now has the invidious distinction of being the first dramatist to attempt to
> introduce bestiality as a theme for comedy.

Set in the near future, *Leda* focuses on a family in which the progressive
parents are determined to discuss sexual matters openly with their
children, in contrast with their own experience. They then find themselves
horrified by an emerging fashion, in which young people take to having
sexual intercourse with their pets or animal acquaintances. Their son
brings home a goose 'with whom he sleeps (in every sense)', as the Reader
delicately put it, and the play ends with the parents realising that they
have been no better than the previous generation at understanding their
children.

Gascoigne's script was witty and at times extremely funny; there is, for
example, a peacock called Tynan who can be heard letting out 'terrible
shrieks', and one scene contains an amusing parody in which a beggar who
'should look as much as possible like Bertold Brecht' begs for money as he
'sings or speaks to very Brechtian music':

> What is happening in my fatherland?
> The country that I was borne and bred in is a highly agriculturalised country
> with intensive stock-breeding boosted by heavy government subsidies.
> Is the government now subsidising vice?
> Is the government now subsidising vice?

None of this could save it: 'I began marking the script for cuts', wrote
Heriot, 'but since the whole of the last act is inadmissible, I see no reason for
listing them'. Hill thought the whole thing might be 'an obscure mockery
of those who advance the exquisitely logical and rational supports for
homo-sexuality'. Indeed, he said he had 'long anticipated the introduction
of "bestiality" on the stage, once playwrights fancy they are victorious
over homo-sexuality'. He even suggested that 'Mr Gascoigne is right to
the extent that every argument which has been advanced in condonation
of homo-sexuality can be applied unchanged in favour of bestiality'. To

make his point, he re-wrote Scarbrough's famous 1958 minute which had replaced the absolute ban on stage representations of homosexuality with a more limited set of principles:

> Every play will continue to be judged on its merits. The difference will be that plays will be passed that deal seriously with bestiality.
>
> Plays violently concerned with bestiality will not be passed.
>
> Bestialities will not be allowed if their inclusion in the piece is unnecessary.
>
> Embraces or practical demonstration of love with animals will not be allowed.
>
> Criticism of the present bestiality laws will be allowed, though plays obviously written for propaganda purposes will be judged on their merits.
>
> Embarrassing displays with animals will not be allowed.

If performed, warned Hill, *Leda* would 'be taken at its face by many', and he had no doubt that 'any play on bestiality will be followed by others'. He argued successfully that it should receive 'a complete refusal'.

When Gascoigne was informed of this decision, he claimed to be 'astonished'. The script did not require any sexual action on stage, being 'entirely cerebral' and having 'no objectionable language'. He wrote a personal letter to the Assistant Comptroller:

> Dear Johnnie,
> I have just got back from four months touring around Europe collecting material for a book, and I gather that while I was away the Jeanetta Cochrane Theatre submitted to you a play of mine, *Leda had a Little Swan*, which they were planning to produce this autumn but which you didn't license. There's a production of it planned by the experimental wing of the Belgian National Theatre in Brussels this winter, and the possibility of one off-Broadway, so naturally it's disappointing not to have it done in London too. The Jeanetta Cochrane Theatre have now replaced it with something else. But in case anyone else should want to do it, I'd be grateful if you could let me know if there were any alterations which would have made it acceptable to your office.

'Johnnie' replied, rather stiffly, that other than removing the bestiality there were 'no alterations which would make it acceptable'.[28]

There were plenty of objections, too, to *Fill the Stage with Happy Hours*, submitted in July 1966. Set in a provincial theatre which is owned and managed by the Harris family, Charles Wood's new play explored the contrast between the performance of fictions and real lives, focusing on the often sordid back-stage relationships. 'Sex', explained Harward, 'is the nigger in the woodpile', with 'some of it perverted'. Particularly concerning was the ambiguity of a scene between a man and a woman in a hotel bedroom, in which she is old enough to be his mother. 'The copy of the play as submitted is deficient in that it does not give details of important stage action', worried Hill; 'I should therefore be inclined to ask for a new MS incorporating details of stage action throughout'. The hotel bedroom scene is clearly the build up to the boy's first experience of sexual intercourse, as he watches the woman in a mirror preparing herself. Heriot did his best to work out what might be happening on stage:

> Reading this scene very carefully, I think that until page nine the woman is only doing her face and adding false hair. Then she goes into the bathroom for a more intimate preparation and Henry watches her in the mirror. I think the text can stay as it is . . . but a firm warning that Harry must not react in a visually sexual way nor imitate what she is doing in the bathroom and that the bedroom light must remain on during this scene at least until she emerges from the bathroom and that when she does she must be adequately clothed.

The script was licensed with around fifty cuts to sexual language and images, as well as a guarantee that there would be 'no physical contact between the artists on stage of a suggestive nature'.[29]

The censorship chose not to intervene over a performance by the Sierra Leone National Dance Troup at Sadler's Wells Theatre: 'I notice that certain female dancers have bare breasts, but I don't think anything should be done', wrote Heriot; 'this company has already been seen by audiences in the provinces—including a number of clergymen'.[30] However, a fertility dance in the Royal Court's production of Wole Soyinka's *The Lion and the Jewel* was a different matter: 'The genitals of the carved figure of the Bale must not be visible to the audience', decreed the Lord Chamberlain; while 'The dance of virility must not include the actual motions and proximities of copulation'. The Assistant Comptroller also queried what the female dancer would be wearing, prompting a 'rude letter from Gaskill' in return: 'I would not dream of asking an actress what undergarment she is wearing beneath a costume which adequately covers her, and I consider it rather indelicate of you to suggest that I should.'[31]

One play which was never licensed was *The Architect and the Emperor of Assyria*, written by the Spanish surrealist playwright Fernando Arrabal, and submitted by the National Theatre in the summer of 1966. Harward described it as 'a disturbing modern play', and recognised it as a significant work—albeit one with problems, so far as the British stage was concerned:

This is certainly a play with serious intentions, but since the intention is to liberate the audience from a conventional rational experience of the play's 'story' it needs to explore the fantastic world of the subconscious with all its unpleasant and morally offensive associations. Also, Arrabal's vision is clouded at times by bitterness and ugliness. This is not entertainment; but it is fascinating and forceful theatre.

Particularly problematic was the juxtaposition of religion and sexuality:

the dialogue . . . implies every kind of unrestrained sexual activity both between these two men, between the Emperor and his mother, between himself and his brother, his wife and others. The Architect helps him to act out his guilt and fantasy memories and acts as judge, executioner and, finally, undertaker—when he carves up and eats the dead Emperor on stage.

Harward evidently regretted the narrowness of attitudes in Britain, which made Arrabal's script hard to approve. Indeed, the terms in which his report is couched would suggest that he had already sought advice within the Office, and was not entirely at ease with the recommendations he was obliged to make:

It is felt that since there is no satisfactory means, at present, of warning a potential audience of the play's content and method of presentation, a large number of alterations must, regrettably, be made. The French theatre audience may have a far more liberal attitude towards this kind of experimental drama, but this may be because they are by temperament more tolerant and self-critical than the British.

Seeking to avoid a confrontation, Cobbold broke with normal practice, and wrote discreetly to Laurence Olivier, admitting that Arrabal's play 'presents considerable difficulties for this office', and that he had

two alternative courses—either to refuse a licence (which I am always reluctant to do if I see any possible alternative), or to make a long list of cuts and alterations which I should require . . . I am very ready to do the latter if that is the National Theatre's wish; but I do not wish to waste everybody's time and possibly cause unnecessary irritation unless you tell me that you are anxious to put the play on and would like to know the extent of cuts which would be required.

Olivier was not going to make things easy for St James's Palace:

My dear Lord Cobbold,

I am very loath to put your office to any unnecessary burdens of course, but my enthusiasm for *The Architect and the Emperor of Assyria* does embolden me to beg you to furnish me with the cuts and/or alterations that would be required before I could feel happy or conscientious about abandoning the idea.

However, the proposed production was dropped after a list of some forty cuts was sent out.[32]

In September, the Royal Court again clashed with the Lord Chamberlain over the mixture of sex with religion in David Cregan's *Three Men For Colverton*, in which 'three hell-fire Evangelists come to a quiet Bedfordshire town to convert it'. Heriot found himself confused—'What the thesis of this play is, I cannot discover; but I am reluctantly compelled to admit that it is at times amusing'—and ten cuts were demanded, all involving religious and/or sexual references. They included references to Christ on the Cross, the immaculate conception, and the Angel Gabriel, all made outside a strictly religious context, as well as a line about 'sloppy loins'. For the Court, Desmond O'Donovan, asked the Comptroller to reconsider: 'I do not think that your readers have perceived the seriousness of Mr Cregan's intentions', he admonished; 'the author is not taking a frivolous attitude either to religion or to sex. The play is concerned with the difficulties of achieving true moral attitudes in both sexual and religious matters in the modern world'. Moreover

The author is, and has been for many years, a school-master and is intensely aware of his responsibilities in this area. My impression from reading your list of cuts is that his integrity has not been appreciated and I wish to say most strongly that the changes that you have asked for would seriously weaken the moral impact that we hope the play will make.

'Nonsense', wrote someone in the Office, and Heriot dismissed this response as 'another piece of disingenuous pleading'. But Gaskill took up the case for the Court, sending the Lord Chamberlain the sort of letter which could have been designed to demonstrate to the Select Committee the frustration of theatre artists:

although we have had many tussles in the past, including one which took us both to Court, I am very surprised by some of your objections to this play. You should realise by now that we do not particularly enjoy fighting these battles and I hope you believe that it is not our intention to harass you with unnecessary problems. The game we both indulge in of exchanging letters about individual lines or passages snatched from their context seems

to me a denial of our artistic integrity on one side and of your concept of
morality on the other. When we talk to you, or your representatives, we have
a perfectly civilised conversation in which you usually concede the dramatic
relevance of the passages you object to and frequently say that you were not
personally shocked but that you fear that they might give offense [sic] to
others. Without a detailed knowledge of every member of every audience
who goes to see every play, I cannot see how you can estimate what will or
will not give offence. There are many things in plays that I see regularly
which are both offensive and distasteful to me on the grounds of morality,
but you have failed to protect me from these passages and I feel, as an adult,
that I have the right to my own assessment and, if necessary, to make my
own protest by leaving the theatre. I do not hope to persuade you of the truth
of my argument but I do feel that the kind of correspondence that we have
over plays is degrading to both of us and slightly ridiculous.

Gaskill also asked that someone should come and see Cregan's play
in rehearsal: 'I feel that you owe it to this theatre, whose integrity you
have called in question, perhaps more than any other, to comply with
this request.' But the Office declined to be drawn: 'In the absence of
the submission of any alternative MS designed to conform to the Lord
Chamberlain's requirements it would, in view of the foregoing, serve no
purpose for a representative of this Office to see the play.' The theatre
backed down and made the required cuts, and the play was duly licensed.
'The actor and actress will not lie down together, but will be sitting together
behind a stock of hay out of sight of the audience.'[33]

Another relatively petty but potentially embarrassing intervention
picked up by the press in the autumn of 1966 involved a revised version of
The Bed Sitting Room performed at the Mermaid theatre: 'The *Daily Mail*
people have asked Mr Hill why a lavatory had been allowed on stage in the
course of this play', reported Johnston; 'I have checked with Mr Heriot
who confirms that there is no stage direction in the MS to this effect'.
Phone calls to the Mermaid discovered that it concerned 'a non-practical
pedestal lavatory', which was 'used as a means of transport—to chase an
actor across the stage'. Johnston conceded that 'I don't think we can make a
fuss about this', but cuts which were imposed including the singing of 'The
First Noel' because 'it equates the child on stage with the birth of Christ';
individual lines such as 'We're doing so well testing these contraceptives
for *Which*', 'doesn't she know God's dead', and 'It's God, good old God';
references to a horse being listed in Burke's peerage as Prince Philip's third
cousin; and the claim that someone has been bitten by a royal corgi. The
company was also warned that 'The actor and actress may only appear in
bed together if the scene is played in a farcical manner'.[34]

World Politics

Another play to cause problems in the autumn of 1966 was Henry Livings's *The Little Mrs Foster Show*, a 'not very political satire' about a rich white widow caught up in a revolution in the Congo. According to the Reader, any 'message' was too obscure to worry about: 'The text is a nauseous blend of Mr Livings at his most whimsical and vague propaganda which may be against war, or against Congolese troops or coloured races insufficiently educated, or against television vulgarity or general bureaucracy.' The main interventions concerned language and visual imagery: 'We cannot have a jet of blood spurting over the face and clothes of the doctor.' The Office also insisted that projected photographs of mutilated African corpses 'must not be horrifying'. Livings travelled to St James's from his home in Lancashire to argue his case, and his subsequent letter tried to apply pressure by revealing that Richard Findlater had invited him to contribute to his forthcoming book on theatre censorship. Livings's letter was permeated with a mocking but subtle irony.

> I now understand that the Lord Chamberlain's licence is universal; and that bugger and sod, however devoid of physical sexual association in people's minds in many parts of the country, still has that association for others and for the government. My naïve hope that I might say it on stage above the Trent was out of the question therefore . . .
>
> I was, as you know, bewildered by your suggestion that 'You had a fair old grip for a woman being forced' could be taken to refer to a vaginal grip. The problem for me is that to explain that it's not is to suggest that it might be.

Livings asked whether 'buggeroo' would be 'an acceptable substitute for "bugger"', pointing out that 'it seems hardly possible that a woman could come within the dictionary definition of bugger'. A large 'NO' written in the margin was the Office's response to his request. In reference to the blood, Livings cited Act Two of Ibsen's *Peer Gynt* as a precedent, where 'the lunatic who thinks he's a pen cuts his throat, and the blood spurts'. This was also rejected: 'I have seen various productions of *Peer Gynt*, and the blood never spurted.' The most that could be allowed was 'a slow stain of blood on the body and the hands of the doctor'. But in respect of the photographs, Livings seems to have managed to pull something of a fast one, when he promised that 'the photograph of mutilated African corpses' would be 'horrifying'. The 'mistake' was spotted at St James's—'Surely he means "not horrifying"'—but it appears that no-one checked up on this. So when the administrator at the Liverpool Playhouse, where the play was to be staged, forwarded the photograph to be used (a very disturbing image of the bodies of some of the sixty people recently killed in a village battle in Northern Rhodesia) her accompanying note to the Lord Chamberlain stated: 'We consider that this one answers your request that it should be horrifying.' To have challenged it at this stage would have risked embarrassment and publicity, and the photograph was quietly approved.[35]

The politics of Livings's play may not have been direct enough to worry the Lord Chamberlain too much, but there were three texts in the autumn of 1966 in which politics featured overtly, causing him considerable problems and embarrassment. All of them involved the United States of America. The first was Kipphardt's documentary drama about Robert Oppenheimer, which now resurfaced; the second was Peter Brook's production of *US*, devised with the RSC; and the third was Barbara Garson's *MacBird*, a loose adaptation of *Macbeth* which attacked the integrity of senior American politicians, including the President, and which was staged by Joan Littlewood and Theatre Workshop.

The situation over *In the Matter of J. Robert Oppenheimer* had been on hold since the summer of 1965, when the RSC had indicated its intention to check the accuracy of the script. In October 1966, a rewritten version was presented privately at the Hampstead Theatre by the RSC, but they also wanted the licence which would allow public performance. Kipphardt's play was based on a 3,000-page transcript of the month-long 1954 Atomic Energy Commission hearings which humiliated Oppenheimer, but it did not limit itself to verbatim documentation of the trial, and included fictional speculations. Following its first performance in Germany in 1964, Oppenheimer had reportedly been ready to sue for inaccuracies.

> Where the play is flawed is not so much in inflating Senator Joe McCarthy, who appears as a dark, looming cloud over Washington, but rather in what Oppenheimer himself sharply calls 'improvisations which were contrary to history and to the nature of the people involved' . . . An even graver distortion is the script's assertion that Oppenheimer felt that in making the bomb, 'we have done the work of the devil'. 'This is the very opposite of what I think', said the real Oppenheimer last week. 'I had never said that I regretted participating in a responsible way in the making of the bomb.'[36]

In 1965, the British press had reported both the RSC's intention to stage the play and Oppenheimer's disapproval of it. The Lord Chamberlain asked the RSC whether they understood the actual views of the individuals represented in the play, and the company said it would send the script to Oppenheimer once the English translation of the original German text had been completed. After a silence of over a year, John Roberts of the RSC came to St James's in September 1966 to discuss how things stood:

Mr Roberts asked me whether it was worthwhile him submitting a script. I said there was no reason why he should not, but that in my opinion, if he did, he should remember the Lord Chamberlain's request regarding the views of Mr Oppenheimer and others.

I also pointed out that whatever anyone might say, plays of this nature turned fact into fiction, but represented the latter as fact. I said I was sure that it would aid him if, in submitting the play, he made it quite plain what was actually verbatim evidence and what was interpolated matter.

On 19 October, the RSC submitted the script for reading, pointing out that 'No objections whatsoever have been raised to the 23 different productions which have been mounted in different parts of the world including most European capitals, Japan and Israel', and that 'No action of any kind has been taken against the Hampstead Theatre Club'. They also emphasised their 'firm belief that this is one of the most important plays of the present generation', and insisted on the authenticity and accuracy of the text: 'It is sincerely believed that the play is a true and honest reflection of the original Hearing and that the statements made and the views expressed by the characters in the play were in fact made and expressed at the time.' No-one, they said, could be damaged by it: 'responsible opinion suggests that no living person represented or mentioned in the play can suffer from a public representation of the amended script'. However, the Lord Chamberlain received another letter from a firm of Lincolns Inn solicitors, acting in connection with the play on behalf of 'a client, who prefers not to be named at the moment'. The solicitors explained that while the RSC had refused to give them sight of the script, they considered it 'likely that our client's name would be mentioned', and asked Cobbold 'to bear in mind, if and when you see this play, that it concerns living persons held in high regard in this country whose reputations could be gravely damaged by its performance'. Although the solicitors chose not to identify their client, the person in question was George Eltenton, an associate of Oppenheimer during the forties; Eltenton had (or had had) communist sympathies, and had been named by Oppenheimer during the hearing as one of several 'intermediaries' keen to share American military intelligence with the Soviets during the Second World War.

Cobbold decided that 'in the light of its history in other countries and at Hampstead . . . it would be foolish to refuse a licence', given that 'with the possible exception of the references to Mr Eltenton, who is an Englishman living in England' no-one could have cause for complaint; 'I certainly do not regard the play as offensive to Oppenheimer'. Nevertheless, the Office took care to cover itself, asking Roberts to confirm that no action was being taken or 'to the best of your knowledge is contemplated' in relation to the Hampstead Club production. They also requested confirmation 'that the dialogue . . . consists entirely of actual evidence given at the Atomic Energy Commissions Security Board hearing held in April 1954, and contains no misrepresentation of fact'. Finally, they asked whether the theatre would be 'prepared to omit the name of Mr Eltenton', substituting a fictitious name and deleting the fact that he was English.[37] The irony and hypocrisy were not lost on Hill: 'We are demanding authenticity, and ourselves requiring deviation from the truth', he observed; 'I don't like this'.

There were further delays before the licence could be issued. Oppenheimer himself had not yet seen the English script, and there was concern at St James's Palace about his likely attitude, and especially whether he might take legal action—and if so, against whom. On 17 November, his American lawyer wrote to say that 'Oppenheimer's objections to a performance in the United States of the Oppenheimer play are unchanged' and that 'He would take every step possible under American law to prevent such a production'. But the RSC lawyer put a crucial gloss on this: 'I believe this letter to be exceedingly carefully worded and I think that the references to "a performance in the United States" and to "American law" . . . are deliberately used.'[38] The fact that Oppenheimer was by now suffering from the throat cancer which would shortly kill him made the risk of legal action in Britain even more improbable, and a licensed public production of Kipphardt's play by the RSC was finally permitted to open in London at the end of November.[39]

US

Even while the RSC was embroiled in discussions with the Office over Kipphardt's play, another production about war and America was causing much more tension and hostility. The script of US—a piece devised by members of the RSC under the direction of Peter Brook—was submitted at the end of September 1966 for proposed production at the Aldwych. Like the Kipphardt play, US might be placed under the umbrella heading of documentary theatre; but it was a very different beast. The starting point for US was an absolute condemnation of America's ongoing war in Vietnam, and while it was not seen by many people (and certainly not by Brook) as a wholly successful theatrical experiment, it did include some chilling ideas and images, not least in a climactic monologue calling for Britain to be subjected to the kind of bombing and destruction currently being inflicted in Vietnam, and for the results to be filmed and shown to people across the world. Only then, would 'we' understand what it was like for 'them'.

As Vice President when Kennedy was assassinated in November 1963, Lyndon B. Johnson ('LBJ') had inherited the leadership of the United States, and subsequently secured a large majority in the next Presidential elections. Under his leadership, America quickly escalated the war in

Vietnam with a policy of 'saturation bombing' and a threat to 'bomb them back into the stone age'.[40] Johnson also sent in ground troops, and tried unsuccessfully to persuade other countries—including Britain— to contribute its own direct military support. As the war continued, the campaign against it would grow into a primary cause of civil unrest and disobedience, particularly among the young. In September 1966, peace protestors managed to infiltrate the stages of a number of London theatres, interrupting performances to make political speeches to their captive audiences. In the same month, the RSC submitted the script for *US*. As the ambiguous title suggests, its focus was as much an analysis of how best to oppose the war, as it was about the war itself.

Charles Heriot, immediately dismissed *US* as 'a piece of hysterically subjective anti-Vietnam War propaganda' and drew attention to specific passages, including 'The torture sequence . . . The Quaker hymn . . . The masturbation verse . . . . Insulting references to President Johnson', as well as parts of the final speech calling for bombings in Britain. But as he noted, 'these are what would be cut in any play'. The real problem lay at a deeper level, and the comparison he offered was revealing: 'The attitude to America seems to me to be dangerous and insulting to an ally', suggested the Reader; 'and since the war in Vietnam is, so to speak, sub judice (would we have permitted a play about the Suez Crisis during the crisis?), the piece is not recommended for licence'.

Cobbold held a meeting with Sir Paul Gore-Booth, the experienced Permanent Under-Secretary of State at the Foreign Office:

> I said that in my preliminary view there was a strong slant throughout the script on this highly inflammable [and] topical subject with . . . political implications. Whilst the decision rested entirely with me, I said that I would welcome FO advice on this point. They need not worry about the obsceni- ties, which I shall deal with in the normal way. I gave him the script. He telephoned me this morning and said that his personal view coincided with mine, but I could not take this as an FO view as he was consulting the S of S. And there were questions of . . . politics and timing involved.

Gore-Booth also raised some interesting questions:

> He asked
> Whether there seemed to be a definite author of the script.
> Whether Shakespeare company was subsidised.
> I said (a) no, (b) yes.

Later on the same day, Gore-Booth telephoned to say that he had now discussed the play with the Foreign Secretary, George Brown, and that

'The FO do not wish to express a view one way or another' since 'the S of S, though he personally thinks this revolting and tiresome stuff, disapproves of government censorship'. 'As I do!' noted Cobbold. Gore-Booth also promised he would 'let the US ambassador know privately about our conversation' at the appropriate time. But the decision was essentially Cobbold's to make: 'I said I entirely accepted this and was only concerned to give them an opportunity of commenting if they wished to.' He told Gore-Booth that

> I had not finally made up my mind but was contemplating saying the present script was unacceptable because so much would be offensive to responsible foreign opinion and suggesting they revise with this in mind and re-submit if they wish to.

Cobbold's next move was to send the script to Lord Nugent, the former and now retired Comptroller. Nugent replied the following day with a three page hand-written letter:

> I fear I can give little advice of any value on this play (if you can call it a play!) because to ban or not is a purely political question on which I am certainly not qualified to judge. If the Foreign Office give it as their opinion that the production of this play at the Aldwych would 'impair our relations with a friendly power' or whatever the phrase is then doubtless the Lord Chamberlain will have to give much weight to this opinion.

However, Nugent suggested that 'perhaps the FO will do well to remember one or two points before rendering such advice', and offered a series of reason why it might be better just to allow the production to go ahead.

1. I imagine that most of the anti-American, anti-war stuff contained in this play has already been published in pamphlets . . .
2. With all the talk in the papers about the anti-Vietnam war demonstrations everywhere and Bertrand Russell staging mock War Crimes Trials in Paris the ideas in this play are not exactly new or earth shaking.
3. I imagine the Royal Shakespeare audiences at the Aldwych are usually the same, very left wing beardies. So the play would be preaching to the converted and I doubt if many new recruits would be won for the anti-Americans.
4. To ban a play always gets more publicity than the play itself. And I think this could probably be explained to that nice and very sensible American ambassador.

Nor had Nugent missed the potential significance of the issues raised by
Gore-Booth:

> I am most interested to read the questions Paul GB asked the Lord
> Chamberlain. Do you think George Brown will try to get the Royal
> Shakespeare's subsidy cut? That would be too good to be true!

Nugent also seemed to imply that it might be better to allow the RSC to go
ahead in order to justify such a draconian response by Brown: 'he couldn't
very well do it unless the play were produced!'

On the same day, the Chairman of the RSC, Sir George Farmer,
interrupted his holiday 'at the Ld. Ch's request' to discuss the play
privately with Cobbold and the Assistant Comptroller. On the afternoon of
30 September, Farmer watched *US* in rehearsal, before visiting Cobbold's
house, as requested, in the evening. Peter Hall and Peter Brook were
present for the later part of that meeting, having had to wait outside in the
street to begin with. Cobbold told Farmer that 'his inclination has been to
refuse a licence', but that he had now decided 'to allow it with certain cuts',
subject to Mr Farmer providing a guarantee of accountability. 'Mr Farmer
pledged his assurances.' Following the meeting, Cobbold wrote to Farmer,
thanking him for cutting short his holiday, and summarising the situation:

> On points of detail, there are a number of cuts which I should require; some
> concerned with references to President Johnson and other political figures;
> others which I should require on grounds of religious objection or obscenity;
> and one relating to drug-addiction . . .
>
> On a more general point: I could not allow any TV monitor scene show-
> ing, or purporting to show, any interviews or discussions with the United
> States personalities. And there are one or two passages where I shall ask for
> modification of comment about America.

But he was also determined to commit Farmer to his responsibility:

> If these points can be met I shall be prepared to give a licence for the script,
> but I shall do so largely on the strength of your personal assurance that,
> having seen the play in rehearsal, you are satisfied that it is not liable to give
> offence to responsible American opinion, and that you will ensure that it is
> played in strict accordance with the licensed script.

Farmer responded carefully:

> When you kindly saw me on Friday evening last you asked for my assurance
> that I was satisfied, having seen the play in rehearsal, that it was calculated

not to give offence to responsible American opinion. Your letter now uses the word 'liable' instead of the word 'calculated' which does alter the emphasis somewhat.

He added: 'I trust you will not think that I am splitting hairs over this.'

On 5 October, Jeremy Brooks submitted the RSC's proposed alternatives to disallowed lines and words. They offered to remove a specific reference to the American president in one song by substituting 'the Yankee leech' for 'the Lyndon leech', but this was also rejected. However, they secured approval for 'amuse myself' instead of 'pull myself off' and—slightly bizarrely—'meditate' for 'masturbate'. A lengthy and impassioned plea was made for the final, shocking monologue to be allowed to remain intact:

> This speech is the climax of the second act. Its images are intended to bring home to an audience what the Vietnamese war would be like for us, if it were fought on English soil. The things described happen every day in Vietnam. The speech is designed to move an audience. No substitution of weaker images would achieve this purpose at this point in the play . . .
>
> We cannot believe that the Lord Chamberlain's intention is to distort the climax of the play and thus undermine the purpose reflected in the title—that the United States and ourselves share at this time an agony of conscience . . . the speech under discussion is totally inseparable from the nature and intent of the whole performance.

The initial response (probably of Hill) was to reject the plea. 'NO', he wrote in capital letters, underlining the word three times and adding three exclamation marks. But Cobbold decided that with the exception of the phrases 'swallowing each other's sick' and 'smell the explosion of frightened bowels', the speech could be reinstated. The RSC substituted 'crawling in one another's sick' and 'the running bowels of fear', and the licence was issued.

On the same day that he signed the licence, Cobbold wrote to David Bruce, the ultra-conservative American Ambassador, to warn him about the production, and to explain his decision to allow it to go ahead:

> Although I am assured by the chairman of the Royal Shakespeare Company, who has seen it in rehearsal, that it is not in his judgement liable to give offence to responsible American opinion, there is, I think, a risk that some people may see an anti-American slant in it. I thought for a time of refusing a licence, but the trouble is that this always causes an enormous hullabaloo and may well do more harm than good. In the end I decided to give a licence after toning some things down pretty considerably, and taking out some personal references to political figures.

On the bottom he added in pen: 'It is all very tiresome!'

There was one more chapter to the story of *US* and the Censor. On 2 November, Jeremy Brooks wrote to the Lord Chamberlain again: 'we are experiencing a certain amount of audience participation which invites ad-lib reply from the actors. They have been warned against this, but are sometimes left with a difficult situation to contain'. Brooks then made a request:

> We would like permission to use the following statement to be read out by the stage manager on occasions which warrant it:
> 'This is an official announcement. The actors are not permitted to speak any words that have not been licensed by the Lord Chamberlain. However, the position of members of the audience who wish to make spontaneous statements has never been clearly defined. This statement has been licensed by the Lord Chamberlain.'

In other words, members of the audience could probably say whatever they wanted—provided the actors did not reply. 'Is not this an incitement to riot?' queried Hill. Keen to avert further confrontations, Cobbold asked his secretary to come up with 'one of your carefully guarded replies please', and a few days later the RSC received a letter informing them that 'official announcements in theatres, not being epilogues or prologues or similar appendices to the play do not require the Lord Chamberlain's sanction'. In other words, 'It's nothing to do with us'. Or even *US*.[41]

On balance, Cobbold's strategic skills had enabled him to steer a successful course around *US* without generating too much adverse publicity for the Censorship. However, the case would be cited to the Joint Select Committee by Peter Hall, as a key example of the potential the Lord Chamberlain had to suppress political comment. Such overt political censorship was judged by most MPs to be irreconcilable with concepts of freedom in a modern and progressive society, and the case of *US* carried significant weight in the parliamentary debate and outcome, and the abolition of the Lord Chamberlain's authority.

MacBird

In the Matter of J. Robert Oppenheimer and *US* both received licences in the late autumn of 1966. A third play about contemporary American politics would have to wait a little longer. *MacBird* was written by Barbara Garson, described in the British press as 'a 25-year-old graduate from the rebellious university of California at Berkeley'.[42] Garson had indeed been amongst hundreds of others arrested during widespread campus student protests against the war, and was the editor of *The Free Speech Movement Newsletter*.

In fact, her playscript had begun life the previous year as a short skit for performances at anti-war events, before evolving into a full-length play. It was published in early 1966, but would only receive its first American performances in February 1967, and in the face of much opposition. In November 1966, the script was submitted to the Lord Chamberlain. Heriot reported:

> An ingenuous, amusing, often tasteless satire on the career of President Johnson . . . with Duncan as President Kennedy (and a cruel drawing in the text of his spouse). The witches are three agitators, a beatnik, a negro and an anti-Vietnam war demonstrator. They prophesy that Johnson will be Senate Leader (as he already is) then Vice President and finally President. The assassination of Kennedy is treated comically and leans dangerously to the opinion that Johnson, if not exactly responsible for it (and the later incidents that befell other members of the Kennedy family), was grateful for it for removing all barriers to his advancement. He dies of a heart attack when he learns that Robert Kennedy (Macduff) has no heart. The piece ends with Robert Kennedy swearing to carry on the 'Smooth Society' policy of Johnson.

The Reader admitted he was out of his depth:

> I am not sufficiently au fait with American politics to say whether this is libellous caricature or not. It does not appear to have been performed in the United States, in spite of the hysterical over-praise on the back cover. Perhaps this is a case for the American Embassy.

Hill had no doubt about the sharpness of the text: 'It is satire, one would almost say on the level of Swift, and as potent.' As he pointed out: 'if the facts alleged were true the writer of the play would be a person of great personal courage'. But he also recognised the political dangers:

> I am afraid that I treat this play very much more seriously than Mr Heriot. It accuses the late President Kennedy, with the connivance of his brothers, of attempting to set up a Presidential dynasty. In an America brought up on the principles of 1775 I imagine that no greater insult can be offered.

Yet according to Hill, 'this does not really concern us'—presumably because Kennedy was no longer around. The real problem was rather the direct association of the current American president with Shakespeare's ambitious regicide:

It accuses President Johnson and his wife, without any equivocation whatsoever, of luring President Kennedy to their home State of Texas and engineering his assassination. Furthermore, since the dynastic ambitions of President Kennedy's brothers constitute a threat, President Johnson is accused of being responsible for the aircraft accident which nearly killed and seriously injured Robert Kennedy, as well as another attempt on his life. President Johnson is also accused of arranging the murder of an associate who would not collaborate in the killing of Robert Kennedy . . . It is furthermore stated that the policeman who is too inquisitive about the assassination of President Kennedy was likewise murdered on official instructions.

In these circumstances, Hill was against licensing:

My own view is that public and open attack of this nature upon the Head of a friendly Power should not be given advertisement in this country but if the bona fides of the persons concerned are equal to their beliefs they should put it on first in their own country and face whatever obloquy or victimization or adulation may come to them in consequence.

Johnston suggested that the Lord Chamberlain consult the American Ambassador, but Cobbold held back on this: 'I think it would be a bit embarrassing for David Bruce to ask his advice.' Instead, he sent the script to the Foreign Office: 'I am afraid I must bother you with another play', he apologised.

It is quite funny and might be taken as a joke. On the other hand, I think the risks of its being taken otherwise are too serious and I am inclined to think that I ought not to let it go on in London, especially if it has not been played in the USA (which I am trying to find out).

The FO response was to suggest 'that it could not be shown here until it had been tried out in the United States', and Cobbold then sent the script to Bruce, explaining the situation to him:

I understand that it has not yet been produced in the States, but is likely to be in the near future. If it is and it does not provoke undue unfavourable comment, then I am prepared to reconsider licensing it here.

If you care to read the play, I hope this view will coincide with yours . . . It is, as a matter of fact, quite funny, but a bit too hot, at any rate if it were produced first in London!

Meanwhile, the play's putative producer, Michael White, told Johnston he had now discovered that the play had indeed been staged in New York, and that he had read a review of it. But the Office nudged the goalposts. White was now instructed that the Lord Chamberlain would only be prepared to reconsider his position if 'evidence could be produced of a considerable run in the United States without undue unfavourable comment'. Bruce had admitted to Cobbold that he had 'a certain admiration for the ingenuity of the author', but that 'it would at present be a mistake for it to be produced here'. As for productions in America and the legal position:

> I have made enquiries about the situation in regard to it at home, and understand it has been shown on several occasions, but I am also told, though I cannot vouch for the accuracy of this statement, it has had no consecutive run.
>
> I am not in a position to pass on whether or not its contents are libellous under American Law; I do feel, however, the text is in almost every respect . . . objectionable, and hope you will not reconsider licensing it until one can judge how it has been received in the United States.[43]

For the time being *MacBird* was grounded, though the arguments would take to the air again in the early months of 1967 when Theatre Workshop got hold of the script.

On 16 November 1966, BBC Radio's Third Programme broadcast an hour-long programme under the title 'Clearly a Case for An Enquiry', a relatively straightforward account of the history of theatre censorship. Compiled and presented by Leslie Stokes, (himself the co-author of a play about Oscar Wilde which had been refused a licence twenty years earlier), its list of real-life characters whose words were spoken aloud by actors included Lord Chesterfield, Bernard Shaw, James Barrie, Benn Levy, Michael Foot and Dingle Foot. The programme focused much of its attention on the Joint Select Committee of 1909, but it was the present situation which it had in mind, not least in its final appeal: 'Let us wish the new Committee well in their unfortunate lot. Let us hope that far from tossing up a coin they will come to a sensible conclusion and that this time something will be done about it.' The following week, the Joint Select Committee began its cross-examination of witnesses.

CHAPTER EIGHT

An Affront to Constitutional Principles (1967)

> The Committee are convinced that the case for removing the powers of the
> Lord Chamberlain over stage plays is compelling . . .
> (Recommendation of the Joint Select Committee on Censorship)[1]

By the time it began interviewing witnesses in November 1966, the Joint
Select Committee had already received written evidence and statements
from a variety of organisations and individuals. The Lord Chamberlain
was given prior access to this material, though, predictably, it was
his secretary who carefully read through it. Equally predictably, Hill
was irritated by what he found, insisting that the criticisms of Cobbold
'misrepresent his activities in the usual misleading way', and that there
was a 'tacit conspiracy of all interested parties to withhold from the public
the true nature of the Lord Chamberlain's work'.[2] Infuriatingly for him,
even the right-wing Bow group—whom he had helped and advised in their
research—had come out strongly in favour of total abolition:

> As the Lord Chamberlain does not and cannot seek to maintain any firm
> set of principles, the main justification for his authority over the theatre
> crumbles. His presence merely ensures that any point of view or cause which
> can give offence must gain general acceptance through other media before it
> can be admitted to the theatre. Moreover the Lord Chamberlain has a more
> insidious effect than the straightforward exclusion of certain points or topics.
> He can and does ban certain theoretically acceptable subjects by refusing to
> approve the mode of language or theatrical device which gives them a special
> force or meaning in a particular play . . . seemingly unaware that in the
> theatre, as in other art forms, the idea and its expression are indivisible.

The Bow Group reached an unequivocal conclusion: 'the Lord
Chamberlain (*and any censor who might replace him*) [my emphasis] is by
the very nature of his position condemned to be approved by the majority
of his contemporaries, to be deplored by posterity but to influence the taste
and morals of neither'.[3]

Hill maintained that the Lord Chamberlain's critics missed the key point and failed to acknowledge the dangers of removing all restraint:

> the matter at issue is not freedom to express facts or opinions, but . . . with the fictional notions of the author presented as fact in the form of plays which may have very great influence over the community whether based on truths or untruths. The liberty demanded by the abolitionists is the liberty to act and speak in public without being subjected to any moral, religious or social responsibilities. Nothing whatever is said of the responsibility to the Community that such freedom implies, nor who shall assess the degree of responsibility.

Nor did he accept that common law was capable of providing the essential protection:

> What can be done under Common Law to control, for example a spate of plays on the subject of 'Juvenile Drug Taking' which whilst not advocating the vice deal in detail in methods and experience, and as such likely to arouse the interest of the immature. Or, a succession of bestial or sadistic plays which are neither indecent nor obscene. After the Moors Murder it would be hard for anybody to suggest that there are not people likely to be affected by this type of work.[4]

But the Lord Chamberlain's secretary was fighting an increasingly lone battle.

Business as Usual

For the time being, the Lord Chamberlain continued to fulfil his authority, but exercising that authority effectively was not getting any easier. On 1 January 1967, John McGrath's *Events while Guarding the Bofors Gun* was submitted for performance at the Edinburgh Lyceum Theatre. Set amongst a group of soldiers doing national service in the 1950s, and depending to a considerable degree on authenticity of language, the script was bound to pose difficulties. Tim Harward, himself not long out of the services, admired its achievement: 'It is an effective piece of theatre', he wrote; 'The situation is real and undershot with tension. The dialogue is accurate barrackroom language.' But this accuracy was the problem, and over eighty changes were demanded:

> 'Baw-lawks' . . . 'sod it' . . . 'pissy-knickered' . . . 'he wondahs if the Almighty might not have a finger up it' . . . 'fine arse on him' . . . 'all the Second Lieutenants have to bend over for the C.O.' (sodomy inferred) . . .

'gobshite' . . . 'fresh frozen pees' . . . 'He's having a crafty J. Arthur' (Troop slang for masturbation) . . . 'I don't give a silent fart' . . . 'shit myself' . . . 'we can always amuse ourselves. Or each other' (Homosexual act or masturbation implied here) . . . 'I'll have a frost-bitten cock' . . . 'Irish bum boy' . . . 'heap of shit' . . . 'your finger up me bum' . . . 'a monkey's fart' . . . 'you've crapped it' . . . 'You may telephone to the late King George the Sixth himself.'[5]

However, the production—directed by a young Richard Eyre—found an ingenious way to outwit some of the attempts to sanitise the language, inventing a non-speaking character by the name of 'Kinnell', who could be conveniently—and loudly—invoked whenever anyone needed to swear. One can almost hear Shaw applauding in his grave.

A translation of Brecht's *The Visions of Simon Machard* also caused some hesitation in the Office:

> This is a Brechtian picture of war as muddle, intrigue, self-gain, self-preservation and suffering . . . It is highly critical, by implication, of French policy and attitudes in 1940, and attention has been drawn to certain statements which may give offence in diplomatic quarters.

In the event, a licence was approved on the grounds that although Brecht's take on war was 'a muddled one', he was 'making a universal human judgement and not a particular historical one'.[6]

Much more problematic was *The Day That Will Not End*, a home-grown play written for performance at the *Colwyn Bay Drama Festival*, which dealt with the 1963 shooting of the American President. 'This is an attempt to make a thriller out of the Kennedy assassination story', wrote Fletcher; despite its claims to be 'a documentary investigation', it was 'very far from being this', since it abandoned solid facts and was 'taken over by the author's theorising' and unsubstantiated speculation:

> His theory is that Oswald was a weakling who was used by ruthless men as a stool-pigeon. According to this theory, he did not even fire the shot. He thought he was being employed to assassinate the Governor of Texas . . .

Fletcher was prepared to recommend a licence, but Hill—without even reading the play—disagreed on the principle that it was based on fiction masquerading as fact:

> A few years ago a play of this kind would not have been allowed on the grounds that it fictionalised a recent political fact and was not in the public interest. According to Mr Kyrle Fletcher the play is reasonable according

to its lights. The decision is thus one of principle—are we to allow plays purporting to recreate the Kennedy assassination or are we not?

My own opinion is that such a play should NOT be allowed.

Johnston agreed: 'A matter of principle is involved here. This is not a documentary investigation—it is theoretical fiction.' He informed the management that the Lord Chamberlain was unwilling to license sections which 'involve the impersonation of living persons, and the attribution to them of dialogue and actions at your discretion', unless they could provide evidence that the characters' real life counterparts did not object. 'I have stalled these people', he told Cobbold, and the play was never licensed.[7]

As we know, there had for some years been tensions focused on the very idea of documentary dramas. Rumours that the enquiry into the Profumo scandal was to be used as the basis for a performance had particularly worried the Censorship, and Hill had now received evidence that such an attempt might be imminent, with a reading of sections of Denning's report by actors at the Traverse Theatre. However, since the report was technically Crown Copyright, the Traverse, reported Hill, 'have been forced to ask HMSO for permission'; HMSO had, in turn, consulted both the Cabinet Office and the Lord Chamberlain's Office:

> I told them that in my opinion, if they decided to accord permission it should be in as generalised a form as possible, so that their authority could not be quoted against the Lord Chamberlain if in fact the piece was put on publicly, and he had to interfere with it. Some phrase such as 'Objection would not be raised to the reading in public of the Denning Report', but in any case not 'approving'!
>
> Probably the effort will be done in a 'Theatre Club', but it may be something of a problem if the Traverse Theatre, which is 'progressive' in the most pejorative sense, decides to do the thing publicly.[8]

There is no evidence that a script about Profumo was ever submitted, but in January 1967 the RSC was allowed to go ahead with a Sunday reading of extracts from deliberations in the American Senate about the invasion of Vietnam, juxtaposed with a performance of a debate by senators in ancient Greece in 405 BC about the possible invasion of Syracuse. The idea for such a juxtaposition had been prompted by suggestions made by William Fulbright, an American Senator known for his active opposition to US policy in Vietnam, that future historians would make just such a link in criticising the American invasion. Irving Wardle in *The Times* compared the effect of the RSC performance to a Bach fugue, suggesting that although the two narratives were 'laid side by side without any attempts to establish links or mutual resonance', the introduction of the character of a historian 'underscored the events as if with a feather dipped in acid'. Certainly, the tone and text of the performance were critical of international powers seeking to expand and impose their Empire: 'As an American, I cannot imagine how annoying it must be to a non-American to have Americans around.'[9] The Lord Chamberlain's Office had chosen not to intervene, on the grounds that while a performance featuring 'impersonation of people involved and stage props and costume <u>would</u> be a stage play', because this was designated as a 'reading' and was presented by 'readers at a table, or sitting in chairs not laid out as a Court', it was outside their remit.[10]

Soldiers

It was a play about the Second World War—and particularly the accusations against Winston Churchill it contained—which really put the cats of documentary drama among the establishment pigeons. The name of its author, Rolf Hochhuth, was already familiar at St James's Palace, his denunciation of the Catholic Church and the Pope for their attitudes and actions during the Second World War in *The Representative* having previously caused long and heated debates. At the end of 1966, Kenneth Tynan submitted the script of *Soldiers*, not yet seeking a licence but stating 'that some comments on the play would be appreciated' prior to a forthcoming meeting of the National Theatre board which would be considering a plan to stage it at the Old Vic the following summer. The Reader—Ifan Fletcher—found much in it to admire: 'Whilst not having the stylistic distinction of the plays of Bernard Shaw', it was 'in other ways equal to the finest scenes of intellectual grappling in *Saint Joan*'. In particular, he described as 'outstandingly interesting' a scene in which Churchill discusses with a Bishop the strategy of bombing cities and killing civilians. Fletcher was aware that the text raised important issues of principle, notably 'the general question as to whether a play dealing with the motives of men who controlled events which influenced the lives of millions should be given public performance so soon after those events have taken place, and within the lifetime of one of the participants'. His own view was that this should not prevent a licence being issued. However, there were also some specific points concerning Air Marshall Arthur 'Bomber' Harris—who, as head of Bomber Command, had been responsible for instituting the mass bombardment of German cities—and, particularly, Churchill himself, who was accused by the play of complicity with the Soviet Union in the 1943 assassination of the Polish leader-in-exile Władysław Sikorski. Hochhuth would later claim that he had firm evidence which proved his claim, but which was hidden in a bank vault; though in fact, much of his research drew on the work of the right-wing historian David Irving, known subsequently as an apologist for the Nazis, and a leading Holocaust denier.

Without reading the script, and basing his assessment on Fletcher's report, Hill attacked the play as 'a gross libel on Sir Winston Churchill dead for only two years, and one which could have been the subject of action were he alive'. Indeed, there was still his son to consider: 'If there are any openings for Randolph Churchill to take action, he certainly would.' Nor were the accusations against Churchill the only issue; 'From what I read the play imputes improper motives to Harris in advocating the bombing of Germany and again could be libellous'. Hill recognised that censoring the play's theme would be contentious: 'I know that where there is a political context to a play the Lord Chamberlain is at his weakest; since the last thing he can afford to be accused of is a political bias.' On the other hand, 'he has a mandate from Parliament to forbid invidious representation'. Beyond the specifics, it was the genre and the principles involved to which Hill most objected:

> I am not surprised that it has been taken up by Mr Tynan since the latest aspect of the activities of the progressive theatre has been to move from the sphere of calculated indecency, through the 'Theatre of Cruelty', to plays which fictionalise real events, in the interests of a policy of antagonism to all in authority.

As we have already seen, this fudging of 'truth' with 'fiction' was a particular bête noire for Hill. 'The whole of this play is imagination, and it is imagination projected as fact through the mouths of living or very recently dead notabilities, and I do not think it should be allowed.' If evidence existed, then it should be presented in a book or pamphlet rather than on the stage, and the accused charged in a court of law. Theatre was not the proper place for airing such matters: 'I can see no future in the policy of giving official approval, if tacitly, to works of fiction, which since they impute words and actions to the living or recently dead, which they never uttered—must be untrue.' For Hill, this was a crucial principle in the battle over the future of censorship:

> I know that what I say would, if acted upon give rise to uproar, and I feel that the growth of this form of play constitutes a very cogent reason why the Lord Chamberlain should either lose the censorship or have his authority endorsed. I still feel that to allow the misrepresentation on the stage of the living or recently dead is wrong, and I would, if the synopsis truly represents the play, disallow it. Even if necessary making a public statement of the general principle why this has been done.

The Office played for time, as the Assistant Comptroller cautiously advised the Lord Chamberlain that he 'could put off a decision until further plans for production are made'. In the meantime, Cobbold wrote to the Chair of the National Theatre's Board, Oliver Lyttleton (Lord Chandos), aware that as a member of Churchill's wartime government he was likely to have strong views on Hochhuth's case: 'I have so far only glanced through the play and am taking it away for the weekend to read it carefully', Cobbold told him; 'It is obviously a difficult one for reasons which you, as a former colleague of some of the leading characters, will be the first to appreciate'. And he added the sort of cosy invitation which so antagonised opponents of censorship when they found out about them:

> I wonder if there is any chance of our having a private and informal word about it. If you are in London next week would you care to look in and have a word, or come and have a drink one evening at my house in St James's.

A few days later, Cobbold duly recorded in an internal memorandum: 'I have talked to Lord Chandos. He is opposed to the National Theatre putting this play on.' Officially—and much to Tynan's chagrin—the National decided to defer their decision until they had a final version of the script in front of them, and—as Chandos and Cobbold had no doubt agreed—the Office took up the same position.

In August, Tynan sent in a revised and supposedly final version of the play which retained the accusations against Churchill but removed the references to Harris. Pointedly, he also asked what the Lord Chamberlain's attitude would be towards a 'private' club production, and whether he would prosecute. Tynan pursued this question through the autumn of 1967, and each time the Office refused to answer, or to make a commitment either way. In October, Tynan arranged to visit Cobbold, with Hill convinced his aim was to secure 'some sort of undertaking that he will not initiate proceedings if the play is produced at a Theatre Club'. Johnston urged Cobbold not to concede:

> May I please make the point that Tynan is being exceptionally treated by being allowed to discuss this play with you—especially after that libellous letter he wrote to me a few months ago. Without wishing to prejudge the issue, I am sure you will stand firm.

Hill was even more insistent he should not be allowed to 'cock a snook at us', as he surely intended:

> I should like to remark that if Mr Tynan obtained an assurance of this kind, he would almost certainly erect a fictitious Theatre Club in a big London

theatre, admission to be obtainable on the flimsiest of pretexts . . . This would demolish any sort of resistance which we are putting up at the moment in an attempt to contain the censorship situation within reasonable bounds . . .

Cobbold played Tynan with the deadest of bats, and then advised both Laurence Olivier and the Director of Public Prosecutions of the gist of his discussions:

> He asked me two questions.
> 1) In view of Press comment about the Berlin production . . . was I prepared to reconsider my attitude to the play? I replied that I was sorry, but 'No'.
> 2) He said that there was now a firm offer of production at a Theatre Club at the Mermaid next February, and asked whether in these circumstances I could state whether or not there was a risk of proceedings being initiated. I repeated that, as stated in earlier correspondence, it was not possible to give any indication.[11]

There the discussions and the proposed production apparently rested—though of course Tynan knew he could probably bide his time and just wait for the end of the Lord Chamberlain's reign.

MacBird

Another political confrontation which emerged in the early months of 1967 centred on the return of *MacBird*. In February, Gerry Raffles informed the Office that Theatre Workshop was planning to relaunch itself in the spring by staging Garson's play at Stratford East with a new company under Joan Littlewood. When Johnston informed him that the Lord Chamberlain was not ready to license this text, Raffles informed the press that Theatre Workshop was considering turning the Theatre Royal into a private club. The Lord Chamberlain's Office readied itself for battle:

> It is quite possible from page 16 of 'The Times' that we shall be faced with another 'Club Effort' over *MacBird* i.e. that Joan Littlewood . . . will attempt to turn the Theatre Royal, Stratford into a Club for the occasion. I think this situation ought not to be allowed to get out of hand, and at the first inkling we should quote the recent 'Royal Court Case' to them, and make it unmistakably plain that we should send the papers to the DPP.[12]

MacBird had finally opened off-Broadway in New York in February, to a reception which *The Times* called 'predictably lukewarm'.[13] Raffles forwarded to Johnston a series of reviews of this production, and simultaneously called his bluff by giving official notification that the Theatre Workshop was prepared to go down the Royal Court route:

> I hope we will be able to show the play to a wide audience . . . but if you can't see your way to allowing full public performance for the moment, I would like, which I trust meets with your approval, to present the play for some private performances for members of the Theatre Royal Club at the Theatre Royal, Stratford.

Cobbold was less keen than Hill to strap on his armour again. He wrote to Sir Norman Skelhorn, the DPP, warning him that the issue of theatre clubs was about to re-emerge and that he was 'disposed . . . to continue the practice followed by my predecessors and myself of raising no objection'. Cobbold was carefully passing on the buck of responsibility: 'It may be that, in the light of the Magistrate's decision in the *Saved* case, you would take a different view and feel that some action should be taken' he observed; 'but that, I think, is a matter for decision by yourself and the Law Officers'. Hill, for one, did not expect the Director of Public Prosecutions to take up the baton:

> My feeling is that the DPP who is on difficult ground with the present mood of Parliament, on all matters affecting indecency and obscenity, won't move unless we force him to, as we did over *Saved*. He has, after all, little to gain and much to lose by pulling our chestnuts out of the fire.

Cobbold advised Sir Paul Gore-Booth, the Under Secretary of State in the Foreign Office, that he intended to give unofficial approval for *MacBird*. He acknowledged it was 'contrary to long established practice for the Lord Chamberlain to give a licence for the play, which is, as you will remember, extremely scurrilous about the President'; but he pointed out that it would be staged either way:

> The Stratford theatre people are now going to put it on in a theatre club for members only (How genuine the 'club' will be I do not know). For my part I should be prepared to turn a blind eye to this . . . whilst feeling that I must refuse official approval, I see no reason to make a fuss about a club perfor-mance even if the club is slightly bogus.
>
> But I have felt bound to let the Director of Public Prosecutions know the facts (without encouraging him to take action) and it will be for him and the Law Officers to decide whether action should be taken.

Skelhorn agreed that 'drastic action should, if possible, be avoided in these cases until the Joint Select Committee has made its report', and that turning a blind eye was the soundest policy.

> Even if the production was in circumstances which must properly be regarded as a public performance I would still feel that pending the report of the Committee, proceedings should only be taken in an exceptionally flagrant case in which the law was being defiantly flouted.

The DPP indicated that he would also seek advice from the Attorney General, and a few days later wrote to Cobbold to confirm he had 'now ascertained that the Attorney agrees with the views which I expressed'.

It was clear that no-one had the stomach to become embroiled in another fight at this time. Well, no-one except Hill—who was almost spoiling for one: 'Having with some pain and difficulty established the fact that the Lord Chamberlain can be pushed only so far', he wrote, 'I am reluctant to see this position abandoned, even with the Censorship Committee in being'. He proposed issuing a warning to the company that if it went ahead with its plan 'The Lord Chamberlain will be bound to test their arrangements, and take appropriate action in consequence'. This would ensure that 'If we do have to prosecute they cannot say they have not been warned'; it might even scotch the snake: 'We may by this means frighten them and thus ensure that their rules and behaviour are such that we don't have to interfere; which obviously we should prefer not to do.' But Hill knew full well what the Office would be up against: 'I have had dealings with Miss Littlewood before', he warned, 'and I would say that any attempt at finding an amicable modus vivendi will be a waste of time'. Here, indeed, was an enemy to be feared: 'being the darling of the Left she will have any number of influential backers in whatever defiance she proposes to indulge in'. Yet perhaps there was an even greater risk for the Censorship in putting their tail between their legs and running away?

> Whether in view of the existence of the Committee the Lord Chamberlain would prefer to avoid a head on collision is not for me to say. But I do feel that if legislation should be a long time coming, and we allow the bogus Theatre Club to re-establish itself, we shall be exposing ourselves to a great deal of ridicule and trouble.[14]

Mrs Wilson's Diary

In the event, *MacBird* proved to be a damp squib. It opened without a licence but was not particularly well received and ran only for a few weeks; there was thus no pressure to secure the licence which would have allowed a transfer to a public venue. Johnston was even invited to attend the show's final performance, as a guest of the theatre, but declined. However, the continuing ability of Theatre Workshop to get under the Censors' skin was immediately demonstrated again in relation to their stage version of a well-known column published weekly in the satirical *Private Eye* magazine. The column purported to be written by the prime minister's wife and to offer an everyday perspective of goings-on in and around 10 Downing Street. In April 1967, Cobbold wrote a confidential memorandum to his Comptroller and Assistant Comptroller:

> I have spoken privately to the Prime Minister about the Stratford Theatre's reported intention to produce *Mrs Wilson's Diaries*.
>
> I said that our normal practice is to allow a good deal of teasing of public figures, but that we should look very carefully at anything affecting private individuals (and should consider Mrs Wilson, to some extent at least, a private individual), and should probably insist on the assurance that the individual did not object.
>
> Mr Wilson agreed that, unless there was anything unduly offensive about Mrs Wilson or other private individuals, it would probably be wise not to refuse a licence.[15]

The script, which Raffles submitted soon afterwards, opens with the news that the Prime Minister has denounced the American policy in Vietnam as 'utterly indefensible' and 'a crime against humanity', and that President Johnson has responded by ordering air strikes on London. Wilson, meanwhile, plans to parachute George Brown, his Foreign Secretary, into North Vietnam with a personal letter to Ho Chi Minh, with the minister depicted as an incompetent drunkard, cheerfully boasting about himself as 'the wonderful Mr Brown'. Wilson and his wife are a colourless suburban couple—almost a pre-echo of the grey puppets used thirty years later by Spitting Image to mock the Conservative Prime Minister, John Major—and they end the play (after America has bombed Greenland by mistake) singing an ode to cocoa and retiring to bed. The script is punctuated with references to current politicians, and the cast list also includes Jim Callaghan (then Chancellor of the Exchequer) and Gerald Kaufman. In one scene, the French President, General de Gaulle, visits 10 Downing Street and discovers a (male) police inspector giving the kiss of life to a (male) French onion seller on the sofa. So shocked is he by this that he utters his famous one word rejection of Britain's application to join the Common Market:

DE GAULLE: Aha. Qu'est-ce que c'est que je vois?
HAROLD: Aha, mon General, bonjour.

DE GAULLE: Le vice anglais!
HAROLD: No no . . . Gladys, more paste sandwiches quick.
DE GAULLE: Non!!!
(*He turns on his heel and strides out*)[16]

Heriot was incensed by the play's mockery of respectable public figures
and his report was scathing:

> I am told that this thing is derived from a series in the periodical 'Private
> Eye'. I have not seen the paper but, judging from the present ms. it would be
> written by Yahoos for Yahoos. This is a sniggering, unfunny, romp about
> the present Prime Minister, his wife and other people in the public view,
> with a touch of the paranoia to be found in the plays of Spike Milligan (plus
> the sudden violent obscenity) . . . in fact, material well down to the level of
> that other paranoiac, Miss Littlewood, who will no doubt be what she calls
> 'producing' it . . . Wild swipes, at undergraduate level, are taken at various
> other public figures. There is, curiously, no attempt at political satire. In an
> odd way, it is a snobbish production—the whole thing is beneath contempt.

In addition to 'all the permissions that will be required from persons
lampooned', Heriot proposed around twenty cuts:

> The delivery man must not have 'a tendency to break wind'
> 'Bollocks!' . . .
> The statue of President Johnson must not be naked. Nor must the private
> parts of the statue be emphasised either with or without a duster . . .
> Wilson must not make any gesture towards them, with or without the duster
> (which must not be there, anyway)
> The whole of George Brown's song
> 'bugger off'
> 'F . . . the Pope'
> the entire appearance of M. and Mme. De Gaulle . . . all references to the
> 'kiss of life' as the 'poof's delight' and 'le vice Anglais'
> 'Balls to your partner Arse against the wall'
> The whole scene with the Queen on the other end of the telephone.

In fact, he recommended complete refusal of a licence because 'the thing is
so cheap and gratuitously nasty, and so completely worthless'.

Johnston sent the script to the Lord Chamberlain: 'It is in poor taste',
he warned him; 'However, in view of your conversation with the Prime
Minister, I suppose it might be allowed with cuts'. As he added: 'All the
principal characters are made to look very silly indeed, but apart from
George Brown's addiction to drink (which I suppose everyone knows) there

is nothing particularly nasty or invidious.' Cobbold agreed it was 'silly stuff', but felt 'pretty sure it would be a mistake to advertise it by refusing a licence'. He asked the Assistant Comptroller to discuss matters with the Prime Minister's secretary, Michael Halls, and Johnston forwarded the script to him at the start of May. 'He thinks the PM will ask Mrs Wilson to read it', he told Cobbold. Perhaps it was not a priority on the Prime Minister's agenda, for a week later the Assistant Comptroller reported there was little news on his response:

> Mr Halls telephoned on Friday to say he had not made much progress with the Wilsons. They had discussed the play but neither . . . had read it. Mrs W. was not too keen to do so, but the PM was still hoping to persuade her to. She was worrying a lot about him, as he is rather under pressure at the moment, and has been very busy speech-writing.
>
> The PM has also spoken to G.B. [George Brown] about the play and says he too ought to read it. He also doesn't want to much, and says he is unlikely to agree to it because (as he says) he has had just about enough of this sort of thing.

Johnston felt obliged to apologise to Raffles for the delay, and suggested to Cobbold that 'If you have a chance to have a word with the PM tomorrow evening, this might be a good idea'. Ten days later, Halls wrote to say that the script had now been read not only by the Wilsons, but also by George Brown, Jim Callaghan and Mrs Callaghan. As a result, further lines for deletion were marked (such as a reference to 'that time Audrey Callaghan got taken short') and these were duly added to the list of cuts.

Mrs Wilson's Diary eventually opened in September with over thirty endorsements. Hill attended the first performance and, surprisingly, described it as 'a jolly romp' with a sense of humour which was 'good-natured and harmless and in no way malicious'.[17] Possibly his response would have been different if the play's targets had been Conservative rather than Labour politicians.

Tricks and Treats

In April, the Lord Chamberlain's Office crossed swords again with the RSC, this time over the Aldwych's hosting of the World Theatre season, which included a week's run of a production by Peter Zadek and the Bremen Theatre Company of Wedekind's *Spring Awakening* (*Frühlings Erwachen*) in its original German. The Office advised the RSC that all previous restrictions—notably those involving physical and sexual action, such as 'the masturbation scene' and the 'physical act of affection' between two boys—still applied. However, five days before the production was due to open at the Aldwych, the RSC's London manager wrote to advise the Lord Chamberlain that he understood from discussions with the British Council and the Assistant Head of Cultural Relations at the Foreign Office that 'if the alterations are rigidly insisted upon the Bremen Theatre Company intend to refuse to come'. 'Their contention', reported Johnston, 'is that this play has been put on all over Europe for the last sixty years without alterations being made'. The Comptroller agreed to meet the RSC's Literary Manager, and a compromise was reached in which the Censorship conceded at least one potentially significant step:

> The director of the play feels very strongly that the one brief kiss serves to emphasise the innocence of this relationship—in fact, these two boys are the only ones who manage to preserve their innocence, because they are able to express themselves simply and directly and without aggressive sexuality. He does not feel that it is possible to alter the way in which it is played.

The kiss seems to have been quietly permitted, but when Johnston subsequently checked the reviews of the production he discovered that other rulings had been ignored: 'Yesterday's *Times* article was probably deliberately sensational, but it referred to flagellation, masturbation and homosexuality.' This did not go unnoticed. 'Disgusted at your pusillanimity in allowing this filthy German play to be performed in London', fumed one correspondent to the Office; 'Country's morals are in a bad enough state without having to see stuff like this on the British stage'. And he questioned 'why you didn't have the guts to stand out for the elimination of the obscenities?'[18]

There were also two major clashes in early 1967 between the Censors and The London Traverse Theatre Company. The first was over the script of Sandro Key-Aberg's experimental piece *Oh!*:

> This play is described as 'Speakies', by which the author presumably means a series of short scenes, performed almost with television technique. It is difficult to find a story—in fact the author would probably repudiate the suggestion that there should be one . . . the multiplicity of short scenes all turn around the question of loneliness, sexual frustration, fear of the bomb, lack of communication and bourgeois stupidity, all adding up to the feeling of hopelessness. The characters are called by letters of the alphabet.

The Reader also noted that 'In some of the scenes the author, following up his attacks on bourgeois stupidity, has obviously gone out of his way to shock'; and he listed twenty-eight examples of language, as well as a 'reference to the Royal family [which] will probably be spoken sarcastically', and others to Lyndon Johnson and to Dorothy Macmillan. 'I'm sad that I am not included', wrote one of the Lord Chamberlain's staff. There were also 'Four references to "thing" which probably involves a double meaning', and an entire section which was too offensive to allow:

> It is a scene between God and Jesus, with Jesus blaming God for having let Him down when He was on earth, suggesting that God was displeased and surprised by the Resurrection, and ending with the suggestion that God is going to send Jesus back to earth against his will.

The manager gave a written promise in relation to 'thing', that 'no double-entendre would be suggested by any stage-business or intonation', and guaranteed that 'no actor impersonates, or attempts to impersonate either God or Christ'. On that basis a licence was issued, but when Hill went to check the show in performance he reported that although there was no problem with the 'thing', some disallowed lines had been included, and in the case of one particular scene the Office had been taken for a ride. 'The stage directions on p. 53 are a deliberate deception', he noted, for he had witnessed nothing less than sexual intercourse occurring—albeit off-stage:

> The sound track started with very gentle little sighs and kissing noises, which gradually became more rapturous, the girl's sighs getting louder and the man giving little groans. These continued to get louder and more frequent—until suddenly there was a little squeak of pain from the girl, followed by more kissing and sighing which gradually became rhythmic and changed to moans of pleasure/pain on the part of the girl and grunts from the man. When the man got to what the irreverent refer to as the short-stroke, he shouted exultingly in time whilst the girl screamed in unison. The noise at last deafened the actors on stage, who were shouting to make themselves heard.

The Assistant Comptroller sent one of his stiffest letters about this 'serious breach of the Theatres Act' to the Licensee of the Theatre, and to the Managing Director of the company involved: 'I am to ask for your assurance that these illegal interpolations will be omitted at once', he seethed, pointing out that it was 'an offence for which there are considerable financial penalties for any additions to be made to the allowed MS of a play'.[19]

The Traverse was soon in conflict with the Office again over *Fanghorn*, described as 'a purple comedy' by its author, David Pinner, 'which is presumably a black comedy tinted with blue jokes'.[20] Pinner had recently won a Drama Bursary from the Arts Council, and the play was to be staged first under private club conditions in Edinburgh before transferring to London. Its director was Charles Marowitz—an old adversary of the Office, and a leading advocate of theatrical experimentation, who had been involved with Peter Brook in some of the RSC's Artaudian experiments. Reporting on *Fanghorn* at the end of February, Tim Harward acknowledged it as 'an effective piece of drama', but said it contained 'a number of disturbing elements', to which he drew attention: 'There is a strong sexual theme, some of it perverted', he reported, while 'the atmosphere . . . warrants close attention'. Overall, 'Despite the fact that the touch is light and the humour real there is an underlying seriousness and concern with sordid detail that have a cumulative and unpleasant fact'. Harward's summary of the 'bizarre plot' highlighted some of these aspects:

> The central character is Joseph King, Secretary to the Minister of Defence, and married to a second wife, Jane, fourteen years his junior. He has a very attractive and sexy daughter, Jackie, by his first wife. As the play opens, Tamar Fanghorn, a lesbian friend and ex-partner of Jane, has been hidden in the house for two days . . . Tamara and Jane have planned to humiliate Joseph by exposing his past and subjecting him to a third degree interrogation. They tie him up, strip him of his clothes and cut off his moustache in the presence of his daughter . . . The play ends with Jane walking out and leaving Tamara with Joseph, who then go to bed together.

This narrative, said the Reader, was 'embellished with a humour that is at times whimsical, flippant, sexual and fantastic'; but it was the 'lesbian overtures' which worried him the most: 'Jackie . . . is depicted as a precocious, sexually informed and desirable victim for Tamara who . . . is shown as a confirmed lesbian who has had a long standing affair with the girl's stepmother.' Harward also noted in relation to the husband that he was 'uncertain whether any resemblance to the present Secretary to the Minister of Defence is intended'.

The Reader compiled a three-page list of specific lines and images which merited consideration, and Johnston sent the script to Lord Nugent, the former Comptroller, for advice. Unfortunately, it was all a bit much for him: 'My dear Johnnie', he replied, 'I do not feel very competent to give an opinion on these symbolic plays. I never go to see them if I can possibly avoid it because I am much too dull witted to get "the message"'. Nugent hypothesised that the play was 'an essay on sensuality and masochism, in the "Theatre of Cruelty" tradition', but he was less shocked by the lesbianism than by certain other elements: 'Is "insert my foot up your frontal pivot" much better than "kick you in the cunt"?' he mused. He was also clear that 'Grandpa's remark about his arse and wiping it with grass is a bit too nasty', and adamant that 'all mention of "the Queen Mum's place" should come out, particularly the line "she can stuff her cabbage"'.[21]

Fanghorn had by now opened in Edinburgh,[22] with *The Scotsman* headline calling it a 'SPLENDID PARODY OF PERVERSION'. The review itself suggested that 'If Ibsen, Genet and Agatha Christie had collaborated on the script of "The Avengers" they might have given us something like *Fanghorn*'.[23] In seeking the licence for the public transfer to London, Marowitz took up the idea that the play was intended (and was seen by audiences) as a parody of a current fashion, rather than a straightforward expression of it. Hill and Johnston held a meeting to test this with the director, the playwright and a representative of Penguin Books:

> The author stated that this was his intention and that eventually the audience realise that they are being 'spoofed', that all the horrors depicted were imaginary ones and the whole show became a burlesque 'Marat Sade' Performance.
>
> All repeated that the audience once it realised the purport of the play treated it as a farce and an occasion for laughter at the expense of Genet, Theatre of Cruelty etc. . . .
>
> All agreed that read at its face value the play was offensive, they agreed that in print it could be so taken, but all seemed sincere in their assertion that it was played and accepted unquestioningly by the audience as a 'send-up' of the current stage trend extolling cruelty and corruption.

Hill remained uncertain about who was doing the spoofing and who was really being spoofed, but Cobbold issued a licence which left the basic theme and narrative essentially intact, while making extensive cuts to the language. In doing so, he followed Lord Nugent's advice:

> Personally, in view of some of the plays that have been passed lately and the extreme sophistication of the modern generation and the things they can read in the Press and in novels and see on television, I have grave doubts whether he would be justified in banning it. I say this with great reluctance because I think it a horrible play although, no doubt, the beardies and intellectuals at the Royal Court or Aldwych for whom I presume it is destined would disagree with me.[24]

In the spring, the RSC submitted Jules Feiffer's *Little Murders*, a dark comedy about contemporary urban life set in New York. The following year, the London critics would vote this the best foreign play of the year, but Heriot found little in it to commend: 'I see nothing very much else in this play except dottiness and dirt—or, if you prefer it, madness and merde', he complained; 'Why the Aldwych theatre should receive subsidies for performing this kind of play, defeats me'. A relatively short list of specific cuts was sent out, but the playwright and the literary manager contested these, insisting the play had already enjoyed 'a successful fortnight in Boston—a very straight-laced town, where there was not a single complaint as to the language'. The argument centred primarily on the use of the word 'shit', which recurred in the script on a regular basis:

> They said this word was not used as an expletive and was fundamental to the play. They had searched most diligently for an alternative without finding one, and the implication was that if the Lord Chamberlain rejected their appeal he would be responsible for the play, already in rehearsal, having to be abandoned.

Hill was in two minds about this; 'it is fair to say that the author, taken at his own standard, is using the word for a serious and powerful purpose', he acknowledged, following a meeting involving himself, Johnston, the author, and the RSC's literary manager; 'We all agreed "faeces" or "excrement" were not acceptable alternatives'. It was a hard one to juggle: 'The use of the word will hardly corrupt', he conceded:

> <u>On the other hand</u>
> 'Shit' is a degrading and offensive word.
>   It is not used in public reading such as newspapers, nor in even the Pocket Oxford Dictionary. It has not hitherto been allowed on the stage . . .
>   If 'shit' is allowed here—the greatest difficulty will be experienced in preventing it from becoming common currency on the stage.

Johnston wrote to the RSC, informing it of the Office's final decisions: 'I fear that the most important one will come as a disappointment to you', he wrote; 'I can only say that the Lord Chamberlain is very sympathetic with the views you expressed, but after giving the matter very careful consideration he feels bound to disallow the use of this word on the stage in any context'. The production went ahead, with 'crap' substituted.[25]

    At the same time it was considering Feiffer's play, the Office was faced with another 'really smelly play'—James Casey's *A View to the Common*, submitted by the ESC and the Royal Court. The play is set in a one-bedroom London flat, and the characters include Doll, Boxer, Big Man, Small Man, Daniel—an 'unemployed ex-mental patient'—and Rex, a one-year old cross-breed dog. Heriot identified a 'pervading stink of poverty, madness and sex; of unmade beds and unwashed dishes, plus a lavatorial voyeurism for good measure, the whole enveloped in obscure Pinterese'. One concern was a scene which opens with the stage direction 'Big Man and Small Man in left bed, Timothy and Daniel in right bed'.[26] There were some explicit issues to address: 'I do not think that the two male couples can be seen in bed. They are all obviously homosexual.' Other elements made them suspicious: 'The Scene on page 10 I <u>think</u> means that Timothy is watching the man and the woman in the park with a dog that rears up on the woman and has an orgasm.' These were both included in list of required amendments sent out in late April, which also disallowed a range of words and phrases, including 'shooting sperm', 'cock', 'spermatic grasshopper', 'inward masturbation', 'Pissing on a man's back', 'penis', 'desolation before and after masturbation', and 'up her Tooting Broadway'. Like Heriot, Fletcher felt there was more at stake than he could fully grasp: 'There seems to be a strong undercurrent of nastiness, but the conversation is frequently so obscure that it is difficult to tell how far the feeling of perversion and sadism would emerge in a performance.' Desmond O'Donovan, the Royal Court's associate director, replied to the list of cuts with his own little dig: 'I am, of course, as usual profoundly disturbed by your expression of his Lordship's sexual and bodily taboo—life.'[27] The amended script was uneasily licensed.

In the early summer the Royal Court also submitted two plays by Joe Orton, *Erpingham Camp* and *Ruffian on the Stair*. 'This is an insipid and intellectually undemanding play of negative value', wrote Harward of the latter. He drew attention to various unacceptable phrases, including 'I'll have the stones off him', and 'knocking it off', and the Office also insisted that 'the actor and actress must not be in bed together', and that a reference to royalty—'furs and garters flying'—should be removed.[28] *Erpingham Camp* required only a handful of more or less minor cuts of language, though the director, Peter Gill, made a special plea in relation to one of the excisions:

> Could we amend the stage direction 'Eileen makes a farting noise' to 'Eileen blows a raspberry', as it is the moment in the play when the leading character in the play reaches a fulcrum of hubris, and it is very necessary that he should receive a non-verbal puncture. We will undertake to make the noise inoffensive.

The Lord Chamberlain refused to negotiate: 'We stand firm.'[29]

He was sometimes less firm if you simply ignored him. In James Casey's *A View to the Common* it seems as if the ESC may have paid no attention to some of the official endorsements; certainly, at least one review refers to the male characters being in bed together, concluding that 'clearly the script discovered the Lord Chamberlain in one of his most indulgent moods'.[30] And in May, it was the Royal Court again, with newspaper headlines announcing: 'THEATRE TO DEFY LORD'S PRAYER BAN'.[31] The Office had originally decreed that Don Haworth's *Oh God I've Left The Gas On* should receive a licence only with an endorsement stipulating that the Lord's Prayer should not be spoken on stage. 'Well there you are', wrote the Assistant Comptroller to Cobbold when he saw the headlines; 'If they do you can warn them . . . and if they persist you can ask the DPP to prosecute'. But the Office knew the DPP was unlikely to do so. The only alternative, Johnston told Cobbold, was to 'ignore the whole thing', even though this was almost certain to 'lead to bigger defiances' in the near future. 'I wonder in fact why we haven't been "defied" before', he mused. To avoid confrontation and head off overt disobedience, the Censorship chose to substitute a deliberately vague endorsement requiring that the Lord's Prayer 'must not be spoken in an irreverent manner'.[32]

Joe Egg

The script which caused most discomfort in the early summer of 1967 was Peter Nichols's dark comedy about caring for a brain-damaged girl, *A Day in the Death of Joe Egg*. Michael Blakemore was to direct it in Glasgow, and in a lengthy letter submitted to the Lord Chamberlain with the script, he did his best to frame and explain the text in ways which might persuade the Lord Chamberlain of its sincerity and significance. 'So unusual is the play that I feel a word about it might not be out of order', he wrote. Blakemore began by indicating that the text submitted was a draft rather than a final version—thus carefully leaving room for manoeuvre and forestalling an outright rejection. He then pointed out that the play was 'to some extent an autobiographical work, the author himself having a child similar to the one described in the play'—a fact which he doubtless hoped would forestall accusations of insensitivity or cruelty. Blakemore went on to try and justify not just the subject but the surprising tone and style in which the piece was written:

> To most people the situation it presents is a shocking and disturbing one, but the intention of the play is certainly not to shock. On the contrary it is to reduce the problem of any of its horrific or mawkish elements and site it firmly in the only area where it could properly be considered; that utterly real and unsentimental environment where it has to be lived and coped with in the first instance. I believe it is an important play because it is the first to approach a problem of this sort without any of that false gravity with which the well meaning outsider is expected to view the misfortunes of another. It has an audacity which only first hand experience could support, and the extraordinary humour of the piece, far from indicating callousness, testifies to considerable courage and tenderness.

As for its 'sexual frankness', this was 'no more . . . than one would expect in the conversation of any intelligent married couple', and not 'out of line with what you have agreed to in other plays'. Blakemore also tried to anticipate what would indeed prove to be one of the Lord Chamberlain's

greatest anxieties—the physical representation on stage of the central
character:

> The writer and myself are agreed that the last thing we want is to unduly
> alarm the audience, who are meant to see the child as do its parents, with
> the daily familiarity of ten years experience. A perfectly normal child actress
> will be asked to play being permanently asleep. The fits to which the script
> refers are small things, immediately perceptible of course to the parents, but
> of little significance to an outsider. I believe the presentation of the child on
> stage will be far less terrible to see than it is to read about on the page.

Heriot had no time for any of this: 'A play about an over-sexed school-
master and his wife with a spastic child by, I suspect, an over-sexed
schoolmaster with a spastic child', was his summing up. He conceded that it
was not necessarily intended to be exploitative, but still had little sympathy:

> In a twisted way, I suppose the author is trying to say something about the
> plight of parents saddled with spastic children, but it is as if he vomited up
> all his bitterness and helplessness and showed the basin (to use an inelegant
> metaphor) to his captive audience.

It would be bound, he thought, to cause widespread anger and revulsion:

> The medical profession and the church are both libelled in a particularly
> juvenile way. Doctors and clergymen will be offended by this play and I
> should think that any woman in the audience who is in similar circumstances,
> will be outraged.

The issue of the child performer also worried him, especially the implication of having her on stage to hear the language and sexual innuendo:

> I must utter a feeble protest about asking a young actress to play the part
> of the child. If she is young enough to look the part then the conversation
> in Act One is unsuitable and even though she appears as a normal child in
> short 'visionary' sequences, the mental burden she will have to carry will be
> heavy. At the same time I realise that a dummy in a wheelchair is not enough
> if our withers are to be wrung as the author intends.

Heriot was undecided about his final recommendation, and so was
Johnston, who found the play 'a bit fruity', with a theme 'unusual, if not to
date unique'. He recognised that Nichols's text had merits, but there was
also plenty to dislike: 'At times it is moving and the author undoubtedly
has a message, but as the reader says he puts it over in a twisted way.'

Blakemore's letter, he said, was 'honest and seems sincere', and the Assistant Comptroller proposed that if they did issue a licence then a note could be put in the programme to indicate the autobiographical starting point. But he still had reservations: 'What sticks in my gizzard a bit is the association of all the sex-talk . . . in front of a spastic child.' Uncertain what to advise, he passed it to Cobbold: 'You will doubtless want to read the play', he suggested; 'On balance I feel it should be given a licence, but it is difficult to estimate the degree of offence taken to seeing it on stage as compared to reading it'. Cobbold was prepared to approve it: 'I do not find any general difficulty in licensing this play', he wrote, 'subject to the cuts and alterations recommended'. However, he agreed that the child actress was a major issue, and proposed asking 'whether Joe could be off-stage or in the wings some or most of the time—or possibly a dummy except when activated'. Johnston phoned Blakemore and asked him to consider whether in preparing a final version of the script it might be possible to at least reduce the time the actress was on stage: 'I suggested that if he can do this there may be fewer cuts.' Hill thought that publicity should warn the audience about the subject-matter, and that perhaps it could have 'a secondary title as in the old days'. *The Tale of a Spastic Child* should do the trick, he proposed.[33]

Nichols has since written—both factually within his diaries and fictionally within his play *Blue Murder*—about the experience of accompanying Blakemore to St James's Palace to discuss the production. He recalls, for example, his own amazement at the suggestion that an innocent and throwaway gag directed by one of the characters to an imaginary dog had been interpreted as a line spoken to the character's own penis ('"Down Rover" to be accompanied by shallow breathing only means one thing to me', Hill had written).[34] Blakemore argued that to keep the girl offstage would take theatre back to the days of Victorian melodrama, and that the use of a puppet or marionette would be 'a crueller joke than anything in the play'. But Johnston was adamant that even though it would not really be a child playing the part, it was also important not to let audiences think they were watching a child listening to sexual discussions between her parents. Better to wheel her off-stage for such exchanges. Presumably, it wouldn't matter that the performer might still hear the lines from the wings, so long as the audience didn't see her hearing them.

Following this meeting, Blakemore sent in a final script. He also pointed out that the publicity 'has made a point of advertising the fact that the subject of this play is a chronically retarded child', and that Nichols guaranteed 'that in all future productions he will include a paragraph in his contract requiring the management concerned to similarly publicise the nature and subject of the play'. In late April, the Office sent out a list of some twenty cuts, most of them sexual references considered too explicit.

A few of them were contested by Blakemore: 'The author has also asked me to put in a word for "Universal Shafting"', he pleaded; 'This was, in fact, the actual name of a firm his wife worked for'.

The Glasgow production was generally well reviewed, and at the end of May, Blakemore wrote again to the Censorship:

> As I rather hoped, in performance the play is far less shocking than it appears on the page. Its honesty and lack of obliqueness are respected by audiences (especially by people who have had first hand experience of the subject themselves) and we have not had a single complaint or expression of shock.

He also asked whether a deleted line about giving a suppository to the child could now be reinstated, since 'it is central to her condition and the daily routines that surround her existence'. In support, he cited a review of the play which had speculated that because of censorship 'the subject may have been softened a shade beyond the point of reasonable honesty'. *The Times* had indeed suggested that the audience was being 'protected—too carefully', and that too much remained 'hidden by the back of the sofa'. Cobbold conceded, and on 6 June the Office informed Blakemore that the line could be restored.[35] As it happens, 6 June was also the date when the Joint Select Committee on Censorship of the Theatre met to read and formally adopt its final report.

The Committee Reports

The Government's Joint Select Committee of 1966–1967 examined far fewer witnesses than its predecessor in 1909 had done. In fact, they interviewed only nine individuals: Lord Cobbold, Dingle Foot (the Solicitor General), John Mortimer (representing the League of Dramatists), Benn Levy (the playwright and MP who had himself introduced a bill to end theatre censorship in 1949), John Osborne, Peter Hall (Director of the RSC), Kenneth Tynan (Literary Manager of the National Theatre), Emile Littler (President of the Society of West End Theatre Managers) and Peter Saunders (a leading member of that Society). However, written evidence was also considered from the Home Office, the BBC, the ITA, the British Board of Film Censors, the Archbishop of Canterbury, representatives of the Roman Catholic Church, the Arts Council, the Bow Group, the Association of Municipal Corporations, the GLC, the Theatrical Managers' Association, the Council of Repertory Theatres, the Association of Touring Managers and the Writers' Guild of Britain.[36]

The recommendation for total abolition (rather than reform) of the existing system was by no means a foregone conclusion at the start of the process. The House of Lords debate in February 1966 which had approved the setting up of an enquiry had recognised that while most parties wanted change, there was no consensus about what form it should take. Even those who favoured abolition were wary of the risk of replacing the status quo with something which might prove to be less consistent, and could end up being more restrictive, by making theatres more cautious as they were exposed to prosecutions and objections from individuals and bodies in a way generally precluded by the Lord Chamberlain's licence. This was broadly the view presented to the enquiry by the Society of West End Managers and the Association of Municipal Corporations, who were both against making any change in the existing practice:

> The main arguments adduced in its favour are that it is quick, simple and cheap: that the Lord Chamberlain by virtue of his office possesses a unique authority which no other censorship body could have; that the licence of the Lord Chamberlain affords adequate and necessary protection to theatre managers: that recent Lord Chamberlains have been increasingly tolerant: and that any change might lead to a greater rigidity and restriction.[37]

If touring shows became subject to the decisions of local authorities, it would, they said, be 'the kiss of death to the theatre in the provinces'.[38] Littler (who had had his fair share of run-ins with the Office) even described the Lord Chamberlain as 'a sort of father confessor'.[39]

Against this, Cobbold himself—with the implicit authority of the Queen behind him—was unequivocal about the need for reform: 'I take the strong view that this arrangement is no longer an appropriate arrangement.' But he argued that some form of pre-censorship should be maintained in order to protect people who 'go to the theatre not knowing exactly what they are going to see'. The evidence showed that 'by far the major part of the prohibitions and cuts by the Lord Chamberlain are concerned with obscenity', but Cobbold was particularly worried about the possibilities of sadism and blasphemy, as well as giving offence to living people. And of course, he 'expressed concern about offensive references to the Royal Family'. However, most witnesses disagreed with his caution, and the Committee noted there was 'the same objection to the establishment of any other compulsory pre-censorship authority as there is against the continuation of the powers of the Lord Chamberlain'.

Cobbold told the Enquiry that he and his colleagues 'always lean over backwards to allow everything through that we think we possibly can'.[40] However, this assertion was challenged by written evidence submitted by Peter Hall on behalf of the RSC, which declared that his claim 'simply does not square with our experience', and that 'expressions in common use on television and the cinema are automatically cut from our plays'.

They cited the examples of the e.e. cummings poem in *The Rebel,* and David Mercer's play *Belcher's Luck,* from which the 'quite inoffensive colloquialism, "you get on my wick"' had been cut on the grounds that '"wick" is rhyming slang for "prick", and that the image of one person getting on another person's prick was an obscene one'. Countering the notion that negotiations with the Lord Chamberlain were simply an acceptable part of a reasonable process, the RSC's submission insisted that while they might be 'charming gentlemen who always treat us with the greatest politeness', to have 'two retired army colonels and a professional civil servant as arbiters of public taste in an art form which they clearly neither like nor understand' was self-evidently absurd. Nor was the process good-humoured or happily resolved: 'Those unfortunate people who have to visit St James's Palace to fight for what they consider to be damaging or unjustifiable excisions invariably come away from such interviews in a state of raging frustration.'[41]

Political censorship—and specifically the recommendation of the 1909 Committee that the Lord Chamberlain should refuse to license plays 'calculated to impair relations with any Foreign Power'—had become a particularly contentious issue. Following evidence from the RSC, Cobbold was asked by the Committee whether his treatment of *US* had been because of its politics; in an effort to sidestep the question, he replied that the material banned had been 'of an abusive nature towards certain individuals which I should regard as near political'. But he also conceded that 'in the melting pot at the moment' were several plays with 'political contents' with which he was 'having difficulties'.[42] In his evidence, Hall 'stressed that the Royal Shakespeare Company felt more strongly about political censorship than anything else, and that "not being able to deal with contemporary subjects in any open way is terribly dangerous"'.[43] Indeed, the RSC argued that theatre could 'never achieve the vitality of which it is capable until it can restore the sense, which it had until the early eighteenth century, that the present is as much "history" as is the past, and requires our understanding in exactly the same detail'.[44] This proved a persuasive line of attack. The notion that States and politicians should be protected from criticism in the theatre seemed—to most people—an anachronism, and the Committee's final report stated unequivocally 'that all political censorship should cease'. It was careful not to criticise Cobbold for his actions or decisions; the problem lay with what he was being asked to do: 'The Committee are not suggesting that in the case of *US* and similar plays the Lord Chamberlain exceeded the powers granted him by parliament. But they consider that the existence of these powers is inappropriate to a modern democratic society.' The situation, then, would not be resolved by changing the executor, but by doing away with the powers.

In arriving at its final decisions, the Committee had four options available to them:

> They could recommend a continuation of the present system, the transfer of the present powers of the Lord Chamberlain to another pre-censorship body, with or without a right of appeal, the establishment of some form of voluntary pre-censorship, or the complete abolition of pre-censorship.

The first option had become untenable: 'The Committee are convinced that the case for removing the powers of the Lord Chamberlain over stage plays is compelling', declared the report; 'Accordingly they recommend that these powers should be abolished as soon as possible'. They then weighed the other alternatives. Replacing the Lord Chamberlain with an equivalent authority would meet few of the objections to the current system, and in any case, there were no takers for the role. There remained the possibility of voluntary pre-censorship—a solution proposed by the 1909 Joint Select Committee. The argument in favour of this was that total abolition might 'hurt more than it helps the cause of freedom of expression in the theatre' since 'various forms of pre-censorship are likely to operate with greater severity'. A system in which theatres were not obliged to secure licences but could opt do so if they wanted a degree of security against prosecution might therefore appear to provide the best of both worlds. But the committee concluded that this would in fact offer 'the worst of both worlds'. Crucially, they accepted the argument put forward by the Arts Council that any unlicensed play 'would invite prosecution' and that the management responsible for putting it on 'would be at a grave disadvantage in court proceedings'. Knowing this, 'commercial managements would be most reluctant to put on unlicensed plays', and a censorship named as 'voluntary' would in effect remain compulsory. Additionally, a new censorship body (perhaps equivalent to the British Board of Film Censors) was 'likely to be less liberal than the Lord Chamberlain', precisely because it 'would not be the final arbiter', and knew that managements had the right to ignore its views; 'the subsidised theatre would have the unwelcome choice of submitting a play to a more rigorous censor or inviting prosecution'. Moreover, despite how it was generally treated, the Lord Chamberlain's licence had never provided an actual guarantee in law against prosecution, and it would be 'an affront to constitutional principles' to establish a system which could bypass the laws of the land and provide a meaningful or absolute insurance against prosecution.

Finally, then, the committee's recommendation was 'to allow freedom of speech in the theatre' and depend exclusively on the criminal law as a safeguard and to exert control:

The anachronistic licensing powers of the Lord Chamberlain will be abolished and will not be replaced by any other form of pre-censorship, national or local. The theatre will be subjected to the general law of the land, and those presenting plays which break the law will be subjected to prosecution.

In the end, they said, it was 'a question of freedom'. After all, there was 'no other form of creative art where the artist may be prevented . . . from placing his work before the public not because it infringes the general law . . . but because it incurs the criticism of a censor who has absolute power to stop its presentation'. It followed from this that 'the onus of proof' fell not on those seeking to abolish the current system but rather on those wishing to maintain it, when 'Parliament does not deem it necessary in the case of any other art medium'. They therefore proposed that the current Obscene Publications Act, which already covered the written texts of plays, but not their performance, 'should be made to extend to the theatre as a whole'. Moreover, in order that this should not inhibit the protection of 'serious playwrights', the controversial section 4 of the 1959 Act—which allowed as a defence against charges of obscenity the fact that the work was judged to be 'for the public good on the ground that it is in the interests of science, literature, art or learning or of other objects of general concern'—must also be applied to theatre performances. The Committee also anticipated the risk that central censorship might be replaced by something worse: 'It would be wrong in principle to leave a local authority to assume the mantle of censor', they declared. To pre-empt this possibility, they therefore proposed 'that it should be made clear, if necessary by amending legislation, that the powers of local authorities in respect of theatre licensing should be confined to such matters as safety precautions'.

The Committee had also done its best to check whether it was true that other laws would offer the State sufficient control of theatre. The Solicitor General, Dingle Foot—who five years earlier had himself attempted to introduce a bill to abolish theatre censorship—gave evidence on this. He suggested that the issue of causing a breach of the peace was covered by the Public Order Acts and the Race Relations Act, 'which should be amended so as to make it clear that they apply to theatres'. The 'rather vague point about a play being "calculated to conduce to crime or vice"' was, in turn, 'almost certainly covered by common law', as was 'the violation of religious reverence' by the blasphemy laws. More problematic was the issue of 'representing in an invidious manner a living person or a person recently dead', and here the Committee suggested that, since no equivalent restriction was automatically imposed on broadcasting or print, 'it would be unjustifiable to legislate on this matter'. Though in any case, it judged that current laws on libel and defamation were 'sufficient to protect living people'.

No-one imagined that abolishing the Lord Chamberlain's duty to license plays for performance was the same thing as abolishing censorship. As the report itself noted: 'Censorship in the widest sense of the word will inevitably continue and by various means control will be exercised over what appears on the stage.' Nevertheless, if Parliament was willing to accept and legislate according to its recommendations, the Joint Select Committee's report marked a decisive—surely a seismic—shift in terms of the freedom of the theatre. It concluded by quoting the words of Lord Chesterfield, who had spoken in 1737 against Walpole's proposal to create what the Committee was now seeking to dismantle.

> If poets and players are to be restrained, let them be restrained as other subjects are, by the known laws of their country . . . Do not let us subject them to the arbitrary will and pleasure of any one man. A power lodged in the hands of one single man to judge and determine, without any limitation, without any control or appeal, is a sort of power unknown to our laws, inconsistent with our constitution.[45]

By aligning itself with Chesterfield, the Committee implicitly condemned the basis and practice of theatre censorship operated over the last 230 years. Legislation would surely follow.

CHAPTER NINE

Let the Sunshine In (1968)

Politically speaking, I am a moron
(Lord Chamberlain's Reader and Examiner of Plays)[1]

A show that could not conceivably be presented on any British stage . . .
(Publicity promotion for *Hair*)[2]

Under the leadership of Harold Wilson and with Roy Jenkins as Home
Secretary, the Labour government achieved some notable domestic and
liberalising reforms. Capital punishment had been removed in 1965—
though clearly against the weight of public opinion, and for a trial
period only—and in 1967 came legalisation permitting abortion, the
Sexual Offences act, which decriminalised private homosexual acts for
most consenting adults, and the Family Planning Act, which led to the
contraceptive pill becoming widely available. In 1909, the report and
recommendations of the Joint Select Committee on Theatre Censorship
had had little direct impact on theatre censorship because no legislation
had been introduced. It was highly unlikely that the 1967 report would
be swept under the same carpet. On the other hand, it was by no means
certain that parliament would accept its recommendations wholesale, nor
how long it would take to construct a bill and take it through parliament.
In the event, it would be little more than a year until the Theatres Act of
1968 would receive royal assent—and a couple of months after that before
it came into force. In the meantime, until the last Reader hung up his last
blue pencil, the band played on. And many of its tunes contained familiar
echoes of previous hits.

In June 1967, the Censorship faced down *You've Had Your War*, with
its second act set in a male toilet. 'The urinal is shown in full view of the
audience and is several times used', noted Harward; 'It is recommended
that this setting be changed'. At one point, a male character enters in
women's clothing, and the licence was issued only after the script had
been altered 'so that all reference to a gentleman's lavatory and to female
impersonation is omitted'.[3] In July, Peter Terson's *Zigger Zagger*—an

unsettling drama about football hooliganism and disaffected adolescents for the National Youth Theatre—required a couple of interventions. 'Harry must not fill his sample bottle on stage', the Office ruled, 'nor must he drop his trousers'. They reluctantly licensed the word 'pee', and refused 'shit', but their main concern was the removal of Harry's trousers in the 'debagging' scene: 'The only part of the actor to be exposed at any time . . . are knees and upper legs', they insisted; 'The actor must wear underpants or trunks and his private parts must be covered by his shirt', and 'the doctor must not make any attempt to inspect his parts'.[4]

In August, the script of Paul Foster's *Tom Payne*, which the innovative and important New York experimental company, La MaMa, had brought to the Edinburgh Festival, was sent back because it left space for the actors to devise. 'Max Stafford-Clark of the Edinburgh Traverse Theatre writes that you have a question regarding the improvisation scene in my play', wrote Foster to Johnston; he explained that the performance was built from 'free form' improvisation; 'I could throw down some meaningless drivel but it would not be true, and insulting to your intelligence'. But the script was licensed only with a string of cuts and with this freedom removed: 'I regret that the Lord Chamberlain has no power to allow a play which includes improvisation.'[5]

In the autumn, Arthur Miller's *After the Fall* suffered a string of irritating but predictable endorsements:

> The actress must not expose her breasts . . .
> Maggie must not grab Quentin above mid thigh, and must not undress beyond brassiere and briefs within view of the audience.
> Maggie's writhing must not simulate sexual intercourse.
> Nothing beyond Maggie's naked shoulders must be exposed in bed or during movement in the blanket.
> Maggie must not be exposed in less than brassiere and briefs when changing.
> . . . any action reminiscent of sexual intercourse is not allowed.[6]

Yet the Censorship was surprisingly lenient towards *What the Butler Saw*. 'Not unfunny', wrote Heriot, 'but, being by Joe Orton, it has, of course, to deviate into tasteless indecencies'. However, the only stipulation they made was that 'all references to Sir Winston Churchill's private parts are to be omitted'.[7]

Politics and Race

One play which stirred things up politically was *Number Ten*, Ronald Millar's adaptation of a William Clarke novel. Millar would later become a speech writer for three prime ministers, credited with adapting the title of a Christopher Fry play for Mrs Thatcher's famous declaration that 'the lady's not for turning'.[8] *Number Ten* included among its characters a British Prime Minister and Foreign Secretary, as well as a number of other more or less fictitious cabinet ministers. It was set 'some time after the next General Election—i.e. some years after 1970', in 'various rooms of Number Ten Downing Street', and the story focused on international confrontations and southern Africa. Ministers are shown arguing about how to respond to events in 'Zimbadia', which is threatening to nationalise its resources and its infrastructure with the support of the Chinese, and at considerable economic cost to British interests. The cabinet is split on whether to undertake military intervention, and whether to form an alliance with the South African government against the Zimbadian president. Heriot found it 'an amusing, exciting play without any personal axes to grind', but he had clearly been warned that it might raise concerns in government: 'I do not know why the Commonwealth Office should be "interested" in it— but I admit that, politically speaking, I am a moron, and that the interplay behind the scenes may be either too close to life or too frequently false to it.' He noted with approval that 'none of the personalities in the play resemble those of their namesakes in the existing cabinet'—with the exception of 'one reference to Lord Wilson of Huyton'—and recommended 'that the Assistant Comptroller read the play to see whether I have missed anything of significance that might agitate the Commonwealth or the Foreign Offices'. In the event, the only change demanded by the Lord Chamberlain was that the name of the capital city of Lusaka—as a real and identifiable place—be altered. Clarke, the author of the original novel on which the play was based, queried the reason for this in a letter to Cobbold:

> It is made perfectly clear in the novel and in the play that Lusaka is the administration capital of a new state including the Congo, Mozambique, Rhodesia etc., i.e. it is not the capital of Zambia, nor is the 'nationalisation' which takes place confined to places now in Zambia.

Confusingly, he then name-dropped the actual president of Zambia: 'Incidentally I sent my friend Kenneth Kaunda an inscribed copy of the novel and got a grateful reply.' And Clarke expressed surprise at the Lord Chamberlain's involvement in such a case: 'May I say as a writer that I am intrigued to find that your Office exerts this type of political censorship. I had thought your activities were confined to faith and morals.'[9]

In August, the Royal Court submitted a very different and potentially powerful political play. *The Nigger Lovers* was written by the Hungarian-born exile from Nazi Germany, George Tabori, best known as the English translator of several of Brecht's plays. 'This is a strong and relentless analysis of white attitudes to the Negro situation in the US', wrote Harward; 'unfortunately, the author has chosen to use a particularly pungent form of naturalism, both in dialogue and accent'. Nearly sixty cuts were made to the language, but in spite of some reservations a licence was recommended: 'All these plays do harm of course in inculcating the attitude they pretend to be combating', commented Hill, knowledgeably; 'But, short of there being direct incitement to go out and commit mayhem there is little we can do'.[10] In the same month, however, a licence was withheld from *White Man, Black Man, Yellow Man, Chief,* a drama about the Klu Klux Klan, described by Heriot as 'a completely worthless piece, full of violence, sadism, obscenity and blasphemy', not to mention 'rubber-shop stuff'. He added that 'I do not know who the author is but his address is French, where, no doubt, there are still some "Boulevard" theatres where stuff like this may be performed'. A disturbing and grisly play this certainly was, as Heriot's summary of even the opening act demonstrates:

> In a prologue, a Klansman castrates a young negro, who dies. The perpetrator, Pike, is a pharmacist, who is lured by a suggestion that he will be promoted in the Klan after initiation to a lonely shack where he finds two figures in robes, one white, one black. The black figure is a negro, Waight, who intends to torture Pike to death, revelling in the grisly details. While he is conveniently out of the way, the other man, Alvin, gets Pike to promise his entire fortune, his shop and business, his wife and daughters as a price for his life and when the negro returns he is overpowered and bound to a cross in place of Pike. The latter now triumphs and gloats over what he is going to do to Waight . . . [who] bets his own testicles against those of Pike that he will be free. At the crucial moment, Alvin double-crosses Pike and we learn that he is Pike's natural son by a young negress whom he has forced . . . Pike is once more bound to the cross and Waight sets about his tortures, first crowning him with barbed wire . . . The negro and the half-negro are about to initiate the crucifixion, nails and all, but Alvin, now positively drooling with hate and sadism, cannot wait and tears out one of Pike's toenails with a pair of pincers . . . Alvin and Waight now play dice for the privilege of beginning on Pike. Waight wins, and after a long, obscenely worded scene, somewhat reluctantly starts to castrate Pike. The latter faints just as the knife touches him and the Act ends with the audience believing that the operation has been performed . . .

The on-stage violence alone would surely have been enough to prevent the play being licensed (it ends with Pike shooting his son and then hammering nails into the feet of Waight who is bound to the cross), but Heriot's judgment was further informed by the changing political climate: 'The trend today is to prevent at all costs the fomenting of racial hatred', he noted; 'only last night I heard an historian begging radio comics to stop making jokes about Pakistani bus-conductors'. And his report concluded, perhaps with an edge of irony: 'For integrational reasons, therefore, this play is not recommended for licence.'[11]

Crossing Genders

Simon Gray's *Wise Child*, submitted in August 1967 by Michael Codron for John Dexter to direct at Wyndham's Theatre, was more awkward to deal with. To Heriot it was 'a vehicle for cheap shocks', being 'permeated by a sneaking kind of perversity'. The key female character, Mrs Artminster, is ultimately revealed to be a cross-dressing man, who has previously been seen playing an apparently lesbian scene with a maid. 'It could never be described as a serious study of homosexuality', worried Heriot. The Comptroller read the script, but it was a complicated example on which to rule. 'Homosexuality is allowed on stage when considered seriously', wrote Penn. 'I do not know whether in this play there is a serious study of homosexuality.' It depended partly on how you counted (or how audiences saw) the cross-dressing, and in trying to predict this and so decide whether they could allow it, the Censorship became tied up in knots:

> If it is thought by the audience that, at the time concerned, Mrs Artminster is a woman and not a man in the two scenes involving her and Janice . . . then these two scenes are lesbianism.
>
> If the audience are clear that Mrs Artminster is in fact a man before these two scenes take place the question of lesbianism does not arise.

Could they trust the director and the actor?

> Michael Codron explained that Alec Guinness is playing the part of Mrs Artminster and it will be clear from very early on that he is a man. He will speak in his own voice, except in the presence of Booker . . . Mrs Artminster drinks as a man rather than a woman, smokes cigars like a man and takes his shoes on and off like a man. In fact except when Booker is present, Mrs Artminster is Mother Reilly rather than Danny La Rue. Codron, however particularly wishes that Mrs Artminster does not remove his wig.

Whether this was sufficiently reassuring—or whether anyone at St James's had a sense of Guinness's ambivalent sexuality—is not clear; but there remained a question of what would actually occur on stage: 'With regard to the kissing, Codron said that this was not at any time a kiss on the lips, it was a peck on the cheek.' After much argument and negotiation, a licence was issued with endorsements against kissing and 'on the condition that, except in the presence of Booker, Mrs Artminster speaks and acts as a man'.[12]

The Office also made a couple of interventions in a show called *Way Out*. 'I have a feeling, though there is nothing definite to show, that there is a lot of transvestism about this show.' To be on the safe side, they cut 'the homosexual guardsman verse' from a song called 'Britains are Having it Hard', as well as the lines 'they suspect he's serving another queen' and 'take your hands off my clappers'.[13]

A homosexual male relationship was at the heart of a serious play by Roy Minton, staged by drama students at the Edinburgh Festival in August 1967. Minton became best known as the author of *Scum*—a banned television play set in a young offenders' institution, later made as a film; but his stage play *Death in Leicester* was described by Heriot as 'a small tour de force'. It focused on two men living in poverty in a London basement, who dream of making a fortune through gambling; 'They have both left their wives with revulsion in Leicester and it gradually dawns that theirs is really a homosexual affinity', reported Heriot. The play was licensed in August 1967 with a modest handful of cuts ('The actors must not lie on the bed together . . . since men and women are not permitted to embrace on beds'), though the Office received a handful of complaints about the subject matter and the relationship. But given the change in the law on homosexuality, how could the Office ban it? As Penn explained:

> The theme of this play is, of course, one that would have been quite un-acceptable even a few years ago, but the Lord Chamberlain must administer the Theatres Act, 1843, with regard to public opinion generally, and as given expression by Parliament, the Press and the Church, public opinion now apparently extends the very greatest tolerance to homosexuals. It is not accordingly possible for the Lord Chamberlain totally to prohibit the representation of these people on the stage as he did in the past.

The time had come for playgoers to take more responsibility themselves, rather than relying on official censorship to protect them:

> The Lord Chamberlain is most sorry that your evening's entertainment should have been spoiled, but he fears that the climate of public opinion being what it now is, it will always be advisable to enquire the exact nature of a play before going to see it.[14]

Early Morning

Edward Bond—and the confrontations over *Saved*—had undoubtedly played a part in bringing forward the end of the Lord Chamberlain's reign, and it was a new play by Bond which would have the distinction of being the last to be absolutely banned before the law changed. *Early Morning* managed to hit at some of the final and most inviolable taboos. Including Queen Victoria as a central character may no longer have been the absolute no-no it recently would have been, but to show her as a cannibal who kills her husband and rapes Florence Nightingale surely was—especially if you insisted, as Bond did, that all events depicted in his play were 'true'. The final Act is supposedly set in Heaven (though it more resembles Hell) and the list of characters also includes not only Gladstone and Disraeli (who sometimes share a bed) but even the Lord Chamberlain; moreover, we gather that Nightingale's care and nursing of wounded soldiers extends to having sex with them just before they die. The whole play was an attack on the Victorian attitudes and values which Bond believed still dominated British society. Harward partly got it: 'There may be some dramatic truth in this nightmarish plot and distorted characterisation', he acknowledged in his report, 'but it is not a normal vision'. Clearly, it went several steps too far:

> It is possible to see this play as a weird phantasmagoria, making a strong, sour statement about power and politics in the Victorian age. But, the defamatory treatment of the chief characters (principally royalty) apart, the play appears to this Reader to be the product of a diseased imagination; cannibalism and lesbianism may be legitimate themes for dramatisation, but not in this context.

Heriot endorsed his judgment: 'I have read the manuscripts and agree with everything Mr Harward has to say about this maniac play', he wrote. The Lord Chamberlain was hardly seeking the publicity and potential embarrassment which was likely to result from another confrontation with the Royal Court, and Johnston sent the script to Lord Nugent, probably hoping for a different suggestion. But Nugent could only agree that it was a 'mad play' which could not possibly be allowed: 'I hoped in a way that I might be able to disagree with both Readers and recommend a licence in some form, but with the best will in the world this just does not seem possible', he wrote:

> I think the author must have a very sick mind, and I cannot conceive that anyone would want to see the play, except possibly in anticipation of the zany treatment of Queen Victoria and her relationship with Florence Nightingale.

The Royal Court was informed that *Early Morning* was unlicensable. It seems unlikely they could have expected anything else—certainly not without agreeing to the sort of extensive cutting which neither they nor Bond would have been willing to accept. The alternative strategy, of course, was to consider turning the theatre into a private club once again. By coincidence or not, in December 1967, Lord Goodman, the Chair of the Arts Council, wrote to Lord Cobbold to make him aware of the emergence of 'a problem connected with club theatres which affects the Arts Council very profoundly and upon which I should very much like to have your entirely confidential guidance'. Cobbold's initial response was something of a non-sequitur:

> We try to keep lists from various sections of the community of people suitable to be asked to cocktail parties, lunch parties, etc. at the Palace.
>
> We try to avoid always asking the top people who are usually already well known to the Queen and Prince Philip, but rather to get hold of some people who are near the top but not necessarily Household names.
>
> If you felt able to jot down for us about twenty names, it would be most helpful.

However, he arranged for his and Goodman's secretaries to organise a meeting, and Goodman promised to provide a list of suitable people to meet the Queen. It is unlikely to have included the name of Edward Bond.

The meeting took place within a couple of days, on 13 December, and Cobbold himself wrote up the key points. Although he does not state that they referred directly to *Early Morning*, it must surely have been some-where in their minds:

> Lord Goodman came in to ask for some private advice (not for quotation) about the proper attitude of the Arts Council towards theatre clubs in present circumstances.
>
> He has been taking the line at the Arts Council that since the Magistrate's decision on *Saved* any theatre club production without the Lord Chamberlain's licence is an offence and the Arts Council ought not to subsidise a theatre while it is committing an offence.
>
> Most of his colleagues on the Arts Council think that this is being unduly stuffy and is bad for the progressive theatre.
>
> Lord Goodman asked whether I had any views or could give him any private indication of my present attitude towards theatre clubs.

It is not quite clear from this whether Goodman was really seeking to find common ground with Cobbold or just testing his intentions. Perhaps he was warning him of further confrontations ahead if the Lord Chamberlain continued to point to the supposed freedom offered by theatre clubs for those whose plays he would not allow in public. Cobbold told Goodman that he 'had always been inclined, within reason, to turn a blind eye to theatre club productions which I regarded as a useful safety valve for specialised audiences', and that he would have preferred to maintain this strategy; 'I had, however, always made it clear that if theatre clubs were silly I might have to test the law', and that he would 'certainly encourage a prosecution in the case of a production which I regarded as going beyond these limits'. He also endorsed Goodman's stated view 'that the Arts Council would be unwise to find themselves subsidising a production which was the subject of a successful prosecution'. In fact, the likelihood of significant disagreements in how the Lord Chamberlain and the Arts Council viewed the same play was another reason why the existing system of censorship seemed particularly problematic.

In January 1968, Bill Gaskill, the putative director of *Early Morning*, wrote to the Lord Chamberlain to say that he had been given no reason for the decision to refuse a licence, and requesting further information. He speculated that there were four different aspects of the play which might be to blame—lesbianism, cannibalism, the presentation of the Lord Chamberlain and the non-sympathetic portrait of Queen Victoria. Which one was it, he asked, with studied naïvety. Contrary to Bond's unequivocal and provocative assertion in the programme and the published text that 'this play is true', Gaskill innocently claimed it was 'not intended to have any historical truth whatsoever', and that 'the work it most resembles is probably Alice in Wonderland', in which 'Queen Victoria is a symbolic figure like the Queen of Hearts'.

Johnston replied on behalf of the Lord Chamberlain to say that 'whilst he understands the play to be a fantasy, that fact does not absolve it from being required to conform to the general criteria upon which plays are judged'. He did not address Gaskill's question directly, or itemise specific details, but he did offer a more general sense of what was wrong with Bond's play:

> *Early Morning* comprises mainly historical characters, who are subjected throughout to highly offensive personalities and untrue accusations of gross indecency. They are selected for insult apparently as being nationally respected figures with long records of devoted service to their country and fellow citizens.
>
> Whilst lesbianism, hetero-sexual perversion, cannibalism and false accusations of murder may be legitimate subjects for some plays, the Lord Chamberlain does not agree that they should be falsely attributed to historical personages of recent date. If allegory is required then the characters should be allegorical.

Gaskill took up the gauntlet:

> Does his Lordship mean that plays which insult 'historical personages of recent date' are automatically banned outright? Would this be true of a play about Lenin and Trotsky, and how recent does the date have to be? Would the play be acceptable if it were about Queen Anne rather than Queen Victoria . . . Would he license the play if the characters were totally non-historical?

In February 1968, Gaskill wrote again to Johnston, saying he had discussed the situation with Bond, who 'feels very strongly that to remove all sense of recognisable historical personages would weaken the impact of the play'. Gaskill also enquired what Cobbold's attitude would be if the Court went ahead with a private club production. In reply, Johnston informed him that 'on the basis of the script now before him, the Lord Chamberlain would feel bound to pass the papers to the Director of Public Prosecutions'. In March, the theatre publicly announced that there would indeed be two 'private' performances of the play at the Royal Court, and Johnston and Hill immediately met with the Director of Public Prosecutions and a representative from the Home Office. Johnston told them that 'The Lord Chamberlain had very strong views about the undesirability of this play, and had warned the producer', but that 'In spite of this warning the Royal Court Theatre was staging two performances on a "Club" basis on Sunday nights'. The matter was therefore out of the hands of the Lord Chamberlain, though he hoped—and expected—that legal action would be taken. More specifically, Johnston and Hill urged that, whereas the emphasis in the prosecution against *Saved* had been on whether the club arrangement was a genuine one, this time it should be on the basis of the legal ruling handed down from that case that there were no legitimate grounds to exempt clubs from the Acts of 1737 and 1843, and that all plays being presented 'for hire' must be submitted to the Lord Chamberlain for licensing. In other words, all cards were at last to be placed on the table. Unfortunately for the Censorship, the Director of Public Prosecutions responded by saying he 'felt diffident in proceeding in circumstances that had been "connived at" by successive Lord Chamberlains for many years'. Johnston would have settled for a bluff—an official letter to the Royal Court warning them of prosecution if they went ahead. But the DPP was no help here either, once again insisting that 'it would be improper for him to threaten proceedings beforehand'. On the other hand, he had no wish to create an embarrassing and possibly public spat between his Office and the Lord Chamberlain, and he asked Johnston whether Cobbold 'would feel "let down" if no prosecution followed'. He also promised to consult with the Attorney General for advice, and indicated 'he would have little hesitation in taking proceedings if the *Saved* presentation circumstances were repeated'.

This was hardly what St James's Palace had hoped for, although Cobbold promised that he would not feel 'let down' by non-prosecution, provided there was consultation with the Attorney-General. He said he recognised that 'successful proceedings against the Royal Court Theatre for Sunday evening "club performances" would stop the private theatre in its tracks, and invalidate a policy of eighty or ninety years standing', and insisted 'he had no wish to create a difficult and possibly disproportionately embarrassing situation'. In other words, the responsibility and the decision were now with the DPP. The Lord Chamberlain had done his bit by passing on the papers and the details, and he was not going to kick up a fuss at this stage, whatever the DPP and the Attorney-General decided. He did, however, speak about the case with the Queen, and subsequently reported (confidentially) that 'HM agreed that this should be put firmly in the Attorney's lap'. She had also, he said, agreed to 'mention the Censorship Bill to the Prime Minister'. In the meantime, bearing in mind that a repeat of a *Saved* type prosecution was still on the table, Cobbold recommended that the Office should take steps 'to acquire necessary evidence' about the circumstances of the club performances, and Miss Fisher, the clerical assistant at St James's, was sent to try and buy tickets. Possibly her acting was not up to Royal Court standards and she was recognised, for she was informed that the performances were sold out. She therefore took out club membership for just over £1, but had to wait 48 hours to receive her card, and was still told no tickets were available. By contrast, reported Johnston, 'A Vice Squad Inspector joined the club without much difficulty, being charged 7/6d for membership, and got two tickets at the same time'.

The two private performances of *Early Morning* were planned for successive Sunday evenings at the end of March and early April, and were actually billed as dress rehearsals. A Vice Squad Inspector attended the first one—as did many newspaper reviewers—and reported, curiously, that 'he reckoned he was incorruptible, but after last night's performance was not sure!' Clearly, the DPP was waiting to see what the press and public reaction was to the performance before deciding his next step. On the 1 April, Johnston updated Cobbold, informing him that the DPP's current thinking was that 'if these two Sunday night performances pass off quickly to take no action', but then to warn the Royal Court that they would be liable to be prosecuted if they gave any further performances. He added: 'This plan is provisional, and depends I gather on the police report, press reaction, what Marianne Faithfull gets up to, etc.'[15] A few days later, however, the Office was instructed that the situation had changed and that the Attorney-General was 'taking a much more serious view' of the case. The reason for this was apparently that there was now evidence that club rules were not being properly observed, because a police officer had been allowed to buy tickets over the counter at the same time as he took out membership, rather than after the requisite delay. 'The Police are going to interview the Royal Court authorities to make them aware that the DPP is aware of, and is taking note of their intentions', reported Johnston. The Comptroller was delighted by the news. 'I think this is terribly funny', he wrote; 'It is a full point for us as Gaskill may think that a prosecution is now certain and possibly under one of the "Obscenity" Acts'. And he added: 'I hope we don't rush to put him out of suspense!' 'Not me!' promised Cobbold.

In the event, the second 'dress rehearsal' was cancelled; perhaps not surprisingly, some senior staff at the Royal Court lost their nerve. The single 'performance' which had taken place was widely reviewed—and widely condemned. Bond himself said the production was seriously under-rehearsed, and the first full and satisfactory production would only prove possible after the Lord Chamberlain had gone. Overall, it is probably fair to say that Cobbold—at least in this case—had secured a winning draw.[16] The DPP held on to the script and correspondence for a few weeks to see what would happen and then returned them to the Assistant Comptroller. 'As you know the Attorney-General has decided against taking proceedings', he wrote; 'He feels that the action taken has drawn attention to the fact that the law has not yet been altered, and had the effect of cancelling a second advertised performance'.

New Plays, Old Problems

Early Morning was not the only Royal Court play to be denied a licence during the final year of the Lord Chamberlain's reign. In August 1967, the theatre submitted a stage adaptation of J.P. Donleavy's *The Saddest Summer Of Samuel S.*—'a straight play in two acts in which a student, Samuel S, discusses with his psychiatrist his failure to make any significant contact with the opposite sex'. Given the subject matter, there was bound to be a long list of verbal amendments required; but the Office was also anxious about physical actions, and requested a copy of the script 'annotated in such a way as to indicate exactly how each scene is to be played'. Donleavy was not prepared to back down over the language. He pointed out that it was 'part of the characterisation' and that 'euphemistic language would produce artificiality at variance with the characters portrayed'. He also argued that the words deemed offensive were 'admitted vernacular in the United States and, as used between two American characters, should not cause problems for a reasonable English audience'. His refusal to compromise antagonised the Censors—not least Heriot:

The arguments in the author's letter seem insolently specious. I simply do not believe that this play is anything more than the most obvious pornography. There have been dozens of previous plays on the same subject that successfully avoided the cloacal indecencies of this text . . . I sincerely trust that the Lord Chamberlain will stick to his guns and refuse a licence to this worthless trash.

Donleavy's script remained unlicensed and unperformed.[17]

Another play which got under the Censors' collective skin in the autumn of 1967 was Peter Barnes's appositely named *The Ruling Class*—'A psychopathic document by a writer with social and sexual chips on his shoulder'. There was certainly much to annoy: 'The author would have us believe that all privileged persons are racked by every kind of perverse desires', wrote Heriot—and the play is indeed both vitriolic and funny about the British elite.

The Thirteenth Earl of Gurney, a chuckle-headed reactionary, after a patriotic speech, puts on a ballet skirt . . . and inadvertently hangs himself in his bedroom while indulging in his private pleasure of <u>nearly</u> hanging himself so that the preliminary symtoms [sic] of strangulation may produce pleasing illusions.

Cuts included references to 'the God of the Upright testicle' and 'the Penis-Christ', and Barnes's play was eventually licensed at the end of December, two months after it had been submitted, and with a list of around sixty endorsements and deletions:

'Upright Testicle . . .'
'Eton education . . .'
'No balls at all . . .'
'Bum-kissing . . .'
'Penis-like . . .'
'I've asked Prince Philip and he's got his finger out . . .'
'Tip of my penis . . .'
'He hasn't been up on the Cross for ages . . .'
'a' those wee priests with empty ass-holes waiting to be filled . . .'
'having intercourse with Princess Margaret . . .'
'I'll vaporize his left ball and paint his genitals green . . .'
'It's called orgasm . . .'
'syphilitic winkles . . .'[18]

Heriot had been rather patronising towards Barnes: 'I am certain that the author thinks that testicle and penis are synonymous', he declared;

but in fact, it was the Reader's own knowledge of anatomy that proved to be lacking. Four days after producing his original report, Heriot wrote again to the Assistant Comptroller to say he had just discovered 'that strangulation (at least as far as hanging is concerned) is accompanied by spasmodic errection [sic] and emission'. He now felt bound to recommend that the entire death scene involving the Earl of Gurney should be deleted. Which it was. 'I might have guessed that there would be something arcanely perverse about such a scene in a play by such an author', he added. It is perhaps surprising he had forgotten that the same issue had arisen during discussions of *Waiting for Godot*.

1968 (and None of That)

The second reading of the government's new Theatres Bill was scheduled for the last week of February 1968. Although the arguments around *Early Morning* dominated the Censorship's agenda in the early part of the year, day-to-day interventions and conflicts continued as ever. In January, Nottingham Playhouse submitted a revised version of Henry Livings's *The Little Mrs Foster Show*. When the usual cuts in language were demanded, Livings renewed his accusations of class (and geographical) bias:

> I accept reluctantly your cuts where I had intended to be dirty, but in the case of 'bugger', 'balls' and 'shit', I must point out that these are variably offensive, according to region and class, and in the case of 'shit' was intended to pin point a class, in the case of 'balls' was intended to be physical and practical, and in the case of 'bugger'—well we've already argued this out at length. 'Pillock', which I believe is acceptable to your Office, is profoundly offensive where I live.[19]

In February, an endorsement on the licence for the RSC production of *Brief Lives*—a show based on the work of John Aubrey—stipulated that 'there must not be any sound of the actor urinating',[20] and for an adaptation of Thomas Mann's *The Magic Mountain*, the Office insisted that 'no erotic sounds are to be heard' from offstage.[21] From a Cambridge undergraduate review they cut a sketch called 'A Round of Summits' because it featured 'a crude political song sung by masks of various heads of State', as well as 'the repeated homosexual gag about the admiralty . . . [and] the business indicated where one actor seems to urinate (I think) on another's lap'.[22] In the case of a Liverpool undergraduate revue, the Reader drew attention to a song depicting the Foreign Secretary as inebriated, and also to one about the French President; 'In view of what we allowed in *Mrs Wilson's Diary*', they decided, 'it would be consistent if we allowed the George Brown song (but cutting the action with the bottle) but disallowed the De Gaulle sketch'.[23] From *You Can't Smoke a Medal*—David Yallop's passionate anti-war play—they rejected the 'thin-guttedly blasphemous' text of 'The Patriot's Creed', a political prayer supposedly recited before battle:

> I believe in England the Power Almighty, creator of Hell on Earth. And in Patriotism it's [sic] only son. Our Lord! Who was conceived by the Chancellor of the Exchequer, born of the Bank of England, suffered under Lloyd George and Winston Churchill, was crucified, dead and buried by anybody that made a penny out of War. It descended into Hell. The Third World War it will rise again from the dead [sic]. It will sit at the right hand of the Conscientious Objectors Board and utter profunditys [sic]about Germans raping our grand-mothers . . . I believe in corruption, the unholy conspiracy of cynical Government. The non-communication with the people. The forgiveness of no one. The resurrection of nothing, and Death everlasting.[24]

The playwright tried but failed to persuade the Office that the speech should not be taken as an attack on religious faith:

> I explained to the Lord Chamberlain that you had no desire to travesty the Creed . . . but that you were using this affirmation of faith as the vehicle for an affirmation, as passionate as possible, of your antagonism to war . . . I am sorry to have to tell you that, as I anticipated, he feels that whatever the motives that prompt the use; the religious attributions of this particular acknowledgement, acquired over centuries of Christian belief, ought to be respected; and he is not prepared to allow a secular version.[25]

Yallop's play remained unlicensed.

In February, the Censors became involved in horse-trading with the RSC over Harold Pinter's *Landscape*, reluctantly being persuaded to pass 'shit', 'dog shit', 'duck shit', 'piss', and 'bog hole'. The company's chairman wrote to express his thanks: 'I am most grateful to you for agreeing that the disallowances to the text should now be limited to "bugger" . . . "bugger all", and . . . "fuck all".'[26] The Office was also surprisingly lenient over Colin Spencer's *Spitting Image*, a fantasy about 'a wave of homosexual pregnancies' sweeping through the country. Heriot conceded that 'the piece is not without its macabre humour', and even though it was 'larded . . . with the usual indecencies', he did not think it should be banned completely: 'In view of the fact that the central incident of this play is, thank goodness, a biological impossibility, it is, reluctantly, recommended for licence.'[27]

In March—only weeks before the MP Enoch Powell's infamous attack on black immigration and racial equality—a musical adaptation

of Clifford Odets's *Golden Boy* for the London Palladium caused a
bit of a wobbly at St James's Palace. 'The whole play has been altered',
raged Heriot; 'Mr. Gibson has taken the extraordinary liberty of making
Golden Boy a negro'. As he explained, 'This tilts everything', and the
result was 'strong meat for a musical, especially at the Palladium'. A
number of specific amendments were made (including 'As the duchess of
Windsor would say, "Black is me!"'), and the theatre was warned that the
black man and the white woman must not be seen in bed together. There
was also the question of a song which made reference to a Black Power
riot.

> I think some warning is necessary. I can imagine a non integration audience
> breaking into a riot itself here. There is a great deal of black-plus-white, not
> to mention Joe's love affair with Lorna that might easily offend the sort of
> audience that frequents the Palladium.

In the end, however, they opted not to intervene over this: 'I think this must
be left as is, as it is difficult to make any restriction.'[28] In the same month,
Norman Beaton's *Sit Down Banna*—'A glum play . . . about three young
West Indians and a girl who come to England to study'—also caused the
Censorship to hesitate: 'This is the worst possible advertisement for racial
integration', complained Heriot; 'none of the new arrivals bother to study
but get jobs with the GLC instead'; there was also 'a hint of drugs . . .
and a never ending succession of dirty rooms and clothes and dreary, un-
tidy parties'. Some of the sexual details and language were deleted, but the
main thrust of the play survived.[29]

From John Lennon's *In His Own Write* at the Old Vic ('A farrago
of Joycian gobbledegook') they cut the name 'Bugger Street' and an
imitation of the Queen, before passing it 'with regrets that the National
Theatre should be debased by the performance of such whimsical and arty
rubbish'.[30] For 'The Miller's Tale' in an adaptation of Chaucer's *Canterbury
Tales*, the management was warned 'that there must be no imitative coital
movements' and that 'the love-making in the tree must be decent'. They
also cut 'the gesture of kissing Alison's fundament', and required that
the sound of the ensuing fart be replaced by 'a token orchestral effect'.[31]
In John Bowen's rewriting of medieval Mystery plays—*The Fall and
Redemption of Man*—there was concern about how far the actors might
go during 'the embrace of Adam and Eve', and the company was warned
that there must be 'no miming of intercourse'.[32] But attempts to intervene
over the language ('We are all aware of the grossness of some of these
early texts') generated more bad publicity for the Censorship. *Plays and
Players*, for example, reported that 'the antique stage censor of St James's
Palace appears determined to end his days in a positive fart of glory', as he

quibbled over the conversion of 'the medieval phrase "Com kis myne ars" into modern English'.[33]

Another play to be refused a licence in the spring of 1968 was *A Fig for Eloquence*, a comedy about a sculptor who makes a statue of her husband but endows it with someone else's sexual organs, disapprovingly described by Heriot as 'one long snigger at the male genitalia'. Initially, this seemed to be more up Johnston's street—'I think it is harmless comedy, and could be licensed subject to certain changes'—but he changed his mind after consulting Lord Nugent:

> Johnnie, I fear I'm a bad person to give an opinion about this play. 1. I'm out of date as to what is passed nowadays and 2. I am too 'square' to know what sort of things are openly talked about by the up and coming generation of intellectuals. In the stuffy society in which I move we don't often talk about 'cock' even under Charles Heriot's more delicate pseudonym of genitalia, and certainly not when females are present.[34]

The Oedipi

Nugent's letter on the merits and language of stage genitalia drew Lord Cobbold's attention to a larger penis problem—the one he had read about in a review of the current National Theatre production of *Oedipus*. Nugent couldn't help wondering 'whether the Lord Chamberlain had seen the "Phallus" that was exhibited' at the Old Vic. The production referred to was the Peter Brook and Ted Hughes version of Seneca's text. 'It is not a pleasant story', Tim Harward had noted when the script was submitted in the spring of 1968, and he drew attention to its 'grisly conclusion' as well as 'some realistically gruesome descriptions', such as the conception and birth of Oedipus, the sacrifice of a heifer and the self-blinding. The Reader suggested they should 'check that there is no action on stage' to accompany such moments, and the theatre duly confirmed there was 'nothing more than the gesticulating of hands whilst the actors are speaking and a slight moan from the chorus'. Slight moans were generally acceptable now, so there seemed to be no problem. Then, just before the production was due to open, Johnston was contacted by the Director of the National Theatre himself:

> Sir L. Olivier telephoned me on Friday evening about this play which opens at the Old Vic tomorrow. It is being directed by Peter Brook who is introducing a Bacchanalian orgy at the end, complete with phalluses as props. He was not too happy about this and asked my advice.
>
> I told him that we did not allow these things in *Moses and Aaron*, and I was sure you would not permit them here. He said he was anxious for the

National Theatre not to cross swords with us, and I got the impression he rather wanted our backing in trying to persuade the director not to overdo this scene.

He then asked if I would come and see the preview this evening, that is if he failed to get his way over the w/e during the final rehearsals. I said that I would, provided of course they submitted complete stage directions for approval.

However, Olivier phoned again on Monday 'to say that he had succeeded in persuading them to tone down the scene', and that 'there are now no phalluses' and 'nothing which will offend anyone'.

Johnston himself attended the opening performance with his wife. 'It was a bold production, with advanced ideas and methods', he reported, 'but I don't think it quite comes off'. It was 'a sort of Doctor Who for adults in a classical setting', said Johnston, and 'I found it boring'. As for the phallus: 'The only action is at the end of the play when the "thing" is brought on and unveiled', he explained; 'The object is golden, about 8 feet high, and shaped to look like an erect penis! It is meant to shock, I think, but is not really obscene or offensive'.[35] Johnston sided with the *Daily Express* reviewer, who wrote that 'it spoils the effect of the play and looks damn silly'.[36] On balance, the Office opted not to intervene: 'Having discussed this with the Ld Ch. it was decided to leave things as they are, and not ask for any stage directions.' Johnston telephoned Olivier and left a message 'to the effect that there was no need for us to discuss this further, unless Sir L. particularly wanted to ring me up'.

But the Office may have been duped. On the opening night, when Johnston saw it, the giant phallus had been brought on and unveiled, and there the performance had ended. But that was not the full or final version. The following week, the *Sunday Telegraph* published a letter complaining bitterly about members of the cast dancing around a giant phallus, to the particular embarrassment of parents seeking to expose their adolescent children to the power and history of classical drama.

> I proclaimed aloud to anyone who might care to listen: 'The ending is filth. It is not part of Seneca's play; it is just plain filth'.
>
> All I got was stares, and unfriendly stares, too, so I added these words 'Typical English filth', and left the theatre.

The correspondent suspected that someone had been telling porkies:

> Since the unruly singing and dancing, particularly among the younger members of the cast, which accompanies this obscene exhibition, was not

performed on the first night, perhaps I may enquire—has the ending that I witnessed been passed by the Lord Chamberlain?[37]

Hill was duly sent to carry out another inspection and supply a detailed testimony of the climax: 'I have no comment upon the play, until the final scene', he reported; 'For this scene a draped object was carried onto the stage. The draping was slowly removed by an actor to reveal a golden penis about seven feet high'. Presumably it had shrunk a little since Johnston had seen it. But perhaps Hill was looking at it more carefully: 'This object, whilst not complete to the smallest anatomical detail was unmistakable', he reported; 'the prepuce was drawn back, to reveal the erect head'. That was when the action started:

> The caste [sic] then appeared on the stage and indulged in frenzied votive dancing, 'jiving' and so on around this sexual organ. They were followed by a modern band of drum, trumpet, trombone etc. which marched twice or it might have been three times round the entire auditorium playing 'Yes we have no bananas'.

For Hill, this was no more than self-indulgence:

> There was no laughter from the audience, the people who appeared to enjoy the whole thing most were the actors—those in the band who were not blowing through instruments had broad smiles and looked from side to side as if for approbation.

Evidently, this was not his idea of a good night out: 'The whole proceedings were considerably drawn out; the slow march of the band round the auditorium seeming interminable to me.' Nor was he convinced that the rest of the audience had been much more impressed than he was:

> There was a good deal of applause at the end of the play, although this appeared more polite acclamation than any overwhelming response to the play. Even so the curtain was raised four times to display the jiving crowd and the golden penis. After this I fled.

However, he acknowledged that it could have been worse: 'I particularly watched to see if any of the actors caressed the "object" during their frenzy, none did so.' And happily, the excitement did not spread to the auditorium: 'There appeared no audible audience reaction to the penis either one way or the other', reported the Secretary, although 'I noticed a faint expression of displeasure on the faces of the only two elderly ladies near me'.

Brook's innovation had been, in part, an attempt to invoke the spirit of the satyr play, which followed the performance of a cycle of tragedies in ancient Greece, juxtaposing the seriousness with comedy and profanity. But Hill found it cheap and gratuitous—and an indicator of how low contemporary theatre had sunk:

> I give it as my opinion that there is nothing in the piece that requires the introduction of a golden penis, and further that most playgoers would find it difficult to find any connection at all . . . The coarse analogy of 'bananas' and 'penis' is as old as the song and that is at least forty years, it was always disallowed to the tenth rate Variety artists who attempted to introduce it into sketches. It is a commentary on the modern theatre that this same coarse joke, presented in an obscene form that no musical artist would have dared to suggest, is put before the audience as high dramatic art.[38]

By chance, the Censorship was simultaneously dealing with another *Oedipus*—this time in Sheffield—and another penis. *Potted Jack* was described by Heriot as 'An extraordinary "potted" pantomime with masturbatory overtones'; this 'rather poor pastiche of *Jack and the Beanstalk*' had apparently arisen out of 'improvisation on the Oedipus theme by the Company who are performing Sophocles' *Oedipus*'. Heriot did not like it at all: 'It looks as if the sub-conscious has been disturbed and something nasty has turned up', he commented. So as well as hacking away all references to masturbation, the Office issued warnings 'that the giant's housekeeper must be adequately clothed', and that the production must be careful to avoid 'too much realism when "blood and entrails spill out" of the goose'.[39]

Final Acts

April brought two new plays by Samuel Beckett; *Come and Go* ('One of Beckett's sillier efforts') required no intervention, but *Eh Joe*—'A mercifully short piece of portentous rubbish'—contained a phrase—'squeeze away'—which made the Reader suspect that 'the whole thing took place during a masturbation'. The phrase was eventually allowed, 'provided no accompanying action'.[40] Paul Foster's *Balls* ('And of course it is') also caused disquiet: 'I don't like the title', said the Reader, 'which refers to two ping-pong balls that pendulum in space during the action'. Hill was not too worried about them. 'As they don't hang together I suggest leave', he suggested. However, the Office did disallow 'all the erotic breathing and laughing'.[41]

But something else in the same month worried them much more:

I see from yesterday's *Times* that the National Theatre (?) [sic] propose to stage *Edward II and* interpret the stage direction 'they embrace' by having two male actors kiss each other.

Edward II was a reputed pederast, and if this report is true, then we shall have our first example of two actors making homo-sexual love in public—a summit of achievement that will crown their efforts to popularise the profession's hobby.[42]

The article itself had claimed that, with one exception, the only precedents had occurred in club theatres during private performances of Wedekind's *Spring Awakening* a few years earlier, and Miller's *A View from the Bridge*. The exception didn't really count, because it had been David Warner as Henry VI at Stratford-on-Avon, kissing his murderer; 'but that was more a kiss of forgiveness'.[43]

Hill pointed out (as he frequently did) that when Scarbrough had finally conceded and agreed to 'the exposition of the homo-sexual theme on the stage', he had specifically drawn the line at 'sexual embraces between males'. He therefore hoped that Cobbold would intervene. Unusually, the Secretary seems not to have noticed that the National Theatre production was actually Brecht's adaptation of Marlowe, and therefore should have required a licence. Assuming it was using Marlowe's text—which was of course exempt—he recommended they should use the 'ample powers of prohibition under s.14 of the Theatres Act'—the St James's Palace equivalent of a red hot poker—which allowed the Lord Chamberlain to intervene over *any* performance he considered likely to lead to a breach of the peace. Regrettably, Cobbold would probably have to wait until after the production had opened since 'presumably he can't know officially what is being done until it is done'.[44] But in any case, Hill was fighting alone, and his suggestion was ignored.

Marlowe surfaced again a few weeks later, when Hill took a phone call from the *Sun* newspaper: 'I understand that the National Theatre at Stratford [sic] intend to stage Marlowe's *Helen of Troy* [sic] with a naked Helen', he reported afterwards. He was also contacted by a Chief Inspector from Stratford-on-Avon Police 'who said they were receiving complaints about the possibility of naked women on the Stage during *Dr Faustus*'. But the Office informed the Chief Inspector that there was little the Lord Chamberlain could do, since although 'in normal circumstances he would not allow a naked woman to walk about the stage', this was not a text which needed to be submitted to him. In any case, 'As the Lord Chamberlain was under sentence to go it was unlikely that he would initiate action except in the most outrageous of cases'.[45]

★

By the spring of 1968 the end was indeed in sight. On 23 February, the Labour MP George Strauss, who had chaired the Enquiry, introduced a bill 'to implement the conclusions of the Joint Select Committee' and thus 'bring to an end the present archaic, illogical and indefensible system of stage censorship which we have tolerated for far too long'. Strauss reminded MPs that the Committee's recommendations had 'achieved unanimity, not only on basic principles, but on all the controversial minor aspects of the problem', and the evidence and arguments they had heard had 'led to the inescapable conclusion' that pre-censorship should be abandoned. 'The more we examined the present system of censorship the more indefensible it appeared in principle, the more ludicrous in practice.' Strauss argued, as many had done before him, that the restriction was faced by 'the playwright alone of all creative artists', and amounted to 'a gross injustice' against the profession. 'Every author of original ideas who has examined in his plays topical, social or political problems which the censor considered respectable people might find unpalatable, has at one time or another come under his ban.' He cited plays by Arthur Miller, Tennessee Williams, John Osborne, Bamber Gascoigne, and the e.e. cummings poem which had been banned from the RSC's *Rebel* anthology; all of these, he said, had been performed or presented elsewhere, but had been ruled unacceptable on the British stage.

> Then there is the political censorship which the Lord Chamberlain admitted he imposes. He has permitted leaders of Communist countries to be presented on the stage in a highly unfavourable light but he has banned the Royal Shakespeare Company's performance of *US* on the ground . . . that it might be considered offensive to the United States . . . he similarly prevented the production of *MacBird*.

To suggest that Cobbold had banned *US* was stretching the facts somewhat, but Michael Foot stressed the same point about ideological bias, and the dangers of suppressing specific views and political perspectives: 'People have forgotten that politics have been the main cause of censorship', he insisted; 'It was political fears which persuaded the original introduction of the censorship and it has very largely been political fears which have sustained it ever since'.

Strauss pointed out that the Lord Chamberlain himself had stated that the duty of censorship 'should no longer reside in a court official', and that no viable alternative had been proposed. 'Lord Cobbold, to our surprise and to the horror of the Chairman of the Arts Council, Lord Goodman, suggested that the Arts Council should take on that responsibility.' But that was impractical and inappropriate: 'Obviously no body can simultaneously discharge the duty of fostering and fettering the art of the theatre.' Strauss was also keen to reassure the House that the abolition of pre-censorship would not 'leave the theatre unrestricted'. However, he contended there was 'nothing wrong in allowing public figures to be satirised on the stage', and that the monarch should not be automatically exempt from this. Even Cobbold had conceded 'that it would be exceedingly difficult to draft acceptable words' to guarantee this privilege, and in any case no equivalent restriction existed in other media. The safeguard, claimed Strauss, was 'that it was unlikely that the public would tolerate for a moment offensive personal references to the Sovereign'.

A number of MPs spoke against the bill, including some who maintained there was no need for change because London already enjoyed 'more theatre, better theatre, and more experimental theatre than anywhere else in the world'; in these circumstances, parliament should be 'very cautious before making too radical a change', and emulating 'the monkey in the story which takes the watch to bits to see how it works and then cannot put it together again'. The Conservative MP Norman St John-Stevas, who had served on the Committee, told the House that while he backed the main proposals contained in the bill, he still maintained that there was 'a good case for forbidding the presentation of the Sovereign upon the stage' and that 'there must be some institutions in any society which should be exempted from satire'. He therefore sought an amendment, either specifically to protect the monarch, or—in order not to be seen to 'single out the Queen for special treatment'—a clause requiring 'that no living person should be presented on the stage without his or her consent'.[46] The opposition had little impact.

On 10 May, the bill was presented for its third and final reading. 'I expected a long and bitter battle over the Bill', said George Strauss, and 'strenuous opposition'; but most of it had melted away. The most contentious issue in standing committee had concerned representations of international heads of state, and of the British royal family. But it was hard to argue with the logic that there should be no such restriction in theatre, as there was none in books or newspapers. Strauss did warn MPs that 'a temporary state of difficulty and unsettlement in the theatre' might immediately follow the legislation:

> Plays may be put on which are objectionable to some sections of the community on political, religious or moral grounds. Voices may be raised, perhaps strong voices, demanding that there should be prosecution, and that the Attorney-General should either permit a prosecution or launch one himself.[47]

But he was confident that any such problems would be short-lived.

On 28 May the bill had its second reading in the House of Lords, with Cobbold again making clear his support for major changes to the system. In his view, 'the most compelling' reason was the recent and continuing growth in film and television. He echoed some of Stevas's concerns about real people—especially the royal family—and still argued that the theatre needed something similar to the 1964 Television Act, which had imposed on the Independent Television Authority a requirement that they should broadcast nothing 'which offends against good taste or decency or is likely to encourage or incite to crime or to lead to disorder or to be offensive to public feeling'. But as another speaker observed, 'the BBC is a far greater potential danger to the things we want to discourage'. Cobbold's predecessor again spoke to support the bill, and the principle that playwrights should enjoy the same freedom as other writers. There was an argument, said Scarborough, that in previous eras live theatre had enjoyed a unique power to influence audiences; but this was no longer the case: 'the numbers who go to theatres are quite small compared to the multitudes who watch television or read paper-back books'. As the Earl pointed out, if society believed it needed 'a guardian of morals'—which was 'something which the Lord Chamberlain has never claimed to be'—then such a person 'would have to begin in those spheres rather than with stage plays'.[48] The Lords followed the Commons in agreeing the bill should continue to its next stage, and following some very minor amendments, officially approved it at the third reading on 19 July. On the 25 July, the Commons also approved the amendments, and on the 26 July 1968, the House was informed that the 1968 Theatres Act, abolishing pre-censorship, had formally received the Royal assent.

Late Eclipses

As the age of Aquarius dawned around him, the Censorship staggered towards the exit, sometimes relishing its last opportunities to wield authority, sometimes longing to be put out of its misery. In May, Edward Bond's *Narrow Road to the Deep North*, set in ancient Japan, was submitted for its premiere at Coventry's 'People in Cities' Conference. Some of the iconography was judged too controversial, and in need of amendment: so 'God' was changed to 'a god', in the line 'How many testicles has God', while the image of a naked figure nailed to a placard was permitted only 'if (a) there was no blood on the dismembered body and (b) the genitals were not visible'. Confusingly, the endorsement added that 'there was no objection to the actor being known to be naked provided that at all times his back was to the audience and his buttocks were covered'. Among the requirements attached to the licence was a stipulation that 'A towel shall be kept between the buttocks of the actor and the audience in such a way as to conceal the split between the buttocks'.[49]

The Office also refused to license Arrabal's *The Car Cemetery*—'A kind of surrealist Passion Play, larded with petty indecencies'. The play was set in 'a large dump for disused cars' and featured a fornicating Christ. 'I hate this kind of Bunuel-like blasphemy', grumbled Heriot, and Johnston agreed that it was 'too much like a parody of the passion' to be allowed.[50] In June, they cut the line 'what goes up must come down' from a Hungarian play, on account of its 'phallic significance',[51] and in July they insisted that the Cardinal was not allowed to issue communion on stage in a revue sketch called *The Revenger of Malfi* ('a poor parody of Webster').[52] In a play about Oscar Wilde set in a prison, they insisted that a character 'must not vomit on stage' and that 'there must be no visual evidence of anything looking like excrement';[53] and in *George the Mad Ad. Man*, they insisted that 'George must not get on top of his wife', and that 'the phallic bottle must not squirt'.[54] From *Caprice in a Pink Palazzo*—a 'vulgar, emetically-whimsical play about promiscuous puppets'—they insisted that 'the embraces between Dianora and Paolo must not be too specific', and that the performance must 'Omit the direction Dianora gets into bed, and curls herself around the bottom half of Paolo's body'.[55] Among the many amendments required in *Lizzie Strata*, they cut the line 'Ooh, that's a huge one, isn't it delicious?', insisted that a bottle 'must not be erotically shaped', warned that 'the girls must not get on top of the men', and challengingly insisted that 'the messenger must not show any visible sign of erection'.[56] From Peter Terson's *The Apprentices* they disallowed the word 'frigging' but accepted the substitution of 'shafting';[57] in *The Rasputin Show* at the Cambridge Arts Theatre they commanded that 'Rasputin must not produce a four foot phallus',[58] and for Arthur Kopit's *Indians* at the Aldwych they required that 'the business of "erotic off-stage noises" must not be over done', as well as ruling against 'any impersonation of President Johnson, Vice-President Humphrey and the President's wife'. They also disallowed the second half of the line 'It seems no less likely than Christ's returning, and a great deal more useful'.[59] Another minor clash with the RSC took place over Paddy Chayefsky's *The Latent Heterosexual*, which was submitted just a couple of weeks before the Lord Chamberlain's demise. This, said the Reader, was 'a very sick comedy indeed', being 'full of the grossness we associate with contemporary American writing'. Heriot proposed a string of cuts, but following a meeting with a representative of the company (at which they debated whether 'sack' was a synonym for 'vagina' or for 'bed'), the Censorship backed down on most of them. Even so, they insisted on cutting 'hot sperm spurting', 'grabbed his pintel', 'unleash his beef', and 'Oh Christ don't stop now'.[60]

During the final days of the Lord Chamberlain's control there was one more moment of embarrassment involving the Royal Court. It centred on *Total Eclipse*, Christopher Hampton's new play about Rimbaud and Verlaine. The text had been passed in August with a few amendments ('There must be no accompanying action to "pissing on them from a great height"'), but when the production opened in September, some of the reviews raised hackles at St James's:

> *Total Eclipse*, a play about homosexuality at the Royal Court, totally eclipses, with strong four letter language, anything previously shown in open theatre . . . [it] shows the actors kissing each other full on the lips.
>
> This is two weeks before the Lord Chamberlain hands in his blue pencil.
>
> And one has the feeling that he is getting his own back on the critics of his office by allowing this play . . .[61]

Taken aback ('Did we license this play—and the kissing?!') they checked the script and discovered that the only stage direction which specified kissing occurred when Verlaine is dead and Rimbaud kisses his hand. Sadly, it was too late for Cobbold to do much about it—though Hampton himself recalls police officers watching a performance, 'to check, presumably, that the cuts had been observed'. The legislation removing the Lord Chamberlain's authority over theatre came into force while *Total Eclipse* was still being performed, meaning the text could be played in full. According to the playwright 'In the second half of the run, the play therefore ran around five minutes longer'.[62]

HAIR Today (and Gone Tomorrow)

The script which marked the Lord Chamberlain's last hurrah—and pursued him through his final six months in control—was an American musical which brought to the stage things that his predecessors over the previous 250 years could hardly have imagined. The central characters of *Hair* are a group of American drop-outs and hippies who reject what they see as the old-fashioned prejudices and attitudes of mainstream society, notably on sex, drugs, race, capitalism and—in particular—the Vietnam war. Already a hit on Broadway, and widely advertised as 'the American tribal love-rock musical' which 'makes *Marat/Sade* look like Peter Pan', *Hair* purported to be a celebration of youth and alternative values. Even if, for its promoters, it was more about making money, Britain—especially the West End, where it was headed—had never seen anything quite like it.

The script of *Hair* was submitted in May 1968, even as the barricades went up in Paris and left-wing revolution seemed in the air across western Europe. Although Harward acknowledged that 'some of the business and language will certainly cause offence', he recognised it as 'essentially serious in its intention'. Which, in his view, was 'to persuade the audience to understand what the psychedelic movement is all about'. In principle, Harward was even ready to recommend it for licence. 'It is not a vicious play', he advised; 'The form is loose and the action freewheeling in order to try and involve the audience and "turn them on"'. He did suspect there would be 'a temptation to ad-lib', but 'recommended that this real and current point of view should be allowed expression'. Hill—from an older generation and conventional background—saw it rather differently. 'This is a demoralising play', he moaned; 'It extols dirt, anti-establishment views, homosexuality and free love, drug taking, and it inveighs against patriotism'. While acknowledging that 'We are'nt [sic] a school of morals', he found much of it intolerable, including stage nudity. 'We should have to put a blanket prohibition over undress male and female', he warned. Then there was the issue of illegal sustances:

> drug taking in this country, which did not exist as a problem ten years ago, is almost solely due to the influence originally of United States theatrical and 'pop' elements . . . Teen-age drug taking is a growing problem and I would remorselessly delete every reference and 'business' relating to drugs—going on trips and so on.

There was more, too: 'Some other parts also want careful thought', wrote Hill; 'Claude for example is a man yet he sings of his "tits" and his "arse" and he has bad times like a woman'. There was only one explanation: 'Presumably a roaring pansy.'

In June, *Hair* was resubmitted by a different management: 'This script is more or less the same as the previous one', complained Heriot, 'but there are differences'. He came down against licensing:

> it still seems to be a totally reprehensible affair. Satire is one thing, but the 'knocking' at every convention and the tacit glorification of drugs and general intransigence inclines me to agree with Mr Hill that, in effect, this piece is dangerously permissive.

He objected specifically to the inclusion of 'Another hymn to drugs', but suspected there might be more references than he was spotting: 'She takes a drag on her joint', he mused; 'This defeats me unless, as I suspect, a "joint" here means a marijuana cigarette'. Representatives of the management—a Mr Verner and a Mr Conyers—came to negotiate. Although 'they were both very pleasant to deal with', Hill and Johnston conveyed to them that 'the Lord Chamberlain had found *Hair* unacceptable as a whole', and that 'although usually there was room for manoeuvre or negotiation', the general judgment in this case 'precluded his agreeing to a request to discuss areas of disagreement'. The management argued that it was a 'quite uncorrupting and beautiful' piece, 'the theme of which was "love"', and even claimed that 'the text was put over satirically' and 'burlesqued in such a way as to destroy all the glamour of, for example, drug taking'. But the Office maintained it was 'permeated with ideals that were quite unacceptable' and 'would be too controversial for British audiences'.

In the light of this, the producers discussed three options: first, to submit a revised script—'I said he could do this', reported Hill, 'but I was a bit pessimistic as to the outcome'; second, to postpone the production and wait for the law on censorship to change; or third, to 'put it on in July as planned and risk the consequences'. To Hill's chagrin, it was then publicly announced that *Hair* would indeed open in mid-July. 'It begins to look . . . as though these people will defy the Lord Chamberlain', he fumed, and the Office must therefore 'consider what our actions should be' and 'make sure of getting tickets for early performances so that we are in a position to provide evidence'. Then a third version of the script was submitted. 'All the drug references seem to be removed', reported Heriot, 'and all the "f . . . s"'. He was now prepared to recommend a licence, subject to some further information ('Details of the Karma Sutra dance') and some more cuts ('one for Prince Philip . . . policemen in the auditorium . . . the business of giving birth to a uniform . . . erotic action . . . burning of the Buddhist monk . . . I'd rather do it myself—a masturbatory reference').[63] In the event, however, the management decided that rather than present this compromised version, and rather than take the risk of prosecution, they would postpone the opening until 26 September—the date from which the Lord Chamberlain's writ would no longer run. Then it could all hang out.

On 18 September, the Assistant Comptroller at St James's Palace took a phone call:

> Mr John Gledhill of Thames TV asked if the Lord Chamberlain would participate in the Eamon Andrews show from the stage of the Shaftesbury theatre after the final rehearsal of *Hair* in the evening of Thursday September 26th.

The image of 231 years of stage censorship ending with the Lord Chamberlain—clothed or unclothed—signing off by dancing for the cameras for a chat show with the cast of *Hair* (perhaps advising that anyone henceforth requiring censorship would be obliged to 'do it yourself') is one to conjure with. But even in the Age of Aquarius, some dignity remained: 'I told him, v politely of course, that I was sure the L C would not countenance the suggestion.' Cobbold added in blue pencil in the margin: 'Quite right.'[64]

And then he was gone.

★

During the 1968 parliamentary debates, many MPs had been keen to pay tributes to Cobbold and to his predecessors; to exonerate them from any possible blame and criticism and insist that for 230 years they had been doing a job which was both effective and necessary. Mr Douglas Dodds-Parker, for example, the MP for Cheltenham, saluted them for having 'carried out this very great service to the country', and for safeguarding the appropriate standards: 'a play that has been passed by the Lord Chamberlain', he declared, 'goes out throughout not only this country but a large part of the English-speaking world with his imprimatur and is therefore accepted as being in good taste'. But the mood of complacency and well-mannered self-congratulation was shattered by a powerful and evocative speech from Michael Foot, the left-wing MP and future leader of the Labour Party: 'I do not wish to stir up controversy at this stage', he declared, 'but I cannot join in the tributes paid to the Lord Chamberlains over these years'. Urged on, perhaps, by the spirits of writers who had been silenced or forced into humiliating compromises, he denied the Lords Chamberlain their collective dignity:

> Like all other censors, they have made themselves utterly ridiculous. That is in the nature of their office. All censors make themselves ridiculous eventually and the Lord Chamberlains have been no exception and that includes the recent Lord Chamberlains.
>
> They have been making themselves ridiculous because their function was quite impossible.

In committing this ancient system to burial, Foot wanted the real damage it had perpetrated to be acknowledged for what it was, not swept away beneath a bland House of Commons carpet of sycophancy: 'What the Lord Chamberlains have done in trying to execute this impossible function is to impose serious hardship on many of the most eminent playwrights of our country', he insisted; 'This is the evil we have set out to do away with'. Nor could Foot let the occasion go without taking a swipe at the absurdly anachronistic world which the Office itself embodied, and which Foot would doubtless have been glad to do away with in its entirety: 'I think that we are making the institution of Lord Chamberlain slightly less ridiculous than it was, although it still retains some of its other ridiculous attributes.' But removing this particular power was a step of huge significance, and Foot did have one heartfelt and very considerable tribute to pay. 'In making him slightly less ridiculous, we are at the same time affording greater freedom to a section of the community who have perhaps contributed more to the glory of our country than any other section has done.'[65]

And their shades cheered.

CHAPTER TEN

Afterwords (1968–1971)

It follows almost as an axiom that abolition of the Censorship would be followed by agitation for the abolition of such Common Law and statutory defences as at present can be invoked by the community . . .

(Lord Chamberlain's Assistant Secretary, 1967)[1]

Have we been missing nudity on the legitimate stage? Have we been missing the wholesale use of four-letter words? Have we been missing the miming of various forms of sexual act?[2]

(Peter Lewis, 'Is This What We Got Rid of the Lord Chamberlain For', February 1969)

It would surely be impossible to construct anything like a full account of how British theatre has been externally censored in the decades since the 1968 Theatres Act became law. This present volume, like its predecessors which covered the period from 1900 to 1959, has placed the practices of the Lord Chamberlain at its centre, drawing extensively on the remarkable archives which document the day-to-day practices of a system of control which was clearly identifiable and relatively overt. Since 1968, there has been no direct equivalent. Yet it would be absurdly naïve to imagine that writers and theatres have been free to stage whatever they want. There is no way to measure precisely, but it might well be argued that some of the restrictions which affect writers and directors today—and certainly the risks of challenging them—are greater than they were before September 1968—even if they are not embodied in law. Of course, even during the reign of the Lord Chamberlain, his authority was by no means the only inhibiting power. St James's Palace was the most obvious and visible manifestation of control, the one which playwrights and theatres had always to consciously accommodate and negotiate; but, as Helen Freshwater points out in her recent analysis, other webs of restraint were as significant and complex then as they are now—and as often invisible—so that in reality, 'the Lord Chamberlain functioned as part of a larger network of censorious forces'.[3]

In more recent times there have been occasions (most famously, during the first run of Sarah Kane's *Blasted* in the mid-nineties) when voices have been heard calling aloud for the return of a theatre censor. Debates about the rights of artists to offend the beliefs and opinions of those who attend (or who don't attend) their performances have often become both passionate and aggressive. In the light of effective campaigns by, in particular, religious fundamentalists, it is even possible to wonder whether some of those who have been silenced might have been better protected by a buffer of officialdom and a protective licence standing between them and their assailants. Yet at times, censorship has also been identified as a badge of status and significance; self-evidently, those who attempt to suppress theatre are acknowledging its potency and its danger as a form of expression. If you are free to say anything you want, then it is often a sure sign that what you say is not seen to matter, or be likely to affect those who see it. After all, one obvious answer to the question of why pre-censorship could be safely abolished in 1968 was that it no longer mattered; that theatre had become less relevant—especially by comparison with other media and art forms. If that has not always proved to be the case, then this may also be a cause for celebration, especially since the attempt to impose silence often has precisely the opposite impact, turning the material into a subject of debate.

In recognising that it is probably inevitable that theatre—like anything which takes place in public—continues to be restricted by a variety of laws which impose limits on freedom, the situation may be complicated by the fact that we need also to consider whether we would have it otherwise, given that 'some censored material may be difficult to defend'. As Freshwater says, 'supporting the right to freedom of expression in all circumstances entails accepting the dissemination of statements or images which are widely judged to be abusive, bigoted, offensive or simply false', and as she points out, 'in practice, almost everyone ends up drawing the line somewhere'.[4] What may sometimes make things even more problematic is the age-old question—so often debated in the Lord Chamberlain's Office—of how far it is acceptable to have a character or a speech expressing opinions which liberal society might consider unacceptable—for example, racist views— within a play which may not necessarily be endorsing them.

Paradoxically, it can also be argued that the existence of censorship actually encourages 'better'—perhaps more subtle—work, by driving the artist away from the explicit and the direct and the specific into metaphor and ambiguity and broader application, probably leaving more space for audiences and recipients. As Freshwater explains, 'creative responses to censorship can produce sophisticated and complicit audiences' who 'become accustomed to listening for the hidden significances which lurk between the lines'.[5] Actually, it is clear that under censorship by the Lord Chamberlain, some audiences became practised in doing just this.

Indeed, St James's Palace sometimes (though not always) connived in it, concentrating on suppressing only what was named or represented.

By contrast, the relaxation of boundaries in September 1968 doubtless encouraged some performances which trod through previously restricted areas just because they could do so, in order to flaunt their new freedom. 'One thing is clear', wrote George Steiner in an article entitled 'Four-letter Tyranny' published some nine months after the passing of the Theatres Act, 'our new total licence has not made art freer or more persuasive'. Steiner claimed that 'such champions of complete graphic presentment as Kenneth Tynan' were now discovering that 'the nude theatre is a bore'. Citing Borges, Steiner declared that 'only the hack needs to spell out what the master commits to metaphor'.[6] Harold Hobson, also, was soon voicing his disenchantment and frustration at 'The dreary repetition of four-letter words that seems to be the London theatres' sole method of taking advantage of the abolition of stage censorship'. Where, Hobson asked at the start of 1970, was the evidence of artists taking proper advantage of the new opportunities? 'It is surprising that this ecstatically hailed era of freedom has so far in London not resulted in any really ambitious attempt to explore total liberty.'[7] A few months later, Hobson reviewed with contempt a play featuring 'ejaculation against a chair', in which 'a prim little bookseller . . . is forced by a gunman to exhibit his private parts'. This was not, he suggested, the sort of image which most of the Lord Chamberlain's enemies and detractors had been fighting for: 'When naïve but excitable dramatists realise why this sort of thing is less sensational than the mere slapping of a woman's wrists in *How the Other Half Loves* the theatre may begin to reap some benefit from the abolition of censorship.'[8]

Of course, Hobson's was only one perspective, limited, perhaps, by an old-fashioned disinclination to recognise that sexuality and politics—and the words we are allowed to say (and the things we are allowed to see)—may often be connected. Mary Whitehouse, bringing a prosecution against the National Theatre's production of Howard Brenton's *Romans in Britain* at the start of the 1980s, saw only a penis (which, like Whitehouse herself, wasn't actually there) and an arse; others saw a brutal colonising regime invading and abusing a powerless and sacred victim. Clearly, the apparent and the physical can themselves act as a metaphor for things unseen and unspoken.

Laws and Effects

While it may not be feasible to summarise what has happened to censorship in the theatre over the four-and-a-half decades since the Lord Chamberlain's role was abolished, it does seem appropriate to close this particular history by glancing at some of the more immediate occurrences which resulted directly from the change in law. Both before and after the advent of the new Act, there was no shortage of people who expressed grave concerns about what would follow; some were anxious about the liberties that playwrights and managers might take, but others worried that, in the absence of a general licence to offer protection, theatre would find itself not freer, but subject to the conservative and sometimes reactionary views of determined individuals and fanatical pressure groups; and that managers and playwrights would become more cautious in what they dared to expose to public scrutiny, so that whatever the intention of abolition, the effect would be to restrict theatre more. J.W. Lambert, the veteran and old school theatre critic of the *Sunday Times*, was never a convinced supporter of the change; in a column published a few days before the new Act passed into law, he predicted that to break with tradition and throw away the expertise built up under successive Lords Chamberlain would have the opposite effect to what the abolitionists were seeking: 'The authority of their licence has deterred, there can be no doubt, innumerable idiots from cramping the intelligent participation of the theatre in a changing society.'[9]

In an effort to avoid handing new opportunities to the 'innumerable idiots' who might gleefully seize every opportunity to impose more restrictive policies and practices on theatre managements and playwrights, MPs and their civil servants had gone to some lengths in drawing up the detail of the legislation to head off 'frivolous' prosecutions. The Act stipulated that: 'Proceedings . . . shall not be instituted in England and Wales except by or with the consent of the Attorney-General', and anyone seeking to bring a prosecution was required to persuade a Justice of the Peace to agree that there was a valid case to answer, and a reasonable chance of conviction. Moreover, the grounds of possible offence cited under the Act were relatively limited: anything which involved 'the use of threatening, abusive or insulting words or behaviour' or was 'likely to occasion a breach of the peace' would be liable, but the terms under which offended members of the audience could apply to have their protests taken up were quite carefully defined, and directly echoed the Obscene Publications Act: 'a play shall be deemed to be obscene if, taken as a whole, its effect was such as to tend to deprave and corrupt persons who were likely, having regard to all relevant circumstances, to attend it'. Again, the Theatres Act crucially enshrined the principle that no conviction could take place 'if it is proved that the giving of the performance in question was justified as being for the public good on the ground that it was in the interests of drama, opera, ballet or any other art, or of literature or learning'. Furthermore, it specifically provided 'that the opinion of experts as to the artistic, literary or other merits of a performance of a play may be admitted in any proceedings for an offence under section 2 of this Act'.[10]

Notwithstanding such provisions, Lambert reasonably pointed out that 'the theatre will be anything but free', since it would remain liable for prosecution under a range of existing laws. 'It will still be technically seditious to "bring into contempt" the Queen, her heirs or successors', he explained, 'or to "excite disaffection against" the Government or either House of Parliament, or the administration of justice', or even '"to promote feelings of ill-will and hostility between different classes"'. Then there were the libel laws, the obscenity laws, and the risk of causing a breach of the peace by, for example, stirring up racial hatred. 'We shall surely see plays in which putting the case for coloured people involves showing whites in an unfavourable light', worried Lambert; and all anyone would need to do to have it closed down, he suggested, was 'to organise a disturbance in order to prove that a performance is likely to provoke it'. He concluded that the overall impact of jettisoning the Lord Chamberlain was that 'a minor irritant would seem to have been replaced by a major hazard'.[11] But no-one knew for sure how things would play out. 'Uncensored plays line up for West End', declared a *Guardian* headline as D-Day approached.[12]

But the newspaper was less confident in predicting what would actually happen. 'The next few months will show just how much freedom theatre managers have without the Lord Chamberlain', it suggested, acknowledging that much would depend on the attitudes and actions of the Attorney General and the police. The general (and largely accurate) assumption was that it would primarily be issues of sex and dress which would generate anxiety. 'Scotland Yard said the matter would be dealt with by officers who look after obscene publications', reported the *Guardian*, and they 'would wait to see how much extra work was involved before deciding whether to increase staff'. However, 'They would not be sending officers to first nights, and would rely largely on information provided by the public'.

Dancing on the Lord Chamberlain's Grave

First out of the blocks was *Hair*, which opened on 27 September—the very night after the Lord Chamberlain's writ ended. A few weeks earlier it had been proudly advertising itself as 'the show that could not conceivably be presented on any British stage'; now it was bound for the West End.

In the Shaftesbury Theatre next Friday evening a number of young people of both sexes will display themselves stark naked before an eagerly expectant audience. They will in effect be executing a triumphal dance over the grave of the Lord Chamberlain in his capacity as licenser of plays for public performance. On Thursday the Theatres Act 1968 becomes law, and, in theory at least, the drama will be able to express its true heart and soul untrammelled by the oppression of authority or even the insidious pressures of convention.[13]

Hair had its share of detractors, variously disgusted by its values and its denigration of authorities. 'Plenty to alarm unwary in hymn to freedom', as *The Times* headline soberly put it, noting in its review that the performance included 'blasphemy, perversion, and other material taboo until yesterday'. But the review also insisted on the show's 'integrity' and that 'its honesty and passion give it the quality of a true theatrical celebration'.[14] And though not all critics agreed, even the *Daily Telegraph* couldn't help buying into the mood: 'it taps the heady Dionysian spring from which all theatre flows', applauded John Barber, writing under the headline 'Let's Be Fair to "Hair"'.[15] Moreover, it acquired supporters in high places, with photographs appearing in the press of an 18-year-old Princess Anne participating in the on-stage dancing which followed each performance, and reports that she had been to see it several times. Certainly, *Hair*, with its now more or less fashionable attack on traditional values and assumptions, became a commercial success—'the biggest hit in London'.[16] To commemorate its third anniversary in 1971, the Dean of St Paul's Cathedral even welcomed members of the cast to take part in a Sunday Communion service, singing songs from the show.

The nudity in *Hair* was supposedly played under 'dimmed lights' (though the front page of the *Daily Telegraph* insisted 'there was nothing dim about the lighting').[17] But the following week, the press announced that *Fortune and Men's Eyes*—a plea for prison reform which focused on homosexuality in a Toronto prison—was to be staged at the Comedy Theatre with the first 'full-light nude scene'.[18] October brought a revival of Colin Spencer's *Spitting Image*, in which a man in a homosexual 'marriage' not only gives birth, but inspires a wave of male pregnancies across the country. No wonder Barry Norman in the *Daily Mail* thought he could hear the sound of 'the Lord Chamberlain spinning in his grave again'.[19] Actually, Spencer's play had been approved and staged earlier in the year, but with a number of cuts. Now it could be presented in full in the West End, where most critics found it inoffensive and sentimental with its unthreatening message 'that homosexuals can lead happy, harmonious and fruitful lives together', and its gentle satire against 'the fears of officialdom when confronted by the unorthodox'. Still, opening performances were greeted with 'a display of overt hostility' by some sections of the audience. To most people, the surprise was that there was enough in the play to upset anyone. 'How did they find the energy to boo?' asked the *Daily Mail*.[20]

It was a different matter with *The Beard*, a much more provocative American import which opened at the Royal Court in early November in late night performances following the main show. Here the sexuality was hetero, but both the language and the imagery were explicit and sustained, and *The Times* defined Michael McLure's play as the production with which the Royal Court 'celebrated the end of stage censorship'. First performed in 1965 by the Actor's Workshop in San Francisco, *The Beard* had purportedly been staged 'at the huge rock and roll Fillmore Stadium to a wildly enthusiastic capacity crowd', with 'light projections and a sound system utilizing rock music'. McLure himself was identified as the author of 'a collaborative autobiography of a member of the Frisco Chapter of the Hell's Angels' and of '99 poems in a mammalian language he calls "beast language"', as well as 'a book length sexual and revolutionary poem'. Readers of *The Times* were informed that he was currently based in San Francisco 'composing post-psychedelic songs' in a style he called 'Cowboy Shiva'. *The Beard*, meanwhile, had a 'history of persistent police interference (involving repeated arrest of the cast)'.[21]

McLure's play has only two characters, named as Jean Harlow and Billy the Kid, but who apparently exist outside of time or place, waiting in a kind of undefined limbo that possibly resembles eternity. According to Norman Mailer's programme note, although 'its surface seems simple, repetitive and obscene', the repetition and revisiting of text embodied 'subway stops on that electric trip a man and a woman make if they move from the mind to the flesh'. It was, said Mailer,

> almost as if two ghosts from the American past were speaking across decades to each other, and yet at the same time are present in our living room undressing themselves or speaking to us of the nature of seduction, the nature of attraction, and, particularly, the nature of perverse temper between a man and a woman.

In any case, it surely went beyond what the Lord Chamberlain could have stomached:

> THE KID: Come here and sit on my lap and I'll let you hold my cock.
> HARLOW: Now wouldn't I like THAT—a chunk of meat hanging from a hunk of meat!
> THE KID: And afterwards you can lick my boots!

At the end of the play, a stage direction informs us that 'He grasps her thighs and presses his face between them, kissing her', while 'HARLOW stiffens and arches her body', and the curtain falls, presumably on her orgasm.

> HARLOW: (Ecstatically) STAR! STAR! STAR! OH MY GOD—! STAR! STAR! STAR! STAR! STAR! OH MY GOD—! STAR! STAR! YOU'RE

NEXT! OH MY GOD—! BLUE-BLACK STAR! STAR! STAR! STAR!
STAR! STAR! STAR! STAR! STAR! STAR! STAR! STAR! STAR!
STAR! STAR! STAR! STAR! STAR!
Curtain[22]

The Lord Chamberlain would certainly have required a blow by blow
account of the actions which accompanied these lines.

The critical response was mixed. 'Outspoken "Beard" not for
squeamish' was the *Daily Telegraph* headline, while *The Times* went with
'Notorious Play Arrives'. 'Drivel, and dull drivel at that', said Harold
Hobson; 'Two players indulge in lengthy but limited obscenities, rasp the
eardrums with strident voices, and are a frightful bore'. Others were more
open: 'there is no question of its force and originality', declared Irving
Wardle in *The Times*; 'Whether you regard it as a jewel or a heap of dung,
it remains indestructibly itself'. The *Guardian* had no doubt that 'the terse
expletives which celebrate the Lord Chamberlain's demise' were crucial to
the power of the dialogue, as the play moves 'remorselessly to its liberating
act of cunnilingus'.[23] But the real question was whether anyone would try
to intervene. As the *Evening Standard* put it, McLure's play amounted to
a direct challenge to 'the nature and scope of present stage censorship' in
a post Lord Chamberlain world: 'If this goes, I suppose, almost anything
goes.' The newspaper allowed that the Royal Court had 'done everything
possible to indicate that this is no play for the prudish, the susceptible or
the conventional theatre-goer', and judged that although it was shocking,
it was permissible under the terms and conditions of the Act: 'its elusive,
ambiguous language guarantees that it is not a corrupting play'. The issue
was 'whether the theatre is free to tackle subjects in a manner already
familiar in novels read by millions'; and the newspaper concluded that
'The answer must obviously be yes'.[24]

For others, including Peter Lewis in the *Daily Mail*, the arrival of a play
which had been 'warded off for so long by the late Lord Chamberlain's
powers' raised a different question: 'Was this forbidden fruit worth having?'
For Lewis, the 'representation of a sexual act on the stage' had struck 'a
blow for freedom' but one we could have done without.[25] In a longer article
published under the provocative question 'Is This What We Got Rid of
the Lord Chamberlain For?' he quoted, as 'one of the first fruits', a short
extract from McLure's play in which the words 'FUCK YOU' are repeated
six times. His article was less a lament for theatre censorship per se, more
a despair that after such a long and hard fought campaign 'to free it from
a foolish, arbitrary and indefensible interference'—a campaign waged
on behalf of writers such as Aristophanes, Sophocles, Strindberg, Ibsen,
Pirandello, Wilde and Shaw—it should turn out that 'when censorship's
citadel fell, the first exercise of freedom resulted in the import of *Hair*, *The*

Beard, and *Fortune and Men's Eyes* from America'. Sadly, concluded Lewis, Britain lacked the writers necessary 'to celebrate the new-found freedom and show us what could be done with it and what we have been missing'; the offerings of the current crop 'hardly seemed worthy of the occasion', and failed to justify the case for freedom: 'Have we been missing nudity on the legitimate stage? Have we been missing the wholesale use of four-letter words? Have we been missing the miming of various forms of sexual act?' asked Lewis; 'Well, we have them now and so far they show little promise of advancing the art of drama'. Lewis also cited a suggestion by the director James Roose-Evans that 'artists need certain obstacles to fight against as a discipline'. Roose-Evans was wary of the danger that theatres would start to include things just because they could: 'Now we're going to have it all. Mass orgies on the stage', he predicted. 'Then communal petting between actors and audience. Then someone will kill a real canary in *Miss Julie*. Then there'll be a pig killing and probably in the end human killing.'[26]

The Beard had not been submitted prior to September 1968, but some plays which had had their applications for a licence turned down could now take their place in public theatres. *Hair*, of course, but also Harold Pinter's *Landscape*, which had been broadcast on the radio in April 1968 but had to wait for a post-Chamberlain world before being staged as conceived. A licence could have been secured under the Lord Chamberlain if Pinter had been willing to do what so many had done before him—namely, compromise over specific words—and possibly he would have conceded this if the Lord Chamberlain's departure had not been so close. But it seems Pinter was unwilling to continue: 'I was tired of it all . . . I didn't want to discuss them.' *Landscape* received its first performances at the Aldwych alongside *Silence* in July 1969, in an RSC production directed by Peter Hall. The differences between the text that was performed and the version which could have been staged a year earlier might seem trivial. The Lord Chamberlain's restrictions had hardly had the kind of impact on Pinter that they did on writers such as Osborne and Bond. Yet the playwright's own analysis is telling: 'The censorship to me was an irritant and a bore', he told an interviewer, admitting that 'it didn't inhibit me from expressing myself except in points of detail'. Then he added: 'But points of detail are important.'[27]

Another recent play to benefit from the change in law was Peter Barnes's *The Ruling Class*, which had been licensed at the end of 1967 in a deal involving some sixty cuts. In March 1969, the full text was played for the first time at the Piccadilly Theatre, and hailed by Harold Hobson as both 'a scorching and savage tragedy' and 'uproariously funny'. Hobson maintained that 'except for *Hair*', *The Ruling Class* represented 'the single considerable gain that the British stage has made from the abolition of censorship'.[28] He was much less keen on another play which could also now be staged publicly and in full, Edward Bond's *Early Morning* ('It was intended to turn my stomach, and it did', he wrote; 'it would not at all surprise me if at subsequent performances some people vomited over their neighbours'). In spite of this, Hobson—and other reviewers—acknowledged *Early Morning* as an important and serious play ('It is a demand for a complete reform of our system of education') and recognised that Bill Gaskill's 1969 production was finally able to give the text the staging it merited, and which it had been unable to receive under the Lord Chamberlain's surveillance.[29]

Peter Lewis's article quoted the theatre impresario Michael White, who was responsible for bringing a range of controversial productions to the London stage: 'I don't think there's going to be trouble over sex', forecast White in 1969, 'I think there's going to be trouble over politics. And that is far more important'.[30] In the late autumn of 1968, White was working with Kenneth Tynan to bring Hochhuth's *Soldiers*—banned under the Lord Chamberlain for suggesting that Winston Churchill was implicated in a secret and successful wartime plot by the Soviet Union to assassinate the Polish leader in exile in a faked air accident—to the London stage. Equally provocatively, Hochhuth's play criticised the allied aerial bombardment and destruction of German cities, and the targeting of civilians. '*Soldiers* seemed to me to pose a searching question', wrote White; 'Even if the enemy had abandoned all moral considerations, was the bombing of civilians justified?' Nor was it just a historical issue. For White, the key scene in the play was an argument Churchill has with a Bishop who is protesting about this strategy, 'which had strong overtones regarding the current bombing of Cambodia'.[31]

With the Lord Chamberlain gone, there was no obvious reason why Tynan and White should not go ahead with the production. But the situation was not that straightforward:

> that was where censorship of the unofficial kind first showed its head, in a very instructive manner. For a long time it was impossible to find a theatre for the play. Howard and Wyndham's turned it down on the grounds that it was 'liable to cause controversy and unrest in the provinces'. So did Moss Empires because, in the words of Leslie MacDonnell, 'I did not read the script but people told me it was anti-Churchill so I said no'.

According to White, 'a suspiciously large number of theatres which were approached found they had prior commitments', while one well-known and influential manager said he 'wouldn't have it in one of my theatres even if it was dark'.[32] In effect, he contends, theatre-owners were 'taking the role of censor unto themselves'.[33]

Soldiers opened at the New Theatre in December, with the theatre 'in a virtual state of siege' because of the threats received, and with extensive security measures in operation.[34] White records that he received 'serious hate mail' from people who accused him of being a Nazi sympathiser', but *The Times* reported that the opening performance 'passed off without incident before a largely German audience'. The production did poorly at the box office.[35] One more or less typical review described it as 'a slightly turgid historical drama', and the Prime Minister, Harold Wilson, called it 'scurrilous'. Worse, the surviving pilot of the plane in which Sikorski had been killed brought a series of prosecutions for libel against playwright, translator, publisher, director, producer and theatre, which ended with an award of £50,000 in damages. White called this 'the Lord Chamberlain's revenge', and it did seem to offer a salutary warning of the downside of operating without the protection of a licence from the crown.[36] On the other hand, the sensitivities around *Soldiers* also remind us that politics in the theatre did still matter. Writing in *The Times* just after the production had opened, Irving Wardle made the point that 'The Churchill legend' was evidently immune from the criticisms of historians or novelists, but that 'when the man is exhibited on a stage, criticism turns to sacrilege'; he also quoted a priest who had commented in relation to Hochhuth's *The Representative*—with its accusations that the Pope had tacitly endorsed the Nazis—'that it would have mattered so little if only the work had not been a play'. Wardle links this with the 'Puritan tradition' and its fear of 'the basic taboo-breaking act by which one man usurps the identity of another'; it is also, he suggests, 'the greatest compliment they have paid to the theatre', since it is rooted in 'awe for all forms of dramatic representation'.[37]

Notwithstanding White's prediction, it was issues and provocations around sexuality which surfaced most frequently—though of course these were often also political. In December 1968, the Royal Festival Hall presented 'A Gala Evening concerning Depravity and Corruption' in aid of the National Council for Civil Liberties and the Defence of Literature and the Arts Society. Produced by George Melly, this 'anarchic three hour entertainment'—was designed 'to raise money for the arts in their eternal fight against the censor and his scissors'.[38] Authors involved included Samuel Beckett, Johnny Speight, John Mortimer, John Bowen, Edward Bond, and Charles Wood, while performers included Nicol Williamson, Rita Tushingham, Sheila Hancock, Peggy Ashcroft, William Rushton, George Melly and the Grateful Dead. 'Astonishing things are about to happen to the balcony scene from Romeo and Juliet', reported the *Daily Mirror* in its preview, predicting that Charles Marowitz's staging 'may well cause some raised eyebrows', since the action was to be played in a double bed. 'Pinnacles of high-flown romanticism' would be 'brought sharply down to bedroom basic', they reported, quoting Marowitz's claims: 'The scene will have lost all its innocence and will become a filthy sex scene between two depraved people. Shakespeare will turn out to be the filthiest author imaginable.'[39] In the event, *The Times* reported that the 'much vaunted' event actually 'had most of the audience waiting for the interval rather than Godot'.[40] Meanwhile, in what was presumably a show of some kind of puritanism, the fascist National Front distributed sick bags at the door.

For all that it shocked and challenged some, *Hair* was essentially a much safer, more contained, and more commercial embodiment of the late sixties sexual and political revolution than the one for which the Living Theatre was striving in *Paradise Now*, which arrived at London's Roundhouse in the summer of 1969—less than a year after the Lord Chamberlain's demise. There was no way the script could have been approved (or even negotiated) under his authority. Apart from anything else, long sections of the performance were not only to be improvised, but to be improvised in response to and with the audience. In fact, one of the key aims was to break down the barriers between audience and actors not only within the theatre building, but in the streets outside. Within the performance, actors and audience were encouraged to remove their clothes and to participate in direct physical and sexual contact. Exiled under fear of prosecution from their homeland in the United States, the company had clashed with the authorities in a number of European countries, and recently been banned while playing at the Avignon Festival. By contrast, although the opening performance was temporarily halted by a police raid, the Roundhouse event went off with comparatively little interference: 'They arrived about 2½ hours after the show's start, when a love pile was building up on stage, consisting of actors stripped to the G-string lying in a heap and stroking each other gently.'[41] But, officially at least, what the police objected to was the fact that members of the audience were on the stage, in defiance of fire regulations which stipulated that where seats existed, people were obliged to sit in them. Following the police intervention, the audience was persuaded to return to the seats, but ten minutes later began tearing them up from where they were nailed down, and moving them onto the stage—thus circumventing the regulations. For subsequent performances the stage itself was removed 'to leave a completely free area, where the audience and actors can mill around', and there were no further significant confrontations. Indeed, the Living Theatre were reportedly pleased to discover that in London—unlike elsewhere—the concerns of the authorities had not extended beyond issues of basic safety.[42]

Backlash

Just over a year after the passing of the 1968 Theatres Act, George Strauss, who had chaired the Joint Select Committee of Enquiry and introduced the resulting bill to the Commons, made a speech to the Council of Repertory Theatres about 'the first year of liberation'. He claimed that the stage was 'just as vigorous, healthy, lively and popular as it has ever been', and that 'experimental theatre in Britain had advanced considerably'. He had no doubt that several plays had been presented which would previously have been banned, and that none of these could be justly accused of indulging in 'pornography for pornography's sake'. Crucially, not a single prosecution had been brought by the Attorney General under the provisions of the new Theatres Act. However, some commentators read the developing situation differently: 'The fact that after almost two years, the Attorney General's office has not received a single complaint from the DPP', wrote the journalist and historian Brian Moynahan in 1970, 'seems to confirm the widespread fear that the Theatres Act, by abolishing the arbitrary pre-censorship imposed by the Lord Chamberlain, would encourage severe self-censorship by theatre managements'.[43] For some, a further step of liberation was required, and in July 1969, the Arts Council made an official recommendation that all laws which permitted prosecution of books and plays on the grounds of obscenity and which 'have been or could be used as a basis for indirect censorship' should be repealed for a trial five-year period, with the Theatres Act of 1968 to be 'brought into line'.[44] 'The so-called permissive society may have its casualties', they acknowledged, but 'repressed sexuality can be toxic both to the individual and society', and was more likely to 'deprave and corrupt'.[45] Above all: 'It is not for the State to prohibit private citizens from choosing what they may or may not enjoy in literature or art unless there were incontrovertible evidence that the results would be injurious to society.' And their report was clear that 'there is no such evidence'.[46] In any case, 'Incitement to criminal behaviour is sufficiently covered by the ordinary law of incitement' so that the Obscenity laws were effectively 'redundant'.[47]

There were plenty of commentators who challenged the Arts Council view. Kenneth Hurren, for example, called it an 'arrogant proposal' and 'a licence to corrupt'; he also accused the 'Theatre people' who had fought against the Lord Chamberlain of 'duplicity' and 'artistic insolence', since one of their key arguments had been that other laws and controls meant his authority was unnecessary. 'There was no hint in such pious pleas that this readiness of artists to submit themselves to the Common Law was merely an interim readiness, a shifty gambit concealing a more arrogant belief.' Hurren strongly objected to the fact that in spite of the almost unprecedented degree of freedom allowed by the new law, 'artists now seek to place themselves above it'.[48] The Arts Council's proposals also met strong parliamentary resistance, with the Conservative MP David Waddington insisting there was 'widespread concern in the country' at where it might lead: 'any change in the present law would be widely regarded not as a step towards a more civilised society but as a step further towards an unduly permissive society'. Even the Labour Home Secretary, James Callaghan, who had replaced Roy Jenkins in November 1967, agreed that he would 'need a great deal of convincing' before he would accept the recommendations, and indicated that there was 'no prospect of time being made available' for a parliamentary debate in the near future.[49] Perhaps the Arts Council and the freedom-fighters had over-played their hand.

The sixties were nearly over, and writing under the title 'I Beg You 1970', the veteran theatre critic, J.C. Trewin, contemptuously dismissed current tastes for vulgar language and bodily display, and called for a new revolution:

> I wish carbon-copy dramatists would realize that the party is over, and that most of us find the looser lingo intensely boring. There is no reason now—if ever there was one—to bait the Lord Chamberlain. We do not want to be reminded any more that this author or the next is a fellow of gallant and independent spirit who knows just how, in Lewis Carroll's word, to uglify his dialogue . . . This applies also to stage nudity and to the rest of the infantilism we have suffered in the cause of freedom.

Trewin was convinced that the fight had not been lost:

> I look forward with confidence to a theatre that will gradually forswear anarchy, seek the lost virtues of elegance and form, and refuse to take 'civilized' as a form of contempt. I do not believe for half a moment that we are naturally a crude, brash nation. The stage can help by ceasing to be a distorting mirror.[50]

Writing again a few months later, Trewin claimed that the removal of the Lord Chamberlain's authority had led to a decline in standards, and that what had been gained had proved to be far outweighed by what had been lost: 'Many of us felt in 1968 that it was just as well the Censor should go', he wrote, 'so that the restlessly articulate cheerleaders of artistic freedom could get something out of their system'. But the result had been a near total let-down: 'It has meant permission to use on a public stage the lingo of a back street brawl.' Trewin believed that the pendulum must inevitably swing back again: 'We are bound to have a reaction', he declared, and derided in the most patronising terms what he saw as the immature obsessions of contemporary playwrights and theatres: 'audiences will weary of the tedium of Baby in one of Baby's moods'.[51]

The Dirtiest Shows

Trewin and Hurren were by no means alone in holding such views, and there was soon evidence that the new decade was bringing with it a reaction against some of the political optimism of the mid-sixties. In June 1970, Harold Wilson and the Labour Party lost power, and the Conservatives under Edward Heath were elected to government. Brian Moynahan wrote his article ('Testing Time for Sex on Stage') within a few weeks of the Tory victory, and to coincide with the opening of Kenneth Tynan's 'erotic revue', *Oh! Calcutta!*, which was widely expected to lead to the first prosecution. John Mortimer—playwright, lawyer and champion of free speech—advised as much when consulted by the show's producer, Michael White: 'I have no doubt that we are seeing a period of retrogression and backlash against permissiveness in the Arts, and that a production of *Oh! Calcutta!* would be at serious risk of prosecution', warned Mortimer; and while he did not himself believe the show was likely 'to deprave and corrupt', he could not guarantee that an Old Bailey judge and jury would share his view. Indeed, he suggested that if there were to be a prosecution, 'the chances of a conviction would be about 50/50, given the present mood of the Courts'.[52]

The title of Tynan's show was supposedly a play on the French phrase 'Quel cul t'as!' (usually translated as 'What an arse you've got!'), which had itself inspired a painting called 'Oh! Calcutta! Calcutta!' by the French Surrealist artist, Clovis Trouille. Trouille's work depicted the buttocks of a reclining woman, tattooed with the fleur-de-lis, and Tynan's multi-authored script consisted of sketches dealing 'with almost every conceivable erotic fantasy and sexual reality that Western man has dreamt up or experienced'.[53] According to promoters of the published script and recordings, it 'playfully challenged taboos by representing the sexual revolution in a series of uproarious skits, dance and naughty musical numbers performed (mostly) in the nude'.[54] A remarkable list of contributors included Samuel Beckett, Edna O'Brien, Jules Feiffer, Sam Shepard, Joe Orton and John Lennon, and although few critics would find many positive things to say, it lasted for almost 4000 performances, and became 'The World's Longest Running Erotic Stage Musical'. Its arrival in London was much anticipated, not least because it had already shocked New York, Los Angeles and San Francisco, where actors had been arrested and a prosecution had been brought—though subsequently dropped. In London, it initially opened at the Roundhouse because, according to Moynahan, West End managements were worried about possible prosecution. However, he had no doubt 'the big theatres will be queuing up for it' if the show and its backers survived without a successful prosecution against them.

The first official complaint about *Oh! Calcutta!* was duly lodged with the police by three individuals who attended a preview precisely in anticipation of making it; Frank Smith, a GLC council member, Conservative agent, and a lay preacher; his wife, Ida; and the Dowager Lady Birdwood, a well known and extreme right-winger, best known at the time for her campaign against 'blasphemy and filth' on television. According to Moynahan, they 'walked straight from their seats in the Round House theatre to Kentish Town police station', and complained that the show was obscene. Smith told the press it was 'crude, amateurish and complete sex from start to finish', and 'my wife has been upset ever since'. He explained that he had only attended 'to see if it was as bad as they said it was', and had discovered 'it was worse'. Indeed it was 'the most depraved show I have ever seen', and made him ashamed of what London had become: 'We are letting this great city become dirty, filthy, morally.'[55]

Their complaint was duly registered with the DPP while the police investigated, with the final decision about prosecution to be taken by Sir Peter Rawlinson as Attorney General. Meanwhile, the Conservative MP John Biggs-Davison tabled a motion in parliament to condemn *Oh! Calcutta!* as 'an insult to human dignity and a disgrace to London'.[56] *The Times* also published a column by the political journalist Ronald Butt, claiming to speak on behalf of 'the majority of ordinary people'. According to Butt, most people were 'hypnotized, repelled and passive before the morally deathly gyrations of their new persuaders', while their human rights were being effectively 'jeopardized by the insidious erosion of the standards to which the majority wants to adhere'. The opening of *Oh! Calcutta!*, argued Butt, 'should bring home to people what is happening':

> Its genre is basically the sort of exhibition of sexual voyeurism that used to be available to the frustrated and the mentally warped in the side-turnings of a certain kind of sea-port. If Mr Tynan and his friends wished to satisfy themselves by this sort of thing in strict private . . . the rest of us would have no cause for any reaction except pity. But, in fact, they seek to thrust it down the heaving throats of the majority: if they could, they would put it on in a major public theatre. As it is they no doubt feel they have secured a certain triumph by staging it in a theatre which is in receipt of public money from the Arts Council.

Butt even claimed that people watching it 'may suffer some moral damage in their attitude to human relationships', and he also warned of 'the ripple effect' on those who did not themselves attend but 'whose conception of what is tolerable is conditioned' by the show's existence and reception. Such shows, he argued, should not even be discussed by critics: 'there is no reason at all why offerings should not be labelled simply "pornographic": not reviewed'. He called loudly for politicians to intervene.[57]

Inevitably, Butt's column provoked both endorsement and condemnation, with the Defence of Literature and the Arts Society quick to dispute the idea that *Oh! Calcutta!* was likely to have 'any corruptive effect or influence at all on its audiences'. They suggested there was 'more genuine titillation' displayed in many advertising posters, as well as 'ample striptease establishments offering a closer view at a fraction of the price'. However, the concern voiced by this organisation seems to have been motivated less by the wish to defend this particular show, and more by the fear that the government would use it as an excuse to consider turning back the clock: '*Oh! Calcutta!* does not pretend to be any more than a light entertainment', they wrote, 'but any return of theatrical censorship will inevitably lead to serious dramatists such as Edward Bond and Fernando Arrabal, who were penalized under the Lord Chamberlain, finding that their plays once again cannot be produced'. The Society insisted that 'to bring a prosecution or to produce new shackles on the theatre at this time would show a lack of common sense', and urged the Attorney General and the DPP not to be persuaded by Butt's 'veiled invitation to take action', or to let themselves be pushed along a road 'that will turn the whole of the artistic establishment of this country against them'. In the forceful and passionate defence mounted by this society, one can detect a real fear that they might lose the battle; even that the hard-won advances made in the name of liberation might go into reverse. Effectively, then, *Oh! Calcutta!* became a test case of the 1968 Theatres Act and of the direction in which things were moving—even though many of those who cared most about artistic freedom would not have chosen this particular production as the one to fight for. As Moynahan noted, a successful prosecution could result in fines of up to £400 (not counting legal costs) and three years in prison.

As for the theatre critics, while most were generally underwhelmed by *Oh! Calcutta!*, few saw anything much in it to be concerned about. In New York, Clive Barnes had called it 'a Most Innocent Dirty Show', finding it so lacking in the eroticism it boasted of that it 'makes "The Sound of Music" seem like "Hair"'.[58] In London, Harold Hobson waxed lyrical about some of the 'breathtakingly beautiful' visual images composed of bodies, comparing them to paintings by Titian and 'the finest sculpture'; yet he found it 'incredible' that most of the sketches were so bad and performed 'with the leaden circumspection of an elephant setting out on the long trek to Katmandu'. Indeed, he thought the overall quality was so low that the only thing which would enable it to survive for more than a week was 'the excited protests of officious guardians of public and private morality who lack the elementary common sense to keep their mouths shut'.[59] For *The Times*, Irving Wardle could see no danger in it: 'In many ways it is a ghastly show', he wrote; 'ill-written, juvenile, and attention-seeking. But it is not a menace'.[60] John Barber in the *Daily Telegraph* talked about the 'laughable insolence' of a performance which 'teeters along the borderline between the indecorous and the obscene'; Tynan, he said, had 'broken through barriers that many people will think better left where they were'. Yet isolated moments were 'stunning' and 'sensational', and he also found 'poetry in its celebration of the human body and much to laugh at in its mockery of sex'. Barber concluded: 'So far as I can judge, I was neither depraved nor corrupted.'[61]

Despite the best efforts of Lady Birdwood, Mary Whitehouse, Lord Longford and their supporters, the Attorney General, Sir Peter Rawlinson, announced in early August that he had decided not to allow a case against *Oh! Calcutta!* to come to court, there being 'no reasonable likelihood that a prosecution . . . would be successful'.[62] Probably he was inhibited by the fact that it came so soon after a new government and its ministers had taken up the reins of power. Lady Birdwood then bombarded MPs with letters demanding the show's closure, and unsuccessfully petitioned the Attorney General to allow her to bring a private prosecution. Frank Smith accused Rawlinson of having 'shirked the issue', and claimed to speak 'for 90 per cent of the public of Greater London when I say it is time this filth was brought to a halt'.[63] He even vowed to fight against his own political party on the issue, since the 'outrageous' decision had 'set back the cause of civilization and a decent way of life in Britain'.[64] Restricted by—as Smith saw it—'the craftily worded Theatre Act 1968',[65] the Attorney General's decision seemed to have left little scope for future prosecutions—at least on grounds of obscenity. Moreover, not for the first or last time, the publicity generated by those seeking to suppress the show became a crucial element in its promotion and financial success. According to White, 'Every paper had a *Calcutta*-based cartoon', and he had no doubt that the show's longevity and financial success was due primarily to 'the Whitehouse factor'.[66]

With *Oh! Calcutta!* another battle seemed to have been won and lost, but the Dowager Lady Birdwood, for one, had not given up. In the summer of 1970 she tried to bring a prosecution against another controversial production, this time because of its mockery of Christianity. It is not hard to see why *Council of Love*, subtitled *A Heavenly Tragedy in Five Acts*, would have been profoundly disturbing to many religious people. Its characters include God, Jesus, the Virgin Mary and the Devil—the last played here by Warren Mitchell, a familiar face to audiences from his portrayal of the racist and right-wing Alf Garnett in the equally provocative television series *Till Death Us Do Part*. *Council of Love* had originally been written in 1893 by Oskar Panizza, a German psychiatrist who, following years of being pursued and imprisoned by the German and Swiss authorities on the grounds that his play was blasphemous, ended his days confined to a Bavarian mental asylum. It is unthinkable that any theatre manager would even have considered submitting an English version to the Lord Chamberlain before 1968, but in August 1970 it was staged at the Criterion Theatre in Piccadilly, in a text translated and adapted by the well-known television satirist, John Bird. The play has scenes in both Heaven and Hell, and is set during Easter 1495; it features a God, who was described in one review as 'a teasily comic, wheezing King Lear'; a Virgin, 'who spends her time knitting'; and a Jesus 'who complains that He suffers from being eaten by His own worshippers'. There is also a Pope, who associates with a group of courtesans. In *The Times*, Irving Wardle had no doubt it was the first post Lord Chamberlain play to really take on the issue of religion and blasphemy—'the first real act of desecration'. At one point, the Devil observes of God that 'No one can accuse him of being a Christian'. For Wardle, the play had 'some aspirations to metaphysical argument', but was primarily 'a jubilant orgy of idol-smashing':

> God the Father appears as a vainglorious dotard who snores through the harp music: the Virgin is a gracious suburban matron with a home-perm and a basket of knitting, and Christ, still in bad shape after the crucifixion ('Second Coming? He hasn't got over the first!'), is trundled on in a wheelbarrow as a feeble-minded wreck. They are not a happy family; even the placid Virgin cannot get it into her head that she is not a member of the Trinity.

Perhaps most surprising is the fact that *The Times* review, while not without criticisms, concluded quietly that 'Altogether it makes a good evening'.[67]

The critics did not all agree that the arrival of such a play in the West End was something to celebrate. 'I tremble to imagine its effect upon a moderately sensitive playgoer unused to the drama of a stage deserted by the Lord Chamberlain', fretted Trewin; 'Pity the poor man, in London alone for an evening and choosing, unaware, the piece with the amiable title'. Trewin described watching *Council of Love* as 'a disastrous experience' and 'as unpleasant as anything I remember'. He rightly noted that under the Lord Chamberlain it 'would not have had the flimsiest chance of creeping upon an English stage', and he was most critical not of the performers or the writer but of the management which, in allowing it to be presented, had shown themselves 'utterly devoid of feeling for the name of the English stage'. In other words, they should have taken on the responsibility of censoring it.

We had guessed that after the legal death of the Censor practically anything might happen on the stage. Now, between them, *Oh Calcutta* and *Council of Love*, have nearly covered the ground. One or two delights remain, I daresay; but connoisseurs of obscenity and blasphemy cannot grumble about neglect![68]

Trewin took comfort only in his confidence that such a piece would not be long remembered, and that the pendulum would swing; in the near future, wrote Trewin, 'we shall find it hard to recall the title of the piece, buried deep among the detritus of the permissive years'. Perhaps history has proved him right. Who now, one wonders, would stage *Council of Love* anywhere—let alone in the West End?

Some attempts were made to bring a prosecution against those involved in *Council of Love* under section 2 of the Theatres Act, but again the Director of Prosecutions ruled there was no case to answer. A private prosecution was then instigated on behalf of Lady Birdwood, under the Blasphemy Law. She claimed to have seen the production four times, and objected to the 'caricature' image of God 'as "an old man, coughing and spluttering and wheezing—alternately, shouting and screaming, wearing a long dirty robe and with matted hair"'. She told the Court that 'When I got home this caricature came between me and the God I worship' and that 'Had she not been a fairly strong person "it could have done me a lot of harm"'.[69] But the case was dropped in February 1971, when it again became clear that convictions were highly unlikely. One other detail of this particular clash worth noting in respect of Trewin's attack on managers is that the original complaint to Scotland Yard came from one Geoffrey Russell. Russell was a 'theatrical impresario', the owner and managing director of the company responsible for the original production of *Salad Days* and for a number of Terence Rattigan's plays, and he would later become Lord Ampthill and Deputy Speaker of the House of Lords. As we know, the majority of theatre managers and owners had never wanted to get rid of the Lord Chamberlain; some wanted him back.

Trewin, meanwhile, continued both to predict and to demand a reaction against the current direction of travel. 'It is, I persuade myself, merely a flicker of fashion', he wrote in early 1971; 'probably, within a decade, we may be looking back with amused tolerance at the post-1968 excesses'.[70] More voices were joining in. A column in *The Times* the previous autumn had described *Oh! Calcutta!* as 'a crime against human dignity', and identified a climate of 'sexual fascism' in which 'the avant-garde world of culture' was reminiscent of the Nazis and Nuremberg, ruled as it was by 'individuals suffering from grave forms of madness', and driven by 'the impulse to destroy others'. The article cited a recent warning by the Bishop of Southwark that 'theatre was being reduced to the level of a lunatic asylum'.[71]

There were signs, too, that the message was getting through to those in power. During a House of Lords debate on mass media communication, Baroness Emmet of Amberley suggested 'that the permissive society had gone so far that the British character was in danger of being undermined'. Significantly, Lord David Eccles, the Paymaster General and Minister for the Arts, expressed agreement, identifying culture and the Arts as 'the pace-setters in the removal of conventions and restraints'. Eccles observed—doubtless in a tone of regret rather than celebration—that it was 'very easy to forget how many things we do now without shame and without risk of disapproval which only a generation ago we should have avoided like the plague'. Presumably thinking in part of the Theatres Act, he maintained that coercion from within the Arts had persuaded governments to change laws and reduce restrictions, and that changes of attitude and practice then spread more broadly through the culture. In his view, it was not the mass media which were the source of the problem: 'They did not make the permissive society', declared Eccles, 'They were presented with it'. How, then, to reverse the process? Eccles reminded the House that Arts Council funding came from taxpayers' money. It was therefore on the Arts Council that he wanted to bring pressure: 'I would not listen to anybody who wanted the return of the censor on works wholly financed from private sources', he declared; on the other hand, 'If the Arts Council could reach some understanding with their clients that takes into account the moral views of those who are putting up the money, I should be very glad'.

Jenny (by now Baroness) Lee—who as part of Harold Wilson's government had been the first Arts Minister—was quick to seek an assurance as to whether Eccles was seeking to reintroduce a political censorship. He batted this away: 'politics are not in my mind or in my speech at all', he claimed. Rather than seeking to introduce formal legislation, Eccles recommended that 'a convention' should be established, with the Arts Council promising 'that public money will not be available for financing works which affront many taxpayers'. And he insisted—as censors usually do—that his proposals were moderate: 'I have been asked whether the convention which we have in mind should include nudity on the stage', he observed; 'So far as I am concerned, nudity does no harm and will not make much progress in our climate'. Representation of the sexual act was a different matter, but he was vague about boundaries. 'I am not going to be drawn . . . into saying that we must have a legal definition of what is filthy and blasphemous', he insisted; and then with a line which could have come straight from St James's Palace at any time prior to 1968, he added: 'we can recognise it when we see it'. But perhaps the most remarkable aspect of Eccles's position was that he focused exclusively on subsidised theatres. True to a system of market economics, the commercial sector could apparently do what it liked so long as it made money![72]

Eccles's proposals were enough to put the wind up those who feared that freedoms recently earned might yet be withdrawn. Yet perhaps the most significant and sinister aspect of his statement was the implication that it was now acceptable—even sensible and desirable—for government ministers to put pressure on the Arts Council so as to shape its policies, and encourage the Arts Council to do the same to its clients. An outraged Jenny Lee published an article under the headline 'Hands Off the Theatres', insisting that during her own time in office 'The Arts Council scrupulously refrained from interfering with the artistic policies of the companies it subsidised'. Perhaps such an easy assumption seems in retrospect slightly naïve, and we might question whether governmental policies and strategies can ever be so entirely excluded from the equation; but Lee was adamant that her duty had been to defend artists and wring from the Treasury 'every penny of financial support she could lay hands on'.[73] Now in opposition, and with ministers declaring their aim was to 'cleanse the permissive society',[74] she mistrusted the shift Eccles was signalling: 'The prospect of having one law for the State-subsidised theatres and another for privately financed activities is too patently absurd', she observed. Moreover, 'the fact that what is in the wind is no straightforward legislation but back-door pressure on the Arts Council does not improve matters'.[75] In fact, 'Its very ambiguities and uncertainties make it rather worse'.

Yet concern about where new freedoms were driving theatre seemed to be increasing. Reviewing *Byron—the Naked Peacock*, a National Theatre adaptation of 'Don Leon', (a nineteenth-century poem celebrating homosexuality and sodomy, and wrongly attributed to Lord Byron), Harold Hobson worried about 'the principle of permissive permissiveness' and where the line should be drawn. 'One of the principal problems of the stage today, and also one of its principal opportunities, is how to make the best possible use of the chances that permissiveness has put into its hands.' On the one hand, said Hobson, Pinter's four-letter words in *Landscape* were 'the paradoxical foundation of one of the most exhilarating rhapsodies in modern drama'. Similarly, 'Peter Brook's liberal treatment of Bottom and Titania' was 'a giant advance'; but the same was not true in all cases, and Hobson concluded that what should not be accepted was 'any use of permissiveness as an end in itself, and not as an instrument for the better accomplishment of an aesthetic aim'. Moreover, writers and directors such as Pinter and Brook—'the glory of our theatre'—needed protection if their work was to shine: 'It is part of the duty of public authorities to see that they are not put at risk', warned Hobson.[76] His argument was close in effect to advocating a distinction based on a difference between high and low art.

The clamour of protest notched up a level in the summer of 1971 with the arrival in the West End of another American revue with its 'catchpenny title'[77] *The Dirtiest Show in Town*, one of the highlights of which was 'four naked couples simultaneously simulating copulation' while 'shouting in unison the Anglo-Saxon monosyllable which has long described the activity'.[78] To Hobson, the show was a 'disgusting travesty',[79] while the *Daily Mirror* ran an editorial headlined 'Garbage on the Stage', which cast the production as 'a gift to those who would like to see censorship return to the British stage'. The performance, they said, was 'repulsive without wit', 'devastatingly dreary', and 'smelly'; its performers 'flop around unclothed . . . indulging in simulated sexual intercourse or simply kissing bare bums'. The whole thing was little more than a 'big boobs, penis and fuzz show' where 'Four-letter words are repeated ad nauseam', and it depended on 'jokes about V D, queers and masturbation'.[80] 'These uninhibited displays are meant to offend and succeed in doing so', reported the *Guardian*; 'though better on the stage perhaps than, for instance, in a railway carriage'.[81] In reality, there was a little more to it than that. Written and directed by Tom Eyen, *The Dirtiest Show* had started off at New York's experimental and acclaimed La Mama Theatre and become an off-Broadway success. It was subtitled 'A documentary of the destructive effects of air, water, and mind pollution in New York City'—though few (if any) of the British critics quite bought that. 'Who do they think they are kidding', asked Irving Wardle in *The Times*, as he easily dismissed the entire subject of pollution as 'a current fashion like nudity and homosexual marriage'. On the other hand, some critics did get beyond shock and outrage to discover a tone of contemporary angst, as well as a satirical perspective on current values. Again, there was little sympathy among theatre critics for the idea of suppression. 'As the vigilantes will doubtless be hovering greedily over this show waiting for some encouragement to swoop', wrote Wardle, 'I had better do my bit for stage freedom and record that I found nothing offensive in it'.[82] 'At least it's a change from Parsifal', wrote Philip Hope-Wallace; 'Okay for children, but don't take the bishop'.[83]

However, some individuals again sought to pressurise the Attorney General into taking legal action, not least Raymond Blackburn, a former and discredited Labour MP who, having spent sixteen months in prison for selling shares in a worthless company, had now reinvented himself as a well-known 'porn-hater'.[84] But again, the Attorney General refused to pursue the case, because 'no prosecution for obscenity would have a reasonable likelihood of success'.[85] Blackburn did manage to convince the police to accompany him to the theatre on the grounds that photographs advertising the show—including 'a group of naked men and women and a nude couple in an embrace'—represented 'an indecent exhibition in a public place'. To Blackburn's disappointment, the police chose not to take

action. 'I consider this decision one which is difficult to reconcile with
the concern which everyone should feel for young persons in danger of
corruption', he declared.[86]

Yet even among those who might in principle have been expected to
support freedom, concerns were growing. In the *Guardian*, Jill Tweedie
accused the promoters of such shows such as *Oh! Calcutta!* and *The
Dirtiest Show* of abusing performers who were in no position to turn down
work or refuse to do what was asked of them: 'actors and actresses are
being more or less ruthlessly exploited for the ego-building and profit
. . . of writers, directors and backers'. There was, said Tweedie, 'something
rotten in the state of both shows', and she argued that the physical and
psychological health of the victims—the performers—was at serious risk.[87]
She was right to worry. In his autobiography, published much later, the
producer of both these shows, Michael White, claims that during one
performance of *The Dirtiest Show* the simulated sexual intercourse became
all too real—entirely against the wishes of the actress involved. Perhaps
what is most disturbing is White's attitude to the assault, both when it
occurred and when revisiting it later. The actress, says, White, 'behaved
like a trooper' during the performance but 'went berserk' when they came
offstage, threatening to accuse the actor of rape 'even though they were
friends and had been working in the Company together for months'. White
recalls that 'there was nearly a huge scandal' but that he had saved the
day: 'fortunately the actress decided that she would not gain anything by
it and that the enemies of free expression would be delighted'. How was it
dealt with? 'I gave the actor a stern frightening lecture and that was the
end of it.'[88] Possibly Tweedie was aware of the case when she voiced her
criticisms of such shows, and even that it could have been more than an
isolated occurrence.

There we must leave it. Of course, none of the arguments or performances
referred to in this chapter any longer had anything to do with the Lord
Chamberlain. How he and his staff must have relished not having to keep
up with them, or even to read about theatre. As the *Daily Mail* front page
had put it on the fateful day of September 1968:

A significant silence hangs over Stable Yard, St James's Palace. The blinds
are down in the offices of the Lord Chamberlain's examiners of Plays. The
blue pencils are laid to rest. The stage censors are out of work . . . There they
are, hanging about watching the sentries pass the window and wondering
how to fill in the empty hours before sauntering up St James's Street to the
Club.[89]

The *Daily Mail* fantastically imaged that the newly-idle staff in the Lord Chamberlain's Office would now pass their time (and earn themselves some money) by rooting through the 'theatrical treasure trove' of scripts stored in the cellars of St James's Palace, and pulling out the sections they and their predecessors had expunged over the last 237 years in order to construct a box-office hit, to be called *The Blue-Pencil Follies*. While this is an amusing enough suggestion, the tone and emphasis seem to imply that the whole history of control and suppression in the theatre amounted to little more than a piece of prolonged silliness. That the censorship may sometimes have acted in ways that might to modern tastes seem rather foolish, but that it didn't really matter very much—that nothing important had been lost. Of course, that is not the whole truth. As we saw at the end of the previous chapter, when parliament agreed to pass the Theatres Act and consign the Lord Chamberlain to the dustbin of history, Michael Foot was one of the few MPs ready to put the boot in and give him a good kicking. But his speech was followed by one from his brother and fellow Labour MP, Dingle, who five years earlier had himself introduced a bill to try and end theatre censorship. Now, Dingle Foot promised the House that for the decision they had just confirmed 'generations of playwrights yet to come, as well as theatre audiences, will have reason to be grateful'.[94] Though censorship continued and continues to operate in a range of complex guises, and in spite of the problems the new freedom brought, Foot's promise has to be true. Whatever else, we at least do not make and watch every piece of theatre with the Lord Chamberlain perched on our shoulders.

Notes

Notes On Archive Referencing

There are two separate archives in the British Library Manuscript Collections on which I have drawn substantially; both come under the general heading: 'The Play Collections':

The texts of unpublished plays submitted for licensing between 1900 and 1968 are referenced here as 'LCP' (Lord Chamberlain's Plays) followed by a year, an oblique stroke, and a box number. This is the referencing system used within the archive and its index.

The material from the Lord Chamberlain's Correspondence Files 1900–1968 is also referenced here as in the archive, using the abbreviation 'LCP CORR' to indicate the archive. Material relating to plays which were licensed is filed separately from that related to plays which were refused licences.

In the case of a *licensed play*, 'LCP CORR' is followed by the title of the play, the year under which it is filed, and a file number.

For an *unlicensed play*, 'LCP CORR' is followed by the title of the play, then 'LR' (indicating 'Licence Refused') and a year.

There is also correspondence relating to plays which were neither licensed nor refused. These are known as 'Waiting Box Plays'. To reference these, 'LCP CORR' is followed by the title of the play, then 'WB' (indicating 'Waiting Box') and a year.

The other archive on which I have drawn extensively is the Lord Chamberlain's Office Files, part of the Royal Archive, and currently held at Windsor Castle. These files contain further general and extensive papers—letters, minutes, memoranda, cuttings, etc.—from the Lord Chamberlain's Office relating to theatre licensing and censorship. This material was evidently kept separate from the material related directly to specific plays submitted for licence, which is held in the British Library collections.

All material cited from the Royal Archive is referenced as in the archive itself; namely: 'RA LC/GEN', followed by an oblique line and one of several numbers under which the material is categorised: 310, 344, 440 or 512. Although the logic for the division and location of files is not always obvious, those labelled 310 were intended to indicate that the focus was the Advisory Board; 344, the Examiners of Plays; 440, the Theatres Act; and 512 apparently indicated Censorship. (The impossibility of maintaining these as discrete categories is evidenced by the fact that 440 and 512 were effectively amalgamated after 1958). The above number is in each case followed by another oblique line and another figure which indicates the appropriate year of the file, and then the individual title which the Lord Chamberlain's Office assigned to it. It should be noted that individual files sometimes contain relevant materials drawn from years other than the one indicated by the file reference number.

I am grateful to Her Majesty Queen Elizabeth II for allowing me access to the relevant sections of the Royal Archive, and for permitting me to make use of and quote from the files.

References are correct to the best of my knowledge. However, many of the plays cited are obscure, and often there is no satisfactory way of checking whether details as recorded in the Lord Chamberlain's Correspondence archives (places and dates of performances, names of authors, etc.) are always correct. Some correspondence (and most of the titles and names as they appear on index cards) are handwritten, and I may have sometimes mis-read. I have tried to indicate with a '[?]' those references over which I am particularly doubtful.

Introduction

1 RA LC/GEN/440/63: 'As to Putting Out an Informed Article on Censorship of Stage Plays'.
2 RA LC/GEN/440/61: 'Major A.G. Douglas Given History and Duties of the Lord Chamberlain re Censorship of Stage Plays'.
3 RA LC/GEN/440/63: '*Daily Telegraph* Offers to Give Lord Chamberlain a Hearing but is Refused'.
4 Memorandum by Ronald John Hill, 10 March 1961. See RA LC/GEN/440/61: 'Mr J.M. Temple, M.P., Suggests New Parliamentary Committee to Give Lord Chamberlain Stronger and More Rigid Directions about Censorship'.
5 Book subtitle to—Judith Clavir Albert, *The Sixties Papers: Documents of a Rebellious Decade* (Westport, Connecticut: Greenwood Press, 1984).
6 *Guardian*, 15 February 1966, p. 6.
7 RA LC/GEN/440/63: 'As to Putting Out an Informed Article on Censorship of Stage Plays'.
8 http://hansard.millbanksystems.com/commons/1900/may/15/london-theatres-supervision-of-plays-etc. The speech was also published as a pamphlet: Samuel Smith, *Plays and their Supervision: A Speech made by Samuel Smith Esq., M.P. in the House of Commons May 15th 1900, and the reply of the Home Secretary* (London: Chas. J. Thynne, 1900).
9 Comment by Ronald Hill after officially watching and reporting on the production. See LCP CORR: *Saved* WB 29. LR (1966).
10 Speech by Dean Acheson, made at West Point, December 1962.

11   See http://africanhistory.about.com/od/eraindependence/a/wind_of_change1.htm
12   See http://www.legislation.gov.uk/ukpga/Eliz2/7-8/66/section/4

Chapter One

1   See Reader's Report by Sir St Vincent Troubridge, 14 August 1961. LCP CORR: 1961/1920: *No Time For Love*. The play was written by James Liggat and licensed for the Palace Theatre, Westcliff-on-Sea, August 1961.
2   Letter from Norman Gwatkin, Comptroller of the Lord Chamberlain's Office, to Henry Sherek, theatre impresario, 28 July 1961. See RA LC/GEN/440/61: 'Mr Henry Sherek Deplores "Filth" in West End Theatre, and Suggests X Certificates for Plays Dealing with Sex'.
3   *Sunday Despatch*, 19 February. See LCP CORR: 1959/1733: *Fings Ain't What They Used to Be*.
4   'Eric Penn, 77, Director of British Royal Pomp'. Obituary of Penn published in the *New York Times*, 17 May 1993.
5   Joan Littlewood, 'Introduction' to Frank Norman, *Fings Ain't What They Used to Be* (London: Samuel French, 1960), no page number.
6   Bill Boorne, 'The Public Say You're Wrong, Mr Sherek', *Evening News*, 14 July 1961.
7   Michael Croft, 'The Inside Story', *Observer*, 22 February 1959, p. 19.
8   Frank Norman, *Fings Ain't What They Used to Be*, p. 61.
9   For all correspondence on this case, see LCP CORR: 1959/1733: *Fings Ain't What They Used to Be*.
10   Frank Norman, *Fings Ain't What They Used to Be*.
11   LCP CORR: 1959/1733: *Fings Ain't What They Used to Be*.
12   In the late fifties they had instigated a prosecution of Theatre Workshop for adding almost an entire new Act to *You Won't Always Be on Top*, but although the company had been found guilty in court, the fines were so nominal, and the publicity for the Lord Chamberlain's Office so negative, that it was Theatre Workshop who had been the real victors. See Steve Nicholson, *The Censorship of British Drama 1900–1968. Volume Three: The Fifties* (Exeter: University of Exeter Press, 2011), pp. 141–47.
13   LCP CORR: 1959/1733: *Fings Ain't What They Used to Be*.
14   *Daily Express*, 13 February 1961.
15   *Daily Mail*, 13 February 1961.
16   *Evening Standard*, 13 February 1961.
17   *Sunday Despatch*, 19 February 1961.
18   *Time and Tide*, 17 February 1961.
19   *Daily Mail*, 14 February 1961.
20   *Daily Express*, 14 February 1961.
21   *The Spectator*, 17 February 1961.
22   See LCP CORR: 1959/1733: *Fings Ain't What They Used to Be*.
23   *The Sphere*, 25 February 1961.
24   See LCP CORR: 1959/1733: *Fings Ain't What They Used to Be*.
25   RA LC/GEN/440/61: 'Mr J.M. Temple, M.P., Suggests New Parliamentary Committee to give Lord Chamberlain Stronger and More Rigid Directions about Censorship'.
26   'What is "Constructive" Criticism?', *Daily Telegraph*, 20 February 1961, p. 15.
27   See LCP CORR: 1961/1592: *Luther*. Licensed for the Royal Court Theatre, August 1961.

28 See LCP CORR: 1961/1425: *The Devils of London*. Licensed for the Aldwych Theatre, March 1961.

29 See LCP CORR: 1960/1012: *Billy Liar*. Licensed for the Brighton Theatre Royal, September 1960.

30 See LCP CORR: 1960/1111: *You in Your Small Corner*. Licensed for the Everyman Theatre, Cheltenham, October 1960.

31 See LCP CORR: 1961/1642: *The Blacks*. Licensed for the Royal Court Theatre, May 1961.

32 *Daily Mail*, 14 July 1961. See RA LC/GEN/440/61: 'Mr Henry Sherek Deplores "Filth"'.

33 'The Public Say You're Wrong, Mr Sherek' . . .

34 RA LC/GEN/440/61: 'Mr Henry Sherek Deplores "Filth"'.

35 See RA LC/GEN/440/60: 'As to The Lord Chamberlain's Jurisdiction over Ballets Africains with Dancers with Bare Bosoms'.

36 *Daily Herald*, 12 July 1960.

37 See RA LC/GEN/440/61: 'Dr G.E. Kelly Complains of African Dancers on I.T.V.'

38 Darlington in *Daily Telegraph*, 28 March 1961; Hobson in *Sunday Times*, 1 April 1962; *Guardian*, 28 March 1962, p. 9; *Daily Mail*, 18 September 1961.

39 See LCP CORR: 1961/1979: *The Knack*. Licensed for the Cambridge Arts Theatre, October 1961.

40 *Daily Mail*, 18 September 1961.

41 See LCP CORR: 1961/1952: *The American Dream*. Licensed for the Royal Court Theatre, October 1961.

42 Wyndham's Theatre.

43 See LCP CORR: 1960/1010: *Lady Chatterley*.

44 *Daily Sketch*, 21 July 1961, p. 13.

45 *Daily Telegraph*, 16 August 1961.

46 LCP CORR: 1960/1010: *Lady Chatterley*.

47 *Daily Telegraph*, 25 August 1961.

48 'Lady Chatterley Causes Another Storm', *Stage and Television Today*, 31 August 1961.

49 'Rehearsal Of "Chatterley" Bedroom Scene Unclothed', *Daily Telegraph*, 25 August 1961.

50 *Yorkshire Post*, 29 August 1961; *Daily Telegraph*, 28 August 1961; *Daily Worker*, 28 August 1961; *Stage and Television Today*, 31 August 1961; *The Scotsman*, 29 August 1961.

51 LCP CORR: 1960/1010: *Lady Chatterley*.

52 See LCP CORR: 1961/1642: *The Blacks*.

53 LCP CORR: 1960/1010: *Lady Chatterley*.

54 *Sunday Pictorial*, 10 September 1961; *Sunday Telegraph*, 10 September 1961.

55 LCP CORR: 1960/1010: *Lady Chatterley*.

56 LCP CORR: 1960/1010: *Lady Chatterley*.

57 *Evening Standard*, 16 September 1961.

58 See RA LC/GEN/440/61: 'Kent Plays Ltd Informed not in Public Interest for Recent Court Trials to be Depicted on the Stage, with Special Reference to that of Crown v Penguin Books'.

Chapter Two

1   Internal memorandum, 10 January 1963. See LCP CORR: 1962/2767: *The Premise*. Licensed for the Comedy Theatre, London, July 1962.

2   Quoted in John Ardagh, 'Changing Words at St James's Palace', *Observer*, 26 August 1962, p. 1 and p. 3.

3   LCP CORR: 1959/1747: *Clown Jewels*. Licensed for the New Theatre, Oxford, February 1959.

4   RA LC/GEN/440/61: 'Lord Chamberlain Declined Invitation to Take Chair at Literary Luncheon held by W. & G. Foyle Ltd. for Mr. Bud Flanagan'.

5   LCP CORR: 1959/1747: *Clown Jewels*.

6   http://www.bbc.co.uk/comedy/beyondthefringe/

7   LCP CORR: 1960/1027: *Beyond the Fringe*. Licensed for the Royal Lyceum Theatre, Edinburgh, August 1960.

8   LCP CORR: 1961/1714: *Beyond the Fringe*. Licensed for the Cambridge Arts Theatre, April 1961.

9   LCP CORR: 1961/2067: *Ssh!* Licensed for the Twentieth Century Theatre, Bayswater, December 1961.

10 LCP CORR: 1961/1804: *The Lord Chamberlain Regrets*. A touring revue written by Peter Myers and Ronnie Cass. Licensed for the Theatre Royal, Newcastle, June 1961.

11 *Daily Herald*, 5 June 1961.

12 *Plays and Players*, July 1961, vol. 8, no. 10, p. 22; *Evening Standard*, 6 June 1961; *New Statesman*, 11 August 1961; *Daily Express*, 5 June 1961; *Evening News*, 29 June 1961.

13 LCP CORR: 1961/1804: *The Lord Chamberlain Regrets*.

14 LCP CORR: 1962/2317: *The Bed Sitting Room*. Licensed for the Marlowe Theatre, Canterbury, February 1962.

15 Presented by Just Actors, under the direction of Theodore J. Flicker.

16 Cited, for example, in http://www.biography.com/people/george-wallace-9522367 and at http://www.npr.org/2013/01/14/169080969/segregation-forever-a-fiery-pledge-forgiven-but-not-forgotten as 'one of the most vehement rallying cries against racial equality in American history'.

17 *Daily Mail*, 12 October 1962.

18 Unpublished manuscript of *The Premise*, LCP 1962/37.

19 LCP CORR: 1962/2767: *The Premise*.

20 *The Times*, 23 July 1962, p. 14.

21 Kenneth Tynan, 'A Rattle for British Babies', *Observer*, 23 September 1962, p. 27.

22 LCP CORR: 1962/2767: *The Premise*.

23 'Looking After Morals of Stage and Nation', *Guardian*, 6 December 1962, p. 2.

24 LCP CORR: 1962/2767: *The Premise*.

25 RA LC/GEN/440/62: 'Mr Dingle Foot, MP's Bill on Censorship'.

26 See RA LC/GEN/440/67: 'Joint Committee on Stage Censorship Appreciation by Lord Chamberlain (Earl of Scarbrough) on Desirability of Continuing Censorship of Stage Plays'.

27 LCP CORR: 1962/2767: *The Premise*.

28 RA LC/GEN/440/62: 'Mr Dingle Foot, MP's Bill on Censorship'.

29 RA LC/GEN/440/63: 'Lord Chamberlain to Discuss Censorship with the Home Secretary with an Additional Reference to Legality of Improvisation'.

30 LCP CORR: 1962/2767: *The Premise*.

31 LCP CORR: 1962/2270: *My Place*. Licensed for the Memorial Theatre, Stratford, January 1962.

32 LCP CORR: 1962/2316: *Zoo Story*. Licensed for London's Scala Theatre, February 1962.
33 *Final Performance* by John Turpin. Licensed for Maidenhead Town Hall, 6 April 1962. See LCP CORR: 1962/2535: *Final Performance*.
34 LCP CORR: 1962/2447: *The Photo Finish*. Licensed for the Theatre Royal, Newcastle on Tyne, March 1962.
35 LCP CORR: 1962/2576: *Happy Days*. Licensed for the Royal Court Theatre, July 1962.
36 LCP CORR: 1962/2718: *The Blood of the Bambergs*. Licensed for the Royal Court Theatre, June 1962.
37 LCP CORR: 1962/2484: *The Scatterin'*. Written by James McKenna, and licensed for the Theatre Royal, Stratford East, April 1962.
38 LCP CORR: 1962/2705: *Fit to Print*. Written by Alastair M. Dunnett, and licensed for the Theatre Royal Nottingham, July 1962.
39 LCP CORR: 1961/2067: *Ssh!*
40 LCP CORR: 1961/1804: *The Lord Chamberlain Regrets*.
41 LCP CORR: 1962/3026: *Send us Victorias*. Written by Pat Wilson and licensed for the Library Theatre, Scarborough, December 1962. He also suggested that Scarbrough 'would probably delete from a play insulting or cutting references to someone who had given birth to a deformed baby due to thalidomide'.
42 LCP CORR: 1962/2580: *Semi-Detached*. Licensed for Coventry's Belgrade Theatre, June 1962.
43 LCP CORR: 1962/2936: *All Things Bright and Beautiful*. Licensed for Bristol's Theatre Royal, October 1962.
44 LCP CORR: 1962/2769: *Under Plain Cover*. Licensed for the Royal Court Theatre, July 1962.
45 LCP CORR: 1962/2773: *The Voice of Shem*. Written by Mary Manning, and licensed for the Theatre Royal, Stratford East, July 1962.
46 LCP CORR: 1962/2783: *The Savage Parade*. Licensed for London's Scala Theatre, July 1962.
47 See RA LC/GEN/440/58: 'Consideration by Home Office of Proposal to Amend the Theatres Act 1843 to Allow the Lord Chamberlain to Attach Conditions to his Stage Plays Licence—not Adopted. Subsequent Decision to License Certain Plays Dealing with Homosexuality'. See also Steve Nicholson, *The Censorship of British Drama 1900–1968. Volume Three: The Fifties* (Exeter: University of Exeter Press, 2011), p. 110.
48 *The People*, 27 March 1960. See LCP CORR: 1959/515: *Look on Tempests*.
49 *Daily Sketch*, 13 September 1960; *Daily Mail*, 10 September 1960. See LCP CORR: 1960/1069: *Compulsion*. Written by Meyer Levin, and licensed for the Pembroke Theatre, Croydon, September 1960.
50 See LCP CORR: 1960/1027: *Beyond the Fringe*.
51 See LCP CORR: 1962/2269: *High on the Wall*. Written by James Morrison, and licensed for the Aberdeen Students' Union, January 1962.
52 LCP CORR: *House of Glass* WB 20 (1962).
53 LCP CORR: 1962/2757: *Escape from Eden*. Licensed for the Lyric Opera House, Hammersmith, July 1962.
54 LCP CORR: 1962/2322: *The Caucasian Chalk Circle*. Licensed for the Aldwych Theatre, March 1963.
55 LCP CORR: 1962/2657: *The Jungle of The Cities*. Licensed for the Theatre Royal, Stratford East, June 1962.

56 LCP CORR: 1962/2931: *The Good Woman of Setzuan*. Licensed for the Citizens Theatre, Glasgow, October 1962.

57 LCP CORR: 1962/3111: *The Rise And Fall Of The City Of Mahagonny*. Licensed for the Royal Shakespeare Company at Stratford-on-Avon, December 1962.

58 LCP CORR: 1962/3040: *Baal*. Licensed for London's Phoenix Theatre, December 1962.

59 House of Commons Debate, 5 December 1962. See Hansard vol. 668, cc 1321-34. http://hansard.millbanksystems.com/commons/1962/dec/05/censorship-of-plays-abolition#S5CV0668P0_19621205_HOC_195

60 See, for example, *Yorkshire Post*, 6 December 1962. See also reports on the debate in the *Guardian*, 6 December 1962, p. 2 and p. 20.

61 See RA LC/GEN/440/62: 'Professor H. Street's Draft on Censorship for his Book on Civil Liberties Checked and Commented Upon'.

62 Harry Street, *Freedom, the Individual and the Law* (Harmondsworth: Penguin Books, 1963), pp. 64–68.

63 RA LC/GEN/440/62: 'Mr Haw Prefers his View on Censorship and is Answered'.

64 RA LC/GEN/440/61: 'Lord Chamberlain Declines Invitation from *Daily Mail* to be Interviewed on Censorship'.

65 John Ardagh, 'Changing Words at St James's Palace'.

66 RA LC/GEN/440/63: 'As to Putting Out an Informed Article on Censorship of Stage Plays'.

67 RA LC/GEN/440/62: 'Mr Dingle Foot, MP's Bill on Censorship'.

68 RA LC/GEN/440/67: 'Joint Committee on Stage Censorship Appreciation by Lord Chamberlain . . .'.

69 LCP CORR: 1963/3181: *All in Good Time*. Licensed for the Mermaid Theatre, Blackfriars, January 1963.

70 LCP CORR: 1963/3196: *The Workhouse Donkey*. Licensed for the Chichester Festival Theatre, June 1963.

71 LCP CORR: 1963/3167: *Stephen D*. Adapted from Joyce by Hugh Leonard, and licensed for St Martin's Theatre, London, January 1963.

72 LCP CORR: *The Night of the Iguana* WB 22 (1963).

73 LCP CORR: *Clap Hands Here Comes Charlie* LR (1963).

74 Heriot refers to this in his Reader' Report on *Who's Afraid of Virginia Woolf?* (13 April 1963). See LCP CORR: 1963/3412: *Who's Afraid of Virginia Woolf?*

75 See *Daily Mirror*, 15 January 1963, p. 2 and *Daily Mail*, same date. See also RA LC/GEN/440/63: 'BBC Scraps its Policy Guide for Writers and Producers, thus Abandoning Censorship'.

76 RA LC/GEN/440/67: 'Joint Committee on Stage Censorship Appreciation by Lord Chamberlain . . .'.

Chapter Three

1   John Osborne, 'Land of the Free' in Osborne, *Damn You, England* (London: Faber and Faber, 1994), pp. 162–64. Originally published in *TV Times*, 31 May 1963.

2   See LCP CORR: 1962/3482: *Ubu*.

3   Article first published in *The Spectator*, 23 November 2013. See http://www.spectator.co.uk/features/9081511/it-all-began-in-1963/ See also Christopher Booker, *The Neophiliacs: The Revolution in English Life in the Fifties and Sixties* (London: William Collins, 1969; London: Pimlico, 1992).

4   *Ibid.*
5   *Daily Mirror*, 6 June 1963, p. 1.
6   See http://family-tree.cobboldfht.com//people/view/490. Also Cobbold's obituary in the *Daily Telegraph*, November 1987.
7   Theodore Flicker, 'Theatre Today', in *Amateur Stage*, November 1962, vol. XVII, no. 11, pp. 13–15.
8   RA LC/GEN/440/65: 'As to The Lord Chamberlain Giving Tape Recorded Interview on Censorship to the *Sunday Times*'.
9   See John Johnston, *The Lord Chamberlain's Blue Pencil* (London: Hodder and Stoughton, 1990), pp. 179–80.
10 RA LC/GEN/440/63: 'Inspection of Plays Likely to Cause Offence'.
11 RA LC/GEN/440/63: 'A Check to be Kept of Cuts'.
12 See LCP CORR: 1963/3133: *The Bed Sitting Room*. Original script licensed for the Marlowe Theatre, Canterbury, in February 1962; this revised version licensed for the Mermaid Theatre, Blackfriars, January 1963.
13 See LCP CORR: 1963/3421: *Looking for the Action*. Licensed for the Prince Charles Theatre in London, May 1963.
14 See LCP CORR: 1962/3040: *Baal*; and 1963/3212: *Baal*. Original version licensed December 1962, revised version February 1963, both for the Phoenix Theatre, London.
15 LCP CORR: *Night of the Iguana* WB 22 (1963).
16 See RA LC/GEN/440/61: 'Demand for Uniformity of Censorship on Films, Television and Stage, as Put Forward by Film Director Anthony Asquith'.
17 RA LC/GEN/440/63: '*Daily Telegraph* Offers to Give Lord Chamberlain a Hearing but is Refused'.
18 *Sunday Mirror*, 12 May 1963, p. 7. See RA LC/GEN/440/63: 'Assistant Comptroller to Discuss Censorship "off the record" with Mr. Lionel Crane of the *Sunday Mirror*'.
19 'The Censors Censor Themselves', *Daily Mirror*, 7 June 1963, p. 2.
20 Unpublished manuscript of *Night Conspirators*, LCP 1963/12.
21 See Mary Crozier, 'Night Assassins', *Guardian*, 7 May 1962, p. 7.
22 LCP CORR: 1963/3290: *Night Conspirators*. Licensed for the Theatre Royal, Brighton, March 1963.
23 Christopher Booker, *The Spectator*, 23 November 2013.
24 See LCP CORR: *Oh! What a Lovely War* 1963/3308 and 1963/3553. Originally licensed for the Theatre Royal at Stratford East, in March 1963; revised version licensed for Wyndham's Theatre in June of the same year.
25 RA LC/GEN/400/63: 'Mr Alan Informed not in Public Interest for Contemporary Court Case and Proceedings in Parliament to be Dramatised, with Special Reference to the Profumo Affair'.
26 See LCP CORR: 1963/3579: *The Representative*. Licensed for the RSC at the Aldwych Theatre, September 1963.
27 See LCP CORR: 1965/4934: *Spring Awakening*. First licensed for the Royal Court Theatre, London, April 1965.
28 See LCP CORR: 1963/3497: *Miss Julie*. This translation licensed for the Victoria Theatre, Stoke-on-Trent, June 1963.
29 See LCP CORR: 1963/3498: *Skyvers*. Licensed for the Royal Court Theatre, London, July 1963.
30 See LCP CORR: 1964/3938: *Fourth of June*. Licensed for the Theatre Royal, Brighton, January 1964.

31 'Annus Mirabilus' in Philip Larkin, *Collected Poems* (London: Faber and Faber, 2003), p. 146.

32 Christopher Booker, *The Spectator.*

33 See LCP CORR: 1963/3492: *Alfie.* Licensed for the Mermaid Theatre, Blackfriars, June 1963.

34 See LCP CORR: 1963/3482: *Ubu.* This version by T.D.A. Vibert, licensed for the Victoria Rooms, Bristol, in June 1963.

35 See LCP CORR: *Figuro in the Night* WB 21 (1963).

36 See LCP CORR: 1963/3630: *Just Wild About Harry.* Licensed for Cambridge University Theatre Company at the Barrie Halls, Edinburgh, September 1963.

37 See http://www.iberlibro.com/Wild-Harry-MILLER-Henry-IDLE-Eric/11879142699/bd

38 See LCP CORR: *Wayward Stork* LR (1963).

39 See LCP CORR: 1963/3412: *Who's Afraid of Virginia Woolf?* Licensed for the Piccadilly Theatre, December 1963.

40 Christopher Booker, *The Spectator.*

41 RA LC/GEN/344/63: 'Mr Coles has a Nervous Breakdown'.

42 RA LC/GEN/440/63: 'Striperama Club, Soho, Convicted of Keeping A Tenement for Use As An Unlicensed Theatre'.

43 RA LC/GEN/440/66: As to Possible Improvisation by Italian Commedia dell'Arte.

44 See LCP CORR: 1963/3412: *Who's Afraid of Virginia Woolf?*

Chapter Four

1   John Arden, 'How many schoolgirls has the Censor raped?', *Flourish*, Autumn–Winter 1964–65 No. 2. See RA LC/GEN/440/64: 'Royal Shakespeare Company—Attack on Lord Chamberlain In First Number of their Magazine *Flourish.* Certain Members of the Company Write Disassociating Themselves from Article'.

2   RA LC/GEN/440/65: 'Lord Chamberlain's Interview with Home Secretary . . . Legality of Large Theatre Clubs . . . Proceedings Against English Stage Company Not Taken'.

3   RA LC/GEN/400/64: 'Mr Philip Oakes Article in "The Queen" Magazine On Censorship'.

4   Question asked in House of Lords, 7 May 1964. See http://hansard.millbanksystems.com/lords/1964/may/07/censorship-of-stage-plays

5   RA LC/GEN/440/65: 'Lord Chamberlain's Interview with Home Secretary . . .'.

6   RA LC/GEN/440/63 'Mrs Whitworth Complains of Offensive Business in *The Tempest* at Stratford On Avon'.

7   *Daily Telegraph*, 21 February 1964.

8   D.H. Lawrence, Letter to Edward Garnett, regarding the rejection of *Sons and Lovers* by Heinemann (3 July 1912). See James T. Boulton, (ed.) *The Letters of D.H. Lawrence: Volume 1, September 1901–May 1913* (Cambridge: Cambridge University Press, 1979), pp. 420–22.

9   See LCP CORR: 1964/4020: *The Rebel.* Licensed for the RSC at the Aldwych Theatre, February 1964.

10 See LCP CORR: *The Screens* WB (1965).

11 See LCP CORR: 1957/578: *Fin de Partie/Endgame.*

12   See LCP CORR: 1964/4213: *Afore Night Come*. Licensed for the RSC at the Aldwych Theatre, June 1964.

13   Helen Brien, 'Reality Too Real for the Censor', *Sunday Telegraph*, 21 June 1964, p. 13.

14   See LCP CORR: 1964/4352: *The Persecution and Murder of Marat as Performed by the Inmates of the Asylum of Charenton Under the Direction of the Marquis De Sade*. Licensed for the RSC at the Aldwych Theatre, August 1964.

15   See LCP CORR: 1964/4338: *Victor*. Licensed for the RSC at the Aldwych Theatre, August 1964.

16   See RA LC/GEN/440/64: 'Mr John Ounsell's Article on "Middle-Brow Starvation"'.

17   Bill Boorne, 'Dare you take your daughter to the theatre', *Evening News*, 2 July 1964.

18   Bill Boorne, 'West End Storm Grows', *Evening News*, 24 August 1964.

19   *Ibid*.

20   *The Times*, 27 July 1964, p. 11.

21   *The Times*, 31 August 1964, p. 8.

22   RA LC/GEN/440/65: 'Lord Chamberlain's Interview with Home Secretary . . .'.

23   See LCP CORR: 1964/3956: *Hang Down Your Head and Die*. Licensed for performance at the Oxford Playhouse, February 1964.

24   See RA LC/GEN/440/64: 'Peter Eade Ltd Discouraged from Embarking on a Musical Play about Lilly Langtry in which King Edward The VII would be Portrayed'.

25   See RA LC/GEN/440/64: 'Margery Vosper Ltd Informed No Objection in Principle to Plays in which King Edward VII is Depicted'.

26   See RA LC/GEN/440/64: 'Peter Saunders Ltd Warned Against the Possibility of a Play Dealing with The Abdication, Including The Characters of The Duke and Duchess of Windsor'.

27   See LCP CORR: 1964/4080: *A Kayf Up West*. Licensed for the Theatre Royal, Stratford East, March 1964.

28   See RA LC/GEN/440/64: 'Mr Claude Astley of Translators' Association and Mr Michael Meyer, Translator of Scandinavian Plays—as Special Case Words'.

29   See LCP CORR: 1965/4934: *Spring Awakening*. Licensed for the Royal Court Theatre, London, April 1965.

30   See LCP CORR: 1964/4291: *Ladies Day*. This adaptation from Aristophanes licensed for the Minack Theatre, Penzance, July 1964.

31   See LCP CORR: 1964/4267: *Entertaining Mr. Sloane*. Licensed for Wyndham's Theatre, June 1964.

32   See LCP CORR: 1964/4285: *Inadmissible Evidence*. Licensed for the Royal Court Theatre, London, September 1964.

33   See LCP CORR: 1964/4421: *Mighty Reservoy*. Licensed for the Victoria Theatre, Stoke-on-Trent, October 1964.

34   See LCP CORR: 1964/4392: *A Scent of Flowers*. Licensed for Golders Green Hippodrome, September 1964.

35   See LCP CORR: 1964/4378: *A Singular Man*. Licensed for the Comedy Theatre, London, October 1964.

36   RA LC/GEN/344/65: 'Resignation of Mr Maurice Coles. Appointment of Mr T.B. Harward'.

37   *Ibid*.

38   See LCP CORR: *Dingo* WB 29 (1964). Submitted by National Theatre, 4 December 1964.

39 See LCP CORR: 1964/4164: *Loot*. Licensed for the Cambridge Arts Theatre, December 1964.

40 From the unpublished manuscript of *Listen to the Knocking Bird*. See LCP 1964/37. Licensed for Nottingham Playhouse, September 1964.

41 See LCP CORR: 1964/4424: *Listen to the Knocking Bird*.

42 From the unpublished manuscript of *Listen to the Knocking Bird*.

Chapter Five

1 RA LC/GEN/440/65: 'Lord Chamberlain's Interview with Home Secretary . . . Legality of Large Theatre Clubs . . . Proceedings Against English Stage Company Not Taken'.

2 See LCP CORR: 1965/4820: *The Homecoming*. Licensed for the RSC at the Aldwych Theatre, February 1965.

3 David Nathan, 'Osborne will pip the Censor', *Sun*, 6 January 1965. See also RA LC/GEN/440/65: 'Lord Chamberlain's Interview with Home Secretary . . .'.

4 See LCP CORR: *A Patriot for Me* LR (1964).

5 RA LC/GEN/440/65: 'Lord Chamberlain's Interview with Home Secretary . . .'

6 Private interview with author.

7 See LCP CORR: 1965/4820: *The Homecoming*.

8 See LCP CORR: 1965/4934: *Spring Awakening*. Licensed for the Royal Court Theatre, April 1965.

9 *Ibid.*

10 See LCP CORR: 1966/709: *Spring Awakening*.

11 RA LC/GEN/440/65: 'Lord Chamberlain's Interview with Home Secretary . . .'.

12 See LCP CORR: *A Patriot for Me*.

13 See LCP CORR: 1965/131: *Little Malcolm and his Struggle against the Eunuchs*. Licensed for Oxford Playhouse, August 1965.

14 See LCP CORR: 1965/4928: *Ride a Cock Horse*. Licensed for the Theatre Royal, Nottingham, May 1965.

15 See LCP CORR: 1965/28: *The Killing of Sister George* and 1965/4869: *The Killing of Sister George*. Licensed for the Theatre Royal, Bristol, April 1965, and in a revised version the following month for the Theatre Royal, Bath.

16 It was rated thus by *Plays and Players* each month between April and December 1966.

17 See LCP CORR: 1966/1113: *Charles Dyer's Staircase*. Also known as *Staircase*, and licensed for the RSC at the Aldwych Theatre, October 1966. The play was later made into a film with Richard Burton and Rex Harrison.

18 See LCP CORR: 1965/4996: *Moses and Aaron*. Licensed for the Royal Opera House, London, May 1965.

19 See LCP CORR: 1965/4996: *Moses and Aaron*.

20 'The mystery of the missing virgins', *Evening Standard*, 26 June 1965.

21 Eric Mason, 'An orgy but not erotic', *Daily Mail*, 29 June 1965, p. 12.

22 See LCP CORR: 1965/4996: *Moses and Aaron*.

23 RA LC/GEN/440/65: 'As to the Lord Chamberlain Giving Tape Recorded Interview on Censorship to the *Sunday Times*'.

24 *Sunday Times*, 11 April 1965, p. 11.

25 RA LC/GEN/440/65: 'As to the Lord Chamberlain Giving Tape Recorded . . .'.

26 RA LC/GEN/440/65: BBC Informed not Possible to Supply Someone to be Interviewed on Theatre Duties in Their Light Nigth [Sic] Extra Programme . . .'

27 See LCP CORR: *Saved* WB 29. LR (1966).
28 See Philip Roberts's account, which draws heavily on the archives of the Royal Court. Philip Roberts, *The Royal Court Theatre 1965–1972* (London: Routledge and Kegan Paul, 1986), pp. 29–30.
29 See LCP CORR: *Saved*.
30 Edward Bond, 'Censor in Mind', *Censorship* No. 4, August 1965, pp. 9–12.
31 See LCP CORR: *Saved*.
32 Edward Bond, 'Censor in Mind'.
33 *Ibid.*
34 See LCP CORR: *Saved*.
35 *Sunday Times*, 17 October 1965. See also LCP CORR: *Saved*.
36 LCP CORR: *Saved*.
37 'Drama in Court—Act One'. *Plays and Players*, May 1966, pp. 66–67.
38 LCP CORR: *Saved*.
39 Roberts.
40 *Plays and Players*, May 1966.
41 *The Times*, 2 April 1966, p. 12.
42 *The Times*, 2 April 1966.
43 LCP CORR: *Saved*.

Chapter Six

1 RA LC/GEN/440/67: 'As to The Future of Stage Censorship—Lord Chamberlain's Discussions with Law Officers and Home Secretary'.
2 See LCP CORR: *Simple Golgotha* LR (1965).
3 *The Times*, 17 November 1965, p. 6.
4 Written by Ewan Hooper and Ernest Marvin. See LCP CORR: *A Man Dies* LR (1965).
5 *Daily Sketch*, 6 October 1965.
6 *Daily Express*, 6 October 1965.
7 LCP CORR: *A Man Dies*.
8 See RA LC/GEN/440/64: 'Following Discussions With Deputation from Religious Drama Society, Archbishop of Canterbury, Roman Catholic Church And Church Of Scotland The Lord Chamberlain Rescinds Absolute Ban On Portrayal Of God And Christ On The Stage'.
9 See LCP CORR: *Strike* WB 24 (1965)
10 LCP CORR: *In the Matter of J. Robert Oppenheimer* WB 24 (1965). See also LCP CORR: 1966/1153: *In the Matter of J. Robert Oppenheimer*. The much revised script was eventually licensed for the Fortune Theatre, London, November 1966.
11 LCP CORR: 1965/140: *The Star Spangled Jack Show*. Licensed for Golders Green Hippodrome, August 1965.
12 *Sunday Times*, 22 August 1965.
13 LCP CORR: 1965/140: *The Star Spangled Jack Show*.
14 *Daily Mail*, 1 September 1965.
15 LCP CORR: 1965/140: *The Star Spangled Jack Show*.
16 See LCP CORR: 1965/434: *Clowning*. Licensed for the Royal Court Theatre, London, December 1965.
17 See LCP CORR: 1965/272: *Twang*. See also 1965/438: *Twang*. Originally licensed for the Palace Theatre, Manchester in November 1965; then the following month in a revised version for the Shaftesbury Theatre, London.

18 See LCP CORR: 1965/272: *Twang*.
19 *Daily Sketch*, 3 November 1965, p. 11.
20 *Guardian*, 3 November 1965, p. 1.
21 See LCP CORR: 1965/272: *Twang*.
22 See *Daily Telegraph* obituary of Milligan: http://www.telegraph.co.uk/news/obituaries/1386241/Spike-Milligan.html
23 See LCP CORR: 1965/4705: *Son of Oblomov*. Licensed for London's Comedy Theatre, January 1965. It was based on a translation of Goncharov's novel by Riccardo Aragno.
24 See RA LC/GEN/440/67: 'As to The Future of Stage Censorship . . .'.
25 Letter from the Prime Minister's Private Secretary to the Home Office, 7 Jan 1966. See David Thomas, David Carlton and Anne Etienne, *Theatre Censorship: From Walpole to Wilson* (Oxford: Oxford University Press, 2007), p. 193.
26 See RA LC/GEN/440/67: 'As to The Future of Stage Censorship . . .'.
27 See David Thomas, David Carlton and Anne Etienne, *Theatre Censorship: From Walpole to Wilson* (Oxford: Oxford University Press, 2007), p. 194.
28 See RA LC/GEN/440/66: 'Lord Chamberlain, or His Representative, Not to Participate in BBC's "Light Night Extra Symposium" on Censorship'.
29 See RA LC/GEN/440/66: 'Special Memorandum, on Lord Chamberlain's Authority to License Stage Plays, Defining His Powers, Administration and Principle'.
30 See http://hansard.millbanksystems.com/lords/1966/feb/17/theatre-censorship
31 *The Times*, 16 February 1966, p. 13.
32 See http://hansard.millbanksystems.com/lords/1966/feb/17/theatre-censorship-1
33 See RA LC/GEN/440/67: 'Joint Committee on Stage Censorship General Correspondence'.

Chapter Seven

1 See RA LC/GEN/440/67: 'BBC TV—Programme on Stage Censorship "Clearly a Case For an Enquiry"'.
2 See RA LC/GEN/440/66: 'As to Performances of *Lucky Chance* . . .'.
3 See LCP CORR:1966/529: *Dickon*. Licensed for the Queen's Theatre, Hornchurch, February 1966.
4 See LCP CORR: *Dylan* WB (1966).
5 See LCP CORR: *Adventures In The Skin Trade* WB (1967).
6 See LCP CORR: 1966/582: *Saturday Night and Sunday Morning*. Originally licensed for Nottingham Playhouse in March 1964, Alan Sillitoe's revised adaptation of his own novel was licensed for the Prince of Wales Theatre, London, February 1966.
7 See LCP CORR: 1966/606: *The Match Girls*. This version licensed for the Globe Theatre in February 1966.
8 See LCP CORR: 1966/774: *Make the Drums Talk*. Licensed for the Toynbee Theatre, London, May 1966.
9 See LCP CORR: 1966/793: *Burke and Hare*. Written by Neil Hastings, licensed for Edinburgh YMCA, May 1966.
10 See LCP CORR: 1966/690: *The Frogs*. Licensed for Oriel College, Oxford, March 1966.
11 See LCP CORR: 1966/673: *Junket*—a revue in 18 scenes, licensed for Devonshire House, Exeter University, March 1966; and LCP CORR: 1966/741: *The Allergy*

(Better known as *Pink Jesus*), written by Cecil P. Taylor, licensed for the Jeanetta Cochrane Theatre, April 1966.

12 See LCP CORR: 1966/751: *Lysistrata*. This translation licensed for The Theatre in Wokingham, May 1966.

13 See LCP CORR: 1966/851: *Italian Straw Hat*. This version licensed for Oxford Playhouse, May 1966.

14 See LCP CORR: 1966/808: *Tristram Shandy*. Adaptation by G.P. Scannell and A.V. Benjamin, licensed for Oxford Playhouse, May 1966.

15 See LCP CORR: 1966/876: *Adam's Apple*. Written by Terence Feely, licensed for Manchester Opera House, June 1966.

16 See RA LC/GEN/440/66: 'Special Memorandum, on Lord Chamberlain's Authority to License Stage Plays, Defining His Powers, Administration and Principle'. Also, RA LC/GEN/440/65: As to an Offensive Reference to The Queen in the Marowitz Production of Doctor Faustus at the Close Theatre, Glasgow.

17 See LCP CORR: 1966/561: *Scandal at Tranby Croft*. Licensed for the Theatre Royal, Brighton, April 1966.

18 See Richard Adam Smith, 'The beginning of the end of discrimination', *Guardian*, 21 August 2008.

19 See LCP CORR: *A Patriot for Me* LR (1964).

20 See LCP CORR: 1966/945: *The Failure*. Written by A.W. Alger, licensed for London's Tower Theatre, July 1966.

21 See LCP CORR: 1966/530: *When Did You Last See my Mother?* Licensed for the Josca Theatre, Headington, February 1966.

22 Private correspondence between Hampton and the author.

23 *Daily Telegraph*, 5 July 1966.

24 See LCP CORR: 1966/530: *When Did You Last See my Mother?*.

25 See LCP CORR: 1967/1774: *Wise Child*. Licensed for Wyndham's Theatre, London, September 1967.

26 *The Spectator*, 17 February 1961. See Chapter One.

27 To be performed by the London Traverse Theatre Company.

28 See LCP CORR: *Leda Had a Little Swan* LR (1966).

29 See LCP CORR: 1966/1047: *Fill the Stage with Happy Hours*. Licensed for Nottingham Playhouse, November 1966.

30 See LCP CORR: 1966/917: *Sierra Leone National Dance Troup*. Licensed for Sadler's Wells Theatre, June 1966.

31 See LCP CORR: 1966/1160: *The Lion and the Jewel*. Licensed for the Royal Court Theatre, London, December 1966.

32 See LCP CORR: 1966: *The Architect and the Emperor of Assyria* WB (1966).

33 See LCP CORR: 1966/1019: *Three Men For Colverton*. Licensed for the Royal Court Theatre, London, September 1966.

34 See LCP CORR: 1966/1037: *The Bed Sitting Room*. Licensed for the Mermaid Theatre, Blackfriars, October 1966.

35 See LCP CORR: 1966/980: *The Little Mrs Foster Show*. Licensed for Liverpool Playhouse, November 1966.

36 *Time Magazine*, 20 November 1964.

37 The name 'Bakerton' was substituted.

38 See LCP CORR: *In the Matter of J. Robert Oppenheimer* WB 24 (1965) and LCP CORR: 1966/1153: *In the Matter of J. Robert Oppenheimer*.

39 Though it would be 1968 before the play received its first performance in the States.

40 The quotation is generally attributed to General Curtis LeMay, the US Air Force Chief of Staff, in 1964.

41 See LCP CORR: 1966/1075: *US*. Licensed for the RSC at the Aldwych Theatre, October 1966.

42 *Daily Mail*, 29 November 1966.

43 See LCP CORR: *MacBird* LR (1966).

Chapter Eight

1 *Report from the Joint Select Committee on Censorship of the Theatre* (London: Government Publications, 1967), p. x.

2 See RA LC/GEN/440/67: 'Joint Committee on Stage Censorship General Correspondence'.

3 *Report from the Joint Select Committee on Censorship of the Theatre*. Appendix 14, pp. 160–65.

4 See RA LC/GEN/440/67: 'Joint Committee on Stage Censorship General Correspondence'.

5 See LCP CORR: 1967/1291: *Events while Guarding the Bofors Gun*. Licensed for the Royal Lyceum, Edinburgh, February 1967.

6 See LCP CORR: 1967/1361: *The Visions of Simon Machard*. This version licensed for Glasgow Citizens Theatre, February 1967.

7 See LCP CORR: *The Day That Will Not End* WB (1967).

8 See RA LC/GEN/440/68: 'Traverse Theatre: Intention to Stage the Denning Report (Profumo Case)'.

9 Quoted in Irving Wardle's review, 'From Syracuse to Vietnam', *The Times*, 27 February 1967, p. 16.

10 The Sunday night performance took place on 26 May 1967. *The Times* reported that 'The Vietnam section, a seated reading from scripts, was prepared by Michael Kustow and Geoffrey Reeves; while the Athenian section, a performance from memory, was the work of John Barton and David Jones.' (27 February 1967, p. 16).

11 See LCP CORR: *Soldiers* WB 26 (1967).

12 See LCP CORR: *MacBird* LR (1966).

13 *The Times*, 27 February 1967, p. 16.

14 See LCP CORR: *MacBird*.

15 See LCP CORR: 1967/1758: *Mrs Wilson's Diary*. Licensed for the Theatre Royal Stratford East, September 1967.

16 From the unpublished manuscript of *Mrs Wilson's Diary*. See LCP 1967/36.

17 See LCP CORR: 1967/1758: *Mrs Wilson's Diary*.

18 See LCP CORR: 1967/1550: *Frühlings Erwachen* (*Spring Awakening*). Licensed for the Aldwych Theatre, April 1967.

19 See LCP CORR: 1967/1349: *Oh!* Licensed for the Jeanetta Cochrane Theatre, February 1967.

20 *The Scotsman*, 8 March 1967.

21 See LCP CORR: 1967/1676: *Fanghorn*. Licensed for the Jeanetta Cochrane Theatre, July 1967.

22 The show opened on 7 March 1967 at the Traverse Theatre Club.

23 Allen Wright, *The Scotsman*, 8 March 1967.

24 See LCP CORR: 1967/1676: *Fanghorn*.

25 See LCP CORR: 1967/1566: *Little Murders*. Licensed for the RSC and the Aldwych Theatre, London, June 1967.

26 From the unpublished manuscript of *A View to the Common*. See LCP 1967/20. Licensed for the Royal Court Theatre, London, June 1967.

27 See LCP CORR: 1967/1553: *A View to the Common*.

28 See LCP CORR: 1967/1578: *Ruffian on the Stair*. Licensed for the Royal Court Theatre, London, June 1967.

29 See LCP CORR: 1967/1588: *Erpingham Camp*. Licensed for the Royal Court Theatre, London, June 1967.

30 *Financial Times*, 21 June 1967, p. 28.

31 *Daily Sketch*, 12 May 1967.

32 See LCP CORR: 1967/1554: *Oh God I've Left the Gas On*. Written by Don Haworth, licensed for the Royal Court Theatre, London, July 1967.

33 See LCP CORR: 1967/1507: *A Day in the Death of Joe Egg*. Licensed for Glasgow Citizens Theatre, May 1967.

34 Peter Nichols, *Diaries, 1969–1977* (London: Nick Hern, 2000). Also, Peter Nichols, *Blue Murder*, first performed 1995. The script published by Methuen, 1996.

35 See LCP CORR: 1967/1507: *A Day in the Death of Joe Egg*.

36 See *Report from the Joint Select Committee on Censorship* . . .

37 *Ibid.*, p. ix.

38 *Ibid.*, p. 88.

39 *Ibid.*, p. 98.

40 *Ibid.*, pp. 34–51. Evidence given by Cobbold.

41 *Ibid.*, pp. 66–71. Memorandum submitted by the Director of the Royal Shakespeare Company.

42 *Ibid.*, pp. 34–51. Evidence given by Cobbold, Johnston and Hill.

43 *Ibid.*, p. 78. Evidence given by Peter Hall.

44 *Ibid.*, p. 70. Memorandum submitted by the Director of the Royal Shakespeare Company (Peter Hall).

45 *Ibid.*, pp. x–xix.

Chapter Nine

1 Charles Heriot, 6 August 1967. See LCP CORR: 1967/1748: *Number Ten*.

2 Quotation taken from *Sunday Times* article, 28 April 1968, previewing the show's Broadway opening.

3 See LCP CORR: 1967/1670: *You've Had Your War*. Written by R. Martin Beech and licensed for the Mermaid Theatre, June 1967.

4 See LCP CORR: 1967/1705: *Zigger Zagger*. Licensed for the Jeanetta Cochrane Theatre, August 1967.

5 See LCP CORR: 1967/1779: *Tom Payne*. Licensed for the Edinburgh Traverse Theatre, September 1967.

6 See LCP CORR: 1967/1420: *After the Fall*. Also 1967/1839: *After the Fall*. Original version licensed for Newcastle, People's Theatre, February 1967; revised version licensed for Coventry Belgrade Theatre, October 1967.

7 Although no licence was actually issued. See LCP CORR: *What the Butler Saw* WB (1967).

8 In a speech to the Conservative Party conference, October 1980.

9 See LCP CORR: 1967/1748: *Number Ten*. Licensed for King's Theatre, Glasgow, August 1967.

10   Again, no licence was actually issued. See LCP CORR: *The Nigger Lovers* WB (1967).

11   See LCP CORR: *White Man, Black Man, Yellow Man, Chief* LR (1967). Written by Edward Hagopian [?], and submitted by Peter Cotes, a veteran of conflicts with the Lord Chamberlain's Office.

12   See LCP CORR: 1967/1774: *Wise Child*. Licensed for Wyndham's Theatre, London, September 1967.

13   See LCP CORR: 1967/1835: *Way Out*. Licensed for King George's Hall, London, W9, October 1967.

14   See LCP CORR: 1967/1762: *Death in Leicester*. Licensed for Adam House Theatre, Edinburgh, August 1967.

15   Marianne Faithful was the pop star/actress playing Florence Nightingale.

16   See LCP CORR: *Early Morning* LR (1968).

17   See LCP CORR: *The Saddest Summer Of Samuel S* LR (1967).

18   See LCP CORR: 1967/1901: *The Ruling Class*. Licensed for His Majesty's Theatre, Aberdeen, December 1967.

19   See LCP CORR: 1968/2045: *The Little Mrs Foster Show*. Revised version licensed for Nottingham Playhouse, January 1968.

20   See LCP CORR: 1968/2140: *Brief Lives*. Licensed for the RSC at Stratford, February 1968.

21   See LCP CORR: 1968/2170: *The Magic Mountain*. Licensed for Hampstead Theatre, March 1968.

22   See LCP CORR: 1968/2169: *Brittle Fashion*. Licensed for ADC, Cambridge, March 1968.

23   See LCP CORR: 1968/1528: *Pantopera*. Licensed for Liverpool Students' Union, February 1968.

24   See unpublished manuscript of *You Can't Smoke a Medal* in LCP Unlicensed List 2, volume 31 (1968). The play was to have been staged by Birmingham Repertory Theatre. Yallop would go on to achieve fame as an investigative crime writer.

25   See LCP CORR: *You Can't Smoke a Medal* LR (1968).

26   See LCP CORR: *Landscape* WB 29 (1968).

27   See LCP CORR: 1968/2174: *Spitting Image*. Licensed for Hampstead Theatre, March 1968.

28   See LCP CORR: 1968/2249: *Golden Boy*. By C.D. & William Gibson. Licensed for London Palladium, May 1968.

29   See LCP CORR: 1968/2220: *Sit Down Banna*. Licensed for Connaught Theatre, Worthing, March 1968.

30   See LCP CORR: 1968/2245: *In His Own Write*. Licensed for London's Old Vic Theatre, June 1968.

31   See LCP CORR: 1968/2224: *Canterbury Tales*. Licensed for the Phoenix Theatre, London, March 1968.

32   See LCP CORR: 1968/2272: *The Fall and Redemption of Man*. Licensed for the Civic Theatre, Scunthorpe, April 1968.

33   Sean Day-Lewis, 'Green Room', *Plays and Players*, June 1968, p. 58.

34   See LCP CORR: *A Fig for Eloquence* LR (1968).

35   See LCP CORR: 1968/2197: *Oedipus*. Licensed for London's Old Vic Theatre, March 1968.

36   *Daily Express*, 20 March 1968, p. 7.

37   *Sunday Telegraph*, 31 March 1968.

38   See LCP CORR: 1968/2197: *Oedipus*.

39 See LCP CORR: 1968/2273: *Potted Jack*. Licensed for Sheffield Playhouse, April 1968.

40 See LCP CORR: 1968/2323: *Come and Go*. Licensed for Maison Française, Oxford, April 1968; and 1968/2326: *Eh Joe*. Licensed for Maison Française, Oxford, May 1968.

41 See LCP CORR: 1968/2327: *Balls*. Licensed for Maison Française, Oxford, May 1968.

42 See RA LC/GEN/440/68: 'National Theatre's Production of *Edward II* and Proposal for Two Homosexuals "To Embrace Each Other".'

43 *The Times*, 25 April 1968, p. 10.

44 See RA LC/GEN/440/68: 'National Theatre's Production of *Edward II* . . . '

45 See RA LC/GEN/440/68: '*Helen Of Troy* by Marlowe, National Theatre, Stratford-on-Avon [sic]—Press Report of Intention to have Naked Helen'.

46 House of Commons Debate, 23 February 1968, vol. 759, cc825–74. See http://hansard.millbanksystems.com/commons/1968/feb/23/theatres-bill

47 House of Commons Debate, 10 May 1968, vol. 764, c760. See http://hansard.millbanksystems.com/commons/1968/may/10/interpretation

48 House of Lords Debate, 28 May 1968, vol. 292, cc1044–104. See http://hansard.millbanksystems.com/lords/1968/may/28/theatres-bill

49 See LCP CORR: 1968/2363: *Narrow Road to the Deep North*. Licensed for Coventry Belgrade, June 1968.

50 See LCP CORR: *The Car Cemetery* LR (1968).

51 See LCP CORR: 1968/2417: *Roundelay*. Licensed for the Ashcroft Theatre, Croydon, July 1968.

52 See LCP CORR: 1968/2449: *Fracas at The Palace*. By H. Forbes-Simpson and P.D. Barrett. Licensed for Watford Palace Theatre, July 1968.

53 See LCP CORR: 1968/2456: *Years of the Locust*. By Norman Holland. Licensed for Church Hall Theatre, Edinburgh, August 1968.

54 See LCP CORR: 1968/2438: *George the Mad Ad. Man*. By Peter Bland. Licensed for St David's Church Hall, Edinburgh, July 1968.

55 See LCP CORR: 1968/2375: *Caprice in a Pink Palazzo*. By John Peacock. Licensed for the Richmond Theatre, Richmond, June 1968.

56 See LCP CORR: 1968/2437: *Lizzie Strata*. Licensed for St David's Church Hall, Edinburgh, September 1968.

57 See LCP CORR: 1968/2477: *The Apprentices*. Licensed for the Jeanetta Cochrane Theatre, August 1968.

58 See LCP CORR: 1968/2476: *The Rasputin Show*. Licensed for Cambridge Arts Theatre, August 1968.

59 See LCP CORR: 1968/2419: *Indians*. Licensed for the Aldwych Theatre, July 1968.

60 See LCP CORR: 1968/2500: *The Latent Heterosexual*. Licensed for the Aldwych Theatre, September 1968.

61 *The Sketch*, 12 September 1968.

62 Private correspondence between Hampton and the author.

63 See LCP CORR: *Hair* LR (1968).

64 See Unnumbered box in Windsor Archive: Special Box Abolition of Censorship Discontinuance of Theatre Licensing.

65 House of Commons Debate, 10 May 1968, vol. 764, cc760–84. See http://hansard.millbanksystems.com/commons/1968/may/10/interpretation

Chapter Ten

1   RA LC/GEN/440/67: 'Joint Committee on Stage Censorship General Correspondence'.
2   Peter Lewis, 'Is This What We Got Rid of the Lord Chamberlain For', *Nova*, February 1969, pp. 62–65.
3   Helen Freshwater, *Theatre Censorship in Britain: Silence, Censure and Suppression* (Basingstoke: Palgrave Macmillan, 2009), p. 15.
4   *Ibid.*, pp. 5, 6.
5   *Ibid.*, pp. 164–65.
6   *Sunday Times*, 22 June 1969, p. 54.
7   *Sunday Times*, 11 January 1970, p. 53.
8   *Sunday Times*, 25 October 1970, p. 29.
9   J.W. Lambert, 'Exit Censor', *Sunday Times*, 22 September 1968.
10   'In Defence of Public Good (Section 3), *Theatres Act 1968: An Act to abolish censorship of the theatre and to amend the law in respect of theatres and theatrical performances.* See http://www.legislation.gov.uk/ukpga/1968/54/pdfs/ukpga_19680054_en.pdf
11   J.W. Lambert, 'Exit Censor'.
12   *Guardian*, 24 September 1968, p. 2.
13   J.W. Lambert, 'Exit Censor'.
14   *The Times*, 28 September 1968, p. 18.
15   'Let's Be Fair to "Hair"', *Daily Telegraph*, 25 November 1968.
16   *Daily Telegraph*, 25 November 1968.
17   *Daily Telegraph*, 28 September 1968, p. 1.
18   See *Daily Mail*, 4 October 1968. The play was written by John Herbert, and had already run for nearly a year off Broadway. It was later made into a successful film.
19   'How Did they Find the Energy to Boo?', *Daily Mail*, 25 October 1968.
20   See *The Times*, the *Daily Telegraph* and the *Daily Mail*, all 25 October 1968.
21   *The Times*, 5 November 1968, p. 5.
22   Michael McClure, *The Beard* (San Francisco: Coyote Books, 1967), p. 15 and p. 93.
23   *Daily Telegraph*, 6 November 1968; *Sunday Times*, 10 November 1968, p. 59; *The Times*, 6 November 1968, p. 14; *Guardian*, 6 November 1968, p. 6.
24   *Evening Standard*, 5 November 1968.
25   *Daily Mail*, 5 November 1968.
26   Peter Lewis.
27   *Ibid.*
28   *Sunday Times*, 2 March 1969, p. 53.
29   *Sunday Times*, 16 March 1969, p. 57.
30   Peter Lewis.
31   Michael White, *Empty Seats* (London: Hamilton, 1984), p. 108.
32   Peter Lewis.
33   Michael White, p. 109. See also Freshwater, pp. 67–74.
34   Michael White, p. 112.
35   Irving Wardle, 'Soldiers Adds to Churchill Legend, without Offending', *The Times*, 13 December 1968, p. 13.
36   Michael White, pp. 109–13.
37   Irving Wardle, 'Hochhuth as Europe's Conscience', *The Times*, 1 December 1968, p. 19.
38   *The Times*, 10 December 1968, p. 2.

39 *Daily Mirror*, 2 December 1968, p. 15.
40 *The Times*, 10 December 1968, p. 2.
41 *Daily Mail*, 10 June 1969.
42 'A new way of living—off stage', *Guardian*, 12 June 1969.
43 'Testing Time for sex on the stage', *Sunday Times*, 26 July 1970, p. 6.
44 *The Obscenity Laws: a report by the working party set up by a conference convened by the Chairman of the Arts Council of Great Britain* (London: Andre Deutsch, 1969), pp. 36–37.
45 *Ibid.*, pp. 33–34.
46 *Ibid.*, p. 31.
47 *Ibid.*, p. 36.
48 Kenneth Hurren, 'Opinion', *Daily Telegraph*, 31 October 1969.
49 http://hansard.millbanksystems.com/commons/1969/jul/24/obscenity-arts-council-report
50 *Illustrated London News*, 10 January 1970, p. 29.
51 *Illustrated London News*, 5 September 1970, pp. 32–33.
52 Michael White, p. 128.
53 Note on cover of *Oh! Calcutta!* (New York, Grove Press, 1969).
54 See, for example, http://www.amazon.co.uk/Oh-Calcutta-DVD-Kenneth-Tynan/dp/B001G0DCYO
55 *Daily Telegraph*, 22 July 1970.
56 *Daily Telegraph*, 23 July 1970.
57 Ronald Butt, 'Politics of Morals', *The Times*, 23 July 1970, p. 8.
58 *New York Times*, 18 June 1969, p. 33.
59 Harold Hobson, 'Skin Games', *Sunday Times*, 2 August 1970, p. 19.
60 *The Times*, 28 July 1970, p. 7.
61 *Daily Telegraph*, 28 July 1970.
62 *Daily Telegraph*, 1 August 1970.
63 *Daily Telegraph*, 1 August 1970.
64 *Daily Mail*, 1 August 1970.
65 *Punch*, 5 August 1970.
66 Michael White, p. 129.
67 *The Times*, 21 August 1970, p. 7.
68 J.C. Trewin, 'Hell's Delight in the Circus', *Illustrated London News*, 5 August 1970, pp. 32–33.
69 See *The Times*, 19 February 1971, p. 4.
70 J.C. Trewin, 'According to Plan', *Illustrated London News*, 20 February 1971, p. 33.
71 Michael Holbrook, 'Art or Corruption', *The Times*, 14 October 1970.
72 House of Lords Debate, 3 February 1971. See http://hansard.millbanksystems.com/sittings/1971/feb/03
73 Jenny Lee, 'Hands Off the Theatres', *Guardian*, 7 February 1971, p. 23.
74 Eccles. See House of Lords Debate, 3 February 1971. http://hansard.millbanksystems.com/sittings/1971/feb/03
75 Jenny Lee.
76 'Old Vice and Virtue', *Sunday Times*, 10 January 1971, p. 38. The script, by Misha Williams, was entitled 'Naked Peacock'.
77 *Punch*, 19 May 1971, p. 683.
78 *Guardian*, 12 May 1971, p. 10.
79 'Old Vice and Virtue', *Sunday Times*, 10 January 1971, p. 38.
80 *Daily Mirror*, 13 May 1967, p. 2.
81 *Guardian*, 12 May 1971, p. 10.

82 *The Times*, 12 May 1971, p. 9.

83 *Guardian*, 12 May 1971, p. 10.

84 *Evening News*, 19 October 1972.

85 See *The Times*, 19 October 1972, p. 4.

86 See *Daily Telegraph*, 25 October 1972 and *Evening News*, 19 October 1972.

87 Jill Tweedie, 'Porn poser', *Guardian*, 11 October 1971, p. 9.

88 Michael White, pp. 135–36.

89 'Comment: The Blue Pencil Follies', *Daily Mail*, 28 September 1968, p. 1.

90 *Daily Telegraph*. See http://family-tree.cobboldfht.com/people/view/490

91 *The Times*, 14 September 2006.

92 *Daily Telegraph*, 13 September 2006.

93 See RA LC/GEN/344/68: 'Presentation To Mr Charles Heriot'.

94 House of Commons Debate, 10 May 1968, vol. 764, cc760–84. See http://hansard.millbanksystems.com/commons/1968/may/10/interpretation

Biographies

This section offers brief biographies of the principal people working for or on behalf of the Lord Chamberlain's Office, and involved in issues of theatre licensing and censorship between 1900 and 1932. In some cases, there is little information. It may also be worth noting that obituaries and tributes are often key sources of information, and that these may tend to be generous in their judgments and emphasis.

LAWRENCE ROGER LUMLEY, 11th EARL OF SCARBROUGH (KG GCSI GCIE GCVO PC DL) 1896–1969

Lord Chamberlain 1952–1963

Son of Brigadier General Osbert Lumley, Roger Lumley was educated at Eton, Sandhurst and Oxford University. He served in the First World War with the eleventh Hussars, and was then elected to Parliament in 1922 as a Conservative MP. In the same year he married Katherine Isobel McEwen. He represented Hull East until 1929, and then York from 1931 to 1937, serving as Parliamentary Private Secretary to William Ormsby-Gore, Sir Austen Chamberlain and Anthony Eden (Colonial, Foreign and Home Secretaries). Lumley 'did not make a splash in the Commons', notes his biography, but since he was 'efficient, decisive, and imperturbable', he was blessed with the 'ideal qualities for administrative and advisory work'. In 1937, he was appointed Governor of Bombay, serving until 1943. According to *The Times*, 'He made such an impression there that he was often spoken of as a potential viceroy'. But, as the newspaper notes, 'This high responsibility did not come his way'. Upon his return from India, Lumley served as an acting Major General during World War II. Following the war, he continued his connections with the Army, as an honorary colonel. In 1945 he served briefly as Parliamentary Under-Secretary for India and Burma, and in the same year he succeeded to the Earldom of Scarbrough, following the death of his uncle. He also chaired a commission on Oriental, Slavonic, East European, and African studies, and is credited with having 'laid the foundations for a new, purposeful era of British scholarship on non-Western cultures and languages'. He served as President of the East Indian Association of the Royal Asiatic Society and of the Central Asian Society, and from 1951 to 1956 was Chair of the governing body of the School of Oriental and African Studies at London University. In 1956 he went as a special ambassador to the coronation of the King of Nepal. Scarbrough was made a Knight of the Garter in 1948, and was Chancellor of the University of Durham from 1958 to 1969. On his retirement in 1963, he became a Permanent Lord-in-Waiting to the Queen. As a Freemason he became Grand Master of the United Grand Lodge of England, and was also Lord Lieutenant of the West Riding of Yorkshire and the first High Steward of York Minster. He died at his home near Rotherham.

Main sources:
The Times, 30 June 1969, p. 16.
Oxford Dictionary of National Biography. See https://doi.org/10.1093/
     ref:odnb-9780198614128-e-34632.

CAMERON FROMANTEEL, FIRST BARON COBBOLD
(KG GCVO PC) 1904–1987

Lord Chamberlain 1963–1971

The son of a barrister, Cameron Cobbold went from Eton to King's College, Cambridge, but left at the end of his first year. His early successes as an accountant and bank manager in France and Italy led in 1933 to an invitation to join the Bank of England, and within two years he had become an adviser to the governor. By 1938, Cobbold was one of the bank's four executive directors, and at the end of the Second World War he became deputy governor, and was fully involved in discussions and negotiations around its nationalisation. He was also central to other major post-war international financial developments, including the setting up of the IMF and the World Bank. In 1949, he was appointed as the Governor of the Bank of England, a post he held until 1961. He is said to have been 'dedicated to serving the national interest and providing sound practical advice to government', and was 'essentially a pragmatist and an able administrator'. In 1962 Cobbold chaired the Malaysia commission of enquiry, and the following year he was appointed as Lord Chamberlain. He had married Hermione, daughter of Lord Lytton, in 1930 having met her during a big game hunting expedition in India five years earlier, while her father was serving as Governor of Bengal. Hermione subsequently inherited her childhood home of Knebworth House, which is where Cobbold spent his retirement, 'able to find genuine and satisfying relaxation in country pursuits'. While Hermione is said to have attended a family party dressed as an underground railway station, her husband was evidently a rather shy man who disliked public speaking. Despite this, he made attempts to open himself and his offices to scrutiny; he was the first governor of the Bank of England to submit to a television interview, and the first Lord Chamberlain to give an interview to a national newspaper. However, while Cobbold's obituary in *The Times* credited him for specific skills and achievements, it was also quite critical, suggesting that he 'tended to organize the Bank on the "divide and rule" principle', and that 'he often failed to get the best out of his relations with his contemporaries', seemingly 'unable and unwilling to engender an atmosphere of personal warmth'. Challenging this judgment, the Queen's private secretary then wrote to the newspaper insisting that 'to his colleagues in the Household, he presented a very much warmer personality' which had 'won both the respect and affection of members of the Royal Family and colleagues'. Moreover, wrote Sir William Heseltine, as 'the first Lord Chamberlain to have come from the professional world', Cobbold had exerted a considerable impact on operations at the Palace, through his 'awareness of the advantages of modern management techniques'. Under his guidance, staff had been recruited 'from a wider base', more fitting 'to the changing circumstances in which the monarchy functions'. Moreover, he declared, it was Cobbold who had put forward a proposal to the Queen for 'the widening of guest lists at Buckingham Palace, to ensure that a broader cross-section of the population of Britain and the Commonwealth was entertained'. One thing which Cobbold seems to have lacked, however, is any real interest in the theatre, which—ironically—may be one reason he was more than willing to be allowed to relinquish his control of it in 1968. Cobbold remained as Lord Chamberlain until 1971, having been appointed a Knight of the Garter in 1970. Happily relieved of censorship duties, he spent his final three years in office tackling 'with singular efficiency' the other duties of his role, including the institution of 'a study of organisation and method at Buckingham Palace'. We are told that he also did 'much to improve the pay and conditions of those in the Household', and undertook noble work to try and ensure that the Queen's expenses should be index-linked. He died in November 1987.

Main sources:

The Times, 3 November 1987, p. 14.

The Times, 5 November 1987, p. 14.

Oxford Dictionary of National Biography. See https://doi.org/10.1093/ref:odnb/40108.

Obituary of Lady Hermione Cobbold, *Daily Telegraph*, 8 November 2004 (see https://www.telegraph.co.uk/news/obituaries/1476087/Hermione-Lady-Cobbold.html).

LIEUTENANT COLONEL TERENCE EDMUND GASCOIGNE NUGENT, 1st and last BARON NUGENT (GCVO MC) 1895–1973

Comptroller in the Lord Chamberlain's Office 1936–1960

Nugent was educated at Eton College and Sandhurst. Five generations of his family had served in the Grenadiers, and he joined the Irish Guards in 1914 and fought in the First World War. He was wounded in 1917, and received the Military Cross. He was invested as a member of the Royal Victorian Order (1927), and served as Equerry to The Duke of York from 1927 to 1937, accompanying him on trips overseas. He was also Brigade Major of the Brigade Guards from 1929 to 1933. In 1935 he married Rosalie Heathcote-Drummond-Willoughby, and in 1936 he became a Lieutenant Colonel. He was invested as a Commander in the Royal Victorian Order in 1937, as a Knight Commander in 1945, and as a Knight Grand Cross in 1952. He held the office of Extra Equerry to King George VI between 1937 and 1952, and to Queen Elizabeth II between 1952 and 1973. In 1960 he received the award of Grand Officer, Legion of Honour, and was created 1st Baron Nugent, of West Harling, Norfolk. From 1960 until his death in 1973, he was Permanent Lord-in-Waiting. Nugent was a lover of cricket and played for the 1st XI at Eton and later for the Duke of Norfolk's XI at Arundel. In 1966 he was made President of the MCC. Nugent had no children, and his barony died with him. Here is part of the obituary for Nugent as published in *The Times* in April 1973 under the headline: 'An Admired Court figure':

> ... He combined the style of an Ouida Guards officer with a spontaneous kindliness and infectious sense of humour that made him welcome in all the many and varied circles in which he moved. 'Tim' Nugent's tall, elegant figure passed easily from attendance at Court to the company of music-hall artists, from the Long Room at Lords to the Turf Club, and wherever he found himself he was among friends. His wide knowledge of the world, capacity for hard work, common sense and tact enabled him to succeed in several difficult roles ...
>
> His letters were models of resourcefulness and tact. He would handle an awkward subject with honesty and candour and his sincerity was so transparent that it never gave offence. His conversation always added to the gaiety of a company, large or small.

Nugent was also praised for efficient organisation of Buckingham Palace Garden Parties and other court events: 'The ordering of all official func-tions fell to him and the silken ease for which they were renowned owed much to his cool judgment and the affection in which he was held'. Turning to his duties in relation to theatre, the obituary declares that Nugent

> managed the delicate and controversial conduct of stage censorship with consummate skill. Harbingers of the permissive society railed against the anomaly of a retired officer of Foot Guards seated in St James's Palace, blue-pencilling theatrical scripts. But the theatre people liked and trusted him and the BBC, over which he had no jurisdiction, often unofficially consulted him. A keen amateur both of straight plays and musical shows, he cut only with reluctance what he knew would be regarded as over the odds by public opinion of the day. Tolerant he was, but hard to fool. When he had passed a script so blameless that it might have been read aloud at a church assembly, he was liable to check on the performance after some weeks when it was being played on a Saturday night in the provinces, remote from St James's Palace.

A couple of weeks later, *The Times* duly published another remarkably fulsome accolade, written by Richard Attenborough and Laurence Olivier, drawing attention to Nugent's 'immense contribution to the welfare of the members of our profession'. However, it is safe to say that not all playwrights, actors and directors who encountered Nugent would have fully subscribed to the tone or sentiments of such compliments.

Main sources:
The Times, 30 April 1973, p. 16.
The Times, 11 May 1973, p. 22.
The Times, 19 May 1973, p. 16.

BRIGADIER SIR NORMAN WILMSHURST GWATKIN (GCVO KCMG DSO) 1889–1971

Assistant Comptroller in the Lord Chamberlain's Office 1936–1960, Comptroller 1960–1964

Gwatkin was educated at Clifton College, Bristol and the Royal Military College at Sandhurst, and in 1918 was commissioned in the service of the Coldstream Guards. He was subsequently invested as a Member of the Royal Victorian Order in 1937, as a Commander in 1946, and as a Knight Grand Cross in 1963, and received the award of Companion, Distinguished Service Order in 1944. He began the Second World War as a Major and ended it commanding a brigade in the Guards Armoured Division, where he was awarded a DSO for his services. After the war, he held the office of Extra Equerry to King George VI between 1950 and 1952, and to Queen

Elizabeth II between 1952 and 1971. He was Secretary and Registrar of the Order of Merit between 1963 and 1971, and was invested as a Knight Commander in 1964. He married in 1957, and had one adopted daughter. *The Times* published two obituaries of Gwatkin, both written by people who had worked alongside him, one in the army and the other in the Lord Chamberlain's office. The first—headlined 'Soldier of High Standards'— focuses on the experience of serving under Gwatkin as Adjutant in the thirties, and describes him as 'a formidable figure with his fierce moustache, his impeccable turn-out and his clanking spurs'. Those who served with him would 'remember him as the epitome of a smart soldier with superb standards, tempered with a bubbling and irrepressible sense of humour', and for having 'helped them to grow up, to assume responsibility, and to realize that soldiering was fun as well as a vocation'. According to the memoirs of another General who encountered him during the war,

> Norman Gwatkin was a man of enormous character. A Coldstreamer, with a high colour, a choleric expression, a loud and infectious laugh, he was loved by our Grenadiers and known as were few senior officers. 'There's the Brigadier!' they would say, chuckling, and I remember one Sergeant adding, and he's an inspiration to the men!... He cheered all men, wherever they were and whatever the circumstances.

The other *Times* obituary, headlined 'Administrative Skill', was written by Sir Terence Nugent, who 'had the privilege of working with him in the Lord Chamberlain's Off.ice for more than twenty years' and was similarly effusive:

> In Norman Gwatkin kindness, courage and gaiety were personified and for a great many people nothing will be quite the same again without him.
>   I had the privilege of working with him in the Lord Chamberlain's Office for more than twenty years and I could not have wished for a more delightful, easy and loyal colleague. Extremely efficient he had a lightness of touch which made it fun to work with him and which seemed to smooth away all problems and difficulties. His training as a guardsman fitted him to tackle the big ceremonial occasions which the Lord Chamberlain's Office was called upon to organize. A quick and decisive worker he was never rattled and he dealt with any unforeseen snags that might arise calmly and with dispatch.

Nugent goes on to talk specifically about Gwatkin's role in relation to censorship:

> In the Lord Chamberlain's absence Norman often had to interview authors or producers and discuss with them the cuts and alterations that were required.

However disgruntled or even angry the author or producer may have been on arrival at Norman's office he almost invariably left convinced that his case would be carefully and sympathetically considered and very likely roaring with laughter at some remark, probably ribald, that Norman had made.

Main sources:

The Times, 3 August 1971, p. 14.

The Times, 4 August 1971, p. 12.

General Sir David Fraser, *Wars and Shadows: Memoirs of General Sir David Fraser* (London: Allen Lane, 2002). See also http://members.chello.nl/~h.w.a.schutte2/operation.htm.

LT.-COL. SIR ERIC CHARLES WILLIAM MACKENZIE PENN (MC OBE KCVO GCVO) 1916–1993

Assistant Comptroller in the Lord Chamberlain's Office 1960–1964, Comptroller 1964–1981

Eric Penn was educated at Eton and read History at Cambridge, before joining the Grenadier Guards. His father had been killed on the battle-fields of France three months before Eric was born, and his mother died when he was fifteen. He was therefore partly brought up by an uncle who was an adviser to George VI, and later the treasurer and private secretary to the Queen Mother. Penn also became a long-standing personal friend of the future Queen Elizabeth, whom he first met in 1940 after returning from Dunkirk. During the Second World War, Penn participated in many operations, winning the Military Cross for leading the night-time capture of a German machine-gun position outside Rome, and serving as a company commander in the closing battle of the Italian campaign. He remained in the army after the war, serving in Germany and Libya and in the Suez Canal, before being chosen to command the 1st Battalion Grenadier Guards, which 'had always been the height of his ambition'. However, an injury sustained in a skiing accident forced a reluctant end to his military career, and he was appointed as Assistant Comptroller in the Lord Chamberlain's office, later graduating to Comptroller. His duties included arranging garden parties, investitures and programmes for offi-cial visits by overseas Heads of State, along with the administration of the royal palaces and the Royal Collection. He also had responsibility for the Central Chancery of Knighthood, the Lords-in-Waiting, the Gentlemen at Arms, Yeomen of the Guard, the Royal Company of Archers, the Queen's Barge-master and the Royal Watermen. As Comptroller, Penn enjoyed jurisdiction over royal styles and titles, the granting of Royal Warrants and matters of precedence, and the licensing of the use of royal arms on souvenirs and commemorative objects. Last but perhaps not least, he was required to supervise the annual swan upping in Berkshire. When Penn died in 1993, his obituaries recorded that 'Sir Eric's greatest attributes were his organizational ability and producer's eye in planning and executing ceremonial occasions, from the weddings of Princess Margaret and Princess Anne to the funerals of the Duke and Duchess of Windsor and Earl Mountbatten'. Indeed, the *New York Times* headlined its obituary 'Director of British Royal Pomp'. Among his other awards and honours, Penn was appointed as an extra equerry to the Queen, and received an OBE for his role as Assistant Adjutant General in London District, where he was 'responsible for ceremonial in the capital', which included, in 1965, the funeral of Sir Winston Churchill. Penn was married to Prudence Stewart-Wilson, with whom he had three children. He was knighted in 1972 and remained as Comptroller until 1981, having, as his *Times* obituary put it, 'served the Queen with dedication for almost half-a-century'.

Main sources:

The Times, 15 May 1993, p. 17.

New York Times, 17 May 1993, p. B8.

https://www.britishempire.co.uk/forces/armyunits/britishinfantry/
    grenadierericpenn.htm.

http://www.thepeerage.com/p25504.htm.

LIEUTENANT COLONEL SIR JOHN FREDERICK DAME JOHNSTON (MC MVO CVO KCVO GCVO) 1922–2006

Assistant Comptroller in the Lord Chamberlain's Office 1964–1981, Comptroller 1981–1987

Born in Burma, where his father was a banker in Mandalay, John Johnston was educated at Ampleforth. He joined the Grenadier Guards at the age of 19, receiving awards for bravery—including the Military Cross—and being mentioned in dispatches for his 'complete fearlessness and brilliant leadership' in battle during the Second World War. His book, *Memoirs of a Tank Troop Leader*, recounted some of his experiences. After the war, Johnston continued in his military career, eventually becoming Commanding Officer of the 1st Battalion in the Grenadier Guards. He retired from the military in 1964, and was appointed as Assistant Comptroller in the Lord Chamberlain's Office, a position he held for seventeen years until the retirement of Eric Penn, when Johnston naturally replaced him as Comptroller. According to one obituary, Johnston not only combined 'military attention to detail with imagination and foresight', but also 'brought an instinctive appreciation of the theatrical to rigid ceremonial' as well as 'a sense of humour and a lightness of touch which enhanced many a royal occasion'. He was informally known as 'Stopwatch Johnnie', on account of his precision. In its obituary, *The Times* described Johnston as 'A consummate courtier', and as one 'who excelled in staging precision pageantry'. *The Daily Telegraph* said he was 'one of the Queen's most popular courtiers' and 'a great favourite with the Royal Family', who lived with his wife and two children in a 'Grace and Favour' home in Windsor Great Park, and was regularly invited to the Queen Mother's birthday lunch. He also kept flat-coated retrievers and was President of the charity Hearing Dogs for Deaf People. One of his finest hours was said to have been organising the wedding of Prince Charles and Diana Spencer, where he was 'expert at reassuring the apprehensive young bride' and 'managed to keep her calm'. Indeed, so successful were his efforts that he was apparently 'rewarded with a kiss from the newly minted Princess'; or, in some accounts, two kisses. By contrast, one of Johnston's less fortunate moments was when photographs of him appeared in the press in full ceremonial gear and holding a handbag (which he was apparently minding for the Queen). Johnston later appeared on the television programme 'What's My Line' as a Grenadier Guard, and clearly had an active interest in performance. Indeed, he served as President of the King George V Fund for Actors and Actresses, chairman of the Combined Theatrical Charities Appeal Council and director of the Theatre Royal, Windsor. He even wrote a valuable—if relatively brief—history of theatre censorship in Britain, *The Lord Chamberlain's Blue Pencil*. A final triumph for Johnston in retirement was his role in overseeing the rewiring of Windsor Castle.

Main sources:
The Times, 14 September 2006, p. 69.
Daily Telegraph, 13 September 2006.
https://www.britishempire.co.uk/forces/armyunits/britishinfantry/
     grenadierjohnjohnston.htm.
John Johnston, *The Lord Chamberlain's Blue Pencil* (London: Hodder & Stoughton, 1990).

CHARLES HERIOT 1905–1972

Assistant Examiner of Plays 1937–1947; Examiner of Plays 1947–1968

Heriot attended Glasgow Academy, Glasgow University and Glasgow School of Art—where he studied Art of the Theatre. He worked in London with Louis Casson on a production of *Macbeth*, spent three years in professional theatre, including repertory work, touring and the West End, and a year with the Lena Ashwell players. He then worked in advertising and journalism, and was a general editor in the book department of Odham Press Ltd before joining the Lord Chamberlain's office as Assistant Examiner of plays in 1937. Heriot served in the Royal Air Force during the War, and became Senior Examiner in 1947. He remained in this post until the 1968 Theatres Act was passed, and was also involved in amateur drama as a director and designer with Letchworth's Settlement Players. Heriot was married to Adelaide Binnie Murgatroyd, a writer and publisher, who died in 1964. On his retirement, a presentation was made to him in the Lord Chamberlain's Office in November 1968, at which he received a cigarette case engraved with the message:

Charles Heriot
Examiner of Plays
1937–1968
From his friends in the Lord Chamberlain's office.

They also gave him 50 Woodbine tipped cigarettes.

Main sources:
RA LC/GEN/440/65 'As To The Lord Chamberlain Giving Tape Recorded Interview On Censorship to the *Sunday Times*'.
RA LC/GEN/344/68 'Presentation To Mr Charles Heriot'.

LIEUTENANT COLONEL SIR THOMAS ST VINCENT WALLACE TROUBRIDGE, 5th BARONET (MBE *Croce di Guerra*, Order of the Crown of Italy) 1895–1963

Assistant Examiner of Plays 1952–1963

Son of Sir Thomas Troubridge, and educated at Wellington College and Sandhurst, Vincent Troubridge traced his ancestry back to Lord Nelson. In 1914 he was commissioned into the King's Royal Rifle Corps, and served in the First World War, where he was wounded at Salonika. He returned to England in 1917 and worked with Army Intelligence, receiving an MBE in 1919 and retiring with the rank of Captain. According to one obituary, his long-standing interest in theatre had first been stimulated in 1913 while studying at a military academy in Baden and attending a German performance of the medieval Morality Play *Everyman*. After the war, he joined the Stage Society and was involved with its Sunday night productions. He also contributed articles to the *Stage*, became front of house manager at the Strand Theatre, and translated several German plays into English. In 1938 he succeeded his father as fifth baronet, and following the Second World War—in which he served on the army's General Staff—he became chairman of the library committee of the Garrick Club, and a founder member of the Society for Theatre Research. He wrote frequently for *Theatre Notebook*, including a series on Early 19th Century Plays which featured in eight issues between 1948 and 1950, and also 'kept up a continuous output of theatrical articles in the national and world press'. A 1951 lecture on Theatre Riots in history—'delivered with tremendous panache'—was published by the STR in 1951 as one of its *Studies in English Theatre History*, and his full length book *The Benefit System in the British Theatre* was published posthumously by the Society in 1967. Troubridge was an adviser for *Theatre Notebook* from 1954 until his death, and remained an active committee member for the Society for Theatre Research until 1961: 'He livened our deliberations in committee with his forthright, occasionally Rabelasian yet always pertinent observations', and 'was always generous in putting at the disposal of the society his vast fund of information'; indeed he 'would take endless trouble in searching out answers to inquiries ... from scholars and students'. In a short obituary in *The Times*, Sybil Rosenfeld wrote that 'theatre research has sustained a severe loss', and that 'No one was more knowledgeable in the highways and by-ways of the nineteenth-century stage'. She noted that 'His reading in this field was wide and his memory prodigious', and that he would 'be much missed from among us'. In March 1949, Troubridge contributed an article to the *Stage* about the history of theatre censorship ('Censorship Under Fire'), and a few months later he wrote a letter to Tim Nugent, the Comptroller of the Lord Chamberlain's Office, to offer himself as an additional Reader. In August 1951, a letter from Gwatkin officially offered him the position, to run for ten years from April 1952: 'It will be a great pleasure to undertake such congenial work under the direction of yourself and my old friend Tim Nugent', he replied. According to his obituary in *Theatre Notebook*, Troubridge 'was well fitted to the onerous task of censorship', because 'there was in him an odd Puritanical streak' and he was 'vehement in denunciation of the lowering moral standards of his day'. In the Lord Chamberlain's Office, he frequently recommended far more draconian censorship than his superiors were ready to endorse. Troubridge had married Pamela Clough in 1939, but there was no issue.

Main sources:

The Times, 18 December 1963, p. 12.
The Times, 27 December 1963, p. 10.
Basil Francis, 'St Vincent Troubridge, Soldier and Scholar, 1895–1964', *Theatre Notebook*, Volume 9, no. 2, Winter 1964/65, pp. 66–8.

IFAN KYRLE FLETCHER 1905–1969
Assistant Examiner of Plays 1964–1968

Of all the Examiners and Readers of plays employed by the Lord Chamberlain's Office during the twentieth century, it is fair to say that none had such a long-standing interest in or commitment to theatre as Ifan Fletcher. Educated at Newport High School, where he showed 'an undue devotion to the dramatic society, the school library and the school magazine', he persuaded his father to open a bookshop in the basement of his antiques business. He formed a Playgoers Society, and became heavily involved in producing plays, being 'very persistent in getting experimental work produced'. He also married an amateur actress, Constance Fry. Fletcher then began to create book catalogues and collections devoted to theatrical material, and in the mid-1930s moved to London to become a theatrical bookseller, opening a successful business in the West End. For his work in this field he has been described as 'a pioneer in the collecting and selling of theatre materials' since he both 'created a demand' and 'inspired new collectors'. But Fletcher's enthusiasms and contributions went far beyond this. After the war, he was instrumental in establishing *Theatre Notebook* as a periodical devoted to British theatre history. It began publishing in 1945, and Fletcher contributed many articles, in due course becoming the editor. He was also a key figure in establishing the Society for Theatre Research, which was launched in 1948, serving as a member of the committee from its inauguration until his own death, and as its chairman between 1952 and 1956. In 1955 Fletcher was similarly instrumental in the setting up of the International Federation for Theatre Research, serving as its first chair. He also helped to found the British Theatre Museum Association, where he took the role of Vice Chair between 1955 and 1957. In addition, Fletcher wrote two books on festivals and court costume. As the tribute to him published by the Society for Theatre Research after his death says of him: 'His creative ideas, his ability to put them into practice, his friendly attitude to people, his wide knowledge, infinite tact and tireless energy all fused to promote the advance of the study of theatre history in this country and, through the IFTR, in other countries also'. If anything, it may seem slightly surprising that Ifan Fletcher should have taken on a role of Examiner of Plays for the Lord Chamberlain.

Main sources:

Obituary in *The Times*, 3 January 1969, p. 8.
Society for Theatre Research, *Ifan Kyrle Fletcher: A Memorial Tribute* (STR: London, 1970).

TIMOTHY BLAKE HARWARD 1932(?)–2017(?)

Assistant Examiner of Plays 1965–1968

Very little is known about Tim Harward. He was born in Madras, studied French and English, and spent 1962 at a Teachers' Training College in the Ardèche. In 1963 he was living in Dublin and based at Trinity College, where he edited a collection of essays about 'Contemporary Patterns in European Writing', contributing chapters on *Le Silence de la Mer* by Jean Marcel Bruller (Vercors) and *L'Étranger* by Albert Camus, as well as the general introduction. His autobiographical note revealed that he 'prefers the Cevennes to the Alps … is a freelance journalist, and writes book and theatre reviews for the *Irish Times*, but prefers people to books'. According to Charles Heriot—who in November 1964 recommended him as a potential replacement for Troubridge as assistant examiner—Harward had been invalided out of the armed forces, and having completed his Arts degree in Dublin had 'done a series of lectures at Oxford and Eastbourne on twentieth century drama' and 'was now at Sussex University doing postgraduate research'. Heriot also noted that Harward 'Has private means and is firmly against taking a nine-to-six job'. Unfortunately, it has not been possible to discover what happened to him after 1968, although he seems to have lived and died in East Sussex.

Main sources:

RA LC/GEN/344/65 'Resignation Of Mr Maurice Coles, Appointment Of Mr T B Harward'.

T.B. Harward, European Patterns: Contemporary Patterns in European Writing (Dublin: Dolmen Press, 1964).

RONALD JOHN HILL 1911–1981

Secretary To The Lord Chamberlain 1953–1976

Hill became a Clerk to the Prince of Wales in 1934, and transferred to the same role in the Lord Chamberlain's Office in 1936. He married in 1942. In 1955, Hill was promoted to the position of assistant secretary to the Lord Chamberlain, and in 1958 he became Secretary in the same Office, a position he retained until his retirement in 1976. Despite his relatively low status in the Lord Chamberlain's Office, Hill had strong opinions on the need to retain a tough theatre censorship and drafted many detailed documents for senior staff to make use of. In the final period leading up to the introduction of the Theatres Act in September 1968, he either chose or was asked to be absent on leave. Hill was also a

Serjeant-at-Arms to the Queen, and was received by her on his retirement at a ceremony at Buckingham Palace. Unfortunately, no further details about his life have come to light.

Note:

Hill's lowly position in the Office and low social status mean that there are no obituaries or other documentation to draw on.

Select Bibliography

Archival Material

The Lord Chamberlain's Correspondence Files (Manuscript Room, British Library)
Lord Chamberlain's Office Files (Royal Archive, Windsor)
The Lord Chamberlain's Collection of Licensed Plays 1900–1968 (Manuscript Room, British Library)
Production Files (V&A Theatre and Performance Collections Archives)
Hansard's Parliamentary Debates

Books, Articles and Unpublished Dissertations
NB Not including playscripts.

Acheson, James (ed.), *British and Irish Drama Since 1960* (Basingstoke: Macmillan, 1993)

Albert, Judith Clavir and Albert, Stewart E. (eds), *The Sixties Papers: Documents of a Rebellious Decade* (Westport, Connecticut: Greenwood Press, 1984)

Aldgate, Anthony and Robertson, James C., *Censorship in Theatre and Cinema* (Edinburgh: Edinburgh University Press, 2005)

Ansorge, Peter, *Disrupting the Spectacle* (London: Pitman, 1975)

Arts Council of Great Britain, *The Obscenity Laws: a report by the working party set up by a conference convened by the Chairman of the Arts Council of Great Britain* (London: André Deutsch, 1969)

Billington, Michael, *State of the Nation: British Theatre Since 1945* (London: Faber and Faber, 2007)

Booker, Christopher, *The Neophiliacs: The Revolution in English Life in the Fifties and Sixties* (London: William Collins 1969; London: Pimlico, 1992)

Browne, Terry W., *Playwrights' Theatre: The English Stage Company at the Royal Court Theatre* (London: Pitman, 1975)

Caute, David, *Sixty-eight: The Year of the Barricades* (London: Paladin, 1988)

Chandos, John, pseud. [i.e. John Lithgow Chandos MacConnell], *To Deprave and Corrupt: Original Studies in the Nature and Definition of Obscenity* (London: Souvenir Press, 1962)

Childs, David, *Britain Since 1945: A Political History* (London: Routledge, 1997)

Coopey, R., Fielding S. and Tiratsoo N. *The Wilson Governments 1964–1970* (London: Pinter Publishers, 1993)

Curtin, Kaier, *'We Can Always Call them Bulgarians': The Emergence of Lesbians and Gay Men on the American Stage* (Boston: Alyson Publications, 1987)

de Jongh, Nicholas, *Not in Front of the Audience: Homosexuality on Stage* (London: Routledge, 1992) de Jongh, Nicholas, *Politics, Prudery and Perversions: The Censoring of the English Stage 1901–1968* (London: Methuen, 2000)

Devine, Harriet (ed.), *Looking Back: Playwrights at the Royal Court 1956–2006* (London: Faber and Faber, 2006)

Doty, Gresdna A. and Harbin, Billy J. (eds), *Inside the Royal Court Theatre 1956–1981: Artists Talk* (Baton Rouge and London: Louisiana State University Press, 1990)

Etienne, Anne, 'Les Coulisses de Lord Chamberlain: La Censure Théâtrale de 1900 à 1968'. Ph.D. dissertation, L'Université d'Orleans, 1999

Findlater, Richard, *Banned!: A Review of Theatrical Censorship in Britain* (London: MacGibbon & Kee, 1967)

Findlater, Richard (ed.), *The Twentieth Century*, Volume 169, No. 1008, February 1961

Findlater, Richard (ed.), *At the Royal Court: 25 Years of the English Stage Company* (Ambergate: Amber Lane Press, 1981)

Florance, John Allan, 'Theatrical Censorship in Britain 1901–1968'. Ph.D. dissertation, University of Wales, 1980

Freshwater, Helen, *Theatre Censorship in Britain: Silencing, Censure and Suppression* (Basingstoke: Palgrave Macmillan, 2009)

Fowler, Jim, *Unleashing Britain: Theatre Gets Real 1955–1964* (London: V&A Publications, 2005)

Green, Jonathon, *All Dressed Up: The Sixties and the Counterculture* (London: Pimlico, 1999)

Hallifax, Michael, *Let Me Set the Scene: Twenty Years at the Heart of British Theatre 1956 to 1976* (Hanover: Smith & Kraus, 2004)

Hayman, Ronald, *British Theatre Since 1955: A Reassessment* (Oxford: Oxford University Press, 1979)

Hewison, Robert, *Too Much: Art and Society in the Sixties 1960–1975* (London: Methuen, 1986)

Holdsworth, Nadine, *Joan Littlewood's Theatre* (Cambridge: Cambridge University Press, 2011)

Houchin, John, *Censorship of the American Theatre in the Twentieth Century* (Cambridge: Cambridge University Press, 2003)

Itzin, Catherine, *Stages in the Revolution* (London: Eyre Methuen, 1980)

Johnston, John, *The Lord Chamberlain's Blue Pencil* (London: Hodder & Stoughton, 1990)

Kitchin, Laurence, *Drama in the Sixties: Form and Interpretations* (London: Faber and Faber: 1966)

Marowitz, Charles, Milne, Tom and Hale, Owen, *New Theatre Voices of the Fifties and Sixties* (London: Methuen, 1981)

Marowitz, Charles, Milne, Tom and Hale, Owen, *Encore Reader: A Chronicle of the New Drama* (London: Methuen, 1965)

Marowitz, Charles and Trussler, Simon, *Theatre at Work: Playwrights and Productions in the Modern British Theatre* (London: Methuen, 1967)

Marr, Andrew, *A History of Modern Britain* (London: Macmillan, 2007)

Marwick, Arthur, *The Sixties* (Oxford: Oxford University Press, 1998)

Moorhouse, Geoffrey, *Britain in the Sixties: The Other England* (Harmondsworth: Penguin, 1964)

Morgan, Kenneth O., *The People's Peace: British History, 1945–1990* (London: Oxford University Press, 1990)

Peter Nichols, *Diaries, 1969–1977* (London: Nick Hern, 2000)

Nicholson, Steve, *The Censorship of British Drama, 1900–1968: Volume One: 1900–1932* (Exeter: University of Exeter Press, 2003)

Nicholson, Steve, *The Censorship of British Drama, 1900–1968: Volume Two: 1933–1952* (Exeter: University of Exeter Press, 2005)

Nicholson, Steve, *The Censorship of British Drama, 1900–1968: Volume Three: The Fifties* (Exeter: University of Exeter Press, 2011)

Nicholson, Steve, *Modern British Playwriting: the 1960s* (London: Methuen Drama, 2012)

O'Higgins, Paul, *Censorship in Britain* (London: Nelson, 1972)

Osborne, John, *Almost a Gentleman: An Autobiography* (London: Faber and Faber, 1991)

Osborne, John, *Damn You, England* (London: Faber and Faber, 1994)

Patterson, Michael, *Strategies of Political Theatre: Post-War British Playwrights* (Cambridge: Cambridge University Press, 2003)

Rabey, David Ian, *English Drama Since 1940* (London: Longman, 2003)

Rebellato, Dan, *1956 And All That: The Making of Modern British Drama* (London: Routledge, 1999)

Rees, Roland, *Pioneers of Fringe Theatre on Record* (London: Oberon Books, 1992)

Roberts, Philip, *The Royal Court Theatre 1965–1972* (London: Routledge and Kegan Paul, 1986)

Roberts, Philip, *The Royal Court and the Modern Stage* (London: Cambridge University Press, 1999)

Sampson, Anthony, *Anatomy of Britain Today* (London: Hodder & Stoughton, 1965)

Sandbrook, Dominic, *Never Had It So Good: A History of Britain from Suez to the Beatles* (London: Abacus, 2006)

Shellard, Dominic, *British Theatre Since the War* (New Haven: Yale University Press, 2000)

Shellard, Dominic, Nicholson, Steve and Handley, Miriam, *The Lord Chamberlain Regrets* (London: British Library Publications, 2004)

Shellard, Dominic, *Kenneth Tynan: A Life* (London: Yale University Press, 2003)

Sinfield, Alan, *Out on Stage: Lesbian and Gay Theatre in the Twentieth Century* (London: Yale University Press, 1999)

Sinfield, Alan, *Society and Literature 1945–1970* (London: Methuen, 1983)

Sinfield, Alan, *Literature, Culture and Politics in Post-War Britain* (Oxford: Blackwell, 1989)

Sked, Alan and Cook, Chris, *Post-War Britain: A Political History* (Harmondsworth: Penguin, 1979)

Street, Harry, *Freedom, the Individual and the Law* (Harmondsworth: Penguin, 1963)

Taylor, John Russell, *Anger and After: A Guide to the New British Drama* (London: Eyre Methuen, 1977)

Taylor, John Russell, *The Second Wave: British Drama of the Sixties* (London: Eyre Methuen, 1978)

Thomas, David, Carlton, David and Etienne, Anne, *Theatre Censorship: from Walpole to Wilson* (Oxford: Oxford University Press, 2007)

Travis, Allen, *Bound and Gagged: A Secret History of Obscenity in Britain* (London: Profile Books Ltd, 2000)

Tribe, David, *Questions of Censorship* (London: George Allen and Unwin, 1973)

Tynan, Kenneth, *Theatre Writings* [selected and edited by Dominic Shellard] (London: Nick Hern Books, 2007)

Tynan, Ken, *A View of the English Stage 1944–1965* (London: Methuen, 1984)

Tytell, John, *The Living Theatre: Art, Exile and Outrage* (London: Methuen, 1997)

White, Michael, *Empty Seats* (London: Hamilton, 1984)

Worth, Katharine J., *Revolutions in Modern English Drama* (London: G. Bell, 1972)

Index